Introduction to Music

Processes and Style

Introduction to Music

Processes and Style

Allen Winold
Richard DeLone
William Christ

*Indiana University
Bloomington, Indiana*

Harper's College Press
A Department of Harper & Row, Publishers
New York Hagerstown San Francisco London

Introduction to Music: Processes and Styles. Copyright © 1976 by Harper & Row, Publishers, Incorporated.

Printed in the United States of America. All rights reserved. No part of this book may be used or reproduced in any manner whatsoever without written permission except in the case of brief quotations embodied in critical articles and reviews. For information address Harper & Row, Publishers, Inc., 10 East 53rd Street, New York, N.Y. 10022.

International Standard Book Number: 0-06-161412-2
Library of Congress Catalog Card Number: 75-45863

Book produced by Ken Burke & Associates
Designer: James Stockton
Copyeditor: Judith Filmore
Picture editor: Ruth Abraham
Text compositor: Applied Typographic Systems
Music compositor: Music Typographers

Acknowledgments

Photographs, paintings, and music examples are reproduced with permission from the following sources.

Photographs and Paintings:

Alinari-Art Reference Bureau: 141, 227

Alinari-Scala: 2, 9, 37, 73, 174

Bettmann Archive: 5, 57, 64 (right), 71, 95, 100, 108, 114, 130, 135 (left), 145, 151, 152, 154, 155, 156, 164, 171, 172, 179, 200, 213, 219 (left), 220, 235, 241, 250, 263, 264, 266, 270, 273, 282, 297

Black Star: 243 (by Roy Zalesky)

Corcoran Gallery of Art, Washington, D.C.: 64 (left)

Culver Pictures, Inc.: 6, 42, 44, 83, 86, 135 (right), 173, 194, 205, 215, 221, 223, 229, 233, 249, 258, 265, 288, 291

Detroit Institute of Arts: 133

Frick Collection: 170, 191

G. D. Hackett: 218

Indiana University: 16 (top and bottom), 53, 234, 243

Magnum Photos: 29 by D. McCullin; 91 by Dennis Stock

Metropolitan Museum of Art: Alfred Steiglitz collection, 89; Rogers Fund, 119 and 120; Gift of Junius S. Morgan, 126;

Harris Brisbane Dick Fund, 146; Munsey Fund, 147; Isaac Fletcher, 167; The Crosby Brown Collection, 130 and 177; Mrs. Henry McSweeney, 177 (right); Mrs. Robert Goeht, 188; George F. Baker, 242; Horace Havermeyer, 253; Stephen C. Clark, 255; George A. Hearn Fund, 277

Musee Cluny: 117

The British Library; 121

Museum of Fine Arts, Boston: 19, 209, 272

Museum of Modern Art, New York: 13, 21, 279

National Gallery of Art, Washington, D.C.: 231

New York Public Library: 131

New York Times: 127

Philadelphia Museum of Art: John G. Gohnson Collection, 26; Louise and Walter Arensberg Collection, 74, 103, and 286

Photograph Giraudon: 1, 192, 219 (right), 271

Rapho Guillumette: Sanford H. Roth, 60; Sherry Suris, 61 and 198

San Francisco Opera: 67 (by Dennis Calloway), 69 (by Ken Howard)

Solomon R. Guggenheim: 206, 295

Walters Art Gallery: 124

Music Examples:

Pages 24, 25, 27, 28, 207: "Yesterday" by Lennon/McCartney. Copyright © 1965 Northern Songs, Ltd. All rights for the U.S.A., Canada, Mexico, and the Philippines controlled by Maclen Music, Inc., c/o ATV Music Group. Used by permission. All rights reserved. International copyright secured.

Page 27: From *Rhapsody on a Theme by Paganini* by Sergei Rachmaninoff. Copyright 1934 by Belwin-Mills Publishing Corporation. Copyright renewed. Used with permission. All rights reserved.

Pages 30, 290: From *Roberta* by Jerome Kern. Copyright 1933 by T. B. Harms, Co. Copyright renewed. Used with permission. All rights reserved.

Page 63: From *The Magic Flute* by Wolfgang Amadeus Mozart. Copyright 1952 by G. Schirmer Associates. Used by permission of G. Schirmer Associates.

Page 65: From *Madam Butterfly* by Giacomo Puccini. Copyright 1963 by G. Schirmer Associates. Used by permission of G. Schirmer Associates.

Page 67: From *Il Trovatore* by Giuseppe Verdi. Copyright 1963 by G. Schirmer Associates. Used by permission of G. Schirmer Associates.

Page 70: From *Aida* by Giuseppe Verdi. Copyright 1964 by G. Schirmer Associates. Used by permission of G. Schirmer Associates.

Page 72: From *Don Carlo* by Giuseppe Verdi. Copyright 1967 by G. Schirmer Associates. Used by permission of G. Schirmer Associates.

Page 91: "They Long to Be Close to You" by Burt Bacharach and Hal David. Copyright 1963 & 1969 by U.S. Songs, Inc., Blue Seas Music, Inc., and Jac Music Co., Inc. New York, N.Y. International copyright secured. All rights reserved. Reprinted by permission.

Pages 204, 207: From *Das Lied von der Erde* by Gustav Mahler. Copyright by Universal Presser Company. Copyright renewed. Reprinted by permission. All rights reserved.

Page 244: From *Rigoletto* by Giuseppe Verdi. Copyright 1965 by G. Schirmer Associates. Used by permission of G. Schirmer Associates.

Page 145: From *La Boheme* by Giacomo Puccini. Copyright 1963 by G. Schirmer Associates. Used by permission of G. Schirmer Associates.

Page 257: From *Rhapsody in Blue* by George Gershwin. Copyright © 1924 NEW WORLD MUSIC CORP. Copyright renewed. All rights reserved. Used by permission of Warner Bros. Music.

Page 260: From *Symphony for Small Orchestra, Opus 21* by Anton Webern. Copyright 1929 by Universal Editions, A. G. Vienna, Used by permission.

Page 262: From *Mathis der Maler* by Paul Hindemith. Copyright © 1934 by B. Schott's Shoehne. Copyright renewed. Used with permission. All rights reserved.

Page 275: From *Pierrot Lunaire* by Arnold Schoenberg. Copyright by Belmont Music Publishers. Copyright renewed. All rights reserved. Used by permission of Belmont Music Publishers, Los Angeles, Ca. 90049.

Page 276: From *Five Movements for String Quartet, Op. 5* by Anton Webern. Copyright by Universal-Presser Company. Copyright renewed. All rights reserved. Used by permission.

Page 280: From *Sonata for Two Pianos* by Igor Stravinsky. Copyright © 1937 by B. Schott's Shoehne. Copyright renewed. Used with permission. All rights reserved.

Page 283: From *Sonata for Piano and Flute* by Paul Hindemith. Copyright © 1937 by B. Schott's Soehne. Copyright renewed. Used with permission. All rights reserved.

Page 285: From *Kinderstüke* by Anton von Webern (Carl Fischer Catalog No. P3129. Copyright ©MCMLXVI by Carl Fischer, Inc., N.Y. Copyright MCMLXVII by Carl Fischer, Inc., N.Y. International copyright secured. All rights reserved. Used by permission of Carl Fischer, Inc.

Page 291: From *Wozzeck* by Alban Berg. Copyright by Universal-Presser Company. Copyright renewed. All rights reserved. Reprinted by permission.

The instinctive and progressive
interest of every man in art, we are willing to affirm with
no qualification, will go on and on, ever fulfilling
hopes, every building new ones, ever opening new
horizons, until the day will come when every man while
digging his potatoes will breathe his own Epics, his
own Symphonies (operas if he likes it); and as he sits of
an evening in his back-yard and shirt sleeves smoking
his pipe and watching his brave children in *their* fun of
building *their* themes, for *their* sonatas of *their* life,
he will look up over the mountains and see his visions,
in their reality—will hear the transcendental strains
of the day's symphony, resounding in their many choirs,
and in all their perfection, through the west wind
and the tree tops!

Charles Ives
Postface to *114 Songs*

PREFACE

This book presents a general introduction to the materials, aspects, forms, and styles of music, with emphasis on the latter. Its coverage of music is broad in scope, including those genres of music most closely linked to other human experience—dance music, song, religious music, program music and music for the theater as well as symphonic and chamber music and "pop" music. It is intended for use in college-level music classes, but it may also serve the individual.

The text is divided into three parts. Part One is devoted to a discussion of the varieties of music and basic aspects of music such as rhythm, melody, accompaniment, counterpoint, harmony, timbre, dynamics, texture, and form in a general sense. Musical form in the specific sense of organizational schemes or plans is discussed in Part Two; the periods and characteristics of musical style are examined in Part Three which is chronologically arranged to show the development of styles of music from medieval times up to the present. Brief biographies of major composers appear in the chapters devoted to styles of music. Further, general terms and concepts necessary for fruitful involvement with music appear throughout the book.

The only prerequisite for beginning the study of this book is a simple knowledge of the names of the pitches in the treble and base clefs and their location on the piano keyboard and the names of the rhythmic symbols and their proportional relation to each other. This information is summarized in Appendix 1.

We wish especially to acknowledge with gratitude the splendid contributions of Raleigh Wilson, Harper & Row editor; Ken Burke and Judith Fillmore, production services; and James Stockton, designer. And, finally, we are thankful for the patience and understanding of our families.

Allen Winold
Richard DeLone
William Christ

CONTENTS

ONE   Materials of Music   1

Part One is devoted to a study of those genres of music most closely linked to other human experiences and to an exploration of the basic elements of music. The opening chapter discusses ten representative examples from a variety of musical styles and uses them as the basis for general discussion of musical elements. Each of the three following chapters is devoted to a more detailed discussion of specific musical elements and processes.

1   Varieties and Aspects   2

Ten Representative Works   2

Lennon and McCartney: "Yesterday"
Shankar: A Raga
Stockhausen: *Gesang der Jünglinge*
Goodman: "Sing, Sing, Sing"
Strauss: *Emperor Waltz*
Schumann: *Carnaval*, "Chopin"
Beethoven: *Op. 95* ("Serioso")
Mozart: *Don Giovanni*, Duettino
Bach: *Cantata No. 80*
Palestrina: *Mass for Pope Marcellus II*, Kyrie

Musical Terms and Concepts   7

| Timbre | Rhythm | Harmony | Form |
| Dynamics | Melody | Texture | |

Musical Genres   15

Referential and Absolute Music   Popular and Classical Music
Performance Media

2   Rhythm, Melody, and Accompaniment   18

Tempo
Meter and Pulse Levels
Rhythm Pattern and Unity
Rhythm and Structure
Texture
Melody
Motives

Intervals
Contour
Variation of Motives
Tonality
Unity and Variety
Cadence
Accompaniment

3   Counterpoint and Harmony   36

Counterpoint in the canon   36

Imitation   Imitative and Nonimitative Sections

Counterpoint in the Fugue 44
Stretto

Counterpoint in Voice Leading 49
Harmonic progression   Traditional Rules of Voice Leading

4 Instruments and Voices 56

Instruments 56
Strings   Brasses   Keyboard Instruments
Woodwinds   Percussion

The Orchestra 59

The Conductor 61

Voices 62

TWO   Forms of Music 73

Part Two is devoted primarily to a study of instrumental works emphasizing aspects of form. Each of the three chapters describes one of the major organizational processes in music—sectionalization, variation, and development. Musical elements discussed in Part One are considered in terms of the way they contribute to the structure of music.

5 Sectional Forms 74

Structural Interrelations 75
Sectionalization   Symmetry and Balance
Unity and Variety   Function and Structure

Sectional Forms 81
Ternary Form   Ritornello Form
Binary Form   Free Sectional Form
Rondo Form

6 Variational Forms 88

Improvisation and Variation in Jazz 90

Figured Bass and Variation 93

Melodic Variations 96

7 Developmental Forms 102

Sonata-Allegro Form 106

Concerto Sonata-Allegro Form 115

THREE Styles of Music 117

Part Three chronologically traces the development of musical style in its sociocultural context. Each of the six chapters is devoted to the study of one of the major periods of music literature, including detailed analyses of representative works. Musical elements and forms discussed in Parts One and Two are considered in terms of the way they contribute to the varied styles of music.

8 Medieval and Renaissance Style (800–1600) 118

The Periods of Musical Style 118

Music in Ancient Cultures 120
Greece and Rome   The Middle East   The Far East

Music of Other Cultures 123

Medieval Sacred Music 123

Early Polyphony 126

Early Secular Music 126

Fourteenth-Century Music 128

Early Dance Music 133

The Madrigal 137

Summary 139

9 Baroque Style (1600–1750) 140

Opera 140
Recitative Style

Instrumental Music 144

Crosscurrents in the Middle Seventeenth Century 144
France   Italy   England   Germany   The Suite

Theoretical Developments 149

Bach and Handel 153

Summary 162

10 Classical Style (1750–1825) 166

Political and Social Setting 167

Classic Composers 170
Mozart and the Concerto   Beethoven and the Symphony

Summary 187
Style Characteristics of Classical Music

11 Romantic Style (1825–1900) 190

Romanticism and Musical Expression 190

Romantic Composers and Styles 192

Song 195

Song Literature After Schubert 203

12 Romantic Style (1825–1900) 208 (continued)

Program Music 208

Berlioz: *Symphonie Fantistique*   Other Program Music

Piano Music 222

Schumann's *Carnaval*   Chopin's *Mazurka, Op. 68, No. 3*

13 Romantic Style (1825–1900) 230 (concluded)

Opera 230

Wagner's *Die Meistersinger*   Verdi's *Rigoletto*
Verdi's *A Masked Ball*   Puccini's *La Boheme*

Other Music 246

Brahm's *Piano Quintet in E. Minor, Op. 34*
Brahm's *Variations on a Theme by Haydn*

Summary 252

Style Characteristics of Romantic Music

14 Twentieth-Century Style (1900–) 254

Style Changes 254

Jazz: A New Idiom 256

Gershwin's *Rhapsody in Blue*

Comparison of Styles 259

The Move Away from Major-Minor Tonality 260

Trends from 1900 to 1945 *267*

Impressionism   Expressionism

15 Twentieth-Century Style (1900–) 278 (continued)

Neoclassicism 278

Serialism: Twelve Tone Technique

Post Romanticism 286

Opera 290

Since 1945 294

Summary 297

Appendices 299

1: The Notation of Pitch 299

2: Annotated Bibliography 303

Glossary/Index 307

ONE

Materials of Music

1 Varieties and Aspects

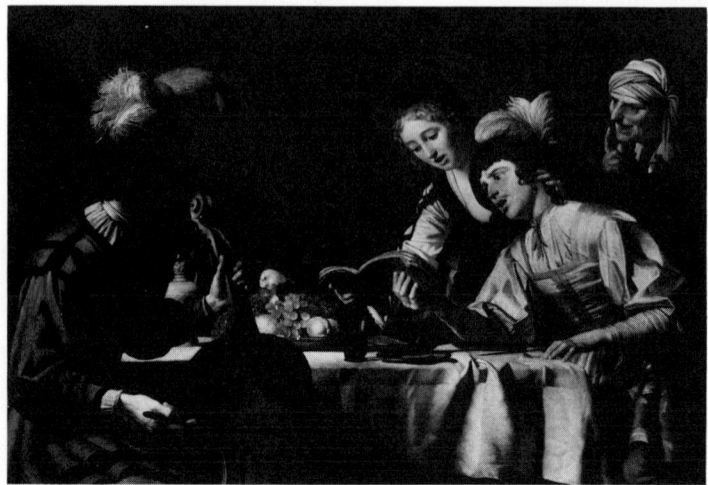

One variety of music has traditionally served as an adjunct to dining. From the 17th century painting Concerto, one can easily imagine that the instrumental and vocal sounds are as delightful to the ear as the fresh fruits are to the palate.

The phrase "That's music to my ears" has been applied at various times to almost everything from the first cry of a newborn baby to the tender strains of a lullaby, from the ring of a cash register to the climax of a Beethoven symphony, or from the roar of engines at an auto race to the electronically amplified sounds of a modern rock group. Music, in its broadest sense, could be defined as anything we want to hear; any narrower definition would eliminate some aural experiences which at least some people would regard as musical experiences. Perhaps the best answer to the question "What is music?" is the reply Louis Armstrong gave when asked "What is jazz?"—"Man, if you got to ask, you'll never find out!"

TEN REPRESENTATIVE WORKS OF MUSIC
This book, however, will not discuss at length the cry of a baby or the roar of an engine; it will be devoted primarily to a study of the masterworks of music in Western civilization and the materials and procedures they exemplify. At the same time we hope to make you aware of the great variety of genres, forms,

2 Materials of Music

and styles of music throughout the world and through the centuries.

Lennon and McCartney: "Yesterday"
They are already a part of history—these four long-haired poet-musicians from Liverpool who called themselves the Beatles. They have not been heard as a group for years and yet their preeminence remains unchallenged. Their songs still embody the sound of a whole generation.

They were always a step ahead of their imitators. By the time hundreds of groups were imitating the strident abandon of "Yeah, yeah, yeah," the Beatles were already exploring the nostalgic subtlety of "Yesterday." While countless groups were adopting their standard instrumentation of two guitars, bass, and percussion, the Beatles had moved on to incorporate in their music the sounds of a Classical string quartet, a Baroque trumpet, or an Indian sitar.

Their songs articulated feelings that could not otherwise be articulated; they discussed subjects that could not otherwise be discussed. Their records became prize possessions; their concerts turned into epic events. They were pacesetters in hair style, dress style, and life style.

And then suddenly it was over. The members of the group separated in 1970 and since then have only been heard as individuals in efforts that seem to prove the truth of the theorem that the whole is greater than the sum of the parts. Other groups ranging from the brash Rolling Stones to the polished Carpenters have come before the public but none have matched the impact of the Beatles. Nor does it seem likely that any will.

Shankar: A Raga
In 1966, one year after the composition of "Yesterday," the Beatles heard for the first time the music of Ravi Shankar, one of the leading musicians of India. They were so fascinated by Shankar as a musician and as a man that they sought to incorporate aspects of his music into their songs and his philosophy into their lives. George Harrison even spent six weeks in India studying with Shankar. Indian music has also influenced Western art music through such men as the French composer Olivier Messiaen and the violinist Yehudi Menuhin. On the other hand, the influence of Western music may be heard in some Indian film music, and India is beginning to produce such outstanding masters of Western music as the conductor Zubin Mehta.

Despite these interactions, the basic attitude toward music and art is vastly different in India and in the Western world. Music for a European or an American is the personal expression of an individual composer or performer; for an Indian, as the critic Ananda K. Coomaraswamy wrote, all art is "an expression of the soul of the people and serves the purposes of life like daily bread." Indian music, dance, and the visual arts all serve to bring man into unity with God.

Indian music differs from Western music not only in its purpose but also in its media and techniques. The most popular instruments—the *sitar*, a plucked instrument with twenty strings, and the *tabla*, drums played with the hands and fingers—are played with astounding virtuosity by musicians like Shankar. Indian music relies mostly on melody and rhythm, with virtually no emphasis on harmonic or contrapuntal aspects. The melodies of classical Indian music are based on melodic formulas called *ragas*. Each of the more than 70,000 ragas has its own emotional character and may be played only on special occasions or at specified times of the year. In long, mostly improvised performances, Indian music can achieve a hypnotic effect and lead the listener to a depth and intensity of feeling unlike that achieved by any other music.

Stockhausen: Gesang der Jünglinge
Karlheinz Stockhausen's *Gesang der Jünglinge* (*Song of the Youth*) is a work that would stretch any definition of music to its limits. Some people might find it too advanced and unusual to be called music at all; others, having heard some avant-garde music written since this work appeared in 1958, might describe it as a fairly conservative example of modern music.

The work was created by tape-recording the voice of a

young boy reading a verse from the Bible; then subjecting these sounds to electronic manipulation to produce other sounds with different durations, pitches, timbres, and degrees of loudness; and finally ordering these in various simultaneous and successive combinations. The resulting work resists description and analysis in the traditional terms of music, but nevertheless is heard by most listeners as a valid aural artistic experience.

Stockhausen is an avant-garde composer in the original sense of the term. He has been in the forefront of many movements ranging from electronic music to multimedia "happenings." In some of his works elements of chance play a role. The score of his *Klavierstück XI* (*Piano Piece XI*) consists of a number of fragments which the performer plays in any order. On a larger scale Stockhausen has envisioned replacing the traditional concert hall with a building devoted exclusively to music where listeners could wander in and out at any time of the day and sample whatever live or electronic music might be playing at the time.

Goodman: "Sing, Sing, Sing"

The music of Benny Goodman was for the late 1930's and early 1940's what the music of the Beatles was for the 1960's. Hailed as the "King of Swing," Goodman led his band on triumphant cross-country tours, produced best-selling records, and even presented concerts in that bastion of symphonic music, Carnegie Hall. "Sing, Sing, Sing," a highlight of Goodman's 1938 Carnegie Hall concert, features not only the clarinet artistry of Goodman, but also the fabulous solo work of drummer Gene Krupa, and the swinging precision of the whole band. The original tune is by Louis Prima.

Goodman has been a great force for creative synthesis in music. Not only a leading jazz performer, he has also become known as a leading performer of symphonic and chamber music; such composers as Béla Bartók, Paul Hindemith, and Aaron Copland have written works for him. In the field of jazz he successfully combined elements of his own native "Chicago style" with other jazz influences. By bringing such outstanding performers as Teddy Wilson and Lionel Hampton into his quartet and big band, he became the first band leader to integrate black musicians and white musicians, long before Jackie Robinson began playing with the Brooklyn Dodgers.

Although in his middle sixties, Goodman continues to play with skill, imagination, and taste. Riding the crest of a wave of nostalgia for the thirties and forties, he could easily play nothing but his old hits. Instead he keeps himself fully abreast of the current musical scene.

Strauss: Emperor Waltz

From the "King of Swing," Benny Goodman, to the "Waltz King," Johann Strauss, Jr., is a geographical leap from New York to Vienna and a chronological leap from the twentieth century to the nineteenth. More than this, it is a move from the dance hall to the ballroom, from the hustle of a democratic society to the elegance of an aristocratic society.

When it was first introduced in the nineteenth century, the waltz created a great furore because it was the first time that men and women could dance with their arms about each other. In his more than 500 waltzes Strauss captured the marvelous combination of sensuality and sophistication that is the essence of the waltz. Each of his waltzes has its own individuality, its own unique characteristics. Some are vivacious, some languorous; some are dignified, some reckless; some are simple, some complex. And yet all bear that special imprint of *wienerische Daseinsfreude* (Viennese joy of living), especially when played with the proper Viennese lilt and phrasing.

Strauss's spirit is very much alive in his native Vienna today. His waltzes, such as *Emperor Waltz, Blue Danube,* or *Tales from the Vienna Woods,* may be heard afternoons in the city park or evenings at lavish balls in the elegant palaces of the city. His operettas are a staple of the city's theaters. His melodies are known and loved by young and old. Perhaps the supreme compliment to Strauss was paid by his contemporary Johannes Brahms, the famous German composer. Brahms once responded to a request for an autograph by writing out the first few bars of the *Blue Danube* and then added underneath the words, "Unfortunately not by Johannes Brahms."

Creator of an art for an heroic era, the man who "freed" music from the constraints of the classicist suffered the ultimate indignity of becoming totally deaf—watching but not hearing the premiere performance of his Ninth Symphony, a utopian vision of the day when "all men shall be brothers."

Schumann: Carnaval, "Chopin"

If imitation is the sincerest form of flattery, then this piece is a magnificent tribute to the Polish composer, Frederic Chopin, written by his German contemporary, Robert Schumann. More than that, this exquisite miniature masterfully captures the sense of longing that was a hallmark of nineteenth-century romanticism. The search for the *blaue Blume*—the blue flower symbolizing the unattainable ideal—was an important aspect of literature, painting, and music.

Schumann's *Carnaval* is a collection of short character pieces depicting figures such as the dreamy Eusebius and the impetuous Florestan (representing two aspects of Schumann's personality) and characters from the Italian *commedia dell'arte* such as Pierrot, Arlequin, Pantalon, and Colombine. The work suggests colorful scenes from a ball, but unlike Strauss's music which was written for real-life, flesh-and-blood dancers, Schumann's music is written for a ballroom of the mind; its characters are all fantasy. The tender strains of "Chopin" are appropriately placed between pieces entitled "Chiarina" and "Estrella," representing the two women in Schumann's life at the time.

In his music and his writings Schumann struggled for the freedom of the creative artist from the strictures of a conservative public. The struggle is vividly portrayed in the last piece of *Carnaval*, "March of the Band of David against the Philistines," with the forward-looking creative artists represented by the Band of David and the backward-looking public and critics represented by the Philistines. This struggle is one that has repeated itself throughout the history of music.

Beethoven: String Quartet in F Minor, Op. 95 (Serioso), first movement.

Perhaps nowhere does the sense of struggle appear more dramatic than in the life and music of Ludwig van Beethoven. He struggled against social conventions that would have limited his freedom and prestige as a man; he struggled against musical conventions that would have limited his scope and imagination as a composer; and he struggled against the most terrible of all afflictions for a musician—deafness. His motto was *per aspera ad astra*—"through struggle to victory."

Perhaps nowhere in his music is this sense of struggle so concisely and cogently portrayed as in the opening measures of the *String Quartet in F Minor, Op. 95* ("Serioso"). Not even the famed opening measures of the Fifth Symphony can surpass the concentrated power and energy of these measures. The opening section is followed by a more relaxed, lyrical passage, but hovering in the background are echoes of the "storm and stress" of the opening. Throughout the movement, mercurial changes of mood from stormy resistance to quiet pleading command the listener's involvement. Beethoven's intensely personal musical language speaks with a vividness and immediacy that would be impossible to capture with words.

Through his life and music Beethoven inexorably changed the course of music history. While his great predecessors like Bach and Haydn were content to write music to meet the demands of the church or nobility, Beethoven insisted that his music should be supported by his patrons, not written for them. While contemporaries like Dittersdorf and Cherubini were content to accept rules of form and harmony largely as they inherited them from the past, Beethoven struck out on new paths, writing passages of music that sound bold and innovative even today.

Mozart: Don Giovanni, Duettino
At first glance the life and music of Wolfgang Amadeus Mozart seemed to be untouched by struggle. The popular image of the composer is one of a happy child prodigy on a triumphant concert tour; the popular conception of his music is one of pure, untroubled grace and serenity.

The success of the child prodigy, however, turned into the difficulties of the mature composer. Even a masterpiece such as *Don Giovanni* found little favor in Vienna, though it did eventually become a success in Prague. Mozart's early death and burial in a pauper's grave may not have been as unusual in eighteenth-century Austria as they would be in twentieth-century America, but they are still evidence of the tragic side of his life. In his mind this tragic side is reflected in such works as the G-Minor Symphony (K 550), the G-Minor String Quintet (K 516), and the *Requiem Mass*.

Don Giovanni is a mixture of almost equal parts of *opera buffa* and *opera seria*—of comedy and tragedy. The opera is based on the life of the famous lover ("Don Juan" in English) whose conquests, we are told, included 640 women in Italy, 231 in Germany, 100 in France, 91 in Turkey, and 1,003 in Spain. And yet in Mozart's opera we only see the Don in his moments of failure with women. Even the peasant girl, Zerlina, who yields to his entreaties in the *duettino* (little duet) "La ci darem la mano" ("Give me your hand"), soon returns to her country boyfriend, Masseto.

The duet is divided into two parts. In the first part we hear the amorous Don urging Zerlina to go away with him, while the peasant girl coyly resists his advances. At the end of the first part the Don passionately pleads, "Andiam, andiam" ("Let us go, let us go"). She finally relents and echoes his words as if to say, "All right, let us go." In the second part they sing together of their anticipated bliss.

Palestrina at the organ with singers reading through his Pope Marcellus Mass.

Mozart's music is marked by a perfection in form and technique that is sometimes compared to that of Raphael in painting. Both creative artists grew up with admirable models to follow. Raphael's father was recognized as a leading artist; his frescoes and paintings still grace churches and palaces in his native Urbino, Italy. Mozart's father was a recognized composer, writing works for patrons in his native Salzburg, Austria. For both artists their chosen medium was as natural for them as their native language.

Bach: Cantata No. 80
Luther's powerful affirmation of faith, "A mighty fortress is our God," has been expressed in the architecture of magnificent churches and cathedrals, but it finds its most sublime expression in the opening chorus of Bach's *Cantata No. 80*. Like the flying buttresses of a Gothic cathedral, the brilliant high trumpet line and its sonorous echo in the bass instruments provide a solid foundation for the elaborate working-out of Luther's melody in the voices and middle instruments. Each phrase of the melody is treated in a separate section. We hear powerful masses of sound piled beside one another like huge stones in a cathedral. Only after careful study and repeated

hearings are we aware of the intricate interrelationships that permeate the work. This is musical craftsmanship of the highest order, and yet it is musical craftsmanship not for the sake of display, but designed to bring out the deeper meaning of the text.

This cantata, with its eight movements for chorus, orchestra, and soloists, was first performed in its present form in 1730 at the St. Thomas Church in Leipzig, Germany. Bach wrote more than 300 cantatas while serving as *Kappellmeister* or music director of various Lutheran churches. His complete works, totaling more than 50 volumes in the Bach Gesellschaft Edition, include both sacred and secular music. But for Bach all music was an expression of faith; he once wrote that even a musical exercise should be written for the glory of God.

Palestrina: Mass for Pope Marcellus II, Kyrie
Giovanni Pierluigi da Palestrina is generally recognized as the greatest master of Renaissance choral music in Italy, and yet his style is really that of the Flemish composers of the time. Although his writing technique has been regarded for centuries as a model for composers, the rules supposedly based upon it bear little resemblance to his actual music. This particular mass, the *Mass for Pope Marcellus II,* has been surrounded for centuries by legend according to which it effected the salvation of Catholic Church music, and yet the known historical facts do not tend to support this. Indeed there is even some question as to the dedication to Pope Marcellus since his pontificate lasted only 22 days. But these matters are peripheral to the essentials of the work itself.

The text of the Kyrie may be translated "Lord, have mercy upon us; Christ, have mercy upon us; Lord, have mercy upon us." The musical setting takes advantage of the fact that the text is short and probably thoroughly familiar to the listening worshippers; it is highly elaborate, with the six vocal lines spun out in intricate relationships. In other mass movements like the Credo, where the text is quite long, Palestrina adopts a simpler musical style so as not to obscure the text. If we compare this mass with the Bach cantata we find that it is like comparing the clean lines and balanced proportions of an Italian Renaissance church with the elaborate lines and exuberant colors of a German Baroque church.

Aspects we are accustomed to hearing in music of later centuries—such as strong changes of mood or tone color—are not of importance in the Palestrina mass. Listening to this music requires an active effort and involvement on our part if we are to appreciate fully its subtle beauties. As Palestrina's great English contemporary, William Byrd, once wrote,". . . a song that is well and artificially [i.e., artistically] made cannot be well perceived nor understood at the first hearing, but the oftner you shall heare it the better cause of liking you will discover; and commonly that Song is best esteemed with which our eares are most acquainted." (From the preface to Byrd's *Psalmes, Sonnets, and Songs of Sadness and Pietie.*)

MUSICAL TERMS AND CONCEPTS
Describing these works in nontechnical terms as we have gives a general idea of their character but does not give any specific information on how the works actually sound. In music, as in any specialized field, we must have a set of commonly understood terms and symbols if we are to communicate effectively with one another. To try to discuss music without terms such as "pizzicato" or "quarter note" is like trying to discuss painting without terms such as "perspective" or "chiaroscuro,"—or, for that matter, to discuss basketball without terms such as "free throw" or "center."

The symbols of music, *notes,* are summarized in Appendix 1 of this book. Many readers are already familiar with these; some may need only a brief review; others, who are encountering notes for the first time, may find a fuller explanation in the module *How to Read Music.* A basic understanding of music notation will enable you to follow the music examples in this book and in other works.

The terms of music and the concepts they embody will be introduced subsequently. Knowledge of these terms and concepts not only enables us to study the forms of music in Part Two and the styles of music in Part Three, but it also

In Botticelli's famous painting, figures are projected against a background of trees, in a manner somewhat analagous to the way foreground rhythmic figures in music may be projected against a metric background.

helps to sharpen our perception of musical sounds and deepen our involvement in musical processes. In this introductory chapter, however, we shall first discuss important aspects of music—timbre, dynamics, rhythm, melody, harmony, texture, and form—and we shall also consider ways in which music may be classified according to genre and type.

Timbre
When you listen to a number of different works such as those presented at the beginning of this chapter, the musical aspect or characteristic that probably strikes your ear most immediately is the different sound, tone color, or *timbre* of each work. Timbre is one of the most important aspects of music and in many ways one of the easiest to understand. You may not realize it but you are attending to differences in timbre constantly as you listen to the sounds of spoken language. The difference between an "o" sound and an "i" sound in the words *love* and *live* is really a difference in timbre. The fact that we are so conditioned to listen for timbre differences in speech may account for our sensitivity to timbre differences in music.

In many compositions timbre remains basically unchanged throughout; piano sonatas, string quartets, or unaccompanied choral works, for example, may have no drastic changes in timbre from beginning to end. Works for orchestra will usually have some striking changes of timbre involving the varied colors of the woodwinds, the rich sonorities of the brasses, the warm sounds of the strings, or the colorful timbres of the percussion. Some works may be written with frequent changes in timbre; indeed the changes in timbre may become more important than any other aspect of the music. Some of the music of the present "pop" scene is characterized by great richness in timbre; the variety of electrically amplified and natural sounds produced at an exciting rock concert may be almost as complex as the variety of pitches at a classical chamber-music concert.

Timbre may be used effectively to evoke emotional associations. Flutes and oboes may be used to establish a peaceful, pastoral mood; French horns may suggest a hunting scene. The use of trumpets and timpani in the opening of the Bach cantata contributes to the festive and powerful character of the music. It is interesting to note that some scholars believe these trumpet and timpani parts were not originally written by J. S. Bach but were added later by his son Friedemann for a special festival performance in Halle.

Dynamics
Another highly accessible and easily understood aspect of music is *dynamics*—that is, changes of loudness. It is usual to associate loud music with characteristics such as power and splendor, soft music with characteristics such as delicacy and grace. An increase in loudness may suggest gathering tension or excitement; a decrease in loudness may suggest release or calm.

Loudness may be described scientifically in *decibels* (the smallest perceivable increment in loudness), but in music it is customary to indicate loudness with the following Italian terms and abbreviations:

pp = *pianissimo* = very soft
p = *piano* = soft
mp = *mezzo piano* = moderately soft
mf = *mezzo forte* = moderately loud
f = *forte* = loud
ff = *fortissimo* = very loud
cresc. = *crescendo* = getting louder (<)
decresc. = *decrescendo* = getting softer (>)
dim. = *diminuendo* = getting softer

As important as timbre and dynamics are, they are not usually regarded as the prime bearers of the musical message. Rather they may be compared in a sense to color in the visual arts. We can still recognize a painting in a black-and-white reproduction, and we can still recognize an orchestral composition in a piano transcription. *Transcription*, the process of changing a work from one medium or timbre to another, has both current and historic interest. Two recent best-selling classical records were transcriptions of Bach works for jazz chorus ("Bach's Greatest Hits" by the Swingle Singers) and for an elec-

tronic instrument called the Moog synthesizer ("The Switched-on Bach"). Bach himself frequently transcribed his own music and that of other composers from one medium to another. Indeed, the process of transcription may be found throughout music history. Listen if possible to such famous transcriptions as Ravel's orchestration of Mussorgsky's piano piece, *Pictures at an Exhibition,* or Liszt's piano transcriptions of violin pieces by Paganini. In some instances transcriptions or arrangements may involve changes beyond those of timbre alone.

Rhythm

In most music the two prime bearers of the musical message are rhythm and pitch. *Rhythm,* that aspect of music concerned with the duration, accentuation, and temporal grouping of musical sounds, is probably the most fundamental and pervasive of all the aspects of music. The strong tendency of listeners to respond to this aspect is revealed when they tap their foot or make some other gesture in time to the beats or pulses of the music. When they do this they are showing their awareness of what we might call the "background" of the rhythmic aspect. Just as in the visual arts we tend to see the foreground figures of a picture against some form of background, so too in music we tend to hear rhythmic figures against some sort of temporal background.

This temporal background in music is made up of beats or pulses—that is, regularly recurring stimuli or points in time. In most works some beats are heard as stronger or more accented than others, and this creates groupings of two beats (strong/weak, strong/weak, etc.), or three beats (strong/weak/weak, strong/weak/weak, etc.), or larger groupings that may be thought of as combinations of these two basic groupings. Listen to the beginning of the Mozart duet for a good example of a two-beat grouping and to the beginning of the Strauss waltz for a good example of a three-beat grouping.

In addition to the basic beats we may also hear beats or pulses moving at faster or slower rates of speed or on different temporal levels. If you listen again to the Bach cantata you will find that you can hear pulses on various levels as shown in Example 1-1. Strong beats are indicated with longer lines. If we compare these to levels of columns in a typical Gothic church as shown in Example 1-1, we can understand how it is possible to speak of "rhythmic" organization in architecture or of "architectonic" levels in music. Indeed it has been said that architecture is frozen music.

The organization of beats into groupings on various levels is called *meter*. The rate of speed at which basic beats are heard is called *tempo*. Choice of tempo seems to have a direct and immediate emotional impact upon the listener, with fast tempos heard as exciting or exhilarating and slow tempos heard as calm and peaceful. Compare, for example, the mood created by the fast tempo of the Beethoven quartet movement with the slow tempo of Schumann's "Chopin." Choice of meter per se does not necessarily have such a general emotional significance, although one may have strong emotional associations with particular marches (two-beat) or waltzes (three-beat).

Against the background created by meter and tempo we hear a foreground of rhythmic patterns that give a composition its special flavor and identity. Rhythmic patterns may be represented specifically in terms of note values or described generally in terms of long and short notes. In Example 1-2 relative length is indicated by the lines beneath the notes.

Melody

The other primary element of music, *pitch*, not only has foreground and background aspects but also what we might call horizontal and vertical aspects. In this section we shall consider the horizontal aspect—that is, the way in which pitches are used in succession. This aspect is usually called *melody*. Since

Example 1-1 Bach: *Cantata No. 80*, "Ein' feste Burg ist unser Gott" ("A Mighty Fortress Is Our God"), No. 1, Chorus, measures 1–2.

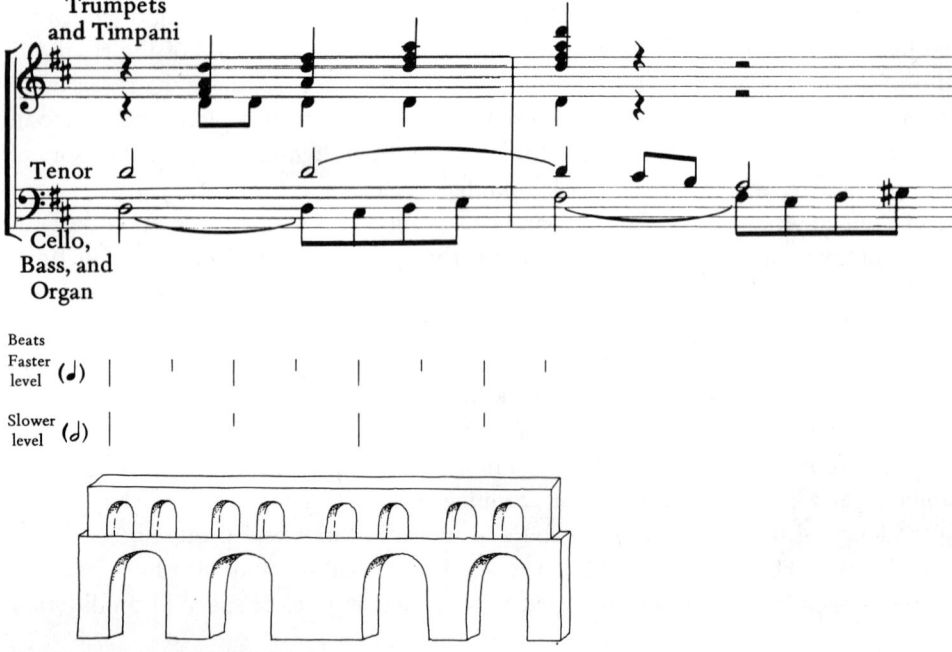

10 Materials of Music

EXAMPLE 1-2 (a) MOZART: *Don Giovanni*, NO. 7, DUETTINO, "LÀ CI DAREM LA MANO" ("GIVE ME YOUR HAND"), MEASURES 1-2; (b) STRAUSS: *Kaiser-Walzer (Emperor Waltz)*, OP. 437, WALTZ 1, MEASURES 1-2; (c) BEETHOVEN: *String Quartet in F Minor*, OP. 95, FIRST MOVEMENT, MEASURES 1-2.

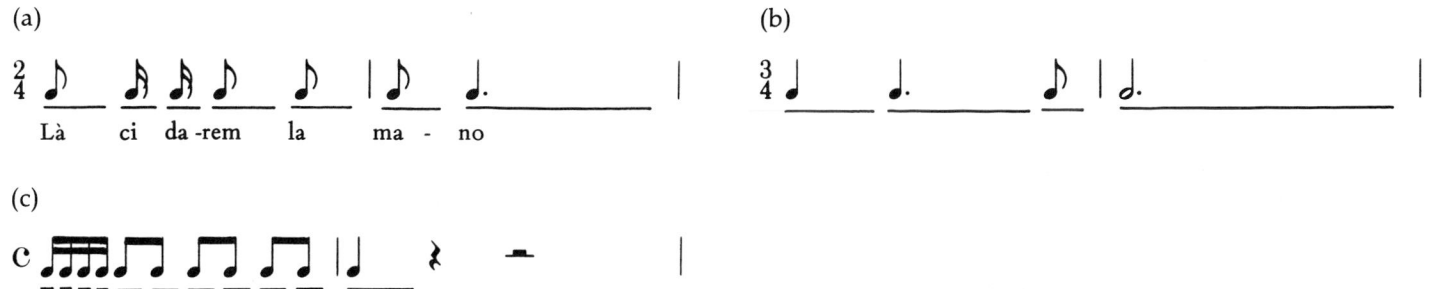

any succession of pitches must involve some aspect of time, any consideration of melody must also involve some consideration of rhythm. When we speak of melody in common usage, however, we are usually referring to the way pitches are used in succession. The vertical aspect of pitch, harmony, will be considered in the next section.

When we consider melody we usually find that the foreground elements claim our attention first. We notice, for example, whether pitches ascend, descend, or remain stationary. Though not as clear-cut as tempo or dynamics, pitch direction may also have some emotional connotations. Ascending melodies may be heard as more forceful or positive, descending melodies as more calm and resigned. All emotional characteristics associated with particular aspects of music—even those associated with tempo and dynamics, and certainly those associated with pitch direction—must be taken as tendencies and not as absolutes. Many passages in music conform to the characteristics we have mentioned, but many others do not.

Another important aspect of melody is *pitch interval*—that is, the musical distance between successive pitches. This may be described specifically with such terms as major third or perfect fifth, or more generally in terms of *steps* (relatively close intervals) and *leaps* (relatively wide intervals). The opening of five familiar melodies may be used to illustrate the concepts of pitch direction and interval. Even if you cannot read music you can easily see in which direction the notes move, and you can see that steps involve movement from adjacent space to line, or line to space, while leaps involve a larger movement. See Examples 1-3 and 1-4 for illustration.

The opening gesture of the Beethoven quartet is all steps. The opening gesture of the Strauss waltz is all leaps. Most melodies contain a balanced mixture of steps and leaps, and of ascending and descending direction as seen in the Mozart duet.

The background aspect of pitch, *tonality*, is probably best understood as the tendency of the pitches in a composition or section to focus upon one central pitch called the *tonic*. In most tonalities there is also a second pitch, called the *dominant*, which is almost as important as the tonic. Thus we can say that the pitch background is organized into strong pitches (tonic and dominant) and weak pitches (the remaining pitches) somewhat in the same way that the rhythm background is organized into strong beats and weak beats.

Most music you will hear will be written in a definite tonality with a clearly heard tonic, and in a definite meter with a clearly heard beat. In some works, however, this will not apply. Though you will probably be able to hear a tonality and meter in most of the examples at the beginning of this chapter, you will no doubt find it difficult to hear these in the Indian raga and impossible to hear them in Stockhausen's *Gesang der Jünglinge*.

Harmony

The vertical aspect of pitch, *harmony*, may be defined as the study of simultaneous pitch combinations or chords. The study of harmony, one of the most complex and fascinating of all the aspects of music, includes not only a consideration of the structure and characteristics of the various chords, but also of the way in which these chords may be connected with one another and the way in which they may be elaborated in the compositional processes of a complete work.

Chord structure may be described specifically in such terms as major triad or dominant seventh chord, or it may be described more generally in terms of consonance and dissonance. Consonant chords sound euphonious: the notes of the chord blend well with each other. Extremely dissonant chords sound harsh: the pitches do not seem to blend as well with each other. Between these two extremes are a variety of mildly

Varieties and Aspects 11

EXAMPLE 1-3 (a) "Jingle Bells"; (b) "Frère Jacques"; (c) "Marines' Hymn"; (d) "Three Blind Mice"; (e) "The Star-Spangled Banner."

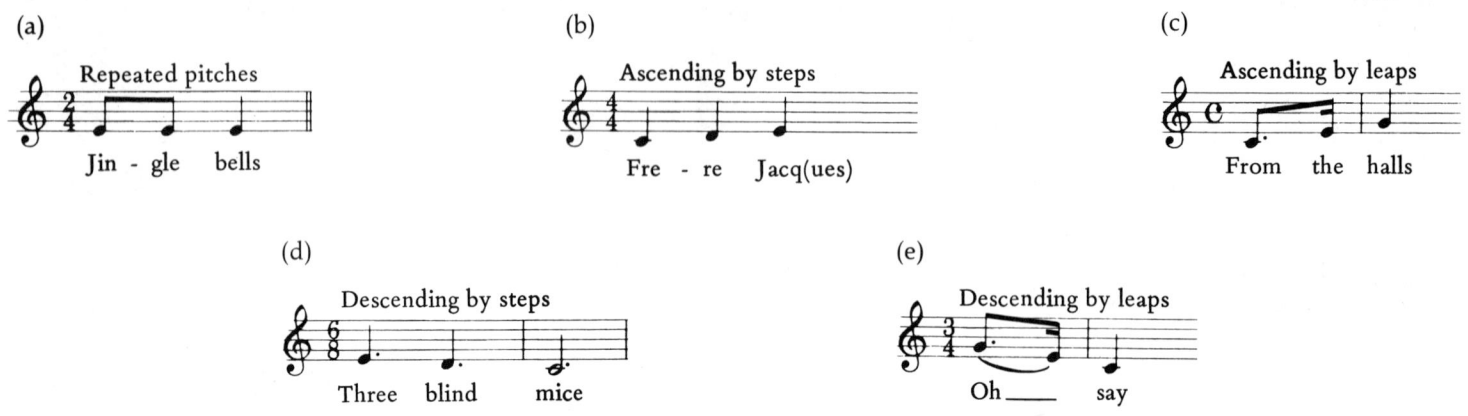

EXAMPLE 1-4 (a) Beethoven: *String Quartet in F Minor, Op 95*, first movement, measures 1–2; (b) Strauss: *Kaiser-Walzer (Emperor Waltz)*, Op. 437, Waltz 1, measures 1–2; (c) Mozart: *Don Giovanni*, No. 7, duettino, "La ci darem la mano" ("Give me your hand"), measures 1–2.

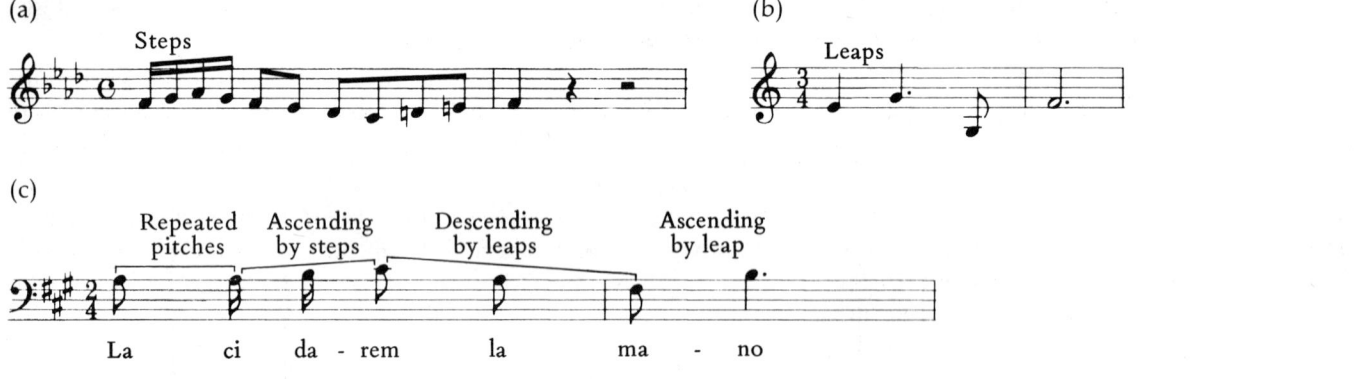

dissonant chords. Consonance and dissonance are subject to contextual factors; a chord that may sound dissonant in the context of one work might sound more consonant in the context of another work.

In general, consonant and mildly dissonant chords have a more relaxing and pleasant effect than extremely dissonant chords. Often, however, listeners will confuse consonance and dissonance with other aspects and will call a work dissonant when in reality it may only have a very rough and unusual timbre or an extremely loud dynamic level. Almost all of the examples at the beginning of this chapter were made up of consonant and mildly dissonant chords, except for some unusual and dissonant pitch combinations in *Gesang der Jünglinge*. In the Indian raga, as in most non-Western music, harmony does not play an important role.

Texture

When we consider timbre, dynamics, rhythm, melody, and harmony, we are breaking the whole of a musical experience down into a series of isolated aspects. It is also important to consider such larger aspects of music as texture and form in which the isolated aspects are combined. We might say that *texture* involves larger aspects of musical space and form involves larger aspects of musical time. Just as texture in cloth refers to the way individual strands of material are woven together to form a fabric, so texture in music refers to the way individual elements of sound are woven together to form a musical fabric.

It is customary to organize musical texture into three main types—monophonic texture: one melody sounded alone; polyphonic or contrapuntal texture: two or more melodies sounded

12 Materials of Music

With undulating swirls and sharp geometric shapes, the Dutch Expressionist Vincent Van Gogh (1853–1890) created a dramatic juxtaposition of disparate textures and shapes in The Starry Night—a fervent protest against the naturalism that pervaded Romantic painting of the 19th century.

simultaneously; and homophonic texture: one main melody sounded with accompanying or subsidiary parts. We could equate these musical types with social types. Monophonic texture is like a single individual; polyphonic texture is like a town-meeting democracy where each voice has a chance to be heard; homophonic texture is like a benevolent dictatorship where one voice is predominant and everything else is subservient.

Monophonic texture is illustrated in the opening two measures of the Beethoven quartet. A single line is heard though it is duplicated or doubled in all four instruments. Homophonic texture is illustrated in the opening measures of the Mozart duet. The melody is heard in the voice part (Don Giovanni) while the accompanying chords are heard in the orchestra. An example of polyphonic texture would be the opening of the Palestrina mass movement. Each of the six voice parts is heard as an important line. Notice in Example 1-5 that the same or similar melodies appear at different times in different parts, a musical technique known as *free imitation*.

Form

Form in music can refer to specific schematic designs such as binary form, concerto form, or *da capo aria* form; or it can refer to general structural principles such as sectionalization, unity and variety, symmetry and balance, or content and function. The study of musical form embraces the study of all aspects. In other words, the study of form in its broadest sense is the study of music itself, as the nineteenth-century esthetician Eduard Hanslick implied in his famous dictum, "Music is form moving in sound."

Because of their fundamental importance, general principles of form will be touched upon in most chapters in this book. Specific formal designs will be treated primarily in Part Two. The varied application of formal principles will be considered as an important aspect of style in Part Three.

As an introduction to the study of form you should consider the aspect of *sectionalization:* the way in which the whole composition is divided and subdivided into sections and subsections. In some works the sense of sectionalization is strongly

EXAMPLE 1-5 PALESTRINA: *Mass for Pope Marcellus II*, KYRIE, MEASURES 1–9.

14 Materials of Music

marked. Notice, for example, how the Mozart duet is broken up into sections marked chiefly by the change from one voice to the other. In other works a sense of sectionalization is circumvented by various means. In the Palestrina mass movement, for example, the first 24 measures form a virtually seamless whole. The sense of sectionalization is avoided because when one voice has a long note or a rest, other voice parts have moving notes that continually contribute to the forward motion of the music. The whole movement has only three large sections corresponding to the three major divisions of the text.

MUSICAL GENRES
Referential and Absolute Music

Just as English literature may be divided into categories such as fiction or nonfiction and into genres such as novel, short story, poem, or others, so too music literature may be divided into various categories, genres, or types. The broadest division of music is into the two general categories of referential music and absolute music. Referential music refers to something outside itself, absolute music does not.

Some inexperienced music listeners tend to think that all music is referential; they expect that every musical aspect or gesture may be translated into a specific emotion, event, or idea; and that every composition may be explained in verbal or pictorial terms. To a certain extent this misconception is rooted in nineteenth-century approaches to music, when writers like E. T. A. Hoffmann tried to give dramatic or programmatic interpretations even for the abstract symphonies and sonatas of the Classical period. Granted that such writings often contained inspiration and insight, they nevertheless were more an expression of the writer's own emotions and ideas than an explanation of the work they intended to discuss.

Just as unfortunate is the mistaken idea that referential music is always highly emotional and subjective, while absolute music is cold, unemotional, and objective. Another related fallacy assumes that referential music is more superficial and less worthy than absolute music.

We would urge you to accept each work of music on its own terms. If it is a referential piece, then by all means you should find out all you can about the text or the program of the piece. If it is a piece of absolute music, however, you should focus your attention on the intrinsic musical aspects. There is nothing wrong if the music calls forth certain associations with people, places, emotions, or ideas, but you should realize that these are your personal responses and they may not have been intended by the composer. You should not regard the categories of referential and absolute music as mutually exclusive. Many works have both referential and absolute characteristics; what differs from work to work is the relative importance of these two characteristics. And finally, you should not confuse attributes of referential and absolute with judgments of expressivity, emotionality, depth, or worth.

Referential music may be subdivided into genres such as dance music, song, religious music, program music, and musical theater. Absolute music may be subdivided into single-movement types such as sectional forms, variational forms, and developmental forms. Absolute music could also be subdivided into such multimovement formal types as sonata, symphony, and concerto.

Performance Media

We could also categorize music according to performance media into instrumental music, vocal music, and miscellaneous or mixed ensembles. Instrumental music may be subdivided into chamber music (music for one to approximately eight players with independent parts) and larger ensembles. Chamber music is usually designated according to the number of players—solo, duo, trio, quartet, etc. Among standard chamber-music combinations are the piano trio (piano, violin, cello), the string quartet (violin I, violin II, viola, cello), the woodwind quintet (flute, oboe, clarinet, bassoon, and French horn), and many others. Larger ensembles include the orchestra, symphonic band, and jazz or stage band. Choral ensembles may also be subdivided into small chamber ensembles and larger choruses. Miscellaneous and mixed ensembles would include chorus and orchestra, ensembles of electronic instruments, and various ethnic ensembles such as the Javanese *gamelan* orchestra.

Popular and Classical Music

There is another way to divide music into two categories that usually creates more problems than it solves. This is the division into popular or light music and classical or serious music. Most people have some idea of what is meant by these terms

Musical Arts Center, Indiana University, Bloomington, Indiana

Music of far-distant times is now enjoying a popular revival and numerous groups of musicians, such as the Pro Arte Ensemble of the School of Music of Indiana University, devote their talents to the performance of Renaissance music on replicas of the instruments of the period.

16   Materials of Music

and could probably decide, for example, that a rock tune in the "top 40" or a theme song from a current film would belong in the first category, while a piano concerto by Tchaikovsky or a symphony by Haydn would belong in the second. However, no adequate terms to describe these categories have yet been found. If we measure popularity by the total number of enthusiastic listeners through the years and not just during one year, then the Tchaikovsky *Concerto No. 2 for Piano* would be more "popular" than the rock song. A theme song from a movie may be quite serious and a Haydn symphony may be light in character. The term "classical" is probably best reserved for a specific period of music history (roughly from 1750 to 1825); for a general stylistic tendency marked by such characteristics as balance, clarity, stability, or restraint; or for a notable accomplishment as when a symphony is called a classic example of colorful orchestration.

Above all, the distinction between popular and classical music, as well as a similar dichotomy between folk music and art music, all too often has implications and connotations of value, integrity, and level of technical achievement that are highly inappropriate. No single type of music has a monopoly on worth, sincerity, or craftsmanship, and no single type of music can be dismissed categorically as inferior, insincere, or incompetent. Like Sir Donald Tovey, the perceptive British music critic, we are not sure if there is such a thing as bad music, but if there is, then we prefer "good bad music" to "bad good music."

We do not reject the idea of standards in music; the works we have chosen to discuss in this book are works that we regard as worthwhile or at the very least interesting. We do urge, however, that each work be considered, as far as possible, with informed and impartial ears. To provide you with at least a beginning basis for this is the purpose of the material in the rest of this book and in the accompanying modules, and such is the hope of the authors who wrote them.

2 Rhythm, Melody, and Accompaniment

Tempo

As was pointed out in Chapter 1, the temporal background of music consists of beats or pulses moving at faster or slower rates of speed and/or at different architectonic levels, the rate or pace of the basic beats being called *tempo*. A large number of French, German, Italian, and English terms have traditionally been used to specify tempos. Some such terms are *allegro* (Italian for "cheerful, bright, or fast"), *animé* (French for "animated"), *lebhaft* (Germany for "lively"), and numerous others. Were you to inspect the score of Aaron Copland's ballet *Appalachian Spring,* for example, you would see that he has indicated *allegro* as the beginning tempo of the work. Immediately, however, the symbol (♩ = 160) appears. This is a far more specific temporal instruction to the players and conductor. In this instance the composer has indicated that the rate of speed for quarter-note beats equals 160 per minute. Musicians use a timing device called the *metronome** to gauge tempi. Most music involves a metronome speed for beats somewhere between 60 and 160 beats per minute. Marches are usually designated at MM120† per minute, so it's easy to see that the quick, exciting pace of this passage is a good bit faster than a typical march. Tempo is a decisive determinant of our perception of rhythm, since rhythm pertains in general to *all* aspects of musical time. Tempo determines to a great extent the rate at which we experience the passing of musical events, and, as we shall see, the relative durations of musical events constitute their rhythm.

Sometimes performers or conductors introduce tempo changes or slight modifications without a cue to do so from the composer's score. You may have noted such modifications in listening to a particular performance. Other words denoting performance considerations other than tempo appear frequently in a score. For example, *vigoroso* (Italian for "vigor-

---

*This clocklike device was invented in 1816 by Maelzel. Metronomic indications are usually prefaced by MM, an abbreviation for "Maelzel's metronome." Beethoven was one of the first well-known composers to systematically employ the metronome.

†MM ♩ = 120, for example, denotes 120 quarter-note beats per minute—that is, 120 ticks per minute, each tick being the duration of one quarter note.

The concentration and contentment of the involved listener is captured in this picture of Degas, which depicts the artist's father listening to Pagans, a popular guitarist of the day.

ously") indicates the aggressive and assertive way in which the player is to approach the opening passage. The letter *f* stands for *forte,* meaning "loud and strong." One other symbol appearing quite often is called a *fermata,* ⌒ ; it indicates that the duration beneath or above it is to be held or sustained for sufficient time to create a distinct musical pause. Fermatas obviously affect rhythm in that their use results in a durational emphasis on whatever sounds are sustained. Sometimes silence is prolonged in music through a similar signal.

Meter and Pulse Levels

The interplay of tempo, rhythm, and meter imparts a unique character and vitality to a particular work. While Copland's ballet *Appalachian Spring* will be further discussed in the last chapter, let us consider certain of its rhythmic aspects now as we become acquainted with the materials of music. Much of *Appalachian Spring's* rhythmic appeal and excitement is in part related to the variety of meter and pulse levels that constitute the rhythmic framework of the piece. This variety is suggested by the succession of different meters that can be observed in the second section by merely thumbing through the score. The meters thus encountered include 4/4 (measure 1), 2/4 (measure 29), 3/2 (measure 50), 7/8 (measure 54), 6/8 (measure 71), and 5/4 (measure 75).

The most characteristic activity of the piece is that associated with 4/4 or common time. To familiarize yourself with common pulse groupings of 4/4 meter consider the line of rhythm in Example 2-1. Establish a quick quarter-note pulse level (beat) as shown on the lower line and intone the rhythm of the example on the syllable *ta.* Continue to tap the quarter-note beat while doing so.

We noted earlier that the rhythm of such a passage is a product of the interaction of durations on different levels;* in this passage those levels are represented by the metered pulse of successive quarters interacting with both quarter notes and their division into eighths. Perform Example 2-1 again, substituting eighths for the quarters on the lower line; doing so presents an aural picture of the pulse level of steady eighths that is also implied by the excerpt. Both levels (quarters and eighths) must be experienced or felt if we are to perceive the rhythm of the passage in the full sense of the word.

Simple triple meter is introduced at several points in the ballet. Simple triple meter involves three beats per measure with regular divisions of the beat by two, four, eight, etc. The most common simple triple meters are as follows:

3/4 (♩ ♩ ♩), 3/2 (♩ ♩ ♩), and 3/8 (♪ ♪ ♪)
Sww   Sww   Sww

The first beat is understood to be accented (strong) while the second and third beats are unaccented (weak). Perform the triple-meter rhythms shown in Example 2-2; in each case establish and maintain the meter while performing the various durations. Note that the use of a dot following the note extends the length of the duration by one-half of its normal value; a dotted half note then is the equivalent of a half note tied to a quarter (♩♩), tied notes denoting continuous sound.

You have probably noticed that in measures in which the basic beat is not represented in the pattern to be read, as in the final measures of the preceding drills, it is necessary to con-

---

*Such levels are indicated by notes and rests signifying different time lengths.

EXAMPLE 2-1 COPLAND: *Appalachian Spring*, RHYTHMIC DURATIONS OF MEASURES 16–23.

EXAMPLE 2-2 TRIPLE-METER RHYTHMS.

tinue mentally the metric pulse as a basis for accurately interpreting the duration(s) indicated.

The preceding examples contain a range of relative durations, each of which may represent a level of pulse (beat) in a given context. The chart on the right reviews common relative durations and their equivalent *rest signs*. The durations are scaled from (relatively) longest to shortest.

Remember that any duration may be assigned *any desired metronomic speed*. A whole note may equal MM 160, if so desired, while an eighth may equal MM 60. A number of factors, including traditions of notation, notational convenience, and composers' whims, may influence such notational decisions.

Relative Rhythmic Durations and Equivalent Rests

𝆹. (𝆹_𝅗𝅥)	dotted whole note	∎.
𝆹	whole note	∎
𝅗𝅥. (𝅗𝅥_𝅘𝅥)	dotted half note	▬.
𝅗𝅥	half note	▬
𝅘𝅥. (𝅘𝅥_𝅘𝅥𝅮)	dotted quarter note	𝄽 (𝄽 𝄾)
𝅘𝅥	quarter note	𝄽
𝅘𝅥𝅮. (𝅘𝅥𝅮_𝅘𝅥𝅯)	dotted eighth note	𝄾 (𝄾 𝄿)
𝅘𝅥𝅮	eighth note	𝄾
𝅘𝅥𝅯. (𝅘𝅥𝅯_𝅘𝅥𝅰)	dotted sixteenth note	𝄿 (𝄿 𝅀)
𝅘𝅥𝅯	sixteenth note	𝄿

20 Materials of Music

Henri Matisse (1869–1954), member of the French Fauves ("wild ones") committed to breaking with the naturalist tradition, fashioned a stylized schematization of motives (repeated and varied lines and geometric shapes) in achieving unity and eloquence of form in his Piano Lesson.

Rhythm Pattern and Unity

Rhythm provides a basis for unity and continuity in most music; it does so in a number of ways. It should be understood from the first that most music is unified in part through the use of rhythm patterns.

Rhythm can create unity via three distinct, related processes: repetition, restatement, and variation—that is, modified or altered repetition. Rhythmic repetition involves the immediate and essentially exact recurrence of a rhythmic figure or pattern—a group of durations that is easily remembered by distinctive arrangement or grouping, called *motive*. Restatement, on the other hand, involves delayed repetition—that is, the reuse of a specific figure or pattern subsequent to the introduction of new or contrasted rhythmic material. The line of rhythm in Example 2-3 illustrates restatement.

Rhythmic repetition is often associated with the similar treatment of melodic—that is, pitch—materials. Such is often the case in *Appalachian Spring;* however, our attention for the time being is directed to the element of rhythmic duration per se. We shall deal later with the combined treatments of rhythm and pitch in conjunction with melodic materials such as motives, phrases, and musical spans.

Although the repetitive treatment of rhythmic patterns is common to dance music, as in *Appalachian Spring,* such unifying use of rhythmic repetition is by no means limited to dance music; on the contrary, the reuse of characteristic rhythmic details is basic to most music. The three passages in Example 2-4 support such a statement. Read their rhythms.

One of the principal means for varying recurring patterns, which if continued throughout tend to become monotonous, lies in the process of rhythmic displacement called *syncopation*.

Syncopation results when rhythmic accents fall on weak beats, those normally regarded as unaccented points in the meter, or weak parts (divisions) of the beat. Syncopation in a number of forms creates considerable rhythmic interest and variety. Several patterns involving syncopation are shown in Example 2-5. Each pattern should be performed.

Rhythm and Structure

Often, rhythm materials dominate other elements of music. For example, the first large section of *Appalachian Spring* evolves out of the opening gesture, which is as follows:

EXAMPLE 2-3   COPLAND: *Appalachian Spring,* MEASURES 19–22.

Statement of pattern | Contrasting rhythmic material | Restatement of original pattern

Rhythm, Melody, and Accompaniment

EXAMPLE 2-4 RHYTHMIC REPETITION IN THREE FAMILIAR PASSAGES: (a) "AMERICA THE BEAUTIFUL," MEASURES 1–8; (b) MOZART: *Symphony No. 40 in G Minor*, FIRST MOVEMENT, MEASURES 1–8; (c) BARTÓK: *Concerto for Orchestra*, FIRST MOVEMENT, MEASURES 39–47.

(a)

(b)

(c)

Bartók: © Copyright 1946 by Hawkes & Son (London) Ltd.; Renewed 1973. Reprinted by permission of Boosey & Hawkes, Inc.

EXAMPLE 2-5 RHYTHM PATTERNS INVOLVING SYNCOPATION. (AN ARROW INDICATES THE POINT OF DISPLACEMENT.)

Mental reference for implied beat division

Musicians generally call such brief yet telling combinations of pitch and rhythm *motives*. Since this figure contains only two different notes, its melodic interest is minimal and its main attraction is, as has been noted, rhythm. The entire section, indeed the entire excerpt, is carried along by the reiterative use of two durations (two short followed by one long) and some slight variants.

Generally speaking, the function of such patterns is that of providing a continuing thread of activity against which new or contrasted activity is projected. Procedures such as this, which provide bases for the extension and growth of compositions into sizable musical structures, are basic to a great deal of well-written and coherent music of many past centuries and of the present one as well. For example, the basic motive appearing in Example 2-6a generates a more or less continuous activity of derivative thematic materials (Example 2-6b-g) which dominate the opening section of the ballet.

Texture

The word *texture* as used by musicians is roughly comparable to the term *composition* as used by painters. Texture refers to the various parts—that is, distinguishable lines or strands—of a piece, or section thereof, and to the relations that such lines have to one another. Textures made of a single musical line are called *monophonic*, meaning one-voiced. Any unaccompanied musical line is monophonic. *Polyphonic* texture (multiple lines) results when the number of individual musical lines are increased to thicken the texture.

Harmony results from the simultaneous sounding of two or more different pitches. Textures in which three or more different pitches (or parts) combine are called *chordal* or *homophonic,* and they are typified by the dominance of one rhythm or melody over other essentially secondary or accompanying parts. The relation of two such parts, one being a duplication of the other at a specific harmonic interval, is called *parallel* motion. A part that moves in counterdirection to another produces *contrary* motion. These terms and others allude to linear relations within a texture.

When a part provides an unchanging pitch reference maintained against other, more varied activity, it is called a *pedal point*. The precise term for motion involving a moving part sounding against one that is stationary or repetitive is *oblique* motion. When the various lines (parts) reveal some individuality or movement, *counterpoint* results. And the activity between two clearly distinguishable parts is called *contrapuntal.*

Melody

Let us now turn to further consideration of that primary element of music called *melody* and its organization. We will use as a point of departure the well-known popular song briefly mentioned in Chapter 1, "Yesterday," by John Lennon and Paul McCartney.

If we wanted to analyze the structure of this song, that is, its text, we would break it down into words, phrases, sentences, paragraphs, and larger units. In a somewhat similar though by no means absolutely parallel manner, we could analyze the music by breaking it down into motives, phrases, periods, sections, and larger units.

EXAMPLE 2-6   COPLAND: *Appalachian Spring,* VARIANTS OF THE OPENING MOTIVE.

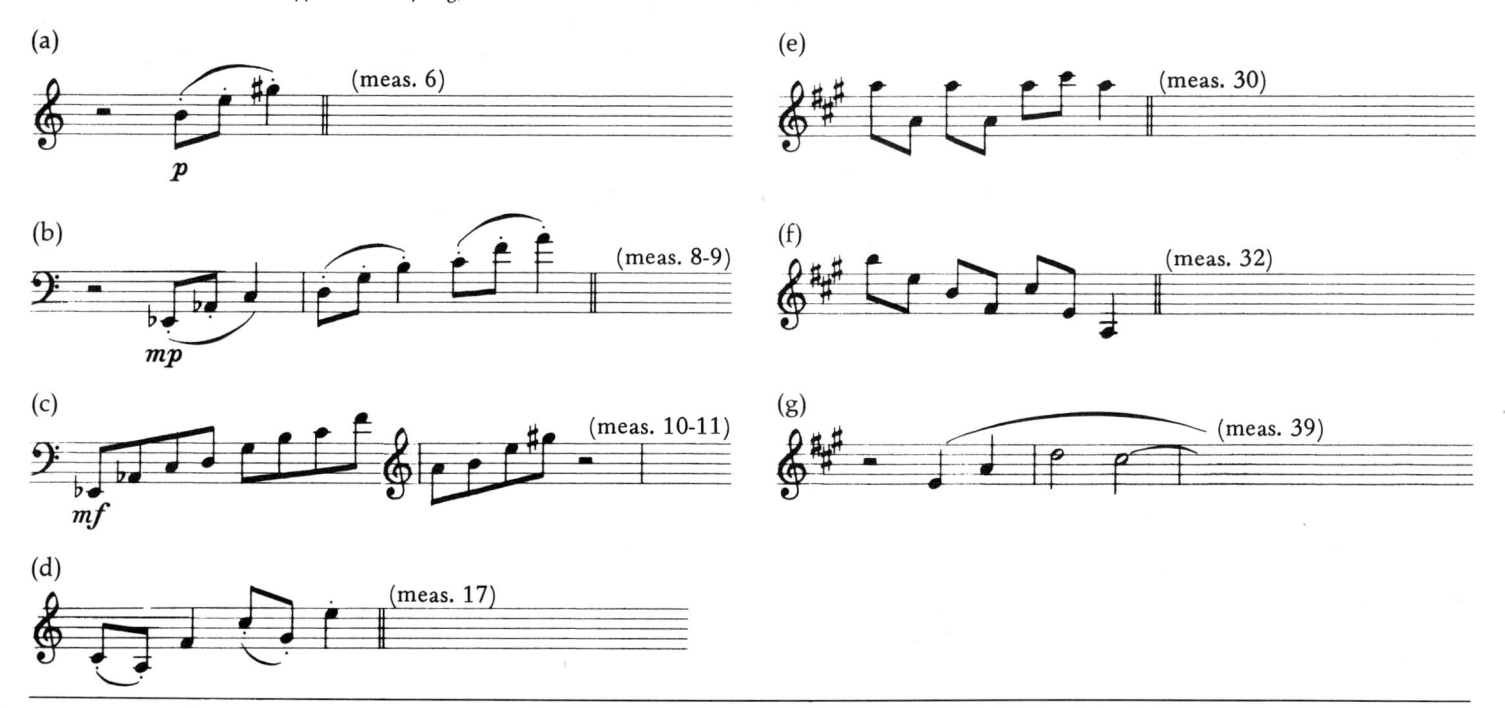

In terms of overall formal structure, "Yesterday" may be divided into four large sections reflecting the four divisions of the poem. The first section presents a distinctive melodic theme or idea, the second section repeats this, the third section introduces a change of melody, and the fourth section brings a restatement or delayed repetition of the original melodic idea. These four processes—presentation, repetition, change, and restatement—are basic to all music and they operate in different ways on different levels of a composition.

The process of change in music may range from subtle changes in only one or two aspects to extensive changes in several aspects. Subtle changes are called *variation*, extensive changes are called *contrast*. Letters or numbers may be used to label units of music. The same letter is used to indicate repetition or restatement (A-A-A or A-B-A); new letters are used for contrast (A-B-C, etc.); the same letter with a superscript is used to designate variation (A-A^1-A^2, etc.). The formal pattern of "Yesterday"—A-A-B-A—is common in many types of song literature. In popular music the B section is sometimes called the "bridge" or "release."

Motives

Having analyzed the larger aspects of form in this song, let us now turn to a consideration of the smallest units—the motives. As we have learned, a motive in music is a relatively short, self-contained, meaningful unit, somewhat like a word or a short phrase in poetry or prose (see Example 2-7).

To qualify as a motive, a musical unit not only must have clearly recognizable characteristics, it must also be used in some form as a significant building block in the structure of a melody. If a set of notes is just used incidentally in a melody or if it appears only in the accompaniment, the term *figure* would probably be more appropriate, but the two terms are sometimes used interchangeably. To understand how motives may be used in a melody, we must first learn to describe their pitch characteristics.

Intervals

We have learned that one important characteristic of pitch is the musical distance or interval between successive notes, and we distinguished narrow intervals or steps from wider intervals or leaps. Now, in order to penetrate more deeply into the musical structure of the works we are studying, we need to develop a more specific set of terms for intervals. Traditional interval designation involves double terms like "major third" or "perfect fifth." The first term is called the *qualitative* name, the second is called the *numerical* name. The numerical name shows the relative distance between two pitches—a second is a narrow interval, a seventh is a wider interval. The qualitative name gives us more exact information on pitch distance. Seconds, for example, may appear in two forms—minor seconds and major seconds. The minor second or half step is the smallest interval commonly used in Western music. Other intervals may be identified in terms of the number of half steps they contain as shown in the following chart:

EXAMPLE 2-7   LENNON AND MCCARTNEY: "YESTERDAY," MEASURES 1–3.

Interval Names and Abbreviations	Number of Half Steps	Examples
Perfect prime or unison or repeated note (P1)	0	C to C
Augmented prime (+1) Minor second (m2)	1	C to C sharp C to D flat
Major second (M2)	2	C to D
Augmented second (+2) Minor third (m3)	3	C to D sharp C to E flat
Major third (M3)	4	C to E
Perfect fourth (P4)	5	C to F
Augmented fourth (+4) Diminished fifth (°5)	6	C to F sharp C to G flat
Perfect fifth (P5)	7	C to G
Augmented fifth (+5) Minor sixth (m6)	8	C to G sharp C to A flat
Major sixth (M6)	9	C to A
Augmented sixth (+6) Minor seventh (m7)	10	C to A sharp C to B flat
Major seventh (M7)	11	C to B
Perfect octave (P8)	12	C to C^1

At this point you are probably wondering if you have to memorize this chart in order to understand and appreciate music. The answer is no. We have included the chart so you may use it for reference, but you do not need to master it as a musician would. You should, however, have a general idea of what we mean when we say that "Yesterday" begins with a descending major second, or that a variation of this motive in measure 5 begins with a descending minor second. (See Example 2-8.)

Movement by seconds gives melodies a smooth flow; movement by larger intervals is generally more assertive and vigorous. Some intervals may be associated with emotions or extramusical ideas. The tritone (diminished fifth or augmented fourth) was known to medieval theorists as the "devil in music"; even in more recent music this interval is sometimes used to express a sinister or at least an exotic character.

Contour

Let us turn from the narrow consideration of the intervals between successive notes to a broader consideration of the overall shape or contour of a motive or a melody. Motives 1 and 2 of "Yesterday" illustrate two basic contoural types—descending contour and ascending contour. Two other important contoural

EXAMPLE 2-8 LENNON AND MCCARTNEY: "YESTERDAY," MEASURES 1–5.

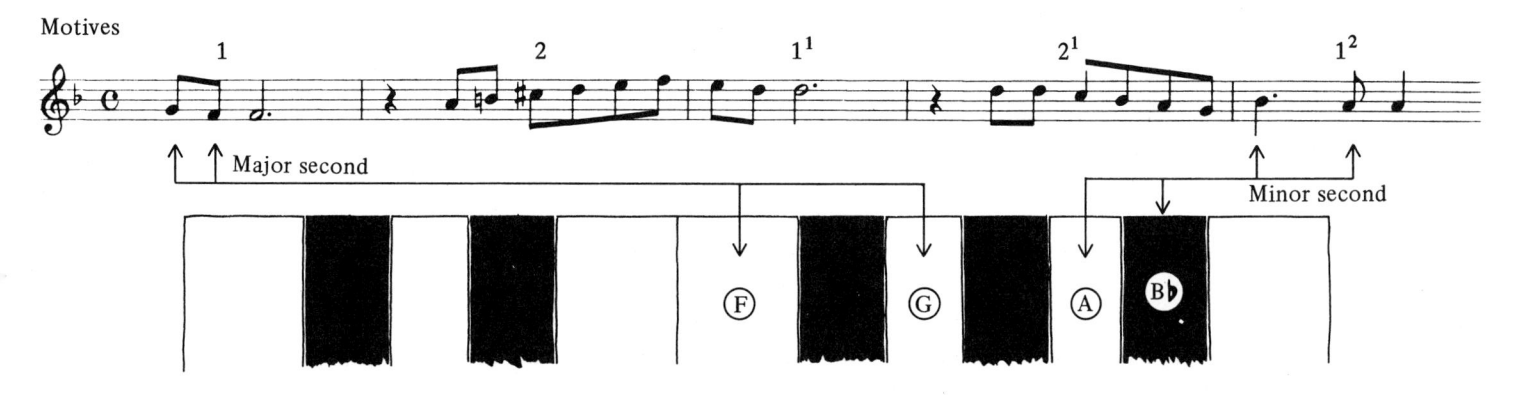

Degas, one of the greatest French painters of the 19th century and very talented in depicting the human form in motion, encapsulates a fleeting impression of a ballerina enjoying the telling glance of an envious admirer.

types, the arch and the inverted arch, are illustrated in Example 2-9. Notice, also, how the whole line of music could be regarded as one large arch contour.

Another contour type is the axis contour in which the pitches seem to cluster around a central axis pitch as shown in Example 2-10. Most melodies will contain a mixture of various contour types.

Variation of Motives

Once we have described the pitch and rhythm characteristics of a motive in its original form, we can then observe how it may be varied in later appearances in a melody. Variation usually implies that one characteristic, either pitch or rhythm, will be kept the same while the other is changed. To hear the variation we must somehow be able to identify the varied motive with the original. There is some evidence that rhythmic characteristics tend to identify a motive more vividly than pitch characteristics. You are more likely to recognize a motive from hearing its rhythm alone than from hearing its pitch aspects without any rhythmic patterning. This may account for the fact that in varied motives it is often the rhythm that is preserved while the pitch is changed. Many of the techniques of pitch variation may be heard in "Yesterday," including transposition, inversion, and interval expansion or contraction.

Transposition means to move a motive or melody from its original pitch location to another pitch location, preserving the relative interval structure and the rhythm. Notice in Example 2-8 how motive 1 is transposed from a beginning pitch of G in measure 1 to a beginning pitch of E in measure 3. Sometimes an entire melody will be transposed from one pitch location to another; a bass singer, for example, might transpose the entire song "Yesterday" down a perfect fifth to fit his vocal range.

Another related technique of pitch variation is *sequence*, a process in which a motive is repeated successively on several different pitch levels. Example 2-11*a* shows how the opening motive of "Yesterday" could have been treated as a sequence. Example 2-11*b* shows how Brahms actually used the technique of sequence to express a sense of importunate desire and tension.

If we compare motive 2 to its variation, motive 2^1, in Example 2-8, we see another technique of pitch variation in operation, namely, *inversion*. Inversion involves reversal of pitch direction—ascending intervals in the original version become descending intervals and vice versa. The inversion in motive 2^1 is somewhat free since the first two notes repeat rather than descend as they would in a strict inversion. Example 2-12 shows the technique of strict inversion as applied by the Russian pianist-composer Rachmaninoff to a melody written by the Italian violinist-composer Paganini. The resulting melody, far from sounding contrived or artificial, has become one of the most famous melodies in music literature and was even made into a popular song.

Interval expansion and *interval contraction* are techniques of pitch variation that involve making the intervals of a motive larger or smaller while preserving their original direction. We have already seen a subtle example of interval contraction in the change from a major second in motive 1 to a minor second in motive 1^2 (see Example 2-8). Other examples of interval contraction and interval expansion may be seen in Example 2-13.

EXAMPLE 2-9 LENNON AND MCCARTNEY: "YESTERDAY," MEASURES 11–14.

EXAMPLE 2-10 SCHUBERT: *Ave Maria*, MEASURES 3–4.

EXAMPLE 2-11 (a) SEQUENTIAL TREATMENT OF THE FIRST MOTIVE OF "YESTERDAY"; (b) BRAHMS: *O liebliche Wangen* (*O Lovely Cheeks*), Op. 47, No. 4, MEASURES 57–59.

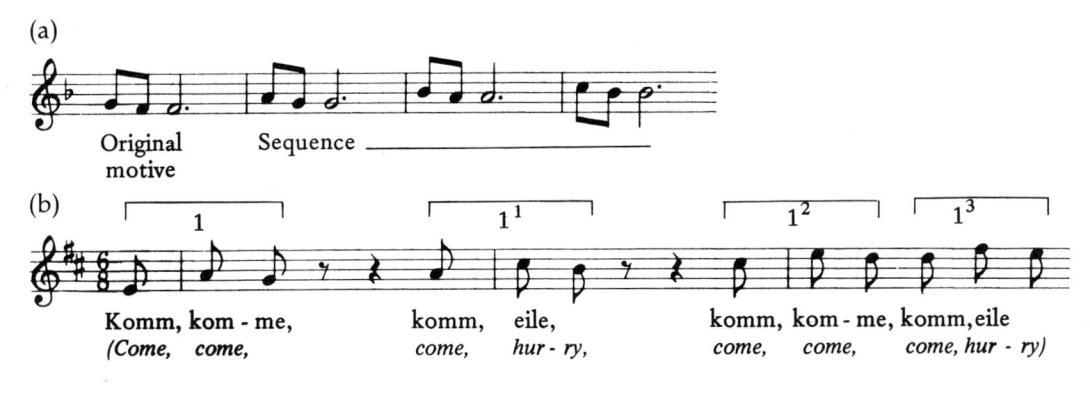

EXAMPLE 2-12 (a) PAGANINI: *Caprice No. 24 in A Minor;* (b) RACHMANINOFF: *Rhapsody on a Theme of Paganini.*

EXAMPLE 2-13 (a) SCHUBERT: *Ständchen* (*Serenade*) (BASED ON SHAKESPEARE), MEASURES 31–32; (b) SCHUBERT: *Ständchen* (BASED ON RELLSTAB), MEASURES 5 AND 11.

Rhythm, Melody, and Accompaniment 27

Variation techniques such as transposition, sequence, inversion, interval expansion, and interval contraction are relatively easy to perceive. Less obvious is the technique of *retrograde*—that is, playing the pitches of a motive or a melody in reverse order. Though an interesting device for the composer, it is almost impossible to perceive as a listener. Try to guess the original motive in Example 2-14a before you look at it in Example 2-14b.

Techniques of pitch variation, as well as those of rhythm variation discussed elsewhere, provide a composition with a sense of unity and coherence. Often several techniques of pitch and rhythm variation will be used in combination, as illustrated in Example 2-15.

Tonality

To this point we have been discussing pitch characteristics as though they existed in themselves without any relation to an underlying structure or background. Though this may be true in some isolated instances, such as the atonal music of the twentieth century, in most instances pitch characteristics will be perceived as foreground details against a background of tonality.

We have already learned that tonality is that quality in music according to which one tone, the tonic, is heard as a focal pitch toward which the other pitches of a particular piece or section all point. More specifically, tonality may be defined on the basis of two criteria—intervallic arrangement and hierarchical ordering. That is, in a specific tonality the pitches will have certain interval relations to each other, and some pitches will be heard as more important than others. To illustrate this let us examine the tonality of F major that was used in our opening song "Yesterday." The intervallic arrangement and hierarchical ordering of F major are suggested notationally and graphically in Example 2-16.

EXAMPLE 2-14 (a) Motive in retrograde; (b) "The Star-Spangled Banner."

EXAMPLE 2-15 Lennon and McCartney: "Yesterday," opening and closing measures.

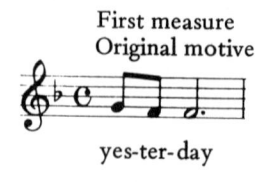

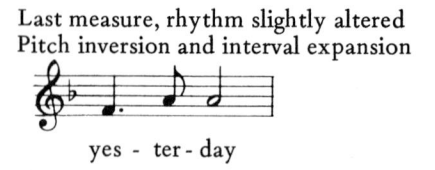

EXAMPLE 2-16 Structure of a tonality.

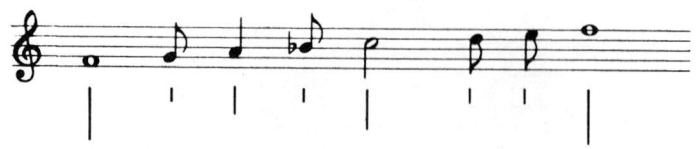

EXAMPLE 2-17 Key signature.

28 Materials of Music

John Lennon and Paul McCartney sport fancy garb, not unfitting for these modern-day troubadours.

Written out in ascending or descending succession the pitches of a tonality form a scale. The intervallic arrangement of a major scale or tonality is major seconds between all degrees of the scale except between the third and fourth and the seventh and eighth degrees where minor seconds occur. Notice that it is necessary to have B flat rather than B natural in order to achieve this intervallic arrangement. For the tonality of D major, the pitches F and C must be sharped in order to achieve the proper intervallic arrangement. To save labor the accidentals (sharps or flats) needed for a particular tonality may be written in a key signature at the beginning of the line.

The hierarchical ordering of pitches in a tonality is suggested in Examples 2-16 and 2-17 by the type of note value in the notational representation and by the length of line in the graphic representation. The *tonic* (F in F major, D in D major) is the most important or strongest pitch in a tonality. It will generally be heard more frequently and longer than other pitches and it will appear at important temporal positions, especially at the end of a section, also frequently at the beginning of a section or at important points in the metric structure such as downbeats. The next most important pitch is the *dominant* (C in F major, A in D major), and these two pitches, tonic and dominant, are sometimes called the *axis* or *polar* pitches of a tonality. The *mediant* (A in F major, F sharp in D major) may also be a fairly important pitch in a tonality. The remaining pitches are generally less important in the structure of a tonality, though they may sometimes be emphasized in a particular melody* For the trained listener each note in a tonality ultimately takes on an individual character and function. The seventh scale degree has a strong tendency to lead to the tonic and is, indeed, called the *leading tone*. The second degree also tends to lead toward the tonic, the fourth degree toward the mediant, and the sixth degree toward the dominant. This explains why motive 1 in "Yesterday" has such a different effect when it occurs on different scale degrees.

*The other notes of a diatonic scale also have similar labels, all of which appear in relation to C major; for example, as follows: C = tonic, D = supertonic, E = mediant, F = subdominant, G = dominant, A = submediant, and B = leading tone.

The seven pitches of a tonality such as we have seen in Examples 2-16 and 2-17 are called the *diatonic pitches*. The remaining five pitches would be the *chromatic pitches*. They may replace or embellish the diatonic pitches. Music written only with diatonic pitches will have a simpler, more straightforward, "folklike" character than music with extensive use of chromaticism. Compare the untroubled serenity created by the diatonic setting of the Schubert song with the dark disquietude created by the more chromatic setting of the Wolf song in Example 2-18.

Major tonalities account for a substantial portion of music literature, but by no means all of it. The next most frequently used type of tonality is the minor tonality. The chief difference between these two tonality types is that the third degree (mediant) of a minor scale or tonality is a minor third (three half steps) away from the tonic, rather than a major third (four half steps) as in the major scale or tonality. Thus the third degree of F minor would be A flat rather than A natural; the third degree of D minor would be F natural rather than F sharp. In addition, the sixth and seventh degrees of a minor scale are variable. For example, in F minor the sixth degree could be D flat or D natural; the seventh degree could be E flat or E natural (see Example 2-19).

Choice of tonality may contribute to the emotional character of the music. There is some tendency to associate major with more positive, happy emotions and minor with more

Rhythm, Melody, and Accompaniment 29

EXAMPLE 2-18 (a) SCHUBERT: *Heidenröslein (Heather Rose)*, Op. 3. No. 3, MEASURES 1–4; (b) WOLF: *Mörike-Lieder*, "IN DER FRÜHE" ("IN THE EARLY MORNING"), MEASURES 1–4.

(a)

Sah ein Knab' ein Rös - lein steh'n Rös - lein auf der Hei - den
(A lad saw a rose stand - ing Rose on the heath - er

(b)

Kein Schlaf noch kühlt das Au - ge-mir; dort ge - het schon der Tag her - fur an mei - nem Kam-mer-fen-ster.
(No sleep yet cools my eye) there goes already the day past my chamber window

EXAMPLE 2-19 MINOR TONALITIES.

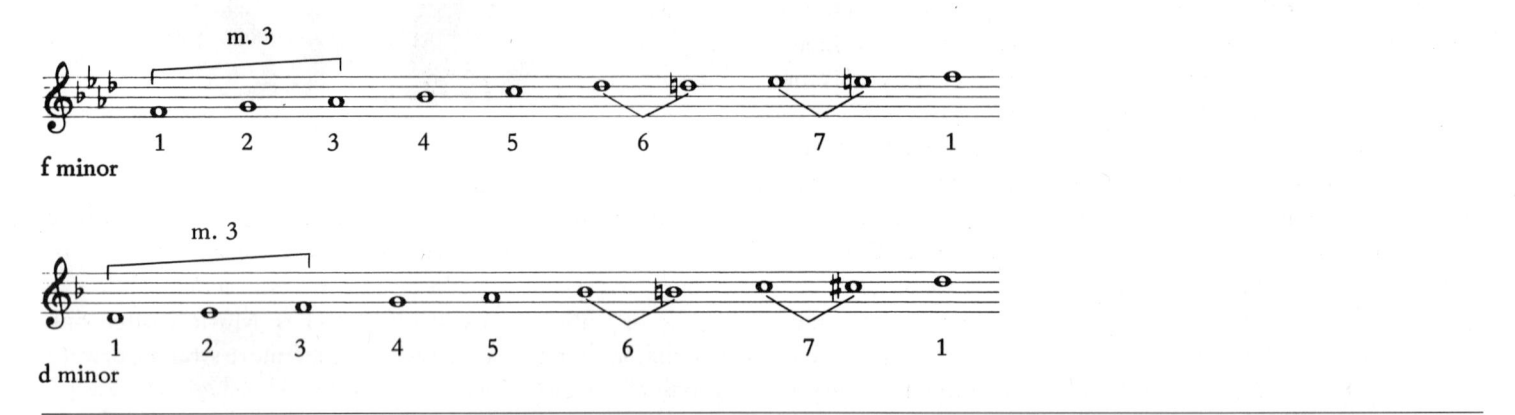

f minor: 1 2 3 4 5 6 7 1 (m. 3)

d minor: 1 2 3 4 5 6 7 1 (m. 3)

EXAMPLE 2-20 PITCH ANALYSIS OF KERN'S "YESTERDAYS."

Scale degrees in d minor: 5 3 4 5 3 4 1 2 3, etc.

negative, sad emotions. That this does not always happen is aptly proven by the fact that the bittersweet sadness of the Beatles' "Yesterday" is expressed in a major tonality. There is, however, another popular song from the 1930's with a very similar title and mood, "Yesterdays" by Jerome Kern, that *is* written in minor (see Example 2-20).

Unity and Variety

One of the most important formal principles in song composition is that of a balance between *unity* and *variety*. Imagine, for example, how a song would sound if it were based on just one motive, or, on the other hand, how it would sound if every word or phrase of the text were set to totally new motives with no repetition or variation of previously heard material. The result would be monotony on the one hand and confusion on the other. Sometimes, it is true, composers deliberately seek to create one of these effects when it is appropriate for the text they are setting, but more often they will seek to create a balance between unity and variety. They will judiciously use the processes of repetition, variation, contrast, and restatement.

The idea of a balance between unity and variety extends beyond motives to such larger units as a phrase. A phrase may

30 Materials of Music

be defined as a relatively complete musical utterance, roughly comparable to a phrase or a short sentence in language. Phrases are often four measures in length. But that this is not always true is shown by phrases in "Yesterday" which could be analyzed as phrase lengths of three measures, two measures, and again two measures in the first part of the song.

Cadence

The end of a phrase is marked by a *cadence*—a musical point of conclusion. The most definite cadence in a piece of music is usually the final cadence; other internal cadences will momentarily stop the music but at the same time they will frequently suggest that the music will go on. Definite, conclusive cadences are sometimes called *full* or *terminal cadences;* less definite cadences suggesting continuation of the music are sometimes called *half* or *progressive cadences.* Cadences ending on the tonic pitch will give a more definite feeling of conclusion than those that do not.

Accompaniment

An essential aspect that is missing in our discussion to this point is any consideration of *accompaniment.* Before we consider this, however, we need to learn something more about chords since most accompaniments involve various treatments or manipulations of chords. A *chord* is simply the sounding of two or more pitches simultaneously. In later chapters we shall study other aspects of chords, but for now we shall merely introduce two chords—the major triad and the minor triad.

A triad is a chord made up of three different pitches. A major triad has a major third and a perfect fifth above the lowest note or "root" of the chord; a minor triad has a minor third and a perfect fifth above this root. As shown in Example 2-21, the same chord may appear in many different forms.

There is a tendency to associate major triads with positive emotions and minor triads with negative, but just as in tonality, this tendency should not be taken for an absolute rule. Both chords are heard as consonant chords—that is, their pitches seem to blend well with one another and their sound is euphonious.

Now that we know at least two types of chords, we can see how a composer might treat them and other chords in the accompaniment of a melody. We have chosen the songs of Franz Schubert for purposes of illustration because his accompaniments not only are uniquely suited to bring out the meaning or mood of the text, but they also are infinitely varied, constituting a veritable catalog of the possibilities of accompaniments and instrumental works as well.

EXAMPLE 2-21 SAME CHORD APPEARING IN DIFFERENT FORMS.

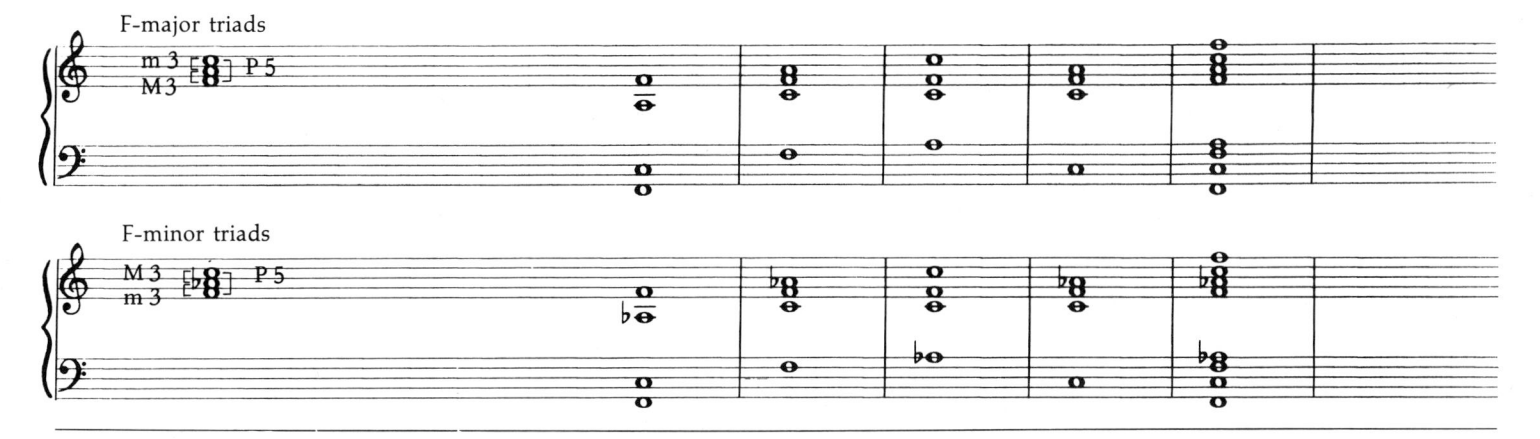

Block-chord accompaniment has a chord in the accompaniment for each note in the melody. It is especially appropriate for the solemnity of *Der Tod und das Mädchen* (Example 2-22).

Sustained-chord accompaniment has one chord sustained in the accompaniment while several notes are sounded in the melody. Schubert uses this type of accompaniment to express the simplicity of *Morgengruss* (Example 2-23).

Repeated-chord accompaniment has several repetitions of a chord in the accompaniment set against each single note of the melody. The pulsating chords in *Aufenthalt* effectively underline the excitement of the opening line (Example 2-24).

Bass-afterbeat accompaniment consists of a low bass note followed by one or more chords in a higher register. A simple bass note followed by a single afterbeat chord is appropriate for the folk-song character of *Heidenröslein,* one of Schubert's most beloved melodies (Example 2-25a). A bass note followed by two afterbeats in a fast tempo vividly portrays the mood of *Ungeduld* (Example 2-25b). A bass note followed by several afterbeats in a slow tempo provides an appropriate background for the tenderly beautiful *Ave Maria* (Example 2-25c).

EXAMPLE 2-22 SCHUBERT: *Der Tod und das Mädchen* (*Death and the Maiden*).

EXAMPLE 2-23 SCHUBERT: *Morgengruss* (*Morning Greeting*).

EXAMPLE 2-24 SCHUBERT: *Aufenthalt* (*Resting Place*).

EXAMPLE 2-25 SCHUBERT: (a) *Heidenröslein (Heather Rose)*; (b) *Ungeduld (Impatience)*; (c) *Ave Maria (Hail Mary)*.

Rhythm, Melody, and Accompaniment 33

Arpeggio or broken-chord accompaniment involves sounding the notes of the chords successively rather than simultaneously. The arpeggios may ascend, descend, or be varied, as shown in Example 2-26.

In addition to treatment of chords, some accompaniments consist of repeated single notes, others of doubling the melodic line in unison, and still others of combinations of various types including some sections in polyphonic texture.

EXAMPLE 2-26 SCHUBERT: (a) *Lob der Thränen (Praise of Tears)*; (b) *Rastlose Liebe (Restless Love)*; (c) *Das Wandern (Wandering)*; (d) *Wohin (Whither)*.

(a)

Lau - e Lüf - te, Blu - men - düf - te
(mild breezes, flower scents)

(b)

Dem Schnee, dem Re - gen
(The snow, the rain)

(c)

Das Wan - dern ist des Mül - lers Lust, das Wan - dern.
(Wandering is the Mill - lers joy, wandering)

34 Materials of Music

(d)

Ich hort' ein Bäch - lein rau - schen
(I heard a brook - let roar - ing)

Counterpoint and Harmony 35

3 Counterpoint and Harmony

A common aspect of music of all cultures, including modern Western civilization, is the idea that music should be governed by rules or at least general principles. Though different cultures have different rules governing the organization of music, virtually all of them do have specific musical requirements and prohibitions that must be followed. When we consider counterpoint and harmony, we find that these aspects of music have also been subject in many periods of music history to the ramifications of a set of rules, a list of do's and don'ts.

Books on music written in the medieval and Renaissance periods usually began with a student asking the master teacher "What do I need to understand music?" and then receiving from the teacher a carefully enumerated and catalogued set of rules about how music should be put together. We could follow this practice and present you with a specific set of rules for writing "good" counterpoint and harmony, but modern music study has tended to move away from the formulation of *a priori* rules toward a more open understanding of counterpoint and harmony, based on a study of what composers in many styles and periods have actually done, rather than attempting to state what they should have done. It is in this spirit that the following sections seek to introduce you to some of the most challenging and at the same time some of the most interesting and vital aspects of music. There is no question but that one's appreciation of music, as well as ability to participate in music making in any number of ways, can be enhanced by gaining some understanding of musical-compositional craft.

COUNTERPOINT IN THE CANON

We can begin by examining a section of a piece by Haydn that reveals an easy mastery of craft in the form of contrapuntal skill—that is, the ability to *combine melodies* or voices so that *each line* is invested with melodic interest and meaning. Textures in which the parts reveal such melodic sufficiency and interest are commonly called *contrapuntal textures*. Example 3-1 shows such a texture. Perform it using available instruments or voices. Note that there are actually just *two* separate lines as such, each of four string parts being doubled (reinforced) at an octave's distance. This being the case, the passage can be real-

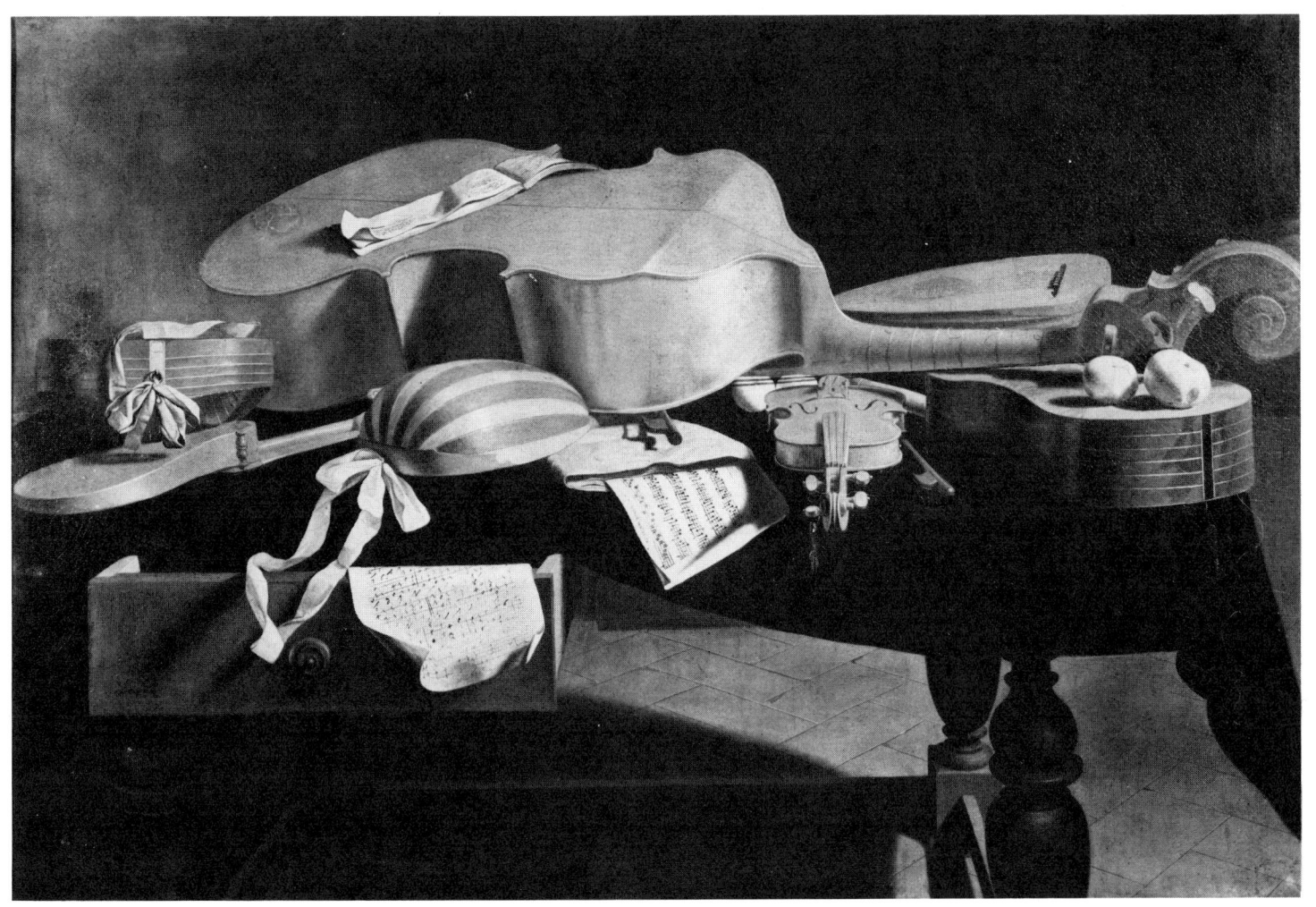

Plucked and bowed stringed instruments, early examples of which are depicted here, have long played a vital part in the evolution of music of Western Civilization—from accompanying the solo lines of the ancients to participating in the later practices of counterpoint and harmony.

ized with just two singers, the one singing the second-violin line and the other, the viola part. To facilitate such a reading, the original version is adapted for two-part singing in Example 3-2*a*. It is a minuet.

The joy of performing a piece such as this minuet by Haydn lies in the fact that both parts share equal roles in the design of the piece; there is no accompaniment as such, but rather a mutual sharing of melodic participation by two complementary voices. Such activity is called *counterpoint*. The particular kind of counterpoint employed here is called *canon*—that is, the consistent *imitation* of one part by the other, maintained throughout an entire composition or section. Canons are similar in organization to rounds; most of us have performed rounds such as "Row, Row, Row Your Boat," "Three Blind Mice," or "Frère Jacques." Such pieces are actually composed of one melody consistently restated by two or more parts. The essence of canons or rounds is imitation, as we have seen.

Imitation

The example cited here is not profound, but it provides easy access to the technique of imitation that often appears in works of more profound impact and meaning. Facility in distributing melodic material among two or more voices in part depends on imitative techniques and the ability to combine voices while observing the limitations of harmony and *voice leading* (an associate of counterpoint). We shall deal shortly with several compositions in which musical craft in the form of various imitative (and other) techniques lies at the heart of the musical unfolding. For the moment, return to the Haydn example just cited.

Counterpoint and Harmony 37

EXAMPLE 3-1 HAYDN: *String Quartet, Op. 76, No. 2,* "QUINTEN," THIRD MOVEMENT, MEASURES 1–11.

A number of features of effective counterpoint occur in Example 3-2a, features that occur here in a very rudimentary form but are nonetheless common to many contrapuntally organized pieces. Note that the two parts seldom move in rhythmic tandem, but maintain some rhythmic individuality in most measures; this is highlighted by their separate entrances. It is also clear that the parts combine to form simple consonances, implying simple harmonic functions such as tonic and dominant in the key of D minor. Play the harmonic reduction in Example 3-2b, comparing its measures with the music in Example 3-2a. The ability of two voices to imply triadic harmony is clearly conveyed here.

J. S. Bach was without question the greatest past master of contrapuntal technique. Composers such as Haydn, who lived after Bach, were emulating him in their compositions when they composed contrapuntally. Most musicians agree that there has never been an equal to Bach's sheer command and inexhaustible technical facility; he remains the unparalleled master of compositional craft. The contrapuntal piece in Example 3-3 is more serious in tone than the Haydn canon in Example 3-1. It is taken from one of Bach's last works, *The Musical Offering,* written in 1747, three years before his death, and dedicated to King Frederick II of Prussia. King Frederick composed the theme upon which the various pieces in *The Musical Offering* are built; it appears in the bass voice of Example 3-3b and is shown separately in Example 3-3a.

Example 3-3b is a three-part composition, but the second voice is not written out; instead the sign 𝄋 is used to indi-

38 Materials of Music

cate the point at which the second voice enters, forming a canon with the first. For a clearer picture of the piece, write down all three parts on a separate piece of paper. Then listen to a recording of Example 3-3b, or, better still, perform it with available resources.

Like the Haydn canon noted earlier, this piece is a product of combined melodies, in this case two markedly different melodies. The first is treated in canon at the unison (meaning at the pitch interval of the unison or prime—that is, the same note) at the time interval of one measure. The resulting con-

trapuntal texture is far more engaging than that of the Haydn canon, containing both independent melodies (two different melodies sounding together) and interdependent melodies (two different voices composed of the same materials). The chordal framework in Example 3-4 reveals, as was the case in the Haydn passage, that triadic chords functioning in a key clearly provide a basis for the harmonic relations that occur. Experiment with the reduction by sounding it on the keyboard while the parts are also performed; note the essentially simple relation between melody and chords. Note also how clearly the

EXAMPLE 3-2 (a) HAYDN: *String Quartet, Op. 76, No. 2,* "QUINTEN," ADAPTATION; (b) *ibid.,* HARMONIC REDUCTION.

EXAMPLE 3-3 (a) BACH: *The Musical Offering*, THEME (COMPOSED BY FREDERICK THE GREAT), MEASURES 1–9; (b) *ibid.*, CANON FOR TWO.

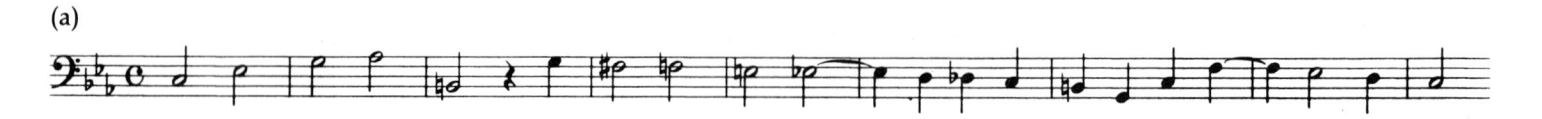

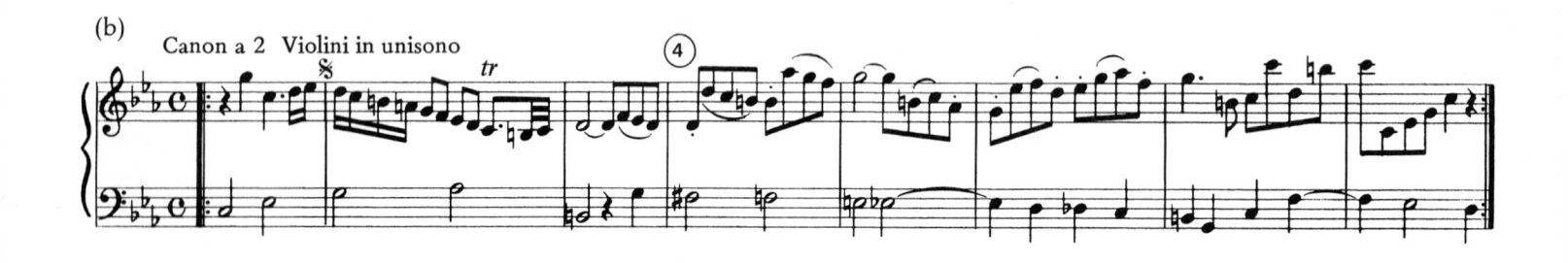

EXAMPLE 3-4 BACH: *The Musical Offering*, CHORDAL FRAMEWORK.

bass theme supports the harmonic and contrapuntal activity of the upper canon parts. In tonal music such as this, melody and harmony act almost as one—harmony limiting and defining melody, melody animating and defining chords.

In this piece contrapuntal craft is remarkably evident, but the impact of the interacting lines and chords is far more than that of a "study" in counterpoint. It is a moving statement by a composer whose mode of expression through counterpoint is as convincing and natural as that of any artist communicating ideas through his craft. The composer has lavished on each part a melodic role that has a unique function in the total design of the passage; the descriptive terms "main voice" or "accompanying part" are not appropriate here.

Imitative and Nonimitative Sections
In both of the canonic pieces noted to this point, imitation is maintained consistently. But contrapuntal pieces built around canons are more the exception than the rule. Pieces such as the one in Example 3-5 are more representative samples of how composers often alternate imitative (sometimes canonic) sections with nonimitative (free) counterpoint. The composition quoted here is one of a collection of fifteen by Bach, written as vehicles for keyboard study as well as models of solutions for different kinds of compositional problems.

We can add considerably to our grasp of both combined voices by holding this gem up to the light and viewing it from several directions. The best way to begin is to become thoroughly acquainted by ear and eye with the piece as a whole. Listen to it several times until you feel you have made the piece a part of you; when you can anticipate in your "mind's ear" each succeeding phrase or event, you have probably really begun to know it.

Like most contrapuntal compositions, this invention reveals an overall equal distribution of rhythmic activity between parts; there is no melody and accompaniment such as one often finds in much popular music or patriotic songs. There is, on the other hand, a marvelous interchange between top and bottom parts of a few pliable musical motives, which are restated, varied by a number of processes such as sequence and key change, and, more importantly, combined in counterpoint

EXAMPLE 3-5 BACH: *Two-Part Invention No. 13 in A Minor,* MEASURES 1–13.

The famous meeting between Bach and Frederick the Great in Potsdam. The master contrapuntalist wove an improvisation on a theme by the king, who deemed him "greater than us all. . . ."

Motive 1:

Motive 2:

Motive 1 is immediately stated in imitation by the lower voice in measure 1, while the top part accompanies with motive 2. The completion of the phrase involves a restatement of motive 1 in the top voice supported by a variant of 2. A final statement of motive 1 closes the first statement or expository section of the invention. The effectiveness of this brief presentation of material is largely a product of rhythmic give-and-take. Note that the slower rhythm of motive 2 provides a simple companion rhythm, a counterrhythm, for the greater activity of motive 1. The pairing of two contrasted and easily recognized rhythms throughout the piece allows them to have easily distinguishable roles in the counterpoint which their simultaneous activity creates. The simple rhythmic contrast of the two motives makes it possible for one figure, 2, to assume a more subordinate role in the piece's unfolding while the rhythm of 1 is usually that of a leading, more actively interesting, voice. This is a common association of parts in which the listener can shift attention from top to bottom and so on as top or bottom assumes a dominant role in the polyphony. There is no more natural association of equal parts than this; it is one that is as much in vogue today as it was two hundred or so years ago. A simple means for experiencing the kind of conversational dialogue seen here is to perform the piece's *rhythm.* Establish a moderate tempo and intone the rhythm. Try to be aware of the shifting location of the dominant voice as determined primarily by rhythmic activity.

Having performed the rhythm of the two combined voices of Bach's *Invention No. 13 in A Minor* gives one a better appreciation of the importance of rhythm in creating counterpoint. This piece is carried along almost without pause by the continuously flowing sixteenths that begin in measure 1 and migrate from one to the other part throughout. Contained only in

in several rhythmic and harmonic contexts. The principal contrapuntal technique used to spin out and extend the piece is imitation, but imitative sections are alternated with nonimitative passages to create a musical design based in part on the contrasts that result. In pieces such as these—inventions, fugues, motets, and the like—a juxtaposition of processes occurs in which primary thematic (motivic) material is stated and treated in imitation, followed by more discursive passages, often nonimitative, in which derivative material is presented in sections called *episodes,* or digressions. In this manner a very common and natural musical growth takes place in which the alternating of statements with digressions from them constitutes the main basis for continuation. Such is the case in the invention cited above. The music is outlined so as to show the two kinds of passages that occur, statements and episodes. Check them over.

The statement passages are built out of two motivic segments:

one voice, such continuous activity at one level (♪) would become boring, but Bach's skillful contrapuntal deployment of sixteenths between two parts, set off by a complementary rhythm in eighths, creates a balance of movement that sustains interest and avoids an overconcentration of activity in either part. It should be clear that counterpoint is as much a product of skillfully combined and interwoven rhythms as it is a result of simultaneously sounded contours and registers of two voices.

The tonal organization of the contrapuntal lines of this invention is simple and transparent; each line consists in the main of melodically outlined chords, making the relation between melody and chordal background quite clear. A harmonic sketch of measures 1-13, the opening half of the piece, appears in Example 3-6. Play the sketch on the piano, or sing it in parts, then relate the sketch to the successive measures of the composition.

The sketch shows the simplicity of harmonic materials that underpin the counterpoint. The pattern of harmonic change, harmonic rhythm, is that of change every beat or half note, thus confirming the simple quadruple meter. The vocabulary of chords includes diatonic triads and occasional seventh chords moving in essentially simple, key-defining progressions. Tonal variety occurs as a result of key changes involving C major, the relative major of A minor, and a closing modulation to the dominant key of E minor. Shown in capsule form this harmonic movement involves a kind of elaboration of the three tones of the tonic triad of the piece—A, C, and E:

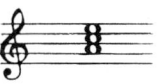

Harmonic movement such as this is very common in tonal music, involving as it does a kind of limited contrast. Note that the sectionalization of the piece is further emphasized by the tonal character of the statement sections—*stability*, as opposed to the instability of the episodic sections, which are typically in a state of flux, providing transitions between *different* keys rather than emphasizing one. Compare, for instance, measures 6–8, a statement, with measures 9–13, which effects a change from C major to E minor. Such complementary relations between material and tonality are prevalent in most tonal music.

EXAMPLE 3-6   BACH: *Two-Part Invention No. 13 in A Minor*, HARMONIC SKETCH OF MEASURES 1-13.

Though virtually unceasing in his efforts to perfect his contrapuntal craft, Bach—the prolific composer and busy church musician—somehow found time to enjoy a musical evening with some of his numerous progeny.

COUNTERPOINT IN THE FUGUE

As engaging as they are for the listener and as rewarding as they are for the player, Bach's inventions do not represent the same peak of artistic expression and mastery of contrapuntal technique as do his numerous organ works or *The Well-Tempered Clavier,* a collection (two volumes) of forty-eight preludes and fugues, composed for the harpsichord or clavichord.

Bach's fugues are very much like his inventions, with certain important exceptions. They are often larger in proportion than the inventions, contain as a rule three or four voices in contrast to the two or three voices of the inventions, begin with solo statements of subject material, and always involve imitative answers at the distance of a fifth or fourth, thus emphasizing the dominant degree or key of the composition. This principle applies to all expository sections of a fugue.

One of Bach's keyboard fugues appears complete in Example 3-7. The piece presented here to represent Bach's fugues was chosen because of several factors: it is short, reveals a number of techniques commonly associated with fugue composition, is relatively easy to perform or read at sight, gives a good picture of Bach's harmonic and melodic idiom, and, most importantly, is a moving and deeply expressive musical statement.

Listen to a performance of Example 3-7 without following the music; then, having become acquainted with the piece by sound, listen again with the music in hand. Listen with an ear for those aspects of the piece that represent (1) a distinctive melodic style, (2) a satisfying formal plan, and (3) any procedures that stand out as heightening your interest as the piece unfolds.

The somewhat plaintive opening statement of the subject of the fugue sets the tone for the entire piece. That Bach was able to solve the problems of handling such expressive and moving melodic statements as occur in this and other fugues in textures involving the intricate weaving of lines without loss of expressivity or formal coherence testifies to his absolute dominance of craft; it is for this and other reasons that he is far more upheld and studied by today's musicians than he was in his own lifetime, a period during which he was by no means so highly revered. Indeed, many of Bach's contemporaries, his

EXAMPLE 3-7 BACH: *The Well-Tempered Clavier, Book II, Fugue in C Minor,* MEASURES 1–28.

sons among them, regarded him as a reactionary upholder of academic tradition rather than a musical "monarch" who explored and perfected the traditions that he inherited, crowning them with masterpieces of unusual brilliance and beauty.

As in the invention noted previously, one's ability to get inside a piece such as this fugue hinges to a great extent on one's ability to interact with the music either by performing the piece on the keyboard or by part-singing or part-reading it using available instruments such as recorders or other woodwinds and strings. Again, such involvement should be prepared by a careful rhythmic reading of the fugue's four distinct parts. Note that the piece begins with steady eighths, distributed between the two top parts in measure 3 and created by the staggered pulses of the syncopation:

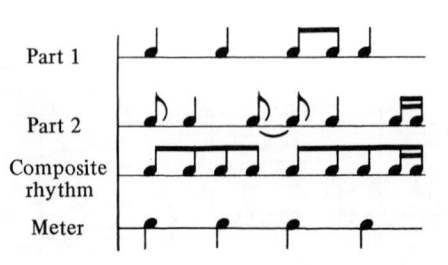

46 Materials of Music

The continuous level of (eighth-note) activity that results, shown on the third line of the preceding figure, is called the *composite rhythm*. Note that the piece gains further rhythmic momentum by assuming a new and quicker composite rhythm at measure 5 and continuing it until the closing section of the fugue, begun at measure 23, wherein eighths are reinstated as the composite rhythm. This sort of division of a fugue (or any piece) via the juxtaposition of contrasted rhythm levels contributes measurably to form. Read this figure, based on measures 7 and 8, in which a composite rhythm of sixteenths results from the distribution of such between three voices, each of which reveals its own individual rhythmic profile while contributing to the composite rhythmic effect as a member of a highly integrated rhythmic unit of three strands (see *A* below). One can easily see that the composite rhythm equates the total activity of the rhythms of all the parts, shown as one line. Multiple pulses from different voices occurring together are not shown, although they clearly affect our perception of accents, rhythm, and meter.

Like most fugues, this one consists of an alternation between expository passages, as found in measures 1-8, and episodic sections, as seen in measures 9-14. A second exposition begins in measure 14, the midpoint of the piece. The episodic passages in this particular fugue, however, are episodic more from the standpoint of key than thematic organization because, as is apparent in measure 10 of the alto part and again in measure 11 in the bass, references to the subject—that is, principal motivic material of the piece—occur throughout the episodic sections as well as in the expository passages of this fugue. The expository passages, mapped out below, are characterized by tonal stability—that is, beginning and ending in the same key—as opposed to motion from one key to another, or *modulation*.*

The outline (see *B* below) pictures the layout of Bach's *Fugue in C Minor* in terms of sectionalization, tonality, and composite rhythm.

As reflected by the outline, the contrapuntal texture of the movement is framed within a very simple formal plan. Two main sections—measures 1-14 and a consequent section, measures 15-28—form the gross sections of the piece. Within those boundaries the simple tonal scheme of C-G-C (I-V-I) is operative. The pattern is like that of a binary dance form. Whereas the opening section is composed of an expository followed by a digressive passage, the entire second section, broken by a

*The brief emphasis on the dominant level in the opening exposition and analogously in subsequent expositions is not considered a change of key.

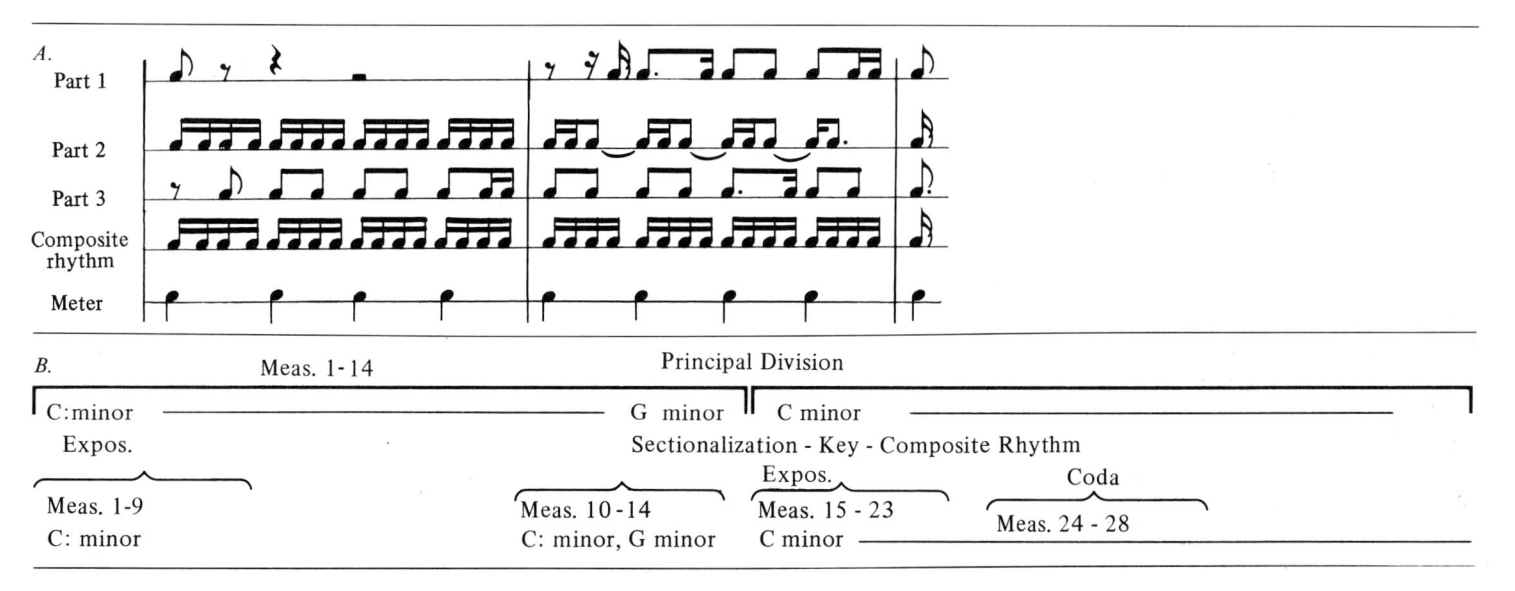

Counterpoint and Harmony

cadence in measure 23, is expository in effect, with brief interludes interspersed as at measure 18. Indeed, the tight-knit organization of the whole piece is in part traceable to the continuing references to the main subject, although at some points their location in the texture tends to obscure them. The player himself must decide to what extent statements of the subject or variants of it should be projected or deemphasized as the piece unfolds; to the extent that the performer must make such decisions, he shapes our perception of the piece and, accordingly, its formal plan.

The formal unity of this fugue, as has been noted, is related to the continuing references to the subjects that occur. By the same token, the subject is given a number of modifications, variations of a sort, that add to its meaning and interest in restatements. Look at a few of the subject variants that are cited in Example 3-8 and locate them in the piece by their measure references. The changes that occur are both intervallic and rhythmic.

The name for rhythmically expanding the subject through the use of note values longer than those of the original statement is *augmentation*. Augmentation of the subject occurs at measure 14, for instance. Note that the augmented version is combined contrapuntally with the original at measure 14, marking the beginning of the second half of the fugue, and that the coda is unified by imitatively treated fragments of the subject; one is shown in Example 3-8g.

Stretto

An important contrapuntal technique called *stretto* occurs frequently throughout the second large section of the piece. Stretto involves a kind of telescoped imitation wherein the imitating voice begins before the initial statement is complete.

EXAMPLE 3-8 BACH: *The Well-Tempered Clavier, Book II, Fugue in C Minor*, VARIANTS OF THE SUBJECT.

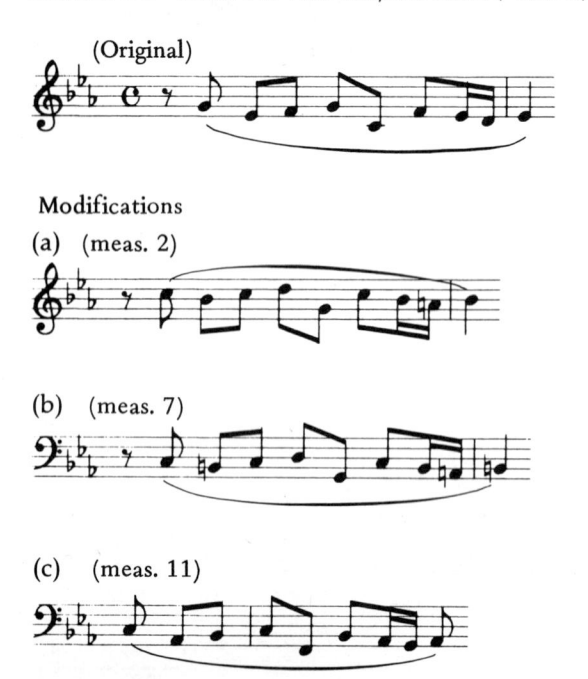

48 Materials of Music

Stretto occurs in this piece in measures 14, 16, and 23, among others. It is characteristically associated with the end of a fugue where its occurrence contributes to the heightening of tension and expectation of close; it may and often does occur in other sections as well. Some fugues have stretto beginnings.

Fugues always begin with a statement of the subject followed by an imitative answer at the intervallic distance of a fourth or fifth, as we have noted. The latter usually emphasizes in one way or another the dominant pitch or key; in this fugue the answering statement of the subject outlines the dominant (minor) triad, G-B flat-D, and closes on the note B flat. However, the answer is not an exact replica of the subject begun a fourth or fifth away, since the opening interval of the answer is changed to a second, rather than a third. Doing so allows the answer to commence with the tonic pitch, C, forming a consonance with the already sounding E flat, and suggesting the tonic triad of C minor. You can speculate as to why an exact transposition of the subject would be less effective here. Literal transpositions of the subject as the basis for answering statements are called *real* answers, whereas intervallically altered answers are called *tonal* answers.

There are a number of additional technical procedures and devices associated with the fugue as well as other contrapuntal forms. It is not practical for us to go into them here, but it is necessary to be aware of the importance of the fugue as a contrapuntal form. It is more to the point that one discovers those qualities in a fugue or any other piece that make it acceptable and attractive as music, rather than as technique alone. Listen again to this fugue and try to determine qualities of this composition, such as unity and variety, continuity, climax, repose, etc., that give it shape. Try also to identify within your mind's ear those melodic or harmonic aspects of the movement that give it special appeal. These may turn out to be details or subtleties of inner voice—movement, key change, sequence, or other aspects of the piece that seem especially attractive—just as a painting, film, or poem may often reveal details or subtleties that have special meaning for us. Most well-written music will reward the attentive listener or performer in one or another way, even though he may reject the general stylistic or formal concept of the piece as a whole. Like a good deal of past music, Bach's often demands a greater effort at acquaintance than is the case with more immediately accessible music; commensurately, the rewards are often more long-lasting.

COUNTERPOINT IN VOICE LEADING

We have looked at several pieces composed in contrapuntal textures, works revealing a number of processes, such as canon, imitation, and stretto, which are part and parcel of many contrapuntal forms. Another side of counterpoint, however, is equally, if not more, germane to a developing understanding of musical organization, one that can sharpen our insights into music of almost any style or form, namely, *voice leading.*

Any music in which lines or parts occur and relate exhibits voice leading—that is, a counterpoint of cosounding parts or voices. This is as true of instrumental music as it is of vocal, and as pertinent to keyboard music as it is to orchestral. Having looked at some aspects of music that are unequivocally contrapuntal, we can explore a few examples of music that are not explicitly contrapuntal in the manner of a fugue or canon, but in which the very basis of counterpoint, melody combinations, is more subtly revealed. We shall begin with an example by Bach (Example 3-9) in which four voices combine to produce a texture of main voice (the soprano) and accompanying voices designed to provide both harmonic as well as contrapuntal (melodic) accompaniment. The focus of the piece is the *chorale melody* sung by the sopranos, given harmonic support artfully enhanced by the altos, tenors, and basses.

To familiarize yourself with this piece read each line separately before performing the full texture. Use the following checklist as a basis for scanning the piece before performing it:

Checklist for Sight Reading
1. Check the key signature and verify from the music the tonality of the piece; note especially the cadences.
2. Check the meter and note the pulse levels that occur.
3. Scan the various voice parts for their contours and intervallic details, noting any wide leaps (a fifth or larger) that occur and noting as well any note alterations used.

EXAMPLE 3-9 BACH: *Es ist gewisslich an der Zeit* (CHORALE), MEASURES 1–10.

Try to account for the relation of any accidentals to the tonality—that is, as temporary leading tones, lower chromatic neighbors, passing tones, etc.

4. Try to assess the relative activity of your line as it relates to the piece as a whole. For example, the alto line of this piece is essentially supportive and has little important linear activity; for that reason it should be treated accordingly, in performance. The bass, on the other hand, has a good deal of variety of rhythm and contour as well as recurring motivic patterns. It should sound as a partner to the *cantus* (main voice in the soprano here) in creating effective counterpoint.

Bach made part settings of more than 200 chorale melodies such as the one that occurs here. The beauty and effectiveness, as well as the performability, of settings such as the one in Example 3-9 can be attributed to a number of factors, such as the appropriateness and simplicity of the chorale tune, the selection of accompanying chords formed by the converging voices (and sounded by an accompanying organ as well), and the unerring judgment of the composer in his fashioning of accompanying voices, the latter being a question mainly of harmonization and voice leading. Voice leading, or "part writing" as it is often called, is a product of the combined intervallic motion of voices—both vertical and horizontal. A direct consequence of combined linear activity can be observed in the various *directional patterns* such as *contrary motion, similar motion, oblique motion,* and *parallel motion*. These terms define the various relations that are created by the simultaneous motion of two or more voices; they are all illustrated by the chorale setting in Example 3-9. For the moment we shall consider the voice leading of the outer parts, the bass and soprano of the piece. These two most active voices create a contrapuntal-harmonic unit that frames the entire texture. To a great extent, soprano and bass delineate the harmonic and melodic structure of the piece. The two outer parts are often called a *two-voice framework*. The name itself implies their role in the piece's structure, as they form a kind of boundary for the voice leading and elaboration of the work's full texture. The two-voice framework of Example 3-9 appears in Example 3-10. Perform it.

One notes immediately the complementary rhythmic relation of the two parts—the eighths of the bass alternating with similar durations of the soprano. Both parts reveal independent rhythms. The voice leading is a product of the two melodies, bass and soprano, each of which is an acceptable melodic part. The effectiveness of their combined activity is a result of the following:

1. Each line reveals a dominance of step motion.
2. A variety of contrapuntal motion is observed. For ex-

EXAMPLE 3-10 BACH: *Es ist gewisslich an der Zeit* (CHORALE), TWO-VOICE FRAMEWORK.

ample, contrary motion occurs in measure 1, beats 1-2; similar motion, motion in the same direction, occurs in measures 3-4, beats 4-5, and in measures 8-9, beginning with the third beat; oblique motion occurs wherever one voice moves while the other remains stationary, as in measure 1.

Summarizing, one can see that *contrary* motion is motion in opposite directions; *parallel* motion is motion in the same direction by the same-sized intervals—e.g., motion in parallel sixths or thirds or fifths; *oblique* motion occurs when only one of the two voices is active (the other sustaining or repeating one note); and *similar* motion results from activity in the same general direction, up or down, by two parts. Return to the chorale in Example 3-9 and discover examples of each type of motion between various pairs of voices. Note the effectiveness of combining different types of motion so that a variety of countermovement occurs at a given point. For instance, the opening upbeat of the piece marks oblique motion between bass and soprano, and contrary motion between soprano and tenor. In measure 5, all types of motion occur, for example, and this is often a clue to the effectiveness of voice-leading details, in that a degree of independence results from the individuality of direction as well as from the different rhythms of the respective parts.

Harmonic Progression

Voice leading is (of necessity) strongly related to, and often a by-product of, chord connection. The linking of successive chords is accomplished by voice leading, and, by the same token, the pitches available are determined by the selection of chords and by the note possibilities that their selection suggests. In some instances chord members connect directly with succeeding chord members, as in moving from measure 1 to measure 2 of Example 3-9. In many other instances, however, decorative pitches such as passing or neighboring tones are introduced to create an effective connection of chords where the use of chord tones alone does not facilitate such connection. Measure 14, last beat, to the end of the setting, reveals considerable use of passing tones to smooth out the connection of chords. A great deal of the eighth-note activity in the bass of the setting incorporates passing and neighboring activity, for example. Check out this statement.

There are a number of other more or less axiomatic principles of voice leading revealed by this and countless other such settings. Note that a leap in one voice is often balanced by step activity in another, as in measure 2. Note also that it is effective to move one part within the chord—that is, by leap from one to another chord tone—while another introduces decorative (nonchordal) activity, as in measure 15.

Playing a significant role in furthering the arts in this century, educational institutions have acquired impressive facilities for this purpose, as exemplified by the Musical Arts Center of Indiana University—Bloomington where some 150 public performances are held annually.

Mastery of voice-leading techniques is the task of composers. However, every performer and person knowledgeable about music can profit measurably from an appreciation of ways in which voice leading operates in well-written music to help create connections of lines, make individual parts playable or singable, and effect the greatest possible expressiveness of parts in any texture, contrapuntal or homophonic. It has been said many times that it is often in composers' handling of details such as voice leading that we, as listeners and performer-critics, recognize the symptoms of musical artistry as opposed to workaday musical outpourings. Any accomplished and responsible performer must heed and attempt to project in performance those details and subtleties of voice leading that can improve his or her performance.

Voice leading, as we have said, is not restricted in occurrence to vocal music; it is a consideration in most music, even when a set number of parts are not operative and "voices" are added or deleted as dictated by other compositional considerations. Smooth voice leading contributes greatly to the impressiveness and contemplative mood of the familiar prelude by Chopin shown in Example 3-11. As many as seven pitches are sounded together at various points, but the basic texture is that of four-part writing similar to that of the chorale noted before. An important feature lies in the more or less consistent doubling at the octave of both the soprano and bass parts. This exploits a capability of the piano, and results in a depth and spread of register not possible with vocal music.

Upon hearing the Prelude, one notes a number of details already cited in the example by Bach. For instance, the contrary motions between outer parts in measures 1–4 is contrasted subsequently by predominately parallel motion between the same voices. Common tones, notes common to two successive chords, are frequently retained in the same voice, as with the notes E flat and C in measure 1, and step motion dominates the entire texture, which, incidentally, is easily sung if the lower octave is omitted.*

Different patterns of voice leading, prolonged for phrases or larger sections, contribute to the variety and impact of the opening of a string quartet movement by Beethoven, shown in Example 3-12. Changes in dynamic level, as well as the textural density—that is, number of parts—complement the opening as well. The first decisive change occurs at measure 19. The reiterated intervals and chords of the opening, which accompany the cello and then the first violin, are replaced by a note-against-note chordal style composed of four rhythmically uniform string voices. Note the dominance of contrary motion between the cello and first violin. They create the two-voice frame. The second violin and viola have less consequential lines and are utilized mainly to fill in the supporting harmonies; they reveal, nonetheless, a good deal of step motion and pre-

*Octave doublings of the bass are often consistently maintained in keyboard or other instrumental works.

EXAMPLE 3-11   CHOPIN: *Prelude in C Minor, Op. 28,* MEASURES 1–4.

dominantly small leaps. A second change of texture at measure 30 incorporates parallel thirds between the upper strings over a sustained triad in the cello and viola. An intensification of dynamics, rhythm, and register is heightened by a contrapuntal separation of the parts in measure 38. All available types of voice-leading combinations occur in this climactic passage

EXAMPLE 3-12 BEETHOVEN: *String Quartet in F Major, Op. 59, No. 1*, FIRST MOVEMENT, MEASURES 1–4, 20–23, 30–34, 38–42.

Counterpoint and Harmony

54 Materials of Music

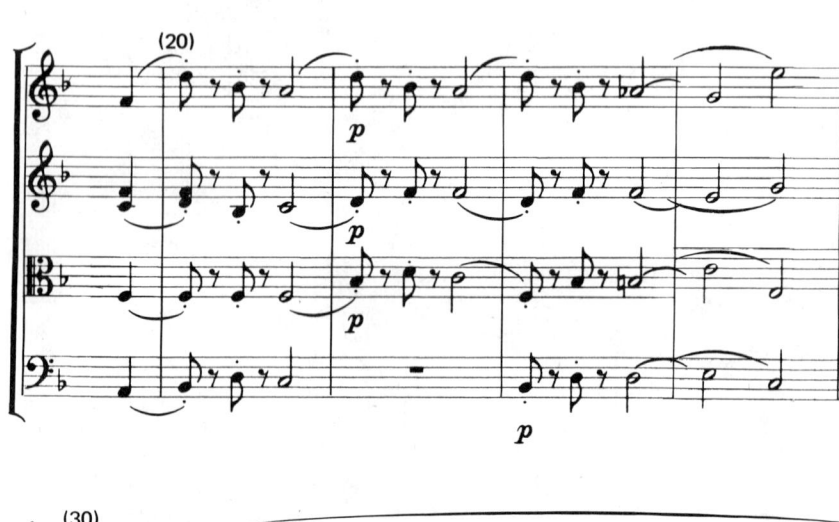

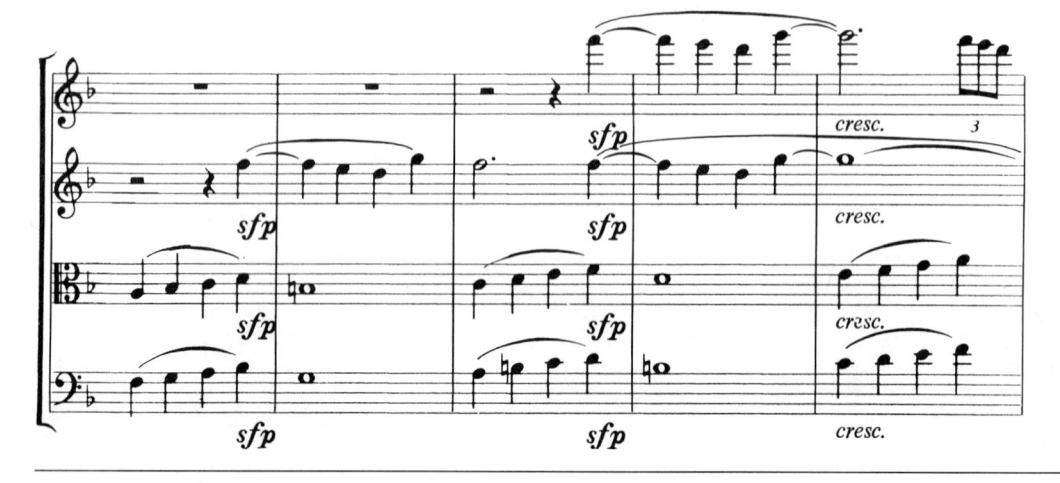

together with some imitative restatement. Although the texture of the passage as a whole is mainly homophonic, it is clear that contrapuntal technique is brought into play to create effective and varied instrumental play. The recognition of ways in which such technique is naturally brought to bear in music such as this, which is far removed in style from the counterpoint of Bach's C-Minor Fugue, is instructive to both informed listening and sympathetic performance of music such as this, which, while not explicitly contrapuntal, is very much indicative of musical craft.

Traditional Rules of Voice Leading
There are several principles of part movement and interval succession that have been operative to varying degrees in tonal music for centuries. Most of these "rules" stem originally from practices associated with vocal composition of the Renaissance and Baroque periods. To a great extent, these rules have been overenforced for didactic convenience as opposed to artistic integrity. Anyone intent on gaining understanding of voice-leading practices in traditional music must be knowledgeable about the rules cited in the Appendix, even though he may find some or all of them irrelevant insofar as his own musical interests and tastes are concerned. Although these rules of thumb apply more specifically to traditional four-part choral works such as Bach's chorales or Josquin's motets, they have considerable application to a great deal of music composed for the keyboard or instrumental ensembles. In some works in which part integrity is largely maintained, traditional part-writing constraints are far more pertinent than in pieces in which free rein is given to the introduction and deletion of parts, and in which integrity of line is not deemed important. In some of the writing assignments in the workbook, awareness of the rules of thumb (see Appendix) will be called for. It is furthermore very much to the point that persons knowledgeable about music be able to determine from a piece to what extent the rules cited in the Appendix have been observed or disregarded by a given composer in a specific context. An ability to determine this reflects both stylistic familiarity and judgment on the part of the observer.

Acquiring technique with counterpoint and voice leading is, as we have said, a task for the aspiring composer or arranger, just as mastering drawing is a must for the novice painter. All artistic skills demand technique and craft. This book is not intended for those whose sights are set on a life of composing; yet it appears that the nourishing of an inclination toward music via listening, composing, or performing demands more than interest and assimilation of facts. For that reason you should realize that your involvement with music, whatever course it may take, will be the more meaningful for whatever first-hand experience you have had in wrestling with the problems of musical construction, even if the outcome is somewhat short of another Beethoven symphony.

4 Instruments and Voices

To this point we have concerned ourselves primarily with such aspects of music as rhythm, melody, texture, counterpoint, and harmony. But we have not considered one of the most important means by which a composer expresses extramusical ideas, namely, the use of *timbre* or instrumental and vocal tone color. McLuhan's famed dictum, "The medium is the message," is borne out in music by the fact that the composer's choice of instruments, voices, or other sound sources such as electronic sounds—in a word, the choice of media—determines to a great extent the expression or the "message" transmitted. Try to imagine funeral music played on a harmonica, a delicate waltz played by a quartet of tubas, or a heroic march played on a banjo, and you will have some idea of what we mean when we point to the close association of timbre and expression.

INSTRUMENTS

Before discussing the human voice, the oldest and in many ways the most marvelous musical instrument, let us consider man-made instruments. These often reflect the cultures in which they evolved—soft reeds and pipes in pastoral societies, bold horns and trumpets in hunting civilizations, genteel instruments such as the lute or the viol in more aristocratic societies, and electronic instruments such as the Moog synthesizer in our own technological society. Modern instruments may be divided into four principal categories or sections—strings, woodwinds, brass, and percussion.

Strings

The stringed instruments form the backbone of the orchestra; there are more of them, and they are usually played more than any of the other instruments. The four instruments of the modern string section include the *violin,* the *viola,* the *violoncello* or *cello,* and the *string bass* or *double bass.* All of these instruments may be played with a bow in a variety of techniques ranging from smoothly connected notes (legato) to short "bouncing" notes (spiccato), or they may be plucked with a finger of the right hand (pizzicato). Stringed instruments can also be used to produce special effects ranging from the whistling sounds of harmonics to the icy chattering of tremolo ponticello.

Stradivari (1644–1737), master builder of some 1000 violins, violas, and cellos, relaxes in his workshop to admire one of his violins—probably little realizing that a fine "Strad" would one day be worth hundreds of thousands of dollars.

The violin, one of the most versatile of all instruments, has a range of expressive possibilities from lyric to dramatic and a large range of pitch and dynamics. In the orchestra the violins are usually divided into two groups, first and second violins. The viola is about four inches longer than the violin and its range is a perfect fifth lower. Though generally used as a harmony instrument or to double melodies played by other instruments, the viola is sometimes entrusted with its own melodies, often of a somewhat melancholy character in keeping with its darker timbre. An octave lower than the viola, the cello has a rich, full, and (to use a well-worn cliché) mellow timbre. The string bass is the largest and lowest of the stringed instruments. Though heard almost exclusively in pizzicato in popular music, the bass is generally bowed in symphonic music and it provides a sonorous bass to the whole orchestra.

You may have noticed that the bass has a slightly different shape than the other stringed instruments. Its sloping shoulders recall the shape of the older predecessors of the modern stringed instruments—the viols, a set of instruments in various sizes which differed from modern stringed instruments not only in shape but also in their softer tone quality and in the fact that they had frets like the guitar. The guitar, though rarely used in symphonic music, is widely used in folk and popular music and is indeed the most popular of all instruments throughout the world. It has descended from such important historical instruments as the Greek *kithara* and the Renaissance

Instruments and Voices 57

Early musical instruments are shown in this woodcut, which probably dates from the 17th century.

lute. In non-Western cultures, plucked stringed instruments are very important, and in recent years even Western audiences have come to know the delightful timbre of such instruments as the *sitar* of India, the *koto* of Japan, and the *bania* of Africa, a predecessor of the banjo.

Woodwinds

The woodwind instruments have the most varied tone colors and playing techniques of all the instruments of the orchestra. They have in common the fact that sound is produced by setting a column of air into vibration by means of an embouchure or mouth hole (*flute* and *piccolo*), single reed (*clarinet* and *saxophone*), double reed (*oboe, English horn,* and *bassoon*).

The flute has a clear, expressive tone quality well suited for lyric melodies; it may also be used for light, agile passage work. The piccolo has a brilliant, penetrating sound that can cut through even the thickest orchestral mass. The clarinet has the largest range of the woodwinds and the greatest variety of timbres—from the dark, rich colors of the low or chalameau register to the bright sound of the upper or clarion register. Saxophones, the most recently invented of the woodwind instruments, are a staple of jazz or rock ensembles but are used only occasionally in symphonic music. The stereotyped use of the oboe is for plaintive, lyrical melodies and that of the bassoon is for staccato, humorous passages, but both instruments are capable of a wide variety of expressive possibilities.

Brasses

The brass instruments, like the woodwinds, produce sound by setting a column of air into vibration. With brass instruments this is accomplished by means of a "lip buzz." Though more unified than the woodwinds in tone quality, each of the brass instruments does have its characteristic uses. *French horns* may be used for stirring horn calls or for warm melodic passages. *Trumpets* are frequently used for passages of a military or fanfare character, but they may also express more lyric passages. *Trombones* and *tubas* are especially effective in four-part chorale passages, but they may also be used for solo passages.

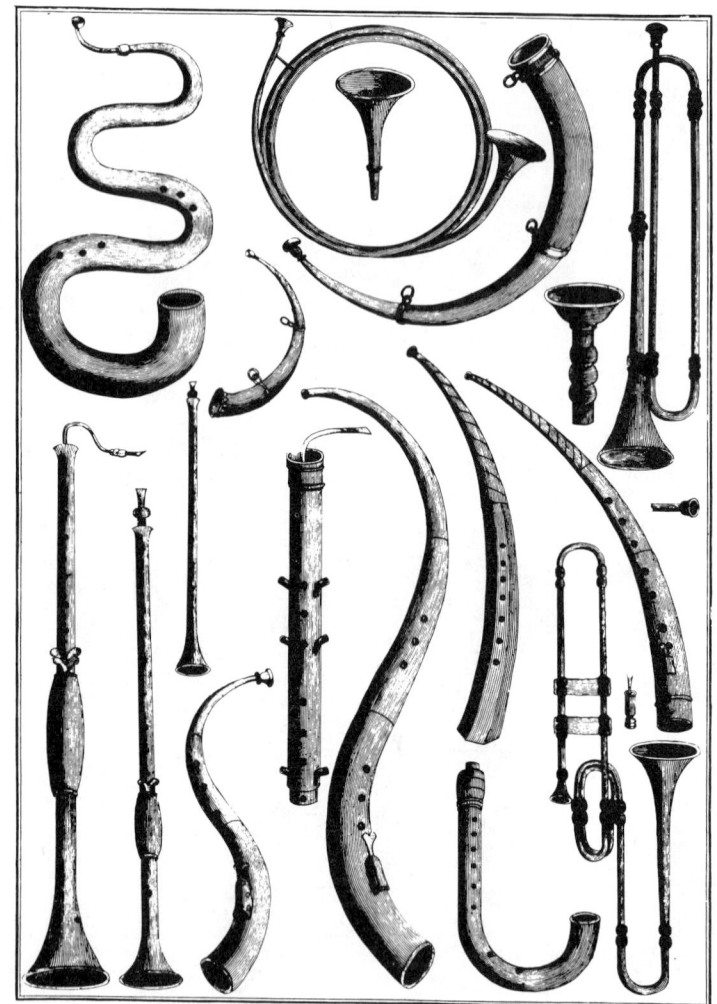

Instrumens de Musique, Anciens, Modernes, Etrangers, à vent, à bocal et à anche.

Percussion

Percussion instruments may be divided into two large categories: instruments with definite pitch and those with indefinite pitch. In the first category the *timpani* are the "senior" instruments both in terms of earliest usage and most frequent usage in the orchestra. Timpani are usually played in sets of two or four instruments, each tuned to a different pitch. Though they are limited in melodic possibilities, they have the largest dynamic range of any orchestral instrument, from an almost inaudible pianissimo to a deafening fortissimo. Other percussion instruments with definite pitch are the *xylophone, marimba,* and *vibraphone*—all instruments with a keyboardlike arrangement of wooden or metal bars, played with mallets. Instruments with indefinite pitch include just about any that can be struck, scraped, rubbed, or otherwise made to sound. The common ones are *snare drum, bass drum, cymbals,* and *triangle.*

Keyboard Instruments

Keyboard instruments, at least in the orchestra, are sometimes considered as stringed instruments, wind instruments, or percussion instruments, or more properly in a category of their own. *Piano* and *organ* are probably known well enough to need no description here. The earlier or historical keyboard instruments may not be as familiar, though they are currently enjoying a rebirth of popularity. The *harpsichord* is similar to the piano except that the strings are plucked by quills set in a jack mechanism, producing a sound that might be mistaken for a guitar. The *clavichord* also resembles the piano except that the strings are struck by T-shaped pieces of metal called "tangents," producing a soft sound that could hardly be heard in a full orchestra but is effective in solo or chamber music.

The *harp* is another instrument that resists assignment to one of the foregoing categories, though it is essentially a plucked stringed instrument. A characteristic effect on this instrument, sounding the notes of a chord in succession, has led to the theoretical term *arpeggio*. Another characteristic effect is the *glissando,* in which the player draws his fingers rapidly over the strings, producing a blurred row of tones.

THE ORCHESTRA

The orchestra, as we know it today, is really a product of the nineteenth century. At that time music left the confines of princely chambers and the churches and moved to the concert halls to be heard not just by an enlightened few but by a large public. Quite naturally, the need arose for a performing organization that was powerful enough to be heard in a large hall and interesting and colorful enough to capture the attention of a less sophisticated audience. In its most developed form, the Romantic orchestra consisted of the following instruments, listed in score order—that is, in the order they appear in the conductor's music:

Woodwinds
Piccolo	
Flutes	I, II, III
Oboes	I, II
English horn	
E-flat clarinet	
B-flat clarinets	I, II
Bass clarinet	
Bassoons	I, II
Contrabassoon	

Brass
Horns in F	I, II, III, IV
Trumpets in B flat	I, II, III
Trombones	I, II, III
Tuba	

Percussion and other instruments
Harp
Piano
Organ
Timpani
Bass drum, snare drum, triangle, cymbals, and other percussion

Strings
First violins	(16–20 players)
Second violins	(14–18 players)
Violas	(12–16 players)
Cellos	(10–14 players)
Contrabasses	(8–12 players)

It is interesting to note that most of the major symphony orchestras of this country and of other countries have personnel virtually identical with that required by the Romantic orchestra. Though some works of late Romantic and early twentieth-century composers call for larger forces, this usually requires hiring extra players beyond those under contract by the symphony orchestra.

Works of the Classic period, and indeed many works of the nineteenth and twentieth centuries, called for generally smaller forces than those indicated. A typical orchestra used by Haydn, Mozart, or Beethoven consisted of pairs of flutes, oboes, clarinets (usual in Beethoven but not used in all works of Haydn and Mozart), trumpets, horns, and timpani, with a

If football games are won in practice, concerts are "won" in rehearsal. The effort this demands from the conductor may be vividly illustrated in this candid shot of Igor Stravinsky rehearsing.

string body with proportions of approximately 12, 10, 8, 6, 4. In Baroque music the usual combinations were much smaller; indeed, much of the music of the Baroque period would be classified today as chamber music, or chamber orchestra music.

In the Renaissance period, instrumentation was not specified, and the groups, generally small, fall in the category of chamber music. It is interesting to note that there is currently some indication on the part of composers and the public for an abandonment of the large Romantic-sized orchestra and a return to smaller chamber-sized dimensions. Just as the Romantic orchestra sprang from the particular cultural and social milieu of the nineteenth century, so too this turning toward chamber music in the twentieth century could be said to result from two cultural factors: (1) the greatly increased use of recorded music, and the fact that with modern recording and reproduction techniques it is acoustically unnecessary to have a huge group of players; and (2) the increased sophistication on the part of audiences for serious music. Thus, in a sense, we might say that, in terms of the performing groups in instrumental music, music has come full circle. This does not mean that the symphony orchestra is "dead," for many serious composers are still writing for it. The recent trend on the part of many orchestras, however, to divide the large orchestra into several smaller orchestras and to present special concerts, school concerts, etc., may be evidence of a new sound ideal.

Most of the large orchestras in the United States and abroad are now on a 52-week basis, including paid vacations. This was not always the case and, as recently as ten years ago, it was not unusual for members of a distinguished professional symphonic organization to be forced in the summer time to seek some other type of employment in order to earn a satisfactory livelihood. Incidentally, in contrast to Europe, where most orchestras are state-subsidized, orchestras in the United States depend on ticket sales for a large percent of their budget, and the rest of it comes from wealthy donors. This system has obvious advantages and disadvantages. With enlightened and broad-minded patronage, the artistic direction of the orchestra is free to pursue those policies that it deems best for the cause of music and the needs of the community.

A typical orchestra musician earns $8,000–$12,000 a year as a member of a string section, and more as a section leader in the string section (i.e., principal second violin, viola, cello, or bass) or a concertmaster (i.e., leader of the first violins). Woodwind and brass players also earn more than the minimum scale since they are, in effect, the soloists of the orchestra. The conductor is usually a person of great international fame, with one result being that he usually is not present at all of the concerts of his own orchestra. Although he oversees the selection of soloists and the programming of pieces, it is typical for him to share his conductorial duties with one or two assistant

60 Materials of Music

The "joy of music" is perhaps nowhere better expressed than in the ecstatic gestures of Leonard Bernstein, seen at a climactic moment of an orchestra concert.

conductors and with guest conductors, allowing him time to go to other orchestras and opera companies for guest-conducting duties himself.

Generally the members of the orchestra are expected to work several "services" per week, each service consisting either of a three-hour rehearsal or a one- to two-hour concert.

It is unfortunate that the general public cannot be present for the rehearsals of a symphony orchestra, for in many ways these are more interesting than the performance. The music for the concert will have been selected well in advance, and in most cases the programs will include at least one soloist. The presence of a star soloist with an international name is usually a good guarantee of box-office success, and it is only rarely that an orchestra will venture to give a concert consisting only of orchestral music without a soloist. The conductor will have thoroughly studied the scores in advance; some conductors will have gone to the extent of memorizing them, although this is by no means a general rule. Members of the orchestra will have access to their own individual parts of the works to be performed several weeks in advance of the first rehearsal for the particular concert. If the work is unfamiliar to them, they will usually "woodshed" the more difficult passages so that they will be prepared for the first rehearsal.

The first rehearsals of a major symphony orchestra, unlike those of an amateur group, are usually quite close to the finished performance. This is only to be expected in an orchestra of paid professionals, especially when the group has been playing together and with the same conductor for many years.

THE CONDUCTOR

What happens in rehearsals depends largely on the personality of the conductor and the nature of the music. If the music is generally familiar and not too difficult, and if the conductor is one who is more concerned with the inspiration of the moment and the excitement of the performance than with the meticulous working-out of details in the rehearsal, it may very well be that the orchestra just reads through the music once or twice in rehearsal and then performs it. In some cases they may read through only sections of the work and actually sight-read portions of the work at the concert. This is fairly rare, however. Some conductors like to play through works several times. They will seldom stop the orchestra during the reading, but will wait until the end and then talk to them about general things that should be observed, dynamics that should be changed, wrong notes that they may have caught, and general admonitions as to the spirit and character of the work. Other conductors tend to stop at the first sign of a mistake, to correct the players in no uncertain terms, and often to rehearse a small portion of a work many times until it is absolutely perfect. The great Arturo Toscanini was famous for his exacting, sometimes tyrannical demands upon his musicians but equally famous for the magnificent results that he achieved. In contrast, Pierre Monteux was more inclined to treat his orchestra like a benevolent father, and to coax beautiful music out of them rather than to pound it into them. In both cases excellent results were achieved, and both of these great conductors of the past have similar followers among today's conductors.

When watching the conductor at a concert, it is generally possible to observe him or her performing two functions. One, generally allotted to the right hand or baton hand, is that of providing the beat for the orchestra. To do this the conductor will move the baton in a pattern such as those illustrated in Example 4-1, which indicates the meter of the particular passage being performed. The other function of the conductor is the expression, and this is indicated in a variety of means. An extended waved hand indicates loud, and a lowered hand with the palm down tells the players to play softly; a hand trembling in imitation of a violin vibrato urges the strings on to a lovely rich sound, and a flick of the wrist helps to establish the notion of staccato for the woodwind players. Some conductors are extremely liberal with such expressive gestures, and indeed it is sometimes tempting to spend more time watching them than listening to the music. Other conductors are far more restrained in their motions and rely on the instructions they have given the performers in rehearsal to convey their notions about the expression of the music.

EXAMPLE 4-1 CONDUCTING PATTERNS.

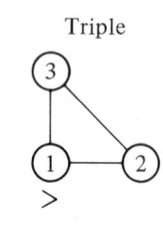

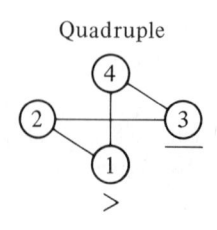

Duple   Triple   Quadruple

VOICES

To illustrate the rich variety of timbres of the human voice, we shall consider some examples of operatic arias (elaborate solo songs with instrumental accompaniment) which constitute the highlights of emotional intensity for "opera buffs." In arias composers display their genius for inventing compelling melodies that delineate the emotion of the character while exploring the unique characteristics of various voice types. Listen to as many of the following as possible, noting the color (timbre) peculiar to each.

Human voices are usually categorized into four general groups, from high voices to low: female voices—soprano and alto; male voices—tenor and bass. The soprano voice is the highest in terms of pitch range and the bass is the lowest. In the broadest sense of the word, voice types are stereotyped in terms of the roles they are generally assigned—i.e., sopranos and tenors (the high female and male voice) assume the parts of the younger heroine and hero, and the altos and basses take such supporting roles as "older" relatives, goddesses, gods, dignitaries, and so on. One senses why this general pattern of "typecasting" has evolved when one compares the brilliance and "youthfulness" of the ringing upper-range male and female voices with the more somber, heavy qualities of the low voices, alto and bass. This convention has created a pattern whereby one may assume generally that the soprano and tenor will carry the lead roles and remaining voices will portray the "character" roles, being somewhat secondary in terms of the parts they play and the arias they sing. This broad generalization does not always apply, as will be seen, since within the individual voice types there are a number of subcategories.

The customary division of the *soprano* voice includes three main types: coloratura, lyric soprano, and mezzo soprano, sometimes called dramatic soprano. The *coloratura* voice is the highest, most agile, and brilliant type, generally being assigned roles the music of which requires the ability to sing at the upper extremities of the range, and to execute fast scales, trills, and other ornamental passages with precision, flexibility, and ease. One of the most memorable of arias for the coloratura

62 Materials of Music

voice is that of the "Queen of the Night," a character in Mozart's last opera, *The Magic Flute* (1791). In this serious allegorical tale, the Queen of the Night, ruler of the realm of evil, sings her memorable song of revenge at the opening of Scene 3, Act II (Examples 4-2 and 4-3).

Another coloratura voice used frequently—one not exploiting the virtual extremes of the upper range, yet requiring the agility of the aforementioned—possesses the capacity to sustain a *broadly* arched melodic line. This voice might be labeled "dramatic coloratura" for lack of a better phrase, since indeed it generally serves a very dramatic function, lending both vocal weight and color, as well as ornamental dexterity. The heroine of the tragic opera *Norma* by Bellini sings one of the most brilliant arias written for this voice type. Norma, High Priestess

EXAMPLE 4-2 MOZART: *The Magic Flute,* ACT II, SCENE 3, "QUEEN OF THE NIGHT" ARIA, MEASURES 1–10.

EXAMPLE 4-3 MOZART: *The Magic Flute,* ACT II, SCENE 3, "QUEEN OF THE NIGHT" ARIA, MEASURES 23–32.

The voice has ever expressed the most profound of human emotions. Its intense appeal is captured in The Pathetic Song *by Thomas Eakins, distinguished American painter of the turn of this century.*

of the Druids, sings her famous aria "Casta diva" ("Chaste goddess") alone before the sacred altar in the hallowed forest of the Druids, lighted by the full moon. Having broken her sacred vows by marrying secretly, Norma turns her voice upward to evoke the benediction of the moon goddess in limpid, ornamental phrases singing "Chaste goddess, who makes silver this ancient, sacred grove, turn your radiant face down on us, unclouded and unveiled . . ." (Example 4-4).

Generally the *lyric soprano* is the "heroine" who is capable of spinning out an opulent, high, clear, "youthful" sound, the personification of the female voice. No one who has heard Butterfly (Cio-Cio-San) of Puccini's *Madame Butterfly* (1904) sing her most popular aria "Un bel di, vedremo" ("One fine day, he'll return") will argue with the generalization above.

Butterfly, a young, beautiful Japanese girl of fifteen, is one of several of Puccini's "little girl" tragediennes, who in this case becomes unfortunately involved with an officer in the U.S. Navy. Their love affair epitomizes the composer's preoccupation with a theme that dominates many of his operas, the tragedy of a young girl who suffers because of her love and devotion to someone she will ultimately lose. In this instance, Butterfly will live to age eighteen and see her beloved desert her to return to his homeland and to his own people. She sings her famous aria near the beginning of Act II, which takes place some three years after their meeting, hoping that although her lover will leave her, he will return, his reappearance being signaled by a wisp of ship's smoke appearing low on the horizon (Example 4-5). Puccini lavished one of his most beguiling melodies on this sympathetic, youthful character, his most loved tragedienne.

Lest one assume that lyric sopranos are doomed to come to untimely ends, it should be observed that this voice type is often used to portray the "soubrette," a shrewd, flippant, quasi-comic young lady who is "old beyond her years" and well versed in the ways of men—and women. Such a character is the maid, Adele, in *Die Fledermaus* (*The Bat*) (1874) by Johann Strauss, the "Waltz King." The merry tale of "the Bat's revenge" comes to a boil in Act II at an elegant costume ball, where both master and chambermaid (Adele) unexpectedly confront one another, the former disguised as a marquis and the latter as a lady of quality—dressed in his wife's most expensive gown and bedecked with her most dazzling jewels! Being informed that she reminds him of someone, the chambermaid (recognizing her master) remains calm and tries to persuade him otherwise by stressing her obvious "aristocratic" attributes—attributes that are "unplebeian" indeed (Example 4-6).

The *dramatic soprano* voice is more rare, since it must combine some of the darkness and intensity of the lower mezzo

Few coloratura arias are more demanding than that penned by Mozart for his "Queen of Evil" of The Magic Flute, his last opera, whose seriousness of purpose presages the impassioned music to follow.

EXAMPLE 4-4 BELLINI: *Norma*, ACT I, "CASTA DIVA" ("CHASTE GODDESS"), MEASURES 1–15.

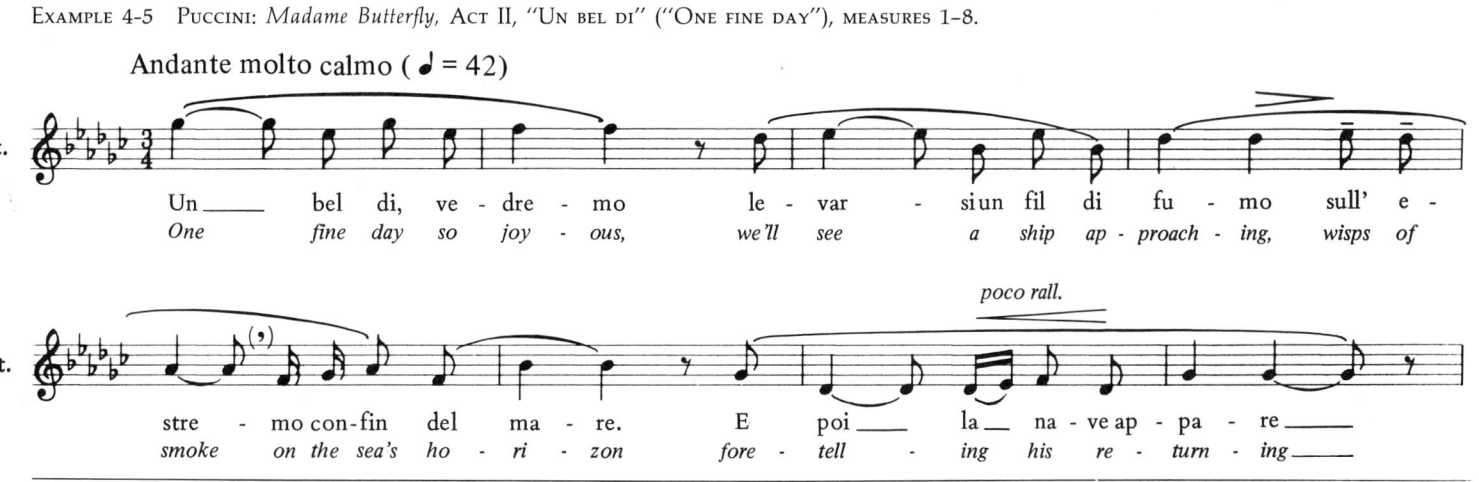

EXAMPLE 4-5 PUCCINI: *Madame Butterfly*, ACT II, "UN BEL DI" ("ONE FINE DAY"), MEASURES 1–8.

EXAMPLE 4-6 J. Strauss: *Die Fledermaus*, Act II, "Mein Herr Marquis" ("My dear Marquis"), measures 1–15.

soprano and yet maintain a high range and brilliant sound. Although roles for this voice appear throughout the repertoire of opera, none displays this noble voice better than does Richard Wagner in the parts created for his heroines. In one of the most colossal works ever written for the musical theater, *Der Ring des Nibelungen* (*The Ring of the Nibelungs*) (1853–1874), Wagner created a memorable role for Brünnhilde, the beautiful, headstrong daughter of Wotan, chieftain of the gods. *The Ring*, a cycle of *four* operas, conceived to play on four consecutive evenings, is a massive drama based on Nordic-Germanic myths. The dramatic unfolding of this mammoth drama culminates in a spectacular panorama, the last scene of *Die Götterdämmerung* (*The Twilight of the Gods*) where Valhalla (Hall of Heroes), the mighty fortress of the gods, and its supernatural inhabitants are engulfed in all-consuming flames. Her mortal hero and husband, Siegfried, slain, Brünnhilde, once loved but now renounced by her father because of her love for an earthling, orders his death bier to be prepared (Example 4-7). She mounts her steed and rides into the flaming bier to join her hero in eternal rest. Ultimately the fire rises into the sky to consume Valhalla itself and brings to an end the world of gods.

The range of the *mezzo soprano* may be that of the dramatic soprano, but it is generally lower, and most characterized by the dark, thick quality of the sound, particularly in the bottom

EXAMPLE 4-7 Wagner: *Die Götterdämmerung*. Act III, "Starke Scheite ("Mighty Pyre"), measures 1–14.

In the operetta Die Fledermaus, the celebrated Austrian composer of popular music, Johann Strauss, Jr. (1826–1889), captured the very essence of Viennese gaiety, as exemplified in the famed costume ball of Act II.

range. The mezzo is usually a "heavy" or "unsympathetic" character, generally an older woman—one notable exception being that of the gypsy, Carmen. Rather than consider the exceptional, let us turn our attention to *Il Trovatore* (1853) by Giuseppe Verdi, another tragic tale of gypsy love. Because the plot is too complex to capsulize here, let us simply turn to Act II, a mountain camp of a band of gypsies. Here an old woman grimly recalls the terrible memories of her mother's execution at the stake (Example 4-8), typifying the mezzo voice.

A curious practice arose in opera, that of assigning male roles to females, particularly to mezzo sopranos. There have been numerous theories advanced to explain this least credible mannerism of opera, since neither the voice nor the figure fit the part. Some interesting observations suggest that perhaps this practice had sexual implications, since women's legs were not normally exposed in tights or pants until this century, or that perhaps there were homosexual overtones. No one is sure. Nevertheless, some important "pant characters" "strut and fret" on stage, from Mozart's *The Marriage of Figaro* of the late eighteenth century to *Der Rosenkavalier* (*The Knight of the Rose*) (1911) by Richard Strauss. One of the famous of such roles is that of Octavian in *Der Rosenkavalier*, a seventeen-year-old nobleman who not only is a forlorn adolescent, loving both

---

EXAMPLE 4-8 VERDE: *Il Trovatore*, ACT II, "STRIDE LA VAMPA" ("THE FLAMES CRY OUT"), MEASURES 1–10.

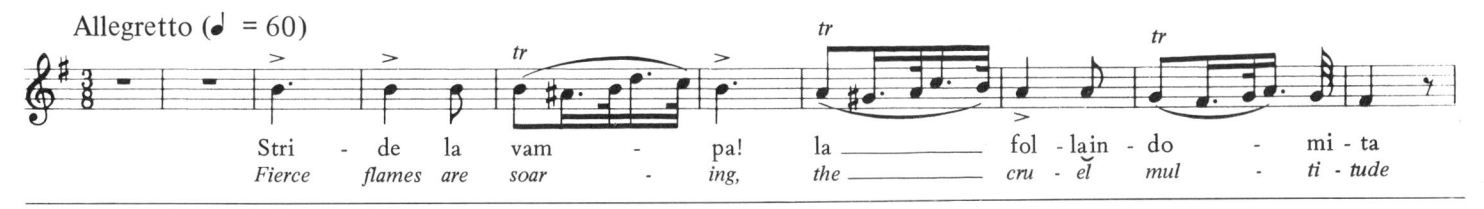

Stri - de la vam - pa! la ____ fol - lain - do ____ mi - ta
Fierce flames are soar - ing, the ____ cru - el mul - ti - tude

Instruments and Voices 67

mature and young ladies on stage, but who also appears disguised as a young servant girl, who in turn is pursued by an amorous male. To sample this voice type, listen to the opening scene of *Der Rosenkavalier*, which begins after a night of love with the Marschallin, Princess of Werdenberg. This treatment of a rather delicate theme offended the sensibilities of many during the early performances, and the opening scene was subsequently modified. It opens to find Octavian kneeling by the bed, embracing the older woman (Example 4-9).

The lowest female voice, and that richest in dark color, is the *alto*, who generally sings matronly supporting parts. One finds Verdi using this voice type most effectively in portraying the role of Ulrica, a Negress fortune-teller in *Un Ballo in Maschera* (*A Masked Ball*) (1859). This opera was subject to censorship because of the political nature of the plot, as discussed in Chapter 13, and Verdi changed the locale from Sweden to Puritan New England and altered the names of the characters to satisfy the official censors. This, one of Verdi's most popular operas, is concerned with a tragic love affair, the dire outcome of which is predicted by the fortune-teller Ulrica. Surrounded by smoking caldrons, she prepares herself for prophecy by darkly calling upon the devil, king of the underworld, to aid her in envisioning the future. Melodramatic though it is, the use of this expressive, low female voice is most theatrically effective (as illustrated in Example 4-10).

The "star of the show," generally speaking, is the ever-popular *tenor*. No one has satisfactorily explained the appeal of these high male voices, which are much less agile than those of females, for example, yet which continue to enchant the audience with their beauty and brilliance. Tenors may be divided into three general voice types—lyric, dramatic, and heroic—although other groupings are possible. These divisions are analogous to those of the soprano voices, excepting the coloratura, where range, color, and size of voice determine the stereotypical role. The *lyric tenor* has a comparatively light voice whose clarity and suppleness makes it ideal for the realization of flowing melodic lines.

For example, Mozart's *Don Giovanni* (1787) tells the story of the life of the famous ill-fated lover, Don Juan, who, in this case, is a baritone. Pitted against this lusty nobleman is the gentlemanly Don Ottavio, a lyric tenor, whose passions are more restricted and restrained (Example 4-11).

The "greatest of them all" in the minds of many opera *aficionados*, "tenor buffs" perhaps, is the *dramatic tenor*, the darling of most opera audiences since the end of the eighteenth century. This is a robust, manly voice which adds power, ardor, and dramatic intensity to what is basically the range of the lyric tenor. Many of the well-known tunes of operas of the nineteenth century were written to be sung by a dramatic tenor, one of the best loved being "Celeste Aïda" ("Heavenly Aïda") from the opening of the first act of Verdi's *Aïda* (1871). This famous work, commissioned for the opening of the new Opera House in Cairo in 1871, is set in Egypt at the time of the pharaohs, and tells the tale of the unfortunate love of Aïda (a slave girl, daughter of the King of Ethiopia) and

*From *Der Rosenkavalier* by Richard Strauss. Copyright © 1947 by Richard Strauss. Renewed 1974 by Franz Strauss. Copyright and renewal assigned to Boosey and Hawkes, Inc. Reprinted by permission.

EXAMPLE 4-9   R. STRAUSS: *Der Rosenkavalier*, ACT I, OPENING, MEASURES 1–10.*

A tempo mosso
Octavian (Passionately)

Wie Du warst! ___ Wie Du ___ bist! Das weiss nie - mand, das ahnt Kei - ner!
All thy soul ___ All thy ___ heart, None can meas - ure all their per - fec - tion.

68   Materials of Music

Seeking to combine the best qualities of Mozart and Johann Strauss, Jr., in a comic opera, Richard Strauss fashioned a ribald stage masterpiece, Der Rosenkavalier, rich with intrigue, burlesque, mistaken identity, waltzes, tenderness, and symbolism (the presentation of a silver rose being the symbol of a marriage proposal). The sexuality of this beguiling work scarcely raises an eyebrow these enlightened days, having become a popular favorite of sophisticates the world over.

Radames (an Egyptian, the valiant captain of the Guard of the Pharaoh). The usual outcome of a love affair between a member of a ruling class and a slave is too familiar to dwell upon here. Rather let us turn to this memorable aria from one of the most popular "grand" operas of all time. "Celeste Aïda" is introduced early in Scene 1 of the first act shortly after the curtain rises on the great ball of the palace of the Pharaoh of Memphis. With little introduction and no time to "warm up," Radames sings his memorable song of love (Example 4-12).

One is tempted to cite other such popular favorites which embellished most of the operas of the nineteenth century, but it is not within the scope of this brief presentation to do so. Seek them out for yourselves, as many of them are already "familiar tunes" to you, no doubt, and hear them within the dramatic context in which they occur. Meanwhile, turn to an even more dramatic tenor voice, the *heldentenor* (heroic tenor),

---

EXAMPLE 4-10 VERDI: *A Masked Ball*, ACT I, SCENE 2, "RE DELL' ABISSO" ("KING OF THE NIGHT"), MEASURES 1–4.

Adagio sostenuto

Re — dell' a - bis - so af - fret - ta - ti; pre - ci - pi - ta per l'e - tra,
King — of the night I sum - mon thee cleave through — the earth's dark cen - ter,

---

EXAMPLE 4-11 MOZART: *Don Giovanni*, ACT II, "IL MIO TESORO" ("MY TREASURE"), MEASURES 8–14.

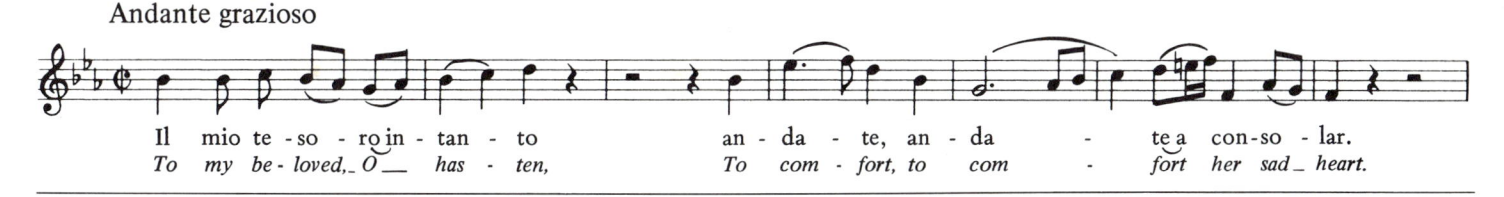

Andante grazioso

Il mio te - so - ro in - tan - to an - da - te, an - da - te a con - so - lar.
To my be - loved, O — has - ten, To com - fort, to com - fort her sad heart.

Instruments and Voices 69

EXAMPLE 4-12 VERDI: *Aïda*, ACT I, "CELESTE AÏDA" ("HEAVENLY AÏDA"), MEASURES 1–8.

Andantino (♪ = 116)
con espress.

Ce - le - ste A - i - da, for - ma di - vi - na, mi - sti - co ser - to
Heav'n - ly A - i - da, beau - ty re - splen - dent, Ra - di - ant flow - er,

di lu - ce e fior,
bloom - ing and bright;

and listen to another excerpt from Wagner's "Ring," from the opera *Siegfried*, in which Siegfried, the youthful hero of the four-opera cycle, will fearlessly accomplish the formidable tasks foretold: the killing of the dread dragon, the giant Fafner, who guards the treasure of the Nibelungs (gnomes) which brings tragedy to whoever takes it from its rightful owners; the rescue of Brünnhilde who is being punished for disobeying her father, Wotan, who takes away her godhood and puts her to sleep on a mountainside surrounded by a ring of magic fire. The central figure is introduced in the third opera of the cycle (*Siegfried*) and by the end of the first act is beginning to play the role ordained. In order to accomplish his deeds of heroism, he must have a mighty sword which he is forced to forge himself after repeated shatterings of those previously made for him. Standing before a glowing forge, he jubilantly fashions "Nothung," the needed sword (Example 4-13).

The middle-ranged voice of the male, the *baritone*, is given some of the most dramatic roles in opera. This voice, heavier and darker than that of the tenors, lends itself nicely to the portrayal of various parts, whether heroic, comic, or villainous. One of the most famous roles of the latter category is that of Scarpia in Puccini's *Tosca* (1900). Baron Scarpia, the cruel and lustful police chief of Rome, covets the love of the celebrated opera singer Tosca, who despises him. The plot revolves around his attempts to win her by torturing her lover, a painter. In the second act, Scarpia uses all his power to win his prize. Being pressured to the breaking point, Tosca says: "How much? What is your price, man?" and Scarpia laughs and replies in his great aria, "I am called venal" (Example 4-14).

Basses are much more common than the equivalent female voice, the contralto. Because of the commanding vocal character, low range, and power of this type of male voice, basses

EXAMPLE 4-13 WAGNER: *Siegfried*, ACT I, "NOTHUNG," MEASURES 1–14.

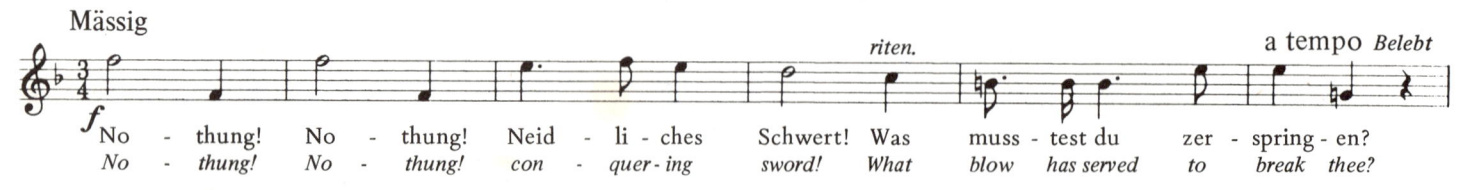

Mässig   *riten.*   *a tempo Belebt*

No - thung! No - thung! Neid - li - ches Schwert! Was muss - test du zer - spring - en?
No - thung! No - thung! con - quer - ing sword! What blow has served to break thee?

Zu Spreu nun schuf ich die schar - fe Pracht, im Ti - gel brat' ich die Späh - ne.
To shreds I shat - tered thy shin - ing blade; the fire has melt - ed the splin - ters.

70 Materials of Music

In fashioning his Nordic superman, the heroic Siegfried, shown here at his forest forge, Wagner unwittingly created a monster image which was to be epitomized, unfortunately, by the "racial superiority" of Hitler's Third Reich.

are often cast as father figures—chieftains, kings, and the like. On the other hand, they often play comic (buffo) roles such as Basilio in *The Barber of Seville*, Leperello in *Don Giovanni*, or Baron Ochs in *Der Rosenkavalier*. The buffo type will not be illustrated here, but let us consider a famous example of the former, excerpted from *Don Carlo* (1867) by Verdi. The tragedy takes place in Spain at the time of the Inquisition, during which troubled time King Philip II (Felipo) and his son Don Carlo fall in love with the same princess. The King marries her and, suspecting his own son of betraying him, gives him over to the Inquisitors to be burned at the stake. Alone in his study as dawn breaks at the opening of Act III, the sleepless Felipo laments the failure of his marriage and sadly contemplates death in a superb monologue, one of the most magnificent solos for bass voice in the operatic repertoire (Example 4-15).

Now that we have become acquainted with some of the materials and processes of music, let us turn to a consideration of the relationships that exist among various sections of a composition, i.e., to the consideration of the overall musical structure—called *form*.

EXAMPLE 4-14   PUCCINI: *Tosca*, ACT II, "MI DICON VENAL" ("I'M CALLED VENAL"), MEASURES 1–7.

Instruments and Voices

EXAMPLE 4-15 VERDI: *Don Carlo*, ACT III, "DORMIRO SOL" ("I'LL SLEEP ALONE"), MEASURES 1–6.

72   Materials of Music

TWO

Forms of Music

5 Sectional Forms

Psychologists tell us that three important hungers or drives influence our lives: *stimulus or sensation hunger, recognition hunger,* and *structure hunger.* The first two are fairly obvious, and it is also fairly obvious how they may relate to music. Stimulus hunger may be satisfied with experiences of the senses. We can listen to music, as Copland has said, on the purely sensuous plane, basking in the sheer pleasure of the sounds. Recognition hunger can usually be met only by interaction with another human being. Music provides a unique opportunity for people to interact with each other, whether it be in the merely passive

Following the practices of Cubism in Man with Violin, *the Spanish genius of this century, Pablo Picasso, fragmented man and violin into an abstraction of figures, lines, and planes—creating form in space much as a composer fashions form in time.*

sense of sharing a listening experience or in the active sense of making music together.

The last hunger, structure hunger, may not be so obvious in its original meaning, but can be illustrated by an experiment with rats raised in a state of sensory deprivation—that is, raised in a totally dark, totally silent environment. Later, when placed in a normal environment, they showed a preference for being on a floor with a checkerboard design rather than a floor that was neutral or without design, even if food were placed on this neutral background. In other words, their hunger for some sort of structure was actually greater, at least for a time, than their hunger for food. Applied to human reaction to music, we can say that structure hunger may be met with a directed perception of form in music.

An artist like Pablo Picasso, for example, creates form in space just as a composer shapes form in time. Sometimes in the visual arts, subjects are presented in a highly representational manner, and we may not be as aware of pure form. Sometimes paintings may be abstract, devoid of any representational aspects, so that our perception of form becomes paramount. Sometimes paintings may represent a compromise between these two extremes as in Picasso's *Man with Violin*. At first we may be aware only of lines, hues, shapes, and an overall sense of form. As we look closer, however, we see that the picture does contain fragments of a man's anatomy and fragments of a violin—notice, for example, the so-called "f holes" from the belly of the violin which appear at the bottom of the picture.

In music the representational element is far less prominent; indeed, in most works it is not present. The perception of form is therefore all the more crucial for rewarding listening. At the same time, it is more difficult to perceive form in the aural arts because we must rely on our memory to sense the structure, while in the visual arts we can move back and forth from one element of the picture to another until we have grasped the sense of structure.

STRUCTURAL INTERRELATIONS

What is form in music? In its broadest sense, form is usually understood to mean the relationships existing among various parts of a composition. More specifically the study of form involves a consideration of the following questions:

1. How is sectionalization created in a composition?
   How are continuity and discontinuity achieved?
   How are various aspects of music used to keep the piece moving forward in time or to more or less stop it?
   How long are the various sections and subsections?
2. How are the aspects of unity and variety used in a composition?
   How much of the composition involves repetition of ideas and therefore leads to a sense of unity or stability?
   How much of the composition involves contrast and therefore contributes to a sense of variety and change?
3. How are symmetry and balance reflected in the composition?
   To what extent are events in one section of a composition balanced by events in another section of a composition?
4. What functions are performed by the various sections of a composition?
   Do they *present* material, *repeat* material, *vary* material, present *contrasting* material, or *return* to previously heard material after contrasting material?
   Are some sections more important than others?
   Do some sections serve primarily as an introduction, a transition, or as a conclusion?
   Are some sections heard primarily as a development or reworking of previous material?
5. To what established formal types does this composition most nearly conform?

This last question should be asked only after all other aspects of the composition have been examined. In other words, we should not start out with the idea that a composition belongs to a particular formal type such as sonata-allegro or ternary form, or theme and variations, and then seek to force the composition into this mold. Rather, we should examine the work with an open mind and then, only after having seen all the details of the composition, come to a judgment as to the general category of form to which it belongs. Let us now examine each of these questions in detail.

Sectionalization

Though some compositions seem to move from beginning to end in a seamless way without stops or pauses, most compositions are marked by fairly clear points at which the forward motion of the music is arrested. These stopping places in the music are usually called *cadences* (from the Latin word *cadere*, "to fall"). The various types of cadences were mentioned in Chapter 2. To provide some review of these, study the cadences in Example 5-1 in terms of their rhythmic, melodic, and harmonic aspects.

Sometimes not all of the aspects of music stop at once. Indeed it is usually the mark of an interesting composer that he knows how to avoid a too obvious sectionalization in compositions. Examine the music in Example 5-2 and indicate which aspects of the music keep moving forward and which aspects contribute to a cadence or sense of stopping.

As we turn our attention to larger aspects and to larger sections of music, we find that sectionalization may be created by the two extremes of repetition and marked change. The literal repetition of a passage of music marks rather clearly the beginning and end of the section. A marked change, especially in the important aspects of tonality, timbre, texture, or themes, usually indicates an important sectional division in a composition. If all four aspects change—that is, if themes (melodic and rhythmic aspects), tonality, texture, and timbre all change—or even if only two or three of them change, the sense of sectionalization is especially clear.

The "Dance of the Reedpipes [or Mirlitons]" from Tchaikovsky's *Nutcracker Suite* is an especially clear example of the use of contrast to create sectionalization (Example 5-3). The second section of this composition begins with an upbeat to

EXAMPLE 5-1 CADENCES.

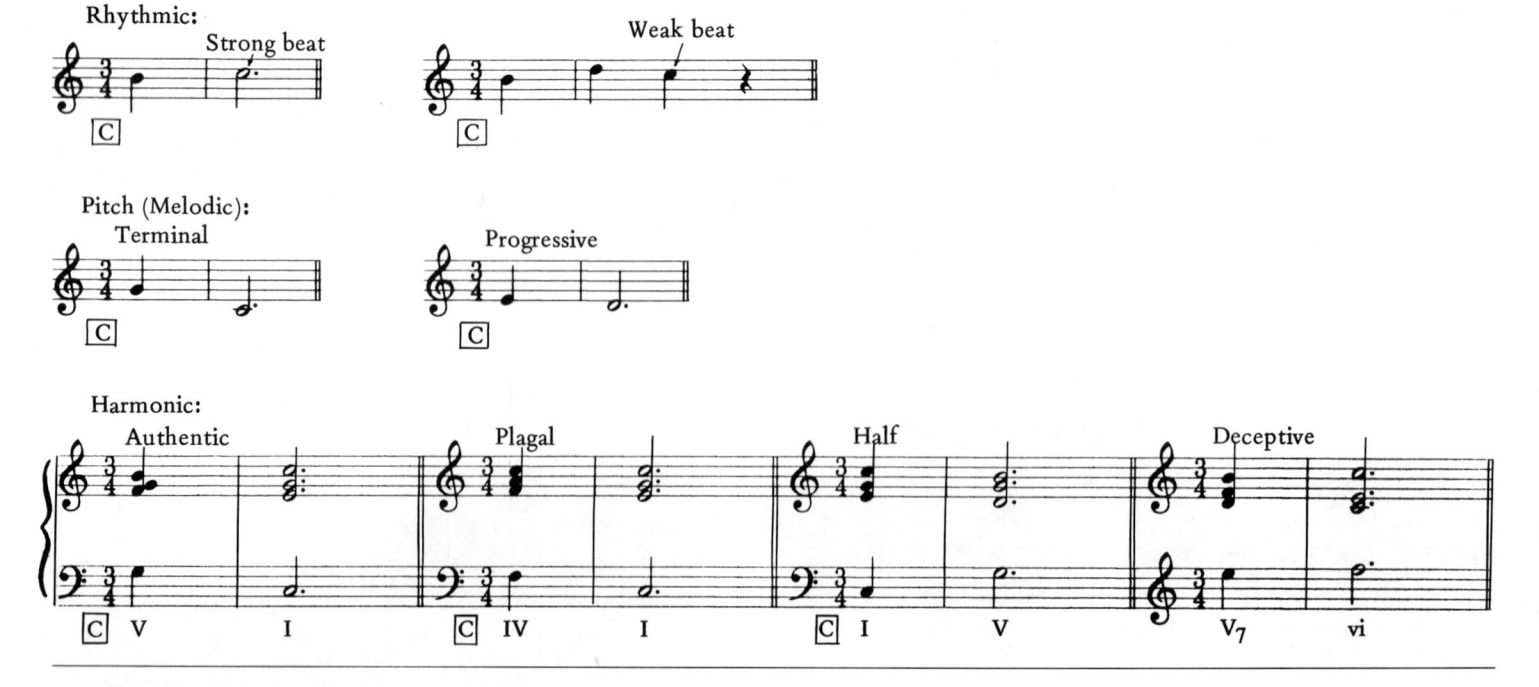

76 Forms of Music

EXAMPLE 5-2 Mozart: *Symphony No. 41 in C Major,* fourth movement, measures 1–10.

EXAMPLE 5-3 Tchaikovsky: *Nutcracker Suite,* "Dance of the Reedpipes." (*a*) Measures 1–5; (*b*) measures 51–52.

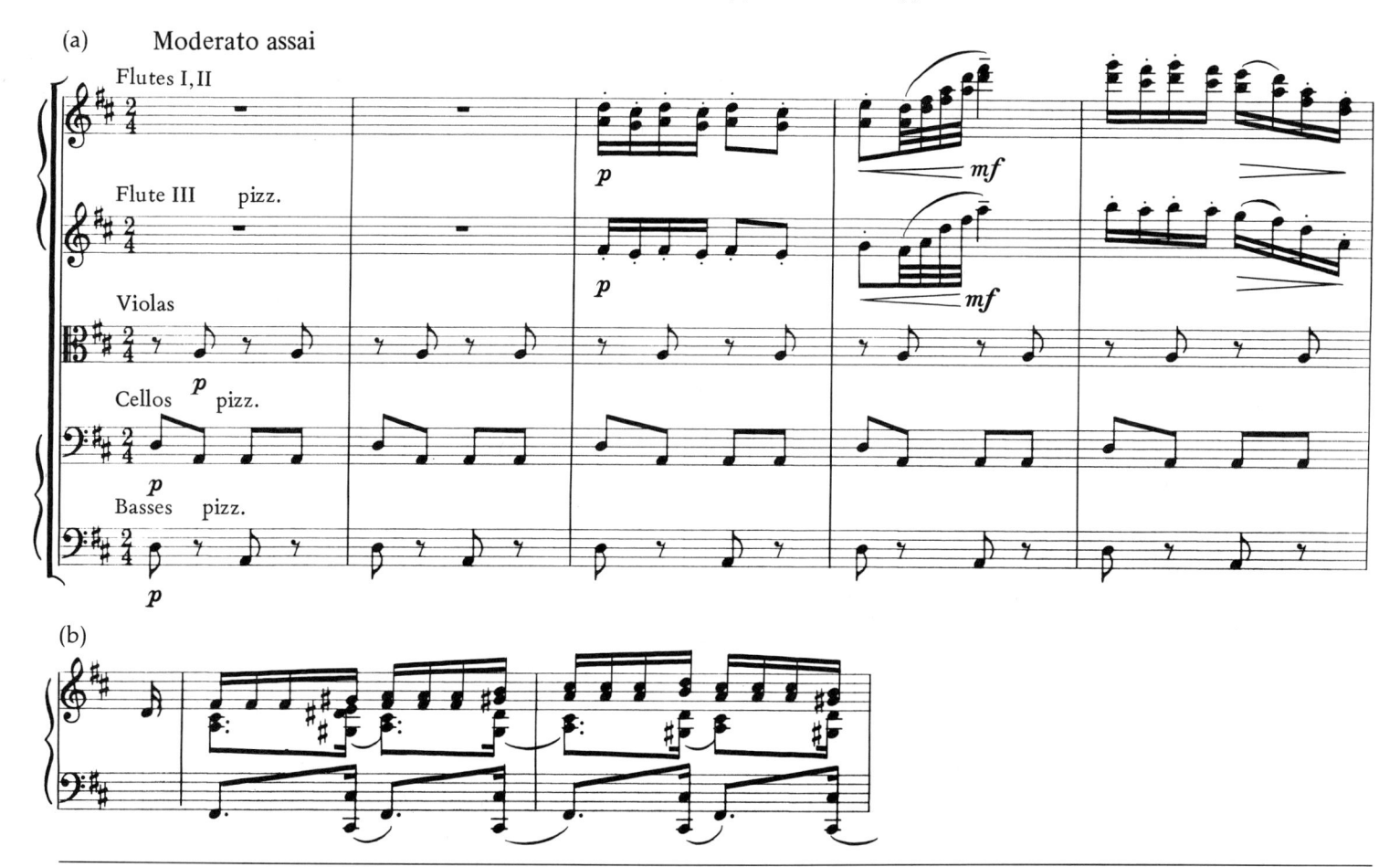

Sectional Forms 77

measure 51, a little more than halfway through the composition. The timbre and texture change from three high flutes with pizzicato strings in the first section to middle and low brasses in the beginning of the second section. The tonality changes from D major to F-sharp minor, and the thematic material changes from basically even-note rhythms and neighbor-tone and arpeggio melodic figures in the first section to primarily dotted-note rhythms and repeated notes and passing-tone figures in the second section. It would be virtually impossible not to hear the strong sense of sectionalization created by these changes.

The use of repetition to create sectionalization can be heard in the opening fourteen measures of the third movement, minuet, from Mozart's *Symphony No. 40 in G Minor*. Notice that the literal and direct repetition of these first fourteen measures, indicated by the repeat sign (:||), establishes them as a single unit in the composition. Throughout this movement, and indeed throughout minuets in general, the use of repetition is an important factor in the creation of sectionalization (Example 5-4).

Unity and Variety

We have already examined the change that occurs in measure 51 of the Tchaikovsky "Dance of the Reedpipes" and have seen that this creates sectionalization. Obviously these changes also create a sense of variety in the composition. At measure 62 the opening theme recurs in the flutes, creating a sense of return and a sense of unity in the composition. At this moment forces of *both* unity and variety are present, for we hear not only the return of the original melody in the flutes and the pizzicato in the low strings, but we also hear a new element—namely, a countermelody in the upper-string parts which adds a sense of variety to this section.

If we turn to Mozart's *Symphony No. 40 in G Minor*, we can find a similar unity and variety between the minuet and the trio. The minuet is in a minor key and features syncopation; throughout this section the full orchestra is usually playing. The trio changes to major, syncopation no longer occurs, and the orchestra is cut down considerably in size. Indeed, this notion of reducing the size of the orchestra, often to just three principal sounding elements, is what originally gave rise to the name "trio" in early examples of the minuet and trio form. Again, however, we can see that the forces of unity and variety are exerting their influence at the same time. Although we have pointed out differences between the minuet and trio which contribute to a sense of variety, we could also point out some similarities between the sections, which contribute to a sense of unity. For example, the triple meter is preserved between both sections, and both the first section of the minuet and the first section of the trio begin on the tonic and move to the dominant. A more superficial point of unity between the two sections is the use of the rhythmic figure quarter-eighth-eighth-eighth-eighth which appears in measures 2, 5, and 8–10 of the first section (see Example 5-4) and in measures 47, 57, and 59 of the second section in Example 5-5.

The search for points of unity and variety can be one of the most meaningful tasks in the analysis of music. Indeed, it was for the purpose of being able to discover such relationships as unity and variety that we undertook to learn the terms and concepts associated with the isolated aspects of music. These isolated aspects of music are of some importance in themselves, but they are mostly important for the way in which they are used in the actual matrix of a composition to create such things as a sense of unity and variety.

Symmetry and Balance

We have already seen that the Tchaikovsky "Dance of the Reedpipes" is in three main sections. The first section is 42 measures in length, the second is 20 measures in length, and the final section approximately 15 measures in length. As you listen to this work, however, the proportions probably will not strike you as being as unbalanced as the figures would indicate. Instead you will probably be conscious of a sense of symmetry or balance in the relationships among the different sections of the composition. This is one of the most interesting aspects of music. A return of a previously heard section does not have to be exactly the same length as the original presentation in order to create a sense of symmetry or balance. Contrast

The cathedral of St. Mark. Notice how the central arch is symmetrically balanced by two arches on either side and the two central domes are balanced by domes to the right and left.

this with the exact proportions seen in St. Mark's Cathedral in the illustration and notice that symmetry is created in the visual or spatial sense by exact proportions on either side of a central figure. The minuet from Mozart's *Symphony No. 40 in G Minor* is 84 measures long including repeats, the trio is also exactly 84 measures in length including repeats, but the return of the minuet, since it is specified to be played without repeats, is only 42 measures in length. Again, however, symmetry is created even with this abbreviated return.

Some composers, like Bartók, in a conscious attempt to create symmetry in their works, have deliberately used the proportions of the Fibonacci series (1, 2, 3, 5, 8, 13, 21, etc.) This is somewhat similar to the use of the golden section in sculpture or painting.

EXAMPLE 5-4   MOZART: *Symphony No. 40 in G Minor*, MINUET, MEASURES 1–14.

Sectional Forms   79

EXAMPLE 5-5 MOZART: *Symphony No. 40 in G Minor,* MINUET, MEASURES 43–60.

Function and Structure

In the two works that we are focusing on in this section, most of the musical material is involved in what might be called *presentation.* It is *thematic*—that is, it expresses significant ideas in the composition rather than merely preparing for these ideas, leading from one idea to another, or extending the ideas. It is interesting to note in the Tchaikovsky composition, however, that when the flutes return after the second section in measure 60, they do not immediately play the opening theme but instead, for two measures, they play an extension or transition from the second section back to the return of the first section. As you listen to this work, pay particular attention to these two measures. Notice how your musical attention is more or less suspended for a brief moment. In a sense you "hold your musical breath" for these two measures and then finally have a sense of arrival at measure 62. For a more extended example of this, listen to measures 296 through 314 of the Beethoven Violin Concerto, last movement, discussed later in this chapter.

With a skillful composer it is not always possible to tell where transitions are occurring. They are sometimes of great beauty and ingenuity, but they can usually be distinguished from presentation sections in the sense that they have a more ongoing motion. Frequently, especially in the Classic period, they occur over a dominant harmony and involve fragmentations of motives heard in the presentation sections. In larger compositions they sometimes involve a modulation from one tonal area to another.

In formal diagrams it is sometimes helpful to distinguish between transition sections and presentation sections by using dotted lines for the former and solid lines for the latter. In sections in which it is difficult to determine whether the transitional nature or the thematic nature is more prominent, one can use alternating dots and dashes to convey this sense of ambiguity.

Letters or numbers can be used to represent the various thematic sections of a composition. A diagram of the "Dance of the Reedpipes" appears in Example 5-6a. Notice the use of

EXAMPLE 5-6 TCHAIKOVSKY: *Nutcracker Suite,* "DANCE OF THE REEDPIPES." (*a*) OVERALL DIAGRAM; (*b*) DETAILED DIAGRAM.

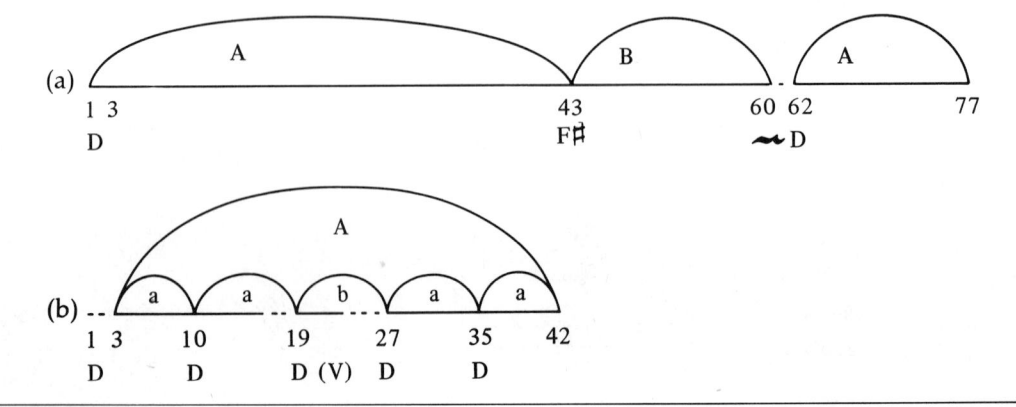

80 Forms of Music

dotted lines in measures 60–62 and the use of A-B-A'* for the main thematic sections. The arched lines over the letters define the beginnings and endings of the thematic sections. The numbers refer to measures, and the letters below the line refer to tonal centers. We could take the first 42 measures and divide them into even smaller groupings, as indicated in Example 5-6b. You can hear the small b section because it is marked by the entrance of the distinctive quality of the English horn. Notice how the principles of repetition, contrast, return and variation, unity and variety, sectionalization, and symmetry operate in this composition on both smaller levels and on the larger level of the entire composition.

This idea of levels of formal activity is one of the most important and one of the most difficult to grasp. Just as there are levels of formal thematic activity, there can also be levels of tonal activity. Notice in Example 5-6b that the whole first section can be regarded in the larger sense in the key of D, but it can also be subdivided in a smaller sense and shown to consist of a movement from D to A and back to D. This sense of hierarchical levels is not unique to music. We can find it, for example, in the division of a country into states, states into counties, counties into cities, and cities into districts and neighborhoods, on down to the level of the individual family groupings with their various members. The comparison, of course, should not be carried too far.

None of the compositions we have studied to this point has an introduction; they all begin directly with a thematic presentation. But many longer works begin with an introduction, and these may be classified into three general types. Some introductions are *nonthematic*—that is, they consist of chords, rhythms, or pitches without a clear-cut thematic shape. Others consist of *fragments of themes* that will later be heard in their entirety in the course of the main thematic sections. Still others are *thematic*, based on material that is not obviously related to material following later in the main presentation sections. This latter type of introduction, which will be studied in Chapter 7, is in effect a presentation section itself, but acts as an introduction in the larger view of the entire form of the movement.

Similarly, the endings of compositions can be of various types. Some are *nonthematic*, consisting merely of a prolonged or reiterated chord or chordal progression. Others are based on *fragments of themes* heard in the main presentation sections in the body of the movement, and still others are *thematic*. Sometimes introduction and coda use the same material and act in the sense of prologue and epilogue for a composition.

SECTIONAL FORMS

Once we have analyzed a composition into its component sections and have considered the aspects of unity and variety, symmetry and balance, and the function of these parts and their interrelations, it is possible to ask ourselves, "Does the form of this particular composition resemble a general class of forms or a specific type of form?"

Ternary Form

Both of the works that we have studied to this point, for example, belong to the category of forms known as *ternary* or three-part form. This form was especially popular in the Classic and Romantic periods (see page 119 for dates), and it continues to be a significant form up to the present day. Its unique balance of unity and variety and its opportunities for symmetry make it an especially effective form. Ternary form in the Classic period is usually characterized by the fact that the individual sections have a sense of completeness. This is definitely true of the first and last sections, and it may be true of the second section, but to somewhat less extent. The first section begins and ends in the tonic key, the second section brings a contrast of key, and the third section returns to the original key and begins and ends in that key.

Binary Form

Binary or two-part form was especially popular in the seventeenth and early eighteenth centuries, during the Baroque period. This form, although it may seem simpler than the ternary form, usually presents more of a problem in analysis. In Example 5-7 we see the prelude from the *Sonata da Camera*,

---

*This symbol, called a *prime* ('), is affixed to letters to denote a variation. For example, A' (A prime) is a varied version of A.

EXAMPLE 5-7 CORELLI: *Sonata da Camera, Op. 5, No. 8,* PRELUDE, MELODY LINE, COMPLETE.

Op. 5, No. 8, by Arcangelo Corelli. That this occurs in two sections is made fairly clear by the double bars and repeat signs appearing at measure 22. In general, we can say that the overall effect of the two sections is one of contrast, and therefore, in general terms, we could label them A and B. If we examine the small phrases within each section carefully, however, we notice that the same phrase ends the A section (measures 19–22) and the B section (measures 39–42). Again we have seen the formal principles of unity and variety in operation simultaneously in a composition.

Example 5-8 presents an interesting formal type, which in effect combines the aspects of binary and ternary form. If we look at the largest aspects of this theme from the sonata movement of Mozart's *Sonata in D Major for Piano, K. 284,* we see that the presence of the double bar and repeat signs—that is, the use of repetition—creates two large sections, and therefore our first analysis of this would probably be in binary form. If, however, we examine the thematic material on the phrase level, we find that it forms a pattern of A-B-A', disregarding the marked repetitions. In other words, because this consists of a presentation, a contrast, and a return, it suggests a ternary or three-part form. The fact that the B and A sections are smaller need not discourage us from finding some ternary characteristics, because we have already discovered in our section on symmetry and balance that it is possible to have progressively smaller sections and still create a sense of symmetry and balance. Theorists have been debating about the proper designation for this form for years. It is variously referred to as binary, ternary, rounded binary, and incipient ternary. If we take the approach that we have recommended—that is, first simply lining up the constituent parts of a composition and studying their interrelationships and their function in

With a native genius for music excelled by no one, Wolfgang Amadeus Mozart was famed in his day for his remarkable keyboard improvisations; he was to become one of the greatest composers of all times.

EXAMPLE 5-8 MOZART: *Sonata in D Major for Piano, K. 284*, MEASURES 1–17.

Sectional Forms 83

the overall structure—we need not be overly concerned about the category into which we put the form. Indeed, the most effective designation for this form might be simply *binary-ternary*, a designation that clearly indicates its twofold nature.

We can expand the idea of presentation, contrast, and return to include more than three sections. Some nineteenth-century symphonies such as the Seventh Symphony of Beethoven expand the idea of minuet-trio-minuet to a five-part structure. By this time the graceful minuet has changed to the faster scherzo and the five-part form is:

scherzo-trio-scherzo-trio-scherzo

which can be simplified in terms of letters as A-B-A-B-A. In some Romantic symphonies two different trios are used:

scherzo-trio I-scherzo-trio II-scherzo (A-B-A-C-A)

Rondo Form

The *rondo* form, used so frequently in lighthearted finale movements of Classic instrumental works, is similar to this five-part form except that there are usually transition sections between the thematic sections. Thus the rondo will give more of an impression of one continuous movement than the five-part scherzo.

The rondo is not limited to any single "ground plan" or ordering of sections. Some possible formal schemes are:

A-B-A-B-A
A-B-A-C-A

A-B-A-C-A-D-A	(used in seventeenth-century keyboard works)
A-B-A-C-A-B-A	(Beethoven's *Concerto for Violin in D Major, Op. 61*, III)

What all these schemes have in common is that every other section is a presentation of the main A theme. This recurring theme is always in the tonic key in the typical Classical rondo form. The other sections provide contrast in key as well as in thematic material.

We shall examine the finale from the Beethoven Violin Concerto in detail, for it not only offers a clear-cut example of the structure and characteristics of rondo form, but also is one of the most effective finales in the concerto literature.

In broad terms this rondo movement conforms to the pattern A-B-A-C-A-B-A. The recurring A theme has many of the characteristics usually associated with rondo themes. It is in 6/8 meter, compound duple meter, and allegro tempo, and has a rollicking, almost folk-dance, character. It opens with an arpeggiated D-major triad figure that is easy to recognize in its subsequent returns. The accompaniment to this theme at first involves only the cellos; later other instruments are added (Example 5-9).

The transition leading from the A to the B section is so interesting that we might be tempted to take it for a thematic section itself. The main reason most analysts would refer to it as a transition is that it does effect a modulation or change of key from the tonic to the dominant (from D to A major). Here again we see how one and the same section of music may simultaneously have two different attributes. We might compare this to a play or movie in which a certain role or character is supposed to perform a relatively minor function in the overall plot, but the actor or actress does such an outstanding job in the role that our attention is irresistibly captured. Marilyn Monroe's first walk-on role in the movies illustrates this. But to return to Beethoven, we can easily identify this "transition" section we have been discussing because it features the horns playing motives that are typical "hunting-horn calls" (Example 5-10).

The B section proper arrives firmly in A major. Thematically it does not differ strikingly from the A theme, except that it has predominantly descending motion in contrast to the predominantly ascending motion of the opening theme. A more striking point of identification involves the texture and orchestration. The theme is presented in alternating two-measure segments, first by the full orchestra and then by the solo violin playing in double stops—that is, playing two notes at the same time (Example 5-11).

EXAMPLE 5-9 BEETHOVEN: *Concerto for Violin in D Major, Op. 61*, THIRD MOVEMENT, MEASURES 1–4.

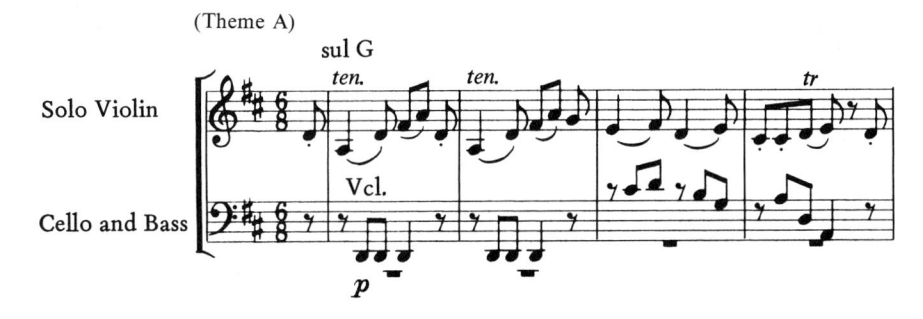

EXAMPLE 5-10 BEETHOVEN: *Concerto for Violin in D Major, Op. 61*, THIRD MOVEMENT, MEASURES 41–49.

EXAMPLE 5-11 BEETHOVEN: *Concerto for Violin in D Major, Op. 61*, THIRD MOVEMENT, MEASURES 59–62.

Sectional Forms 85

Ludwig van Beethoven is depicted in this sketch as the epitome of the genius whose concern with his creation was so great that he was not aware of the disorder about him. Early foreseeing the future role Beethoven was to play, Mozart remarked, "Keep an eye on him—he will make a noise in the world some day."

The C theme brings a sense of contrast in almost all musical aspects. The tonality changes to G minor, the character changes to a rather pensive songlike character, and the bassoon expresses an important melodic role, sharing phrases of the melody with the solo violin. When the bassoon has the melody, the solo violin weaves graceful arabesques around it (Example 5-12). Note that this C section has a form itself, namely, the binary-ternary form that we discussed earlier.

Ritornello Form

Baroque solo concertos and concerti grossi were frequently cast in a form similar to the rondo—the *ritornello* form. In this form a schematic section of music appears at the beginning of the work and then recurs several times throughout the movement with contrasting sections, usually for the soloist or solo group (concertino) in between. The principal difference between this form and the Classical rondo is that the ritornelli or returning sections (the word *ritornello* actually means "little return") occur in different keys in the ritornello form, whereas they return in the same key in the rondo form. A typical ritornello form for a first or last movement of a Baroque concerto might be as follows:

Themes	Tonalities	Comments
RI*	In tonic key	Full orchestra states thematic material
SI	In a related key	Soloist(s) play sequential figures based either on motives from the R section or upon new material
RII	In a related key	Full orchestra states thematic material; may be somewhat shorter than RI
SII	In a related key	Soloist(s) play(s) sequential figures based on the motives from R section or upon new material
SIII	In tonic key	Full orchestra states thematic material

*R = ritornello section; S = soloist(s) section.

This form may be extended by adding more ritornello and solo sections. It is found in many of the movements of the Brandenburg Concertos of Bach and other works of the Baroque period.

EXAMPLE 5-12 BEETHOVEN: *Concerto for Violin in D Major, Op. 61,* THIRD MOVEMENT, MEASURES 127–130.

Free Sectional Form

Sectional forms continued to be used in the nineteenth and twentieth centuries. Many works of music fall in the category of ternary or rondo form, or they may be in a *free sectional* form, in which there are clear sections and some element of return, but no adherence to a strict established pattern such as binary, ternary, or rondo. This formal type will be discussed in detail in the next-to-last chapter in connection with George Gershwin's *Rhapsody in Blue.*

A more radical approach to form is represented in some avant-garde works by composers such as Karlheinz Stockhausen. Some of these works, such as *Mikrophonie I* and *II,* are written in what may be called "moment form" or "now form." Essentially such works are sectional, but, unlike Classical or even early twentieth-century sectional forms, no importance is attached to the ordering of the sections. They could occur in almost any order; indeed, in some of his works Stockhausen advises the audience that they may enter and leave the performance at any time, sampling as much or as little of the work as they wish. It is interesting that this approach to musical form reflects a "nonlinear" structure similar to much avant-garde poetry and drama, or, to translate it into the popular arts, we find the same approach in the television variety and comedy-revue programs. Marshall McLuhan has perceptively described such developments as a change to a "field theory" approach, and compares these developments with those in modern physics. However one might describe it, this is one more instance in which an aspect of music—in this case, the aspect of form—may be seen to be influenced by current sociocultural trends.

6 Variational Forms

Not all music exists in notated or printed reproduction. Indeed some musicians through the ages have shaped some of their most moving and expressive utterances by improvisation. Many of us associate improvisation primarily with jazz, and not without justification. But the *spontaneous* invention of musical ideas has been part of several past and present styles. Improvisatory techniques and procedures representing the abdication of compositional controls by the composer to the player constitute a significant influence in much current music, including jazz and avant-garde musical theater.

Far from being limited to occurrences in this century, improvisation has played varying roles in Western (and Eastern) music from the vocal embellishments of the early priests' chanting to the eloquent and complex organ improvisations of Bach, the virtuosic fantasies of Chopin and Liszt, and the intricate and soaring cascades of saxophone and trumpet sonority by such twentieth-century artists as Charlie Parker, John Coltrane, and Dizzy Gillespie. If there is a single musical process shared in common by all these musicians, past and present, it is the process of *variation*. We shall see how variation plays an important part in the technique of improvising. In this chapter we shall study a number of compositions selected from several centuries of practice, the focal point of this study being the process of variation.

The music literature composed for small ensembles during the past four hundred or so years includes some eloquent musical statements. Both improvised as well as notated compositions for small ensembles have in common the employment of variation, a technique providing both the constraints and flexibility that have appealed to and served so effectively the needs of virtually all inspiring musical creators from Josquin to Stravinsky, Bach to Debussy, and Chopin to Ives.

The rapport and electricity of small-group performance—in which each player is responsible for a separate and often equally important musical line, as in the string quartet, the wind quintet, or the small jazz ensemble—is unmatched by any large musical ensemble. Although the symphonic orchestra, oratorio chorus, or combined forces of the orchestra and voices of the opera are impressive in sheer numbers, variety of sound,

Improvisation occurs in art forms other than music, as exemplified in this painting (Improvisation No. 27) by Kandinsky, the innovative Russian artist who is said to be the creator of the first abstraction and who blazed the way into the world of "new" art of the 20th century.

and potential contrasts of intensity and expression, the small ensemble has played a role in the past development and present exploration of musical style and performance that has existed since the Renaissance and before. The symphonic orchestra and large mixed chorus are relatively recent innovations, stemming from the eighteenth and nineteenth centuries.

Size and spectacle in music have not always assured durable and lasting effect. With the exception of solo performance there is no more rewarding medium of expression for instrumentalists than that of the small ensemble of two, three, or four players wherein each player must be self-reliant. This medium is roughly comparable to the small vocal ensemble composed

Variational Forms

Raw emotion, showmanship, and sophisticated musical skills are creatively wed in varied personal musical statements inspired and fused by a central idea.

of three or four singers, whose ancestry in music predates the instrumental ensemble.* The role of the player and the degree to which his performance is determined by the composer has varied a great deal throughout the course of the development of small-ensemble music. In some works, such as the Baroque trio sonata or the contemporary jazz ensemble, improvisation by some or all of the players is a major factor in the creation of the piece, whereas in more formally organized works such as those composed for the string-quartet medium consisting of two violins, a viola, and cello, the composition's performance represents the realization of highly specified and carefully notated instructions of the composer, offering limited possibilities for individual interpretation by the player. Like the symphony and concerto, the string-quartet medium represents a highly formalized mode of expression; in recent times a number of twentieth-century composers have organized pieces in which far greater latitude is given the player to invent, select, and improvise, in effect to share in the creative aspects of music as well as its performance. There is no better example of this duality of roles shared by the performer than in jazz.

IMPROVISATION AND VARIATION IN JAZZ

The essence of jazz is improvisation. The most easily recognized and typically most engaging characteristics of most jazz are rhythmic, melodic, and timbral, but its most essential structural components are (1) an ongoing and unwavering metrical pulse (beat), and (2) an underlying harmonic progression. There is very little jazz in which these components are not present for the most part. This is true because jazz by definition is an improvised expression, and jazz improvisation, although commonly centered initially on some melodic theme, is predicated on a rhythmic-harmonic background. The improvising player invents a series of melodic variations against the commonly agreed-upon background. The melodic passages invented by the player—usually a saxophone, trumpet, trombone,

*Throughout history voices and instruments were used more or less interchangeably, pieces being invented and improvised without specific performance instructions.

clarinet, flute, piano, string bass, or guitar player (subject to changing vogues in instrumentation)—depend to one degree or another on a rhythmic relation to the ongoing beat and a harmonic association with the ongoing harmonic progression, usually at least eight or twelve measures in length, repeated as many times as desired. The audible relation of the player's melodic improvisations to an initial melodic theme may be easily discerned or completely obscured, depending to a great extent on the facility, fantasy, and resourcefulness of the player. Any traditional "standard" melody such as "Moonlight in Vermont" or "Yesterdays" may serve as the basis for a jazz rendition, just as may a contemporary popular song such as "Up, Up, and Away" or "Close to You." The essence of jazz is essentially one of performance style and presentation rather than raw material as such. The most indigenous jazz raw material is *blues,* constituted of a twelve-measure harmonic progression (and a number of possible variants) over which any of a number of melodic themes may be stated. Perhaps we can bring this discussion into better focus by constructing an artificial jazz passage based on the song "Close to You." A simple arrangement of the piece is shown in Example 6-1. Sing the line while a pianist or guitarist supplies the accompaniment or a modification of it.

The improvising jazz player uses a melody such as this as a point of departure or basic line for his own inventions and elaborations. In some improvisations the player adds and changes relatively little, leaving the basic line essentially intact and clearly recognizable. Such is the case in Example 6-1*a* wherein embellishments and slight modifications enrich and color the basic line, leaving its essential features such as its contour and accented notes largely unaltered. Compare variation 1 (Example 6-1*b*), an imagined saxophone or trumpet improvisation, with the original. The elements of this variation are mainly rhythmic: long notes such as the half note in measure 1 of the theme are broken up into a figure (♪ ♩.); notes are stated in different durations so that those of the theme (♩♩♩♩) become ♫♫ ; long notes are replaced by a series of connective shorter values, as in measure 3; and rhythmic

90 Forms of Music

EXAMPLE 6-1 BACHARACH: "CLOSE TO YOU." (a) OPENING SECTION, MEASURES 1–11; (b) VARIATION 1, MEASURES 1–8; (c) MAIN STRUCTURAL PITCHES; (d) VARIATION 2, MEASURES 1–9; (e) SKETCH.

(a) Slow and steady

Variational Forms 91

(b)
Variation 1
  Slow and steady

(c)

(d)
Variation 2
  A little faster

(e)

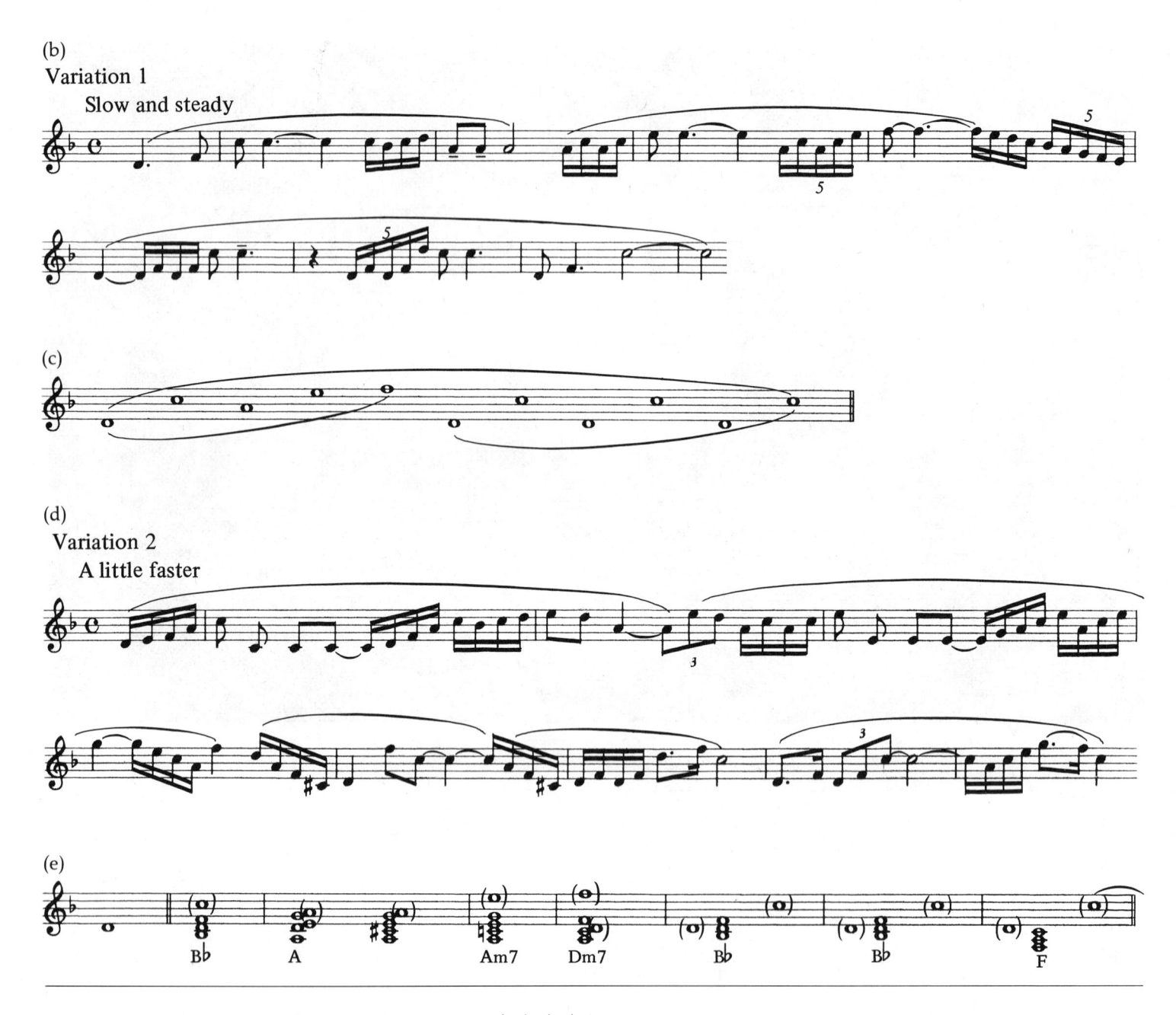

patterns are stated in more elaborate variants such as ♪ ♩ ♪ ♩ becoming

    𝄽 ♬♬♪ ♩.

The latter figure contains a *quintolet*—that is, the division of a given unit (in this case a quarter note) by five equal-length durations, here five sixteenths. Quintolets occur three times in this variation and form a recurring element in it. Note that the structure of the theme is retained in the variation; those

notes that most determine the contour of the melody as well as form its rhythmically stressed notes (long notes and on-the-beat notes) are prominent in the improvisation. The result is a simple elaboration of the theme.

The main structural pitches of the tune are shown in Example 6-1c. The division of the melody into two contrasting segments, the one showing a rising contour from d to f (the interval of a tenth), the other based on repetitions of the span from d to c, a minor seventh, is evident. Awareness of such a division helps the player to exploit characteristics of the melodic contour in improvisation.

A second variation is shown in Example 6-1d; compare it with the previous one. This variation exploits more the harmonic aspects of the theme as well as rhythmic embellishments of various pitches of the melodic contour. Example 6-1e shows a simplified measure-by-measure reduction of the theme to its basic melodic pitches (shown parenthetically) above the accompanying chords. The simplicity of the harmonic materials makes them susceptible to elaboration and embellishment. Relate the variation in Example 6-1d to the sketch in Example 6-1e. Some of the processes noted in the invention of variation 2 include:

1. Rhythmic repetition in a different octave of a basic pitch, as in measures 1 and 3.
2. Adding rhythmic activity by embellishing a basic-pitch step motion above or below, as in measure 1, last beat.
3. Arpeggiation—that is, stating in melodic succession the various members of the accompanying chord—as in measures 3, 4, 5, 6, etc.
4. Embellishing a given basic pitch by leaping to the note a step above (or below) it before moving to the basic pitch, as in measure 4 (notes g and c sharp).

Whether improvised or recorded as part of a written composition, the processes noted herein, together with others, are basic to the techniques of expansion and embellishment that are the essence of musical growth and development. Try to master these two variations through both study and actual performance with your voice or instrument.

FIGURED BASS AND VARIATION

Both improvisation and variation techniques flourished during the Baroque era, ca. 1600 to 1750, a period of immense musical growth and development in Italy, France, Germany, and England. Baroque composers such as Bach, Handel, and Purcell often fashioned vocal or instrumental compositions by creating a series of variations based on a recurring bass melody called an *ostinato*. (The use of ostinati is quite prevalent in twentieth-century music, especially current pop and rock pieces.) The ostinato provided a bass accompaniment for the invention of melodic and harmonic materials heard with it. In some pieces each recurrence of the ostinato theme coincided with a distinct and clearly marked passage or section, set off by a cadence and/or other formal division. Each such passage or section was regarded as a variation. In other pieces, such as the one discussed herein, a more continuous musical flow occurred, uninterrupted by periodic cadences.

Following a brief recitative, an ostinato appears in the song of Example 6-2a, a portion of which is illustrated. It begins with an unaccompanied statement of the ostinato in the bass part (indicated on the score). As a result the listener is cued to the ostinato basis of the piece and can devote attention to the newly invented materials presented with it. Seven statements of the ostinato provide a foundation for the 35-measure song in which a solo voice is accompanied by strings. Listen to a performance of the entire piece or perform the portion quoted with available resources, if possible. Note that the character of the ostinato, while clearly melodic, is simple and unobtrusive; for these reasons it recedes easily into the background as accompaniment and in no way detracts from the activity of the main voice. Another name for such ostinati is *cantus firmus*, meaning "fixed melody." Compositions constructed on ostinati such as the one cited herein were commonly called *passacaglias*.

The ostinato in Example 6-2a supplies a smooth countermelody for the top voice; its rhythmic accents clearly define the simple triple meter of the piece. Taken together, the bass and soprano form a two-part contrapuntal-harmonic framework that is rhythmically effective, having both continuity of activity and sufficient diversity of parts to be interesting. The two parts move independent of each other, having separate contours and making use of different melodic intervals.

The opening measures of the two main voices are shown in Example 6-2b. Perform them using guitar or trombone for the lower part. Be aware of relations between the parts that help create satisfactory two-voice counterpoint. Identify the kinds of harmonic intervals formed and note uses of dissonance. You will note that the dissonances between the outer parts are

EXAMPLE 6-2 PURCELL: *Dido and Aeneas*, "THY HAND, BELINDA." (*a*) RECITATIVE AND SONG, MEASURES 1–23, (*b*) OUTER VOICE FRAME, MEASURES 10–23.

(a) Recitative

Thy hand, Be-lin - da; dark - - ness shades me: On thy bo - som let me rest: More I would, but Death in-vades me: Death is now a wel - come guest.

Song

When I am laid, am laid in earth, may my wrongs cre - ate no trou - ble, no trou-ble in thy breast;

94 Forms of Music

(b)

generally products of decorative patterns involving step embellishments of consonances. Note furthermore that the tonality of the piece, G minor, is defined by the ostinato's semitone descent from the tonic g to the dominant d, followed by a restatement of the tonic g. The beauty and warmth of the soprano melody are striking. The artful text setting and the graceful line make this composition attractive for both performers and listeners. Notice how the line expands gradually to a climactic point and then descends near the end to the cadence. It is one of Purcell's best-known pieces. One is hardly aware of the repetitions of the bass ostinato because the composer has avoided similar repetitiveness in the vocal melody in favor of a more or less continuously unfolding line imbued with a variety of motivic elements. The composition of the vocal line is worked out so that the end of a line of text, as in measure 13, does not coincide with the end of a statement of the ostinato. The two melodies' phrases are staggered so as to create continuity, thereby avoiding the stop-and-go effect of periodic, tandem phrase endings.

You have probably noticed the sets of arabic numerals written vertically below various pitches of the ostinato. These relate to the improvised component of the piece, a harmonic background, supplied by a keyboard player. In Purcell's time many instrumental and most vocal-instrumental ensemble pieces such as this used a keyboard instrument such as the harpsichord, clavichord, or organ to supply the underlying harmonies or to invent more elaborate accompanying counterpoint; the latter was often determined by the skill of the player involved. Baroque composers such as Bach, Purcell, Handel, and others employed a shorthand code called *figured bass* or *thorough bass* to denote in a simple way the chords to be sounded above the different bass notes of a composition. The precise arrangement and elaboration of the indicated chords was determined by the player as he improvised. Only the bass notes with figures appeared on his music. You have probably already related this antiquated system to the process by which

Based on a poem by the famed Roman poet Virgil, Dido and Aeneas is one of the earliest operas in English (1689), still performed today.

Variational Forms 95

today's musicians often denote accompanying chords via a set of chord symbols such as G7, D, Dm7, etc.* The two procedures have a great deal in common, since both provide a kind of minimal instruction for the player, assuming sufficient skill and knowledge on the part of the player to invent. In this composition the accompanying chords are also voiced in the strings. More often than not, however, the keyboard was charged with supplying the accompaniment, often in conjunction with a low string or wind that reinforced the keyboard bass part.

The figures (numbers) generally define the harmonic intervals to be added above the bass note. Notes without figures are harmonized with complete triads. It should be understood that the importance of figured bass is mainly historical; it has not been in vogue since the end of the Baroque era. We can gain a better insight into Baroque music, however, if we understand figured bass as a cue to the tonal basis of many compositions of the time. And our appreciation of the role of improvisation in music is enhanced by the knowledge that a great many pieces of Baroque music were not notated in their finished form by their composers. On the contrary, many pieces were a product of minimal instructions by the composer, consisting of a notated main voice, a keyboard bass line, and a simple coding for on-the-spot invention of accompanying parts. Figured bass as a vehicle for improvisation disappeared from the compositional scene during the nineteenth century. It is interesting to note that in the twentieth century improvisation continues to enjoy a role in art music as well as pop music and jazz quite comparable to, if not more important than, that of improvisation in Baroque music.

Variation involves repetition combined with change; in order to create a variation something must be retained while modifications are introduced. In the piece by Purcell just studied, the retained element was represented by a repeated melodic figure in the bass, a bass ostinato. The song itself consisted of a more or less continuous melody and accompaniment, the latter constituting the retained and essentially *unchanged element* of the piece. The unchanged element is frequently represented by a set harmonic progression that recurs intact throughout a composition while a variety of melodic events are invented in the form of a series of sections or phrases, each having in common the same harmonic basis. Such compositions are commonly known as *chaconnes.* The chaconne, like its counterpart the passacaglia, was essentially a product of the Baroque period. Bach's unaccompanied chaconne for solo violin, from a suite for solo violin, is perhaps the best known of such compositions.

The principle of fashioning a composition around restatements of a basic chord progression, often eight or twelve measures long, has far outlived the period during which the procedure was developed. We noted earlier that there is no procedure more basic to jazz improvisation than that of improvisation based on repetitions of a given chord sequence such as the blues progression. Although the terms chaconne and passacaglia are sometimes used interchangeably, the significance of the principles that they represent is important, chaconne denoting a series of more or less unbroken variations invented on a recurring chord progression. The distinction between the two terms is of far less consequence than an understanding of the processes to which they allude. The music in Example 6-3 is taken from a series of variations based on a harmonic progression by Handel, a contemporary of J. S. Bach and one of the most revered composers of the eighteenth century. Handel (unlike Bach) enjoyed fame and monetary reward during his lifetime. The chord progression that acts as a cantus firmus for the piece is shown preceding the music itself. Only two of fifteen variations are shown here.

MELODIC VARIATIONS

In the passacaglia by Purcell and the chaconne by Handel, a combination of materials was involved. The passacaglia involved a bass ostinato supporting a freely invented vocal melody; in the chaconne by Handel the relation was one of a

---

*Another elaborate system of chord symbols combines Roman and Arabic numerals to designate chord types, relationships, and the general arrangement of the notes of each relative to the lowest pitch, for example, I-ii^6-I$^6_4$-V^7-I. The Roman numerals indicate the scale degree on which each chord is built (I = tonic, ii = supertonic, etc.) and the Arabic numerals function as described in regard to figured bass.

EXAMPLE 6-3 HANDEL: *Passacaille* (CHACONNE). (*a*) HARMONIC PROGRESSION, MEASURES 1–4; (*b*) *ibid.*, MEASURES 1–12.

harmonic theme in the form of a recurring four-measure progression providing a basis for a series of passages involving freely invented melody in the top voice.

Both chaconnes and passacaglias by definition involve combined events, the one repeated, the other freely unfolded, whereas *melodic variations* are composed by modifying a single melodic line, whose accompanying materials and texture may or may not be subsequently modified. There are several common procedures for varying and elaborating melodies; we dealt with a few of them in the beginning of this chapter. Awareness of some of the processes outlined herein can add measurably to one's understanding of ways in which musical material is extended, reshaped, and made interesting through repetition. By the same token, a grasp of some of these simple techniques of variation can provide a useful source of improvisational and inventive techniques for both performance and composition.

In Example 6-4 a familiar melodic phrase undergoes a number of variational treatments in subsequent repetitions. Familiarize yourself with the original version in Example 6-4a, taking note of the essential rhythmic and tonal characteristics of the melody's structure. Sing it several times, then sing or

EXAMPLE 6-4 Mozart: Melodic variational techniques, measures 1–4.

(a) **Andante**

(b)

(c)

(d)

(e) **Piu vivace**

simile

(f)

(g)

(h)

(i) (Andante)

98 Forms of Music

otherwise perform the variations of the melody that follow. Note the descriptive terms associated with the different variational procedures, many of which are fundamental tools of melodic development and extension.

The following melodic variations in Example 6-4, illustrating several techniques of variation, are based on a march theme composed by Mozart for use in his opera *The Magic Flute*:

(a) *Original*—as composed by Mozart.
(b) *Rhythmically varied*—by altering note values or dividing notes into two or more shorter ones.
(c) *Change of direction*—usually called *melodic inversion*; this amounts to a reversal of direction of each interval, retaining all integral sizes.
(d) *Figuration*—this involves the embellishment of the basic pitches of the theme's rhythm and contour via the addition of more or less stereotyped patterns and figures.
(e) *Arpeggiation*—this amounts to stating the tones of the theme together with the various members of its accompanying harmony in a linear (i.e., horizontal) succession. The result is essentially one of broken chords.
(f) *Retrograde*—the theme is stated backwards.
(g) *Change of mode*—the theme is stated in its parallel minor (or major) mode; in this case the change is from F major to F minor.
(h) *Augmentation*—the theme is stated in longer note values, often doubled; the original tempo is maintained.
(i) *Change of meter*—in this case the meter is changed from simple duple to compound duple. Note that the beat unit becomes a dotted quarter note, the regular divisions of which involve three as opposed to two notes of equal length.

The processes cited here represent only a smattering of the wealth of means devised by composers for varying and embellishing melodic materials. Only a few such techniques have generally agreed-upon "stock" labels. The principle of melodic variation being understood, we can proceed to a composition in which it is more fully explored.

Some of the most inspired compositions written in the past two centuries, as well as in the current one, are those in which composers systematically exploit the potential of thematic material through variation. Although varied repetition in one or another guise can be found in most pieces, the particular type referred to here is called *theme and variations.* These pieces are usually cast in the form of a thematic presentation section, often eight, twelve, sixteen, or so measures long, followed by a series of more or less distinct sections each of which constitutes a varied restatement of the theme presenting specific solutions to the problem of variation. These variation types are sometimes relatively complete pieces in themselves; in other cases they are movements of works composed of three or four contrasting movements (a movement is a piece within a larger work). Brahms's *Variations on a Theme by Haydn*, discussed in Chapter 13, is an example of the former; the well-known movement by Mozart dealt with here illustrates the latter. These compositions as a rule did not call for improvisation, as did many pieces written during the Baroque period. Figured bass had been largely abandoned by the second half of the eighteenth and nineteenth centuries, during which time the composition of theme-and-variations pieces flourished. By the same token, the ostinato variations such as the chaconne and passacaglia ceased to play an important role in the formal plans of composers during the Classic period and the nineteenth century, despite a number of exceptions.*

It should be noted that the term *theme* has different connotations in music, and its meaning is somewhat dependent on context. For the present we shall refer to theme in the restricted sense of a melody of significance to the structure of a piece, often being the initial and central melodic substance from which the piece is evolved. The theme of the first movement of Mozart's *Sonata in A Major for Piano, K. 331*, the basis for six variations that are in part based on it, is shown in Example 6-5. Perform the melody or listen while another person plays it at the keyboard; then listen to a recording of the entire movement. The basic melodic pitches of the theme are shown

---

*The finale of Brahms' Fourth Symphony is a passacaglia.

By age six, Mozart became the darling of nobility, captivating his royal audience with his phenomenal talents as player and improvisor; but Dame Success, so easily conquered by the child prodigy, proved to be a fickle mistress, as Mozart reached final musical maturity, spending some eight years "hovering between hope and anxiety."

following the music. Relate them to the *tema* (Italian for "theme") and be prepared to try to see their connection to the variations that follow. The lovely melody of this piece and each of the subsequent variations reveal distinguishing rhythmic characteristics; each is set off by some recurring rhythmic pattern as well as by other aspects of organization such as dynamic level, articulation, mode, or texture.

The meter and tempo of the theme are maintained up to variation 5, whose tempo is adagio. The concluding variation (6) is delineated by both a change of meter to 4/4 and a change of tempo to allegro. Within the framework of 6/8 meter, the composer has invented rhythmic patterns of sufficient variety to help sustain interest in five variations. Our understanding of compound duple meter as well as the potential of rhythm to create form can be enhanced by a knowledge of this movement.

The six variations of this set by Mozart are related and contrasted through many more means than rhythmic. Each variation retains the tonality and to a great extent the harmonic structure of the theme. Furthermore, a number of more subtle aspects of the theme such as note articulation and melodic decoration contribute to the overall unity of the entire piece. Perhaps the simplest and most crucial aspect of the overall melodic unity of the movement is revealed by the basic pitch line, the first eight measures of which appear in Example 6-5b.

Listen to the melody of variation 1 while looking at the basic pitches as shown in Example 6-5b. In spite of the rhythmic diversity of the line, it is easy to relate it to the original because the basic pitches are very much exposed. The change of pace and mood of the variation results in part from the decorative treatments of the basic thematic pitches that occur. Note that the two basic notes of measure 1, for example, are embellished by notes a step below or above them. The note C sharp is embellished by its lower step, B sharp; the note E is similarly decorated by the D sharp that passes from C sharp to E and connects the two. Notes that act as step links between basic pitches by step motion from and returning to the basic pitch are called upper or lower *neighbor tones*. The F sharp in measure 1, occurring after E and returning to E, is a neighbor tone. Find other examples of passing and neighbor tones in variation 1; there are several of both.

Variation 2 contrasts with the previous one by virtue of the characteristic repeated notes as well as by the quickening of activity suggested by the divisions of eights into four thirty-second notes. The sequential character of the theme's basic contour is clearly maintained in the sequential motivic repetition of the first four measures. Note also the addition of a new element in the triplets of the accompaniment.

Variation 3 adapts the basic pitch line and harmonic structure of the theme to the minor mode (A minor). Note that a change of mood also results from the smooth (legato) articulation and continuous activity of the main voice. Variations 4 and 5 return to the major mode of the theme, variation 4 involving a greatly expanded registration and fuller sound and variation 5 presenting a marked change of tempo and point of relative relaxation in the movement. Note that repetition both in the main voice and in accompaniment occurs as in variation 2. Observe also the ornate and dextrous melodic figuration that occurs, involving a variety of *step* embellishments of basic pitches.

100 Forms of Music

EXAMPLE 6-5 Mozart: *Sonata in A Major for Piano, K.331.* (a) First movement (tema), measures 1–18; (b) basic pitches of the measures 1–8.

(a) Andante grazioso

(b)

The final variation (6) is in the nature of a coda, a passage appropriate to and signaling closure. The deliberate character of this closing variation is in part related to the 4/4 meter and quick tempo. The full chords introduced periodically in the accompaniment punctuate the drive toward cadence. Step embellishments (passing and neighboring tones) occur and broken chords (arpeggiation) contribute to the heightened pace, as intensification of dynamics and sudden dynamic shifts create a feeling of climax. The basic pitch line of the theme is clearly evident in this variation, as it has been throughout the piece.

This composition offers ample evidence of the valuable potential of the variation principle as a vehicle for the fashioning of effective and expressive music. An important aspect of this and many variation movements lies in the essential simplicity and transparency of the theme itself. It appears that many composers have related the ideal simplicity of a theme to its potential for variation and elaboration. Indeed, if the listener is to be expected to grasp the essence of a theme and relate its design to a series of potentially diverse and often complex variations, then the structure of the theme itself will in all likelihood be more easily perceived in inverse relation to the complexity of it. Such seems to have been the view of a great number of composers of variations, among them such contributors as Bach, Mozart, Haydn, Beethoven, Brahms, and Stravinsky.

Developmental Forms   101

7 Developmental Forms

Composers will probably tell you that most of their compositions result more from hard work than spur-of-the-moment inspiration—even though the initial ideas or "germs" out of which many great works of art have been fashioned often arrive in the form of gifts of inspiration. Although many musical ideas may have arrived unscheduled, the processes by which they were finally transformed into acceptable if not outstanding works of art are well known to creative persons under the names of hard work, artistic craft, and skill. And such artistic effort usually (as in the case of such rare geniuses as Brahms, Beethoven, or Bartók) involves a great deal of planning, sketching, revising, and retouching.

The one essential musical process that makes greater demands on compositional skill, judgment, and craft than most is the process of musical *development*. An artist such as Cézanne or Picasso may have been inspired by a particular image, face, or even geometrical pattern to the extent that he was impelled to capture it on canvas. And although the initial image or design may occur in a split second, it is only through a number of more or less systematic procedures or routines such as sketching, drawing, mixing paints, actually applying brush strokes to the canvas, and painfully retouching and reshading that a fine painting is produced; the processes of painting and composing, not to mention more mundane crafts such as carpentry and bricklaying, are also long on demands for blood and sweat. It may have been an awareness of this fact of artistic life that prompted the cliché that "great art is produced by 10 percent genius and 90 percent hard work."[*]

In this chapter we shall concentrate on a musical form that has framed some of the greatest compositional inspirations as well as the greatest models of compositional craft, effort, and genius combined. The form dealt with here is typically described (like fugue) as a *developmental form*, an expression whose meaning is often elusive.

An intriguing aspect of music is the fact that pieces or movements within pieces lasting as long as several minutes

---

[*]Alfred Barnes, an art historian and collector, who founded the Barnes Foundation, Merion, Pennsylvania.

A leading spirit of 20th century painting, Duchamp, the French avant-garde painter, shunned artistic tradition, as exemplified in his execution of The Sonata. Ironically, though, he affixed a title which has been traditionally applied to various types of instrumental music dating from the 12th century.

are commonly based on materials such as motives, melodies, or chord patterns constituting only a very short span of time—as brief as two or three seconds' duration. Such is the case, for instance, in the brief theme in Example 7-1, which forms the main thematic material, for a composition of several minutes.

By the same token, the familiar blues progression (Example 7-2) often provides the basis for many minutes of inventive and exciting jazz improvisation, supplying a recurring harmonic-rhythmic framework for the melodic variations and fantasies of skilled performers such as Charlie Parker, Miles Davis, John Coltrane, Count Basie, Ella Fitzgerald, and others.

Whether improvised or composed, the crux of musical growth and extension is *musical development*. The work "development" has special significance in considerations of musical form. It denotes those processes by which a composer expands, varies, and restates materials so as to produce a work of considerable scope that unfolds a logical and convincing thread of musical activity. Such activity assumes elements of both continuity and contrast. In the history of Western music and despite its diversity, there exist only a modicum of composi-

EXAMPLE 7-1 BRAHMS: *Symphony No. 4*, FIRST MOVEMENT, MEASURES 1–4.

104 Forms of Music

The immortal Ella Fitzgerald "sings the blues," one of the many-splendored facets of jazz growing from the folk music of the blacks. The blues were spread throughout the southland following the Civil War by itinerant black troubadours who, with guitar or banjo in hand, improvised their soulful laments.

tions and perhaps even fewer composers who reveal in their music that elusive and rare capacity to create musical developments that sustain the interest of players and listeners beyond the presentation stages of their musical ideas.

Although most music reveals some processes by which musical ideas are extended or expanded—i.e., sequence, imitation, variation, etc.—there are several traditional musical forms, the crux of which is development. These forms, such as sonata-allegro form and fugue, are generally referred to as developmental forms as opposed to sectional forms, such as ternary form and the rondo, in which the juxtaposition of contrasted sections rather than development of opening material throughout constitutes the principal basis for the growth and shape of the piece.

EXAMPLE 7-2 BLUES PROGRESSION IN B FLAT.

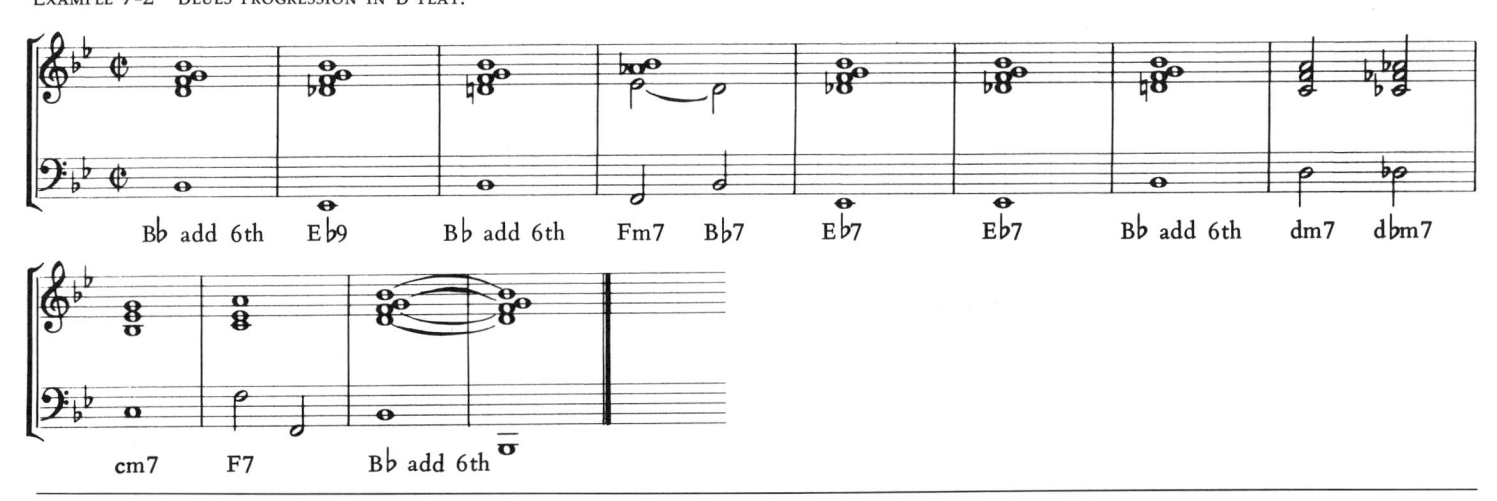

Developmental Forms 105

SONATA-ALLEGRO FORM

Musical-formal procedures are seldom discovered or newly invented. Impressions that certain kinds of forms or procedures simply appeared on the scene at a given time or resulted from a particular composer's activities are an effect of the over-segmentation of music history and chronology into separate periods and eras without sufficient attention to the transitions that link them and make possible the assimilation of ideas of one group of composers by another. No better evidence of such false impressions exists than in the case of sonata-allegro form, commonly viewed as an innovative formal procedure of the second half of the eighteenth century. Although it is true that composers working in the second half of the eighteenth century were largely responsible for the establishment and refinement of this uniquely effective and satisfactory compositional procedure, it is nonetheless true that sonata-allegro form under a different guise was in principle already operative during the Baroque era in numerous dance movements cast in a prototype called *rounded binary form.*

The rounded binary form of Baroque dances provided a clear precedent in the contrapuntal writing of many Baroque composers such as J. S. Bach, Handel, Corelli, and others for the formal patterning of instrumental movements by composers of later homophonic styles such as Haydn and Mozart. Although the contrast of style that is represented by the works of Bach and Mozart is on the whole a very pronounced one, the transition that links their styles, accomplished for practical purposes while Bach was still a young man and before Mozart was born, capitalized on and exploited many formal procedures shared by both, even though one or the other may be said to have been more instrumental in the refinement and molding of one or the other form or process. This applies directly in the current discussion of developmental forms in that Bach and his colleagues established and perfected the binary form that served as a catalyst for later exploitation and refinement by Mozart, Haydn, and Beethoven in their sonata-allegro movements.

A model binary dance form from which the sonata-allegro pattern evolved is found in the movement by Domenico Scarlatti (Example 7-3), which is framed by two (repeated) sections, A and B, each punctuated by a definitive cadence. Section A closes in the key of F major, the dominant key of the principal tonality of the piece, B flat, confirmed again at the final cadence of the piece. The entire Andante is clearly evolved from the thematic material presented in measures 1-4, as a careful hearing of the movement will confirm.

Of most importance to our consideraton of the relation between binary form and the sonata-allegro form that evolved from it is the section begun at the measure following the cadence on F (the dominant) in measure 22. Section B clearly evolves from the same material and characteristic rhythm (like a dance rhythm) stated in section A. The composer has fashioned a *development* of that same material, however, in that he casts it in a new light, so to speak, by manipulating the harmonization so as to avoid a strong, stable definition of key (this is commonly described as *tonal instability*). The composer further modifies and intensifies the movement of the voices through the addition of a third (inner) contrapuntal voice based

EXAMPLE 7-3   D. SCARLATTI: *Andante for Klavier,* COMPLETE.

Developmental Forms 107

Unrivaled harpsichord virtuoso and prolific composer for that instrument, Domenico Scarlatti (1685–1757) is considered to have been the founder of the modern keyboard playing, with all its brilliance, technical fluency, and virtuosic display.

on the counterline first stated in the lower voice at measure 1. The section is brief, moving steadily toward the cadence at measure 31 which defines the dominant (F) of the principal key, B flat, thus preparing the listener for the restatement (return) of B flat that follows. Note that the listener's expectation for such a return is heightened by the silence of measure 32.

The essential feature of this brief derivative section is that the passage (measures 23 to 31) is clearly fashioned out of music first presented in the prior section. Measures 23–31 unfold a miniature *development* of section A in that a number of processes combining both restatement and change occur. These involve tonal, melodic, and textural changes. Furthermore, the section, lacking clear tonal definition and stability of its own, depends harmonically on what is to come, the return to the main key.

A final clue to the relation between pieces of this sort and the sonata-allegro form to which we shall turn shortly lies in the clear restatement of the work's opening at measure 33. Although the composer manipulates its close so as to avoid literal repetition, there is no question but that the listener experiences the satisfaction of a real recalling of the movement's opening in all respects—tonal, thematic, textural, and harmonic. Composed about 1730, this movement provides a solid precedent and groundwork for the subsequent expansion of this formal pattern into a marvelous repertoire of instrumental works composed by Haydn, Mozart, Beethoven, and Mahler.

One may generalize that the Baroque binary form provided a framework for the structuring of pieces based on characteristic dance rhythms such as those found in the dance suites of the time. Unified by recurrences of characteristic rhythm patterns, these pieces typically contained two main sections, the latter of which occurred as a logical outgrowth of the first, continuing to develop material (thematic, rhythmic, and textural) introduced in the opening section. What seems to have been very instrumental in the transition from binary dance movements to the sonata-allegro design is the inclusion in many, but by no means all, binary forms of a brief return toward the close of the piece to the opening materials and tonality of the piece. The inclusion in many such movements of these brief recapitulatory passages, sometimes a phrase or less, gave rise to the term *rounded* binary form—that is, rounded in the sense of returning to the beginning of the piece. As will be seen, formal return, as found in the Baroque rounded binary structure, along with the assumed inclusion of distinctly developmental material, is universally recognized as an essential feature of sonata-allegro design; indeed, in the eyes of some writers, return is the single most psychologically important feature of sonata-allegro design.

Although the Baroque binary *dance* form ceased to function as such in subsequent eras, two-part form in general has by no means become archaic. Composers in the twentieth century especially have utilized the two-part form frequently. Besides serving as the framework for many theme-and-variations movements, two-part form appears frequently in folk songs, pop music, and jazz. Many traditional "standards" such as "Laura" are cast in a two-part structure, although this sectional form has retained little of the internal development that characterized the more unique dance form by which movements like the one in Example 7-3 were clearly spawned.

Let us turn now to a movement of a later work for string quartet (two violins, viola, and cello) intended to be performed for a small audience. This is an example of *chamber music*—the genre of music that contains some of the most personal and craftsmanlike musical statements in the entire repertoire of music. This quartet, like most such compositions of its time—the Classic period (1750–1825)—consists of four contrasted movements in the order of fast, moderately fast (minuet), slow (adagio), and very fast (presto). (More frequently, the minuet movement is the third movement, with the slow movement the second.) The movements are related tonally in that the keys of the end movements are usually the same—in this quartet, G major—and the middle movements typically offer variety of key or, as in this quartet, mode.

The opening movement of most instrumental works is usually the one in which the composer reaches a level of maximum input; one seldom encounters compositions such as chamber pieces, sonatas, concertos, or symphonies (which are in fact sonatas for orchestra just as the string quartet is a sonata composed for a small ensemble of strings) where the emotional and musical content of the later movements overshadow that of the first. The movement excerpted in Example 7-4 is no exception.

It is perhaps significant that first movements such as this are almost invariably framed in sonata-allegro form, a pattern

EXAMPLE 7-4 HAYDN: *String Quartet in G Major, Op. 17, No. 5,* FIRST MOVEMENT, MEASURES 1–90.

Developmental Forms 109

Section B
From trans.

Theme 1

Theme 3

110 Forms of Music

Developmental Forms 111

that is viewed as one of the most satisfactory compositional procedures from the standpoint of composer, listener, and player. The sonata-allegro design is also sometimes used for closing movements, and sometimes for slow movements as well. The term sonata *allegro* is actually misleading in that it need not imply an allegro (fast) tempo as a requisite for a particular movement.

To form a good picture of sonata-allegro form and to relate it to the model from which it emerged, first consider the Haydn quartet (Example 7-4) from the standpoint of a rounded binary form. (For the sake of brevity, and since Haydn has concentrated most of the significant melodic material in the top voice, the first-violin part, only that part is quoted in Example 7-4.) We can subsequently isolate those aspects of the movement that are unique and by which it can be distinguished from the embryonic binary form from which it emerged, or apparently was emerging via compositions such as this.

The first movement is divided into two gross sections (A and B), implied by the composer's retention of the traditional double bars signaling repetition at measure 33 and at the piece's close. A glance at the material opening section B reveals that it is derived from measure 15 of section A and further study will reveal that virtually all the materials explored in section B are derived from section A. In that respect, section B can correctly be described as a logical outgrowth of, or development arising from, section A. Their relation is not unlike that of an antecedent-consequent pair of musical phrases or grammatical constructions—extended here to encompass two sections of music, the one 33 measures long, the other 56. Note also that section A begins in G major and closes with a strong cadence emphasizing the dominant key of G, D major; their relation is like that of I to V. Section B departs from D major, moves through E minor, delineated by a cadence in measure 58, and returns to G major, coinciding with the return of the opening of section A at measure 69. The material heard from measure 69 to the last half of measure 81 is a compacted recapitulation of section A; this is the rounded part of the two large sections. A closing section, called a *coda* or codetta (little coda), follows. It heightens the impression of finality and reaffirms the tonic key.

It has probably occurred to you that there are really two formal operations taking place here on different levels—while the movement consists of two large sections, signaled by the repeat signs emphasized by the strong cadence on D in measure 33, you recognize at the same time *three* formal events superimposed on the traditional *binary* sectionalization. The first of the three large units corresponds to section A, but section B clearly reveals a division into a section of tonal digression and instability coupled with a fanciful and imaginative treatment of various motives and figures derived from section A—namely, musical development.

Now that we have considered the movement in broad terms, let's look in more detail at the thematic materials and processes Haydn used to flesh out his sonata-allegro design. First he poses a three-measure vigorous theme which is repeated with a two-measure extension, clearly establishing the key of G major and fixing the main theme in mind. The first violin, having thus led the way to a dominant cadence, gives way momentarily to imitative statements (second violin, cello, and then viola) of the opening motive of theme 1 (called the *head motive*), but it then resumes its lead role (in the second half of measure 10), leading to a tonic cadence that closes themegroup 1. When an abrupt change of key to the relative minor (E minor), a transition ensues, leading to theme 2 at measure 23.

In contrast to theme 1, theme 2 is more restrained, being less angular and lacking the syncopations (rhythmic irregularities) that characterize theme 1's opening. Note also that there is a change of key (often done to signal the introduction of new thematic material) and a change of dynamic level as well. One is made amply aware that new thematic materials have been presented. Haydn does not dwell as long on theme 2 as he did with the main theme, but rather enters into an agitated closing section whose brief function appears to be that of preparing the way to the dominant key to end the exposition (section A).

Next we hear the transition previously mentioned, which opens section B, and, beginning at measure 37, a brief development of theme 1, which is interrrupted by the appearance of a new theme at measure 48. (This is not an unusual occurrence, as composers frequently introduce new thematic materials in their development sections.) Theme 2 reappears in a different key from its initial statement and evolves into a running passage at measure 59, which begins a lengthy preparation for the important return of the opening material introduced at measure 68. The melodic neutrality of the extended passage in sixteenth notes heightens the listener's expectation for the subsequent psychological "reward" of the return at measure 68.

The development section is followed by a compacted version of the exposition (called *recapitulation*). Here themes 1 and 2 reappear, both in the tonic key now, with the movement being brought to a close with a coda that firmly reestablishes the home key and gives the movement its conclusive end.

Sonata-allegro form, then, is predicated on several essential features, most of which occur to some extent in rounded binary pieces. These features include the following:

1. The exposition often contains two or more discrete themes or motives in contrast to the monothematicism (incorporation of only one significant melodic subject) of most binary-form pieces. This factor varies considerably from composer to composer and, in some composers such as Haydn and Mozart, from piece to piece.
2. The opening section involves the establishment of the key of the movement followed by modulation to the dominant or other related tonality and a marked cadence therein closing the exposition.
3. A section follows the expository passage and is devoted to development and the fanciful restatement and recasting of materials derived from the exposition; the development may contain newly invented materials; the development section is almost invariably unstable tonally, allowing for the display of harmonic relations, colors, and progressions without systematic reference to key or definitive harmonic cadences.
4. A full-fledged restatement of the exposition in the main key of the piece, called the *recapitulation,* follows the development.

To sum up, the main features of sonata-allegro form are profiled in the outline that appears below.

Sonata-Allegro Design

Exposition	Development	Recapitulation	Coda
One or more distinct themes or motives	Free invention based on development of material(s) from exposition	Restatement of exposition	Extension beyond closing point of exposition
Tonic . . . related key	Tonal digressions	Tonic key	Tonic reaffirmed

The movement by Haydn that we have studied (Example 7-4) was selected from Haydn's early compositions; it is indicative of a stage in Haydn's development in which the master was still formulating a style and techniques which were to serve him effectively until the turn of the nineteenth century. Haydn's use of sonata-allegro form reveals, as we have seen, a formulative and transitive stage in musical-stylistic development which effected a link between the Baroque and Classic eras via the use of formal procedure common to both, despite the highly contrasted musical styles that adopted and modified rounded binary form to their respective stylistic needs.

The purpose of this unit of study has been to gain a broader perspective of the various options and potentials of sonata-allegro design, so that it may be understood as an essentially simple and flexible procedure whose use, various modifications, and adaptations by a number of highly skilled composers have made it one of the most uniquely serviceable principles in the history of Western music. That a formal principle could serve effectively the needs of so many composers over a period of more than two hundred years, including such individual and original composers as, say, Haydn and Hindemith, Brahms and Bartók, Schubert and Stravinsky, and Beethoven and Barber, to name a few, implies how significant a principle it was and still is. This suggests as well its importance to the listeners, performers, and composers of today.

The sonata-allegro principle, like most effective formal procedures, appears in a number of modified versions. Its essential simplicity and accessibility may be cited as reasons for the use of sonata design by composers in a number of modifications, some of which appear to have been dictated by the demands or capabilities of a particular style or genre. The most obvious of these is found in the modified sonata-allegro design that occurs in many Classic and Romantic concertos.

114 Forms of Music

The repertoire for string quartet begins with the quartets of Haydn and Mozart, whose creative efforts established this genre of instrumental ensemble music—the veritable backbone of chamber music—and established many of its forms, practices, and procedures.

CONCERTO SONATA-ALLEGRO FORM

The early developers of the solo concerto such as Mozart and J. S. Bach were faced with the problem of structuring large solo-orchestral movements through the use of unified musical materials that were effective for both the solo instrument, usually the piano or violin, and the symphonic ensemble with which the soloists interacted. You will learn that in Baroque music this problem was largely solved through the introduction of a kind of returning theme called a *ritornello,* which was stated at the opening of the piece and restated periodically throughout, often varied or in different keys, thereby providing a rondolike pattern of alternating statements (ritornelli) and digressions in which the soloist assumed the dominant role. The music given to the soloist in such digressions or episodes was appropriate to virtuosic display and elaboration. In many works, such as the solo concertos of J. S. Bach, these solo-centered passages were derivative of sequential motivic or rhythmic elements of the ritornello theme, thereby establishing a loose developmental relation between the tutti and solo sections. (Recall the discussion of ritornello form in Chapter 5.)

Much different is the practice of Mozart, in whose music one finds a far more unified, symphonically appropriate handling of the concerto form than that of his Baroque predecessors. In essence, Mozart adapted the formal ingredients of the sonata-allegro pattern to suit the combined solo and symphonic resources of the concerto of his day by providing *two* expositions, a so-called double exposition. This was followed by a development, recapitulation, and coda. The coda was highlighted by the introduction of an extended passage given over largely to the virtuosity of the player, a passage often improvised on the spot by the composer-performer. This passage, called a *cadenza,* was actually a highly *elaborated cadence.*

The double exposition of the concerto, usually occurring in the opening movement, provided for the presentation of the main themes of the piece (always two or more) by the orchestra alone, followed by a solo presentation of the same themes. The orchestral exposition was marked by the retention of the *tonic* key throughout. The key changes that typically defined sonata expositions were reserved for the solo exposition, which as a rule highlighted the solo instruments as well as allowed for some dialogue between solo and orchestra. The concerto-sonata form comprised a kind of amalgamation of two procedures—the three-stage sonata-allegro pattern plus the adaptation of that pattern to the alternation of tutti-solo on a far more unified and integrated basis than had been the case in earlier solo and orchestral concertos.

Later composers such as Beethoven, Schumann, Tchaikovsky, Brahms, and Bartók introduced further modifications into the concerto-sonata pattern to the extent that Mozart's model is often virtually abandoned. This is perhaps most easily noted in the frequent shortening or avoidance of the separate orchestral exposition. It must be said that in most cases the expositional presentation of materials seems based largely on the suitability of the various themes to orchestral or solo presentation, some materials being reserved for one or the other alone. In recent modifications of the concerto first-movement form, composers concerned with an economic use of (formal) time and resources—as well, perhaps, as a more integrated formal design—have often abandoned the traditional sectionalization of tutti followed by solo expositions in favor of a highly integrated dialogue.

The current century has witnessed tremendous diversification and stylistic change in all art. Despite the many marvelous innovations and provocative changes in musical style, performance, and form that have occurred during the past seventy or so years, many, if not a majority, of the composers whose works and artistic creeds have most affected and diverted the various streams of twentieth-century music have continued to base some of their pieces on sonata-allegro form. This is true despite the fact that to do so, while at the same time incorporating materials and processes indicative of the changing times, has not always produced the happiest of results. The listener, however, must judge the success of these attempts to wed this traditional procedure with the musical materials of today, because in the hands of a few it is still a viable mold for the creation of masterpieces of music.

THREE

Styles of Music

8 Medieval and Renaissance Style (800–1600)

The word "style" comes from the Greek word *stylos* or the Latin word *stilus*, and it originally referred to the instrument that writers used to scratch letters on wax tablets. Later the word was applied to the personal manner of expression of the writer, and then by extension to the characteristic manner of expression in any art. In music the term "style" has a broad variety of applications. It may refer to the style of a specific composer—Wagner's style, Debussy's style—or, even more specifically, to a composer's style at a particular period—Beethoven's middle-period style, Stravinsky's Neoclassic style. It may refer to a particular national group—French style, Flemish style, American style— or to a particular chronological period—sixteenth-century style, the style of the 1930's. It may refer to the manner of expression appropriate to a given instrument or genre—symphonic style, trumpet style, jazz style.

The term "style" may be used in a general sense to denote the particular attitudes, approaches, or spiritual ideals of a person, a group, or an age. It may be used in a more specific sense to denote specific ways in which composers or groups of composers have used the aspects of music, such as rhythm, melody, harmony, texture, and instrumentation, or the forms of music. Style in music can be considered without any relationship to other arts, or it may be considered in relationship to these arts. The very fact that many terms appear in discussions of two or more arts indicates the possibility of tracing parallel developments in the styles of various arts.

THE PERIODS OF MUSICAL STYLE
In the designation of historical periods of musical style, the borrowing of terms from other arts is especially obvious. Problems can arise, however, if we attempt to apply too literally the original meaning of a particular stylistic term. For example, the term "Renaissance" denoted a rebirth of interest in the art of classical antiquity in literature, sculpture, painting, and architecture. In music, except for some minor developments, this rebirth of interest in classical antiquity is not of any great significance. The terms in the following list, therefore, should be regarded as representing simply historical labels rather than signifying any direct parallels with the other arts. The

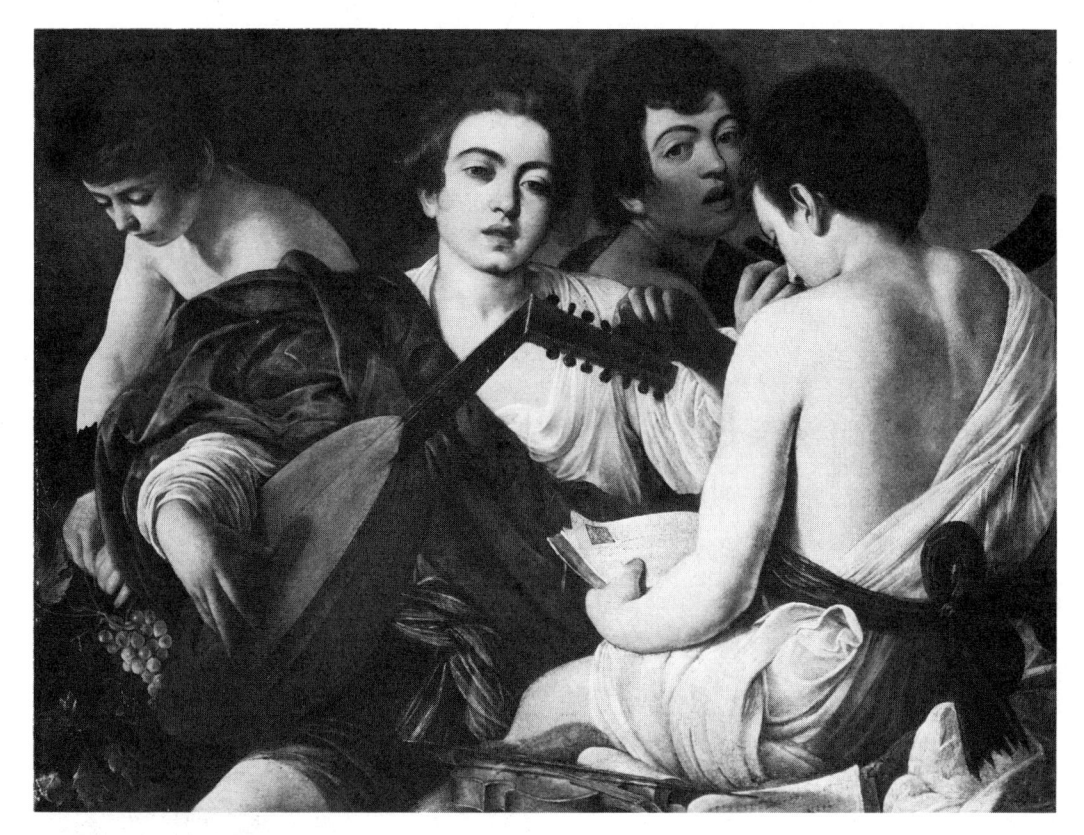

At the same time that Caravaggio was founding a naturalistic school of painting in Rome in the latter half of the 16th century, as exemplified by his painting, The Musicians, composers like Palestrina were bringing the art of Renaissance polyphony to a point of classic perfection.

dates given for the periods are approximate and subject to different interpretations by various authorities. The main periods appear to the left and schools within these periods are idented under the main periods.

Antiquity (?B.C.–A.D.350)

Patristic (350–600)

Early Middle Ages (600–850)

Romanesque (850–1150)
    St. Martial school (1100–1150)

Gothic (1150–1450)
    Notre Dame school (ca. 1200)
    Ars Antiqua (1200–1300)
    Ars Nova (1300–1400)
    Burgundian school (1420–1450)

Renaissance (1450–1600)
    Flemish school (1450–1600)
    Venetian school (1527–1612)
    Roman school (1550–1725)

Baroque (1600–1750)
    Early Baroque (1600–1650)
    Middle Baroque (1650–1700)
    Late Baroque (1700–1750)
    Rococo (1725–1775)

Viennese Classic school (1750–1825)

Romantic (1800–1910)
    Early Romantic (1800–1850)
    Middle Romantic (1850–1890)
    Late or Neo-Romantic (1890–1910)

Twentieth century
    Impressionism (1892–1918)
    Expressionism, atonality, serialism, Neoclassicism (1900–1945)
    Electronic music, automated music, aleatory music, multimedia (1945–   )

Willi Apel has pointed to the interesting fact that approximately every 300 years, significant changes in musical style have taken place which were signaled usually by the publication of a treatise containing the words "new music" in some language—*Ars Nova* (1300), *Nuove Musiche* (1600), *New Music* (1900). Other writers have divided music history into three large areas—the pre-Baroque period prior to 1600, the common-practice period* extending roughly from the seventeenth through the nineteenth centuries, and the contemporary period or twentieth-century period. Until recently, the common-prac-

*The expression "common-practice period" refers to a body of musical works based more or less on a common set of harmonic, melodic, and rhythmic principles, even though they may differ in their character and style.

Considered an alien oriental instrument contributing to sensory pleasure, the harp was condemned by the famed philosopher Plato.

tice period counted for a disproportionately large percentage of music heard and studied. The advent of the long-playing record, the increased availability of old music and old instruments, and increasing openness toward new music have fortunately changed that picture. Ultimately we would hope that the listener would come to take a period of music on its own terms, not expecting to hear the sounds of a Wagnerian opera in the sounds of a Baroque instrumental suite, and not expecting the consummate harmonies and symmetrical forms of a Classical symphony in a modern aleatory or electronic composition. In the sections that follow in this chapter, we shall not attempt a broad overview of all the details of music history, but shall instead take a "post-hole" approach, concentrating on an indepth examination of a limited number of works, together with some consideration of the sociocultural backgrounds against which they arose.

Before beginning our survey of the best-known Western styles of music, let's digress briefly to consider the music of less familiar cultures. To begin you should be aware that throughout history music has been closely associated with the rituals of church, synagogue, and temple. From the psalmist's injunction to praise the Lord with "timbrel and dance . . . with stringed instruments and organs . . . with loud cymbals . . . and the high sounding cymbals" (Psalm 150) to the skillful and effective use of music in a modern televised revival campaign, music has played an important role in religious and other ceremonies of almost every kind. We shall survey briefly the development of sacred music, focusing on those aspects that seem especially interesting or of special significance for the development of the art of music.

MUSIC IN ANCIENT CULTURES

Greece and Rome

In ancient Greece music was an integral part of the religious and civic ceremonies, and training in music was an essential aspect of education, as can be seen in numerous references in the writings of Plato, Aristotle, and others. Though fewer than twenty fragments of Greek music itself have come down to us, we do have an extensive body of historical, descriptive, and theoretical writings on music. According to these we learn that each scale or mode in Greek music was supposed to have a specific "ethical" character. Aristotle says, for example, "All agree that the Dorian harmony (i.e., scale type) is more sedate and of a specially manly character" (*Politics,* trans. by H. Rackham, Harvard University Press, 1950, p. 674). We also learn that instruments were regarded as having certain definite characteristics. The *aulos,* an oboelike reed instrument, was considered appropriate for the orgiastic character of the Dionysian rites; the *kithara,* a plucked-string instrument, was appropriate for the restrained character of the Apollonian rites. Incidentally, these two terms—Apollonian and Dionysian—have been carried over into modern writings about music

120 Styles of Music

Not until the 16th century were Jews to participate in music outside the ghetto, but then began a long and illustrious tradition sparked by Salomone Rossi (1587-1630), pioneer composer of works for violin and polyphonic music for the Jewish service, a collection of whose sacred works is illustrated by a synagogue facade as shown here.

and other arts. Apollonian denotes restraint and objectivity; Dionysian denotes emotionalism and subjectivity.

Similar ideas linking specific musical characteristics to specific emotional characteristics occur throughout history. The eighteenth-century "doctrine of the affections" set forth an elaborate scheme of such relationships. In our time echoes of this concept may be found in such things as the controversy over the use of certain instruments such as the guitar, or certain types of music such as rock or jazz, in religious ceremonies.

From the descriptions of performances and from the few surviving notated examples, we conclude that Greek music was mostly monophonic. Plato, however, uses the term *heterophony* to describe the use of a primitive form of polyphony in this music. Heterophony consists of the simultaneous presentation of two versions of the same melody in two different parts. In Greek music this usually involved a simple version of the melody presented by the singer at the same time an elaborated version was presented by the instrumentalist. We are not certain as to the exact nature of melody and rhythm in Greek music, but we do know that it was closely tied to the inflection of poetry.

We know even less about the theoretical aspects of the music of ancient Rome, but we do know that it played an important role in civic and religious rituals. Incidentally, the story of the Emperor Nero fiddling while Rome burned is questionable, but Nero probably did play the *hydraulis,* a water-powered organ.

With the establishment of Christianity the polytheistic cults of Greece and Rome were gradually suppressed. In some regions of Italy, however, it proved difficult to eradicate the last vestiges of allegiance to the ecstatic practices of the Dionysian cult and to substitute the more restrained rituals of the Christian Church. Forbidden by the Church to dance, followers of the Dionysian cult found a way to circumvent this prohibition. They would claim to have been bitten by the tarantula spider and would insist that the only "cure" for this was to execute a frenzied dance to get the poison out of their systems. Whether this is historically correct or not, it led eventually to a type of music called the *tarantella* that was used to accompany these dances. A modern example of this dance form may be heard in the finale of Mendelssohn's "Italian Symphony."

The Middle East

It is possible to show some direct influences of ancient Greek and Roman music on early Christian music, especially through Byzantine music, the music of the eastern branch of early Christianity. A more direct and interesting connection, however, can be made with Jewish music. Just as the New Testament springs from the soil of the Old Testament, the music of the early Christian Church was nurtured to a great extent by traditions of Jewish music. The Old Testament abounds with references to music. We learn that the music in the Temple in Jerusalem was performed under the direction of a group of highly trained professionals, the Levites. A large group of instruments were used especially to signal the entrance of the priests. After the destruction of the Temple in A.D. 70, instrumental music ceased to be important. The one historical Jewish instrument still in use today is the *shofar*, an instrument made from a ram's horn and having a highly distinctive though somewhat crude-sounding timbre. In modern Jewish services the shofar is sounded at the rites celebrating the New Year.

Vocal music in the Jewish service has an unbroken history extending over 6,000 years. Verses of the Bible were chanted in a style not unlike that of the later plainsong or Gregorian chant of the Catholic Church. They were based on the use of "melody types"—that is, short melodic patterns or formulas. Some of the Psalms have inscriptions that were actually indications of which melody type should be used.

The practice of using melody types is also a prominent feature of Arabian music. Two other features of special interest are the use of intervals smaller than the half step and the use of characteristic complex rhythm patterns often set in metric schemes that alternate 2 + 2 + 2 + 2 and 2 + 3 + 3. The main instruments of Arabian music include the *'ud*, a plucked-string instrument that was the ancestor of the medieval lute and eventually of modern instruments such as the mandolin; the *rebab*, a bowed-string instrument; and the *arghool*, a woodwind instrument with one pipe for a drone (a sustained low note) and one pipe for the melody.

Music also played an important role in the religious ceremonies of ancient Egypt as evidenced through written documents and iconography—that is, the study of pictorial representation. It is interesting to note that apparently there was a substantial change in the character of the music of the Old Kingdom (before the eighteenth century B.C.) and the New Kingdom (after the sixteenth century B.C.). The former was more calm and objective, the latter more emotional and subjective—a difference that we have already encountered in Apollonian and Dionysian aspects of Greek music.

The Far East

To underline the idea of the universality of some musical practices, we can mention that the music of India, like other cultures we have discussed, also makes use of the melody types, called *ragas* in classical Indian music. The number of ragas has been variously placed as low as six or as high as 800, according to various theories and localities. Each raga has not only unique melodic characteristics but also individual emotional connotations. Indian music is also characterized by the use of smaller intervals and interesting rhythm patterns. Indeed, the level of sophistication in both pitch and rhythm aspects of melody reached in Indian music can be astounding.

One of the most interesting aspects of Chinese music is the so-called *huang chung* or basic pitch. Perhaps the best way to understand this is to compare it to the tuning fork of the pitch A, which was kept for many years in our own American Bureau of Standards. This pitch established the norm or standard for use in music. The Chinese, however, went beyond this and believed that the huang chung was responsible for the success of their society. The fall of a dynasty in ancient China was attributed to the loss of the true huang chung. It would be difficult to imagine a modern government being toppled by the loss of the correct pitch. This attitude in ancient China, however, indicates the important, sometimes mystical power of music. Confucius (551–478 B.C.), like Plato, assigns music an important role in the preservation of a sound state. In the T'ang and Sung dynasties (roughly from the seventh to the thirteenth centuries A.D.) Chinese music reached a high degree of perfection, and colorful orchestras with hundreds of performers were used for religious and state ceremonies. At other times, however, as during the reign of Emperor Shih Huang Ti 259–210 B.C.), the extensive preoccupation with music came to be regarded as inimical to society, and all music and instruments were ordered destroyed. An echo of this action, which is in itself a backhanded tribute to the power of music, could be found in the recent order of the Chinese government banning Western music, and the excesses of some who sought to destroy all existing Western instruments in China. Since that time, however, the possibility of an exchange of musical cultures of the West and China has been reopened.

The pitches of Chinese music were derived from the huang chung by a series of perfect fifths. If we assume that the pitch of the huang chung was approximately D (as most scholars agree) and then move up by perfect fifths, we reach the tones D, A, E, B, and F sharp. If we arrange these in scalar order we find they form the pentatonic (five-note) scale of D, E, F sharp, A, and B, which we have already learned is the basis not only of Chinese music but of other early music. Rhythmically, ancient Chinese sacred music was characterized by the extensive use of long tones, possibly not unlike the slow intoning of a chorale or hymn in the Christian tradition.

MUSIC OF OTHER CULTURES

To this point we have been discussing the religious music of several cultures, all of which are quite different, but all of which have at least one point in common—they all have left to us a significant body of written information on the theory and practice of music. Indeed, in many cases our knowledge *about* the music is often far more complete than our knowledge *of* the music, how it actually sounded in practice. We now turn to a group of cultures which have in common the fact that they have not left us such extensive written descriptions of the theory and practice of their music. These cultures would include most of Africa, the Pacific, and the original cultures of North and South America. Instead of basing our knowledge on written records or iconography, we depend more on field research, based on the assumption that we can learn something about the style of these musical cultures by hearing present-day performers who have preserved the original traditions relatively uncorrupted by outside influences. The term "primitive music" that is sometimes used to describe the music of these cultures is unfortunate, for in many instances the music reaches a high degree of complexity and sophistication. The art of drumming in African music, for example, has been a great source of inspiration for many Western players and composers.

The great variety of styles in these musical cultures makes it difficult to formulate any meaningful and relevant generalities. We could point out, however, the fact that many of them share a common belief in the miraculous curative power of music. The medicine man of an African tribe or an American Indian tribe employs specific types of songs for specific types of illnesses, just as he employs specific drugs. Furthermore, these curing songs are usually the secret property of the medicine man and only pass to a trusted assistant on his death.

Actually, the union of music and medicine is by no means limited to African and Indian tribes. It is symbolized in Greek culture by the fact that Apollo was both the god of music and the god of medicine. One of the earliest preserved written prescriptions is an Egyptian document specifying the use of music for an illness.

With this brief background let us return to consideration of the styles of music of our cultural heritage, beginning with early liturgical music.

MEDIEVAL SACRED MUSIC

The coronation of Charlemagne in A.D. 800 provides a logical starting point for our brief survey of the development of musical style. The significance of this period in the history of Western-European culture can hardly be overestimated. The confluence of Roman civilization and Byzantine civilization produced architectural masterpieces like the cathedral in Aix-la-Chapelle. Brilliant administrators working under Charlemagne were responsible for the codification of laws in the various parts of his realm, the spread of classical learning and literature, and attempts at the unification of language. Charlemagne, realizing that the Roman Catholic Church could serve as a means of unifying the vastly different peoples of his enormous empire, promoted the exclusive use of Latin rather than the many different vernacular languages, and he standardized the liturgy—that is, the forms of public worship—including the musical portions thereof.

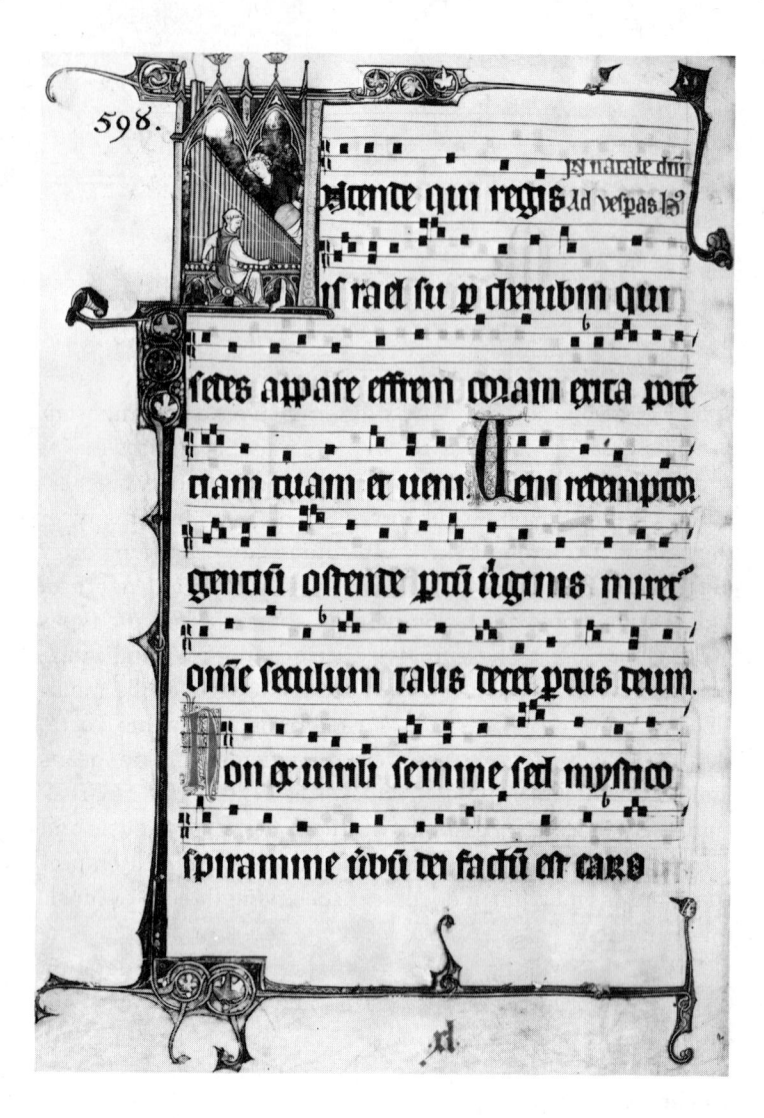

One category of the vast corpus of Catholic liturgical chant is that for the service of the daily hours (Matins, Lauds, etc., as distinct from the Mass), collections of which are contained in various books entitled Antiphonary, such as the Beaupré Antiphonary of the 13th century—a page of which is shown here.

Mass Proper	Mass Ordinary
Introit	Kyrie
	Gloria
Collect	
Epistle	
Gradual	
Alleluia or Tract	
Gospel	Credo
Offertory	
Secret	
Preface	Sanctus
	Canon
	Agnus Dei
Communion	Ite missa est or
Post-communion	Benedicamus Domino

The Mass is shown here in its present-day form. In the early centuries of the Christian era, the Mass consisted primarily of items of the Proper; the items of the Ordinary were added gradually, many of them at the time of Charlemagne and later.

The music of the Mass and the Office came to be known by the general term of "Gregorian chant." It was named after Pope Gregory I, who reigned from 590 to 604, but his role in the codification of this music is a subject of debate. Though the main task of collecting and standardizing this music was accomplished at the time of Charlemagne, the history of Gregorian chant covers over a thousand years, from the earliest singing of the followers of Christ in the first century to approximately 1400. The preserved repertoire of Gregorian chant numbers nearly 3,000 melodies, which have several features in common. They are all monophonic (single line), and they are tonally based on the Church modes (see the Index). One of the charms and, at the same time, one of the problems of Gregorian chant is its rhythm. Exact details of the performance were not specified in the music, but it is probably meant to be

Gregorian Chant

The two major divisions of the liturgy are the Mass,* representing the commemoration of the Last Supper, and the Office, the Services of the Hours celebrated eight times a day by the clergy. The Mass can be divided into two main portions: the Proper, containing items whose texts are changed from day to day, and the Ordinary, containing items that remain the same for every day. In the following list, *italicized items* indicate those that were sung in a simple reciting style. The remaining items were subject to more elaborate musical treatment.

*The name derives from the last item of the Mass—"*Ite missa est*" ("Depart, the congregation is dismissed.")

sung in a free-flowing rhythm with occasional long notes at the end of phrases, leading to a flowing, supple performance that has an almost hypnotic, compellingly beautiful effect on the listener, especially when the music is heard in a resonant cathedral.

There are also important differences in the style of Gregorian chant. Example 8-1 shows the simplest kind of musical setting, a prayer tone for the Collect. Example 8-2 is the beginning of an Introit. Notice that it has a larger variety of pitches and that in some cases groups of notes are bound together into one compound symbol. These notational signs of the Middle Ages are called *neumes,* and the practice of singing each syllable to two, three, or four notes is called *neumatic singing.*

Since many specific details of this notational system are unknown, the precise interpretation of these symbols is a matter of conjecture, one version being the transcription into modern notation which appears below in Example 8-2b.

Gregorian chant is especially suited for settings of the liturgy in Latin. With the recent substitution of the vernacular language (English, in our case), the use of the Gregorian chant in churches has been considerably diminished. Gregorian literature is important, however, not only for its influence upon succeeding generations of musical style, but also because even today it can convey to us in a remarkable way some of the ineffable essence of the medieval spirit.

In addition to the points we have discussed, Gregorian

EXAMPLE 8-1 GREGORIAN CHANT: PRAYER TONE FOR THE COLLECT.

Per Do - mi - num nos - trum Je - sum Christ - um . . . . tu - um

EXAMPLE 8-2 GREGORIAN CHANT: BEGINNING OF AN INTROIT. (*a*) IN NEUMES; (*b*) IN MODERN NOTATION.

(a)
Intr. 8.
Ad te levá - vi á - niman me - am: De - us me - us

(b)

EXAMPLE 8-3 GREGORIAN CHANT: BEGINNING OF AN ALLELUIA.

[Solo] [Chorus]
Al - le - lu - ia _____ *Al - le - lu - ia _____

Building on the impetus begun in the late Middle Ages, secular music was to flourish—even in The Men's Bath as so vividly portrayed by Albrecht Dürer (1471-1528), famed German painter and engraver.

chants can be shown to differ from one another in terms of their forms, ranging from free or "through-composed" forms to repetitive forms such as the aaa, bbb, aaa form, which is used for some Kyries. Among other types of Gregorian chants are the *hymns,* in which the smoothly flowing varied rhythms of the standard Gregorian chant yield to a more regular poetic form and a more metric, almost jingling rhythmic organization; the *conducti* or processional songs; and the *laudes,* or festive ceremonial songs.

EARLY POLYPHONY

It is entirely possible that Western art music might have continued as single-line music which would gradually have become more complex both rhythmically and melodically. Music of other cultures tended to follow this pattern, especially in Arabia, China, India, and Africa. Something happened to Western art music, however, which was to make its development radically different from that of other cultures. At some time and for some reason, people began adding a second, third, fourth, and even more parts to the single-line chant. They began the development of what we would later call *polyphony* or *harmony.* This development has been compared to the idea of perspective in painting, or to the idea of the artistic treatment of space in architecture. It may have arisen because of some unconscious artistic desire or (less likely in the view of most scholars) simply because untrained singers were not able to sing along with the original line of pitch.

The earliest developments in polyphony, called *organa,* are first described in tenth-century treatises. At first they were extremely simple, almost crude-sounding, at least to our ears. The basic idea was merely the addition of a second voice placed a perfect fourth or a perfect fifth below the original chant. Gradually this second voice began to depart from its rigid "shadowing" of the original voice and to move in oblique or contrary motions, especially at phrase endings. As fascinating as it would be to trace this history of polyphony, we shall instead move from the sphere of sacred music to that of secular music.

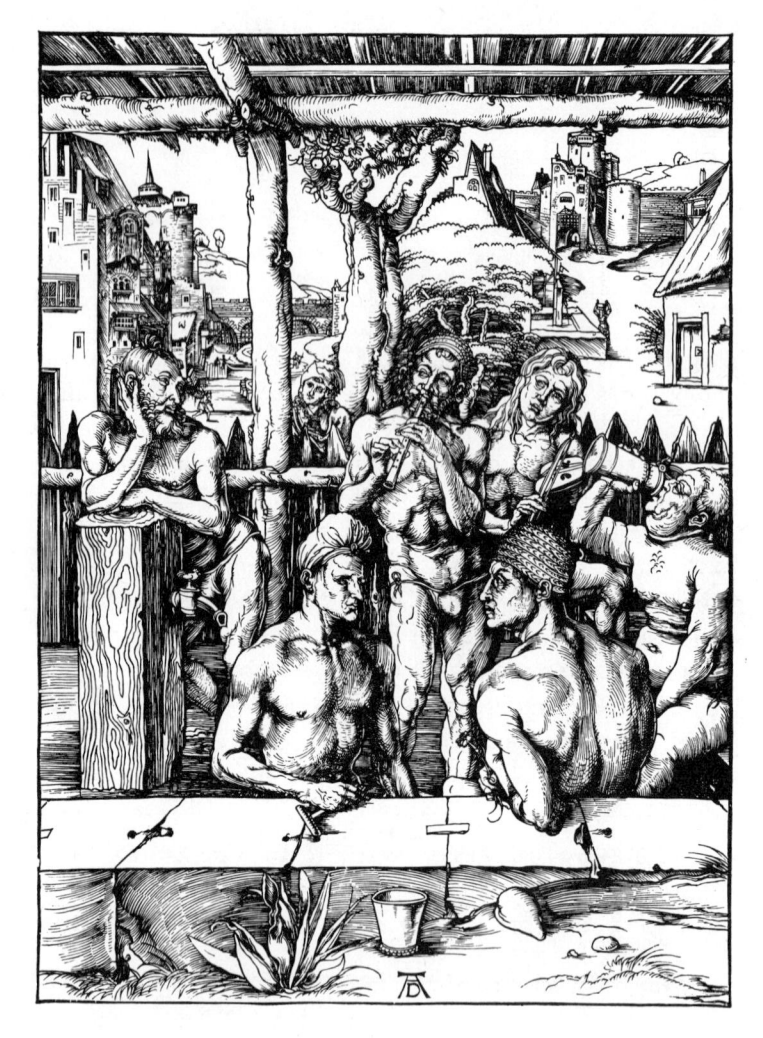

EARLY SECULAR MUSIC

Looking back through recorded time, we see that music, drama, and dance constitute our most basic modes of artistic expression. Further, the word, spoken or sung, whether in epic poems, dramas, or other literary forms, is a well-recognized legacy of primitive and more sophisticated cultures. In most societies, whether quite primitive or highly sophisticated, music and dance of various forms has heightened the dramatic effect of the message being conveyed and evoked emotional responses in the perceptor. In early cultures this was particularly true of religious rites and ceremonies, wherein these three entities were wedded to strengthen the impact of the message being conveyed.

One is hard pressed to speak definitively on this subject in terms of primitive cultures since theirs was commonly an oral (nonrecorded) tradition. Further, with the encroachment of more sophisticated cultures, the old was abandoned, or at least modified, to accommodate the new. Two facts stand out, however, in regard to their cultural life. First, it centered on the recounting of epic myths or folklore, often in a singing narrative style with incidental dancing and ceremonials—often religious. Second, whether or not the performer was a medicine man or minstrel, or the audience actively or passively involved, music, drama, and dance filled a need and a demand in primitive societies that is no less real today. Whether reflected in the Stone Age cave drawings in France of early man wearing an animal mask, bearing a bow, and dancing after a herd of reindeer, or told in the creation myths of the Indians "before the people came," these three expressive forms of artistic endeavor were combined to capture the imagination, and to allow people to see themselves in an existence other than their common one.

Songs constituted a most significant genre of early secular music. In fact, the earliest preserved example of written music is a song coming from the ancient Near East civilization of Ugarit and dating probably from 1800 B.C. The clay tablets on which the song was written were discovered in the early 1950's in Syria and were finally deciphered after fifteen years of work by scholars from the University of California. The top four lines of the tablets contain the text written in the Hurrian language. Very little of the text can be translated but it appears to be a love song or a hymn to a god of love. The bottom six lines contain instructions for performing the music. Richard Crocker believes that the melody is in a diatonic seven-note scale, not unlike our diatonic system, and that the music was meant to be sung to the accompaniment of the lyre, an ancient plucked-string instrument.

Aside from this song and a few fragments of Greek songs, we have very few early preserved secular songs. We do have a body of songs from the *goliards*, wandering students of the

An ancient Hurrian song written in cuneiform signs. The song text is written on the top four lines; instructions for the performance of the music are given on the bottom six lines.

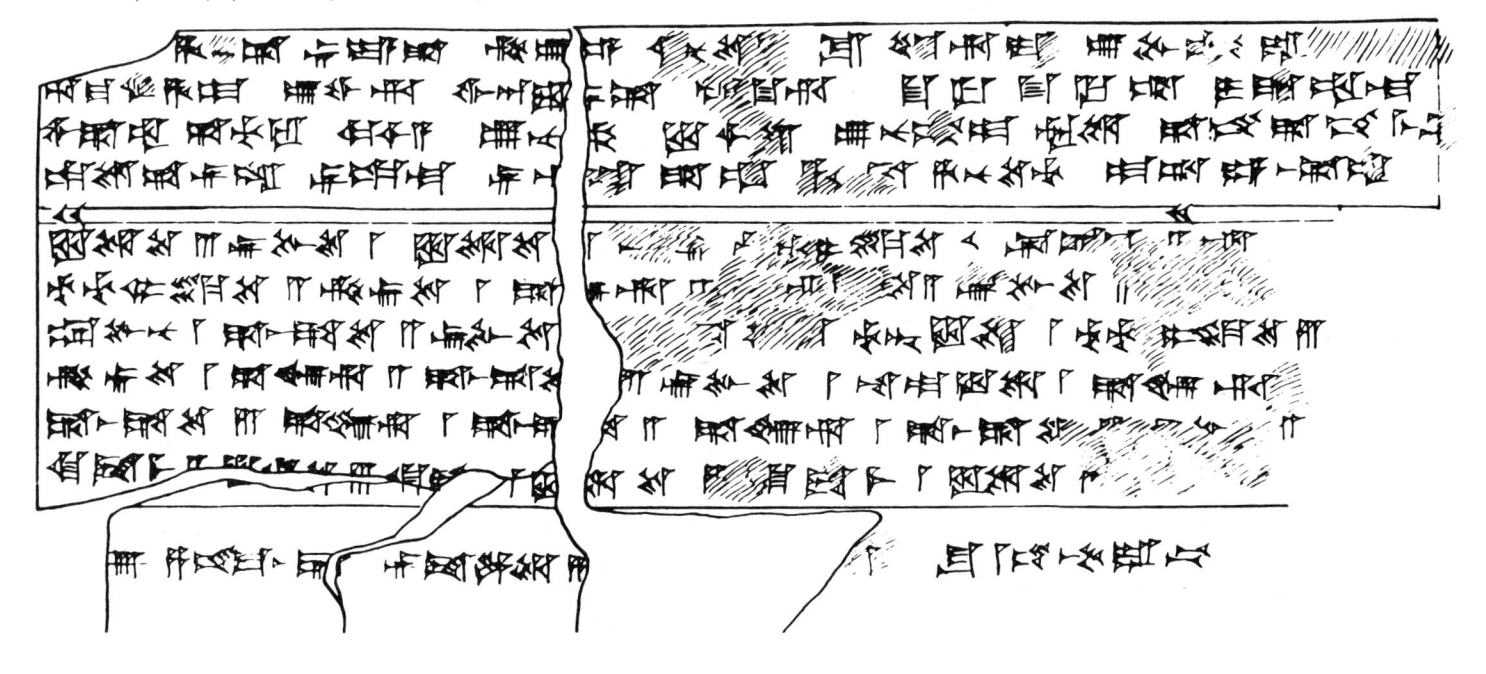

eleventh and twelfth centuries. Much of the music for these songs is either missing or unclear. The texts are concerned with subjects remarkably similar to the subjects of student songs throughout history—drinking, sex, and satire. The present generation of students is perhaps unique in adding to that venerable trio of subjects songs that are permeated with genuine social concern. Some of the early goliard songs have become known to modern audiences through Carl Orff's *Carmina Burana,* an exciting but highly modernized and freely interpreted version of these early songs.

The goliard songs were sung in Latin, just like the sacred music of the period. Among the earliest songs written in the vernacular—that is, the spoken language of a country—were the *chansons de geste* (songs of heroic achievement) written in France. These songs were not only works of art but also important media of communication. Medieval people could learn of the deeds of national heroes through works such as *The Song of Roland* just as we learn of the deeds of political figures through the evening news on television.

These vernacular songs were sung by *jongleurs,* professional entertainers who were not only musicians but also actors, acrobats, and animal trainers. They were usually wandering "free lancers," but occasionally they became attached to a royal household and became known as *minstrels.* Jongleurs and minstrels were primarily performers rather than poets and composers. Among the earliest known secular composers whose names have come down to us were the *troubadours* of twelfth- and thirteenth-century France. These were noblemen poet-composers who wrote songs mostly about love but occasionally dealing with other subjects such as the beauties of nature or religion. Troubadours lived in southern France; in northern France similar "gentleman amateurs" were known as *trouvères.* Both terms are dialect variants of the same root word meaning "inventor." Over 6,000 troubadour and trouvère poems have been preserved, but melodies for only about 1,500 have come down to us. Among these is a trouvère song (Example 8-4) attributed to no less a personage than Richard Coeur de Lion (1157–1199). This song was written in *ballade* form (A-A-B), one of the most widely used forms in all of music history.

Not only did songs abound, but considerable theatrical activity occurred in the medieval secular world, fostered by the wandering minstrels who sang, acted, and danced the ancient secular legends, stories, and heroic tales from village to town—for instance, *Le Jeu de Robin et Marion* (*The Play of Robin and Marion*) by Adam de la Halle, a French trouvère of the thirteenth century. Interestingly enough, minstrels took a satirical, ribald bent, were concerned with the "common man" (not gods, goddesses, or other mythological figures), and most often took a comical view of life and its idiosyncracies. *The Play of Robin and Marion* played for at least a century following the death of the famed bard who created it, and is considered one of the first examples of comic opera. It consists of scenes, dialogues, refrains, and tuneful interchanges among eleven characters, one of the most popular tunes being an old French folk song "Robin m'aime" ("Robin My Love"), Example 8-5.

Lest one assume that France had a monopoly on secular music during medieval times, it should be observed that Germany had its "troubadors." The *Minnesingers,* like their French counterparts, were primarily aristocrats or noblemen. The *Meistersingers,* on the other hand, were middle-class poet-musicians in fifteenth- and sixteenth-century Germany who formed themselves into guilds just as silversmiths and cobblers formed themselves into guilds. The meistersingers had elaborate rituals and strict rules for the composition of songs, practices that were vividly characterized in Richard Wagner's opera *Die Meistersinger* (*The Mastersinger*).

FOURTEENTH CENTURY MUSIC

Although meistersinger guilds continued to exist up to the eighteenth century, the unaccompanied solo song ceased to be a significant art form after the sixteenth century. Indeed, even in the centuries of its highest development, monophonic song literature was surpassed in importance by polyphonic works, both sacred and secular. The fourteenth century produced a rich literature of polyphonic secular song, highlighted by the

EXAMPLE 8-4   RICHARD COEUR DE LION: *"Ja nuns hons pris,"* BALLADE.

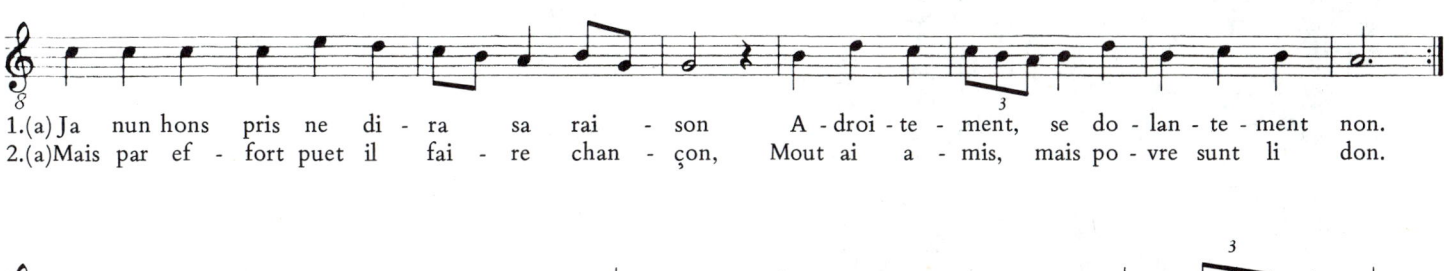

1.(a) Ja nun hons pris ne di - ra sa rai - son A - droi - te - ment, se do - lan - te - ment non.
2.(a) Mais par ef - fort puet il fai - re chan - çon, Mout ai a - mis, mais po - vre sunt li don.

3.(b) Hon - te i a - vront, se por ma re - an - çon Sui ça deus y - vers pris.

    1.(a) Indeed, no captive can tell his story   2.(a) But with an effort, he can make a song.
         Properly, unless it be sadly.   I have many friends, but poor are their gifts.

        3.(b) They will be put to shame, if for ransom
           I am held here for two winters.

EXAMPLE 8-5   DE LA HALLE: "ROBIN M'AIME" ("ROBIN MY LOVE"), MEASURES 1–14.

Ro - bin m'ai - me, Ro - bin m'a, Ro - bin m'a de - man - dé - e
si m'a - ra. Ro - bin m'a - ca - ta co - te - te d'es - car - la - te
bonne et be - le, sous - kai - nie et chain - tu - re - le, a - leur - i - va! Ro - bin
m'ai - me, Ro - bin m'a, Ro - bin m'a de - man - dé - e si m'a - ra.

Medieval and Renaissance Style (800–1600)   **129**

The tradition of serenading one's lady-love at her window is probably one of the oldest in music. This Florentine woodcut shows a group of frottolists serenading at carnival time.

1. How many vocal parts and how many instrumental parts do you hear?
2. How many different melodic ideas do you hear?
3. How are these melodic ideas arranged? Into which form do they fall?
4. Can you say anything about such details as the meter, the scale basis and/or the harmony, especially the kinds of cadences used?

The answers to these questions give us a fairly typical description of the style of this music. Written for three parts—although not clearly specified as such—it is assumed that it is meant to be performed with one part sung and the other two parts played on instruments. There are really only two main melodic ideas in this entire composition, and we shall designate them A and B. These alternate in the following scheme: AB, AA, AB, AB. As shown in Example 8-6, the top line is basically in compound duple meter while the bottom lines suggest simple triple meter. Notice that there are frequent triads in the composition, but that the endings of phrases are usually on an open-fifth sonority. Notice also the stylized cadences.

Now that you have studied this work, try to imagine it as it was sung for the first time in the fourteenth century, probably in a richly adorned princely apartment, perhaps with Machaut himself participating in the performance. Realize that this was the time, in the fourteenth century, when one of the most famous sayings was *"Wo Gott eine Capelle erichte, da baue der Teufel ein Wirtshaus an"* ("Where God builds a chapel, the devil adds a tavern"). This could be taken as a symbol of the times. Though there was great piety—and it was reflected in some of the magnificent churches, ranging from the perpendicular style in England to the flamboyant style in France and the *Hallenkirchen* style in Germany—there was also an enormous importance given to secular arts. The cultural leadership and the center of power had passed over to the cities and the citizens of the cities, and they used this to explore extremes in decoration in clothing, to delight in the colorful writing of Chaucer (ca. 1340–1400), to make great strides in science and technology, and to work toward the realization of rational political goals and establishments.

outstanding works of Machaut in France and Landini in Italy.

The most noted French composer of the century was a cleric, the canon of Rheims. Guillaume de Machaut (ca. 1300–1377) did write sacred music, including one of the earliest complete polyphonic settings of the Ordinary of the Mass, but his musical genius is perhaps nowhere better shown than in his charming secular songs.

In his *ballades, rondeaus, virelais,* and *lais,* Machaut adopted forms which had been developed several centuries before in the art of the *troubadours* and *trouvères,* courtly poet-musicians who sang of love, nature, and religion in beautifully sensitive monophonic songs. Machaut adopted the formal outlines and some of the melodies of these earlier songs in his secular music, but added to them a polyphonic richness and a sense of rhythmic and melodic development that was lacking in the earlier music. His rondeau "Quant ma Dame" may be taken as representative of this genre of music. Since this work is relatively uncomplicated and easy to hear, we would recommend that you listen to it first and then try to answer the following questions before reading the text.

Guillaume de Machaut (ca. 1300–1377). Love presenting to the famed composer of the Ars Nova three of her children, "sweet Musing, Pleasure and Hope."

■ Guillaume de Machaut, an important French composer and poet, is generally considered to be the outstanding composer of that segment of the Middle Ages where musical style is often referred to as *Ars Nova* (new art). More specifically, the term refers to French music of the latter half of the fourteenth century, which differs in style from that preceding in that it is more secular, lengthy, and rhythmically complex.

Born in Rheims, Machaut followed a career common to many musicians of the times in that he studied theology, took the Holy Orders of the Church, and devoted most of his adult life to its service. About the age of 20 he became secretary to the King of Bohemia, and subsequently served the Duchess of Normandy and King Charles V of France. In 1337 he became canon of Rheims where he remained for the rest of his life.

Machaut lived in a time of unrest and change. The supremacy of the Church was weakened—it was torn with bitter struggles between rivals for the papacy and openly criticized for the corruption and scandals involving some of its high officials. The foundation was being laid for the Protestant Reformation to come. Europe was involved in the Hundred Years War, which contributed to discontent, the end of feudalism, and the rise of independent and rival states and cities. Important for the arts was the rise of patronage external to the Church and a renewed interest in secular life as evidenced by Dante's *Divine Comedy* and Chaucer's *Canterbury Tales*.

Machaut was the man for the times—he was both conservative and innovative. His liturgical motets, for example, follow traditional lines, whereas his contrapuntal rondeaux are in the "new style." He is best known for his famous *Messe de Notre Dame* (*Mass of Our Lady*), a four-voice polyphonic setting based on segments of Gregorian chant in which the various parts of the Mass are musically related to form a unified whole. This represented a distinct departure from past practice, which permitted the music director to select parts of various works to be combined in the performance of the Mass.

Machaut wrote music of unusual solemnity and magnificence, but which was filled with the poetic, human sentiments of chivalric verse. In so doing he became the outstanding composer of his day.

EXAMPLE 8-6 Machaut: "Quant ma Dame," rondeau, complete.

1.4.7. Quant / ma da - me / les / maus
3. qu'en / grant dou - ceur / mon / cuer
5. dont / qui les / biens / a / droit

d'a - mer / / m'a - prent,
tient / et / / e - sprent,
sa - veure / / et prent,

2.8. el - le / me puet / plus dous; / aus - - - si les biens a - pren - - - dre,
6. riens n'est / / c'est / / le - gier a com pren - - - dre.

132 Styles of Music

In this painting by Pieter Breughel the Elder (about 1525-1569), peasants choose partners at a wedding to engage in one of man's oldest forms of expression.

EARLY DANCE MUSIC

Like singing, dancing was part of historical and primitive cultures long before the advent of notated music. A great deal of information about the range and development of religious, ritualistic, erotic, and recreational activities is contained within the story of dance, according to many historians such as Willi Apel, Curt Sachs, and others. Traditional dances have served to appease the gods, bring forth rain, induce magic spells, hypnotize, heal the wounded or sick, seduce, and express the exuberance of new-found freedom, love, or the joy of living. Dance was developed and shaped by the Greeks into an expression of artistic beauty for its own sake. During the Middle Ages, a period of Church dominance and rigid Church controls, dancing was frowned upon if not totally excluded from day-to-day social activities.

Dancing gained a strong hold in folk activities during the fourteenth century, a period during which music also occupied a favored position in the lives of many common as well as courtly people in leading European nations such as France, England, and Italy. An early example of the wedding of dance and music occurred with the advent of an instrumentally performed melody called an *estampie,* which in the views of some historians is clearly "in the style" of a dance. One such historical instrumental dance piece is shown in Example 8-7. Since the term *estampie* comes from a word meaning "to stamp," one may deduce the nature of this particular dance as reflected partly in the recurring accents and note groupings of the melody.

It's easy to foot-tap or move to the steadily swinging beats of this estampie. And it is this characteristic physical impulse

EXAMPLE 8-7 ESTAMPIE (INSTRUMENTAL DANCE) OF UNKNOWN ORIGIN, FIRST SECTION—MAIN VOICE.

Medieval and Renaissance Style (800–1600)

to move that is as typically associated with dance music of any time as the urge to participate vocally is with song. It seems entirely logical that the two activities often complement one another.

Most of us have danced or yielded to the impulse to move to the rhythm and pulse of music. Earliest recorded attempts at inventing music have been associated in part with dancing, and the coactivities of music and dance continue to form part of many of our lives. The ritualistic dances of primitive people, such as those that inspired Stravinsky's famous ballet *The Rite of Spring*, and the gyrations of the rock-and-roll-accompanied dancing of the past twenty or so years reflect the variety of music and related physical movement that forms only a glimpse of dance, both formal (ballet) and spontaneous (rock and roll). It seems likely that our irresistible urge to move to music will not be suppressed in the near future, nor in all probability will the rhythmic characteristics of dance music.

SACRED MUSIC OF THE FIFTEENTH AND SIXTEENTH CENTURIES

We left our survey of the development of sacred music with the first tentative steps toward polyphony in the tenth and eleventh centuries. The climax of this early development of polyphony was reached in the music of the Notre Dame school (ca. 1200). A typical work by Perotin, a leading composer of the latter half of the Notre Dame period, would have the original Gregorian chant in long notes in the bass, with two more rapidly moving rhythmic parts above it. These added parts had no separate text, but beginning around 1200, composers began to add original words to the upper parts. The French word for "word" is *mot* and the resulting compositions became known as *motets*. At first the Latin words were pious commentary on the meaning of the original text. Later, in keeping with the medieval spirit of combining the sacred and the secular, French words, sometimes even love songs, were used as texts for the upper parts. In the fourteenth century, the motet was somewhat neglected as a form in favor of the secular forms described in the previous section. But in the fifteenth and sixteenth centuries, it returned and became the most significant form of polyphonic composition. Indeed, in some cases, full motets were supplied with a change of text and became Mass movements in the so-called *parody technique*.

Ave Maria,
gratia plena,
Dominus tecum,
virgo serena.

Ave, cuius conceptio,
solemni plena gaudio,
coelestia terrestria
nova replet laetitia

Ave, cuius nativitas
nostra fuit solemnitas,
ut Lucifer lux oriens
verum solem praeveniens.

Ave, pia humilitas,
sine viro fecunditas
cuius annuntiatio
nostra fuit salvatio.

Ave, vera virginitas,
immaculata castitas,
cuius purificatio
nostra fuit purgatio.

Ave, praeclara omnibus
angelicus virtuitibus,
cuius assumptio
nostra glorificatio.

O mater Dei,
memento mei. Amen

Hail Mary,
full of grace,
the Lord is with thee,
serene Virgin.

Hail, whose conception,
full of great jubilation,
fills Heaven and Earth
with new joy.

Hail, whose birth
brought us joy,
as Lucifer, the morning star,
went before the true sun.

Hail, pious humility,
fruitful without a man,
whose Annunciation
brought us salvation.

Hail, true virginity,
immaculate chastity,
whose purification
brought our cleansing.

Hail, glorious one
in all angelic virtues,
whose Assumption
was our glorification.

O Mother of God,
remember me. Amen.

The text and translation of the motet "Ave Maria," by Josquin des Prez, is given here (see Example 8-8). The work is performed by four-part chorus, with medieval instruments doubling the voices. Although the fifteenth and sixteenth centuries are sometimes referred to as "the golden age of a

Josquin des Prez
(ca. 1445–1521).

■ Few details are known about the life of Josquin des Prez, despite the fact that this Flemish composer was one of the great contrapuntalists of his day. Born in Burgundy he became a choirboy and later a canon and choirmaster. He left the Netherlands in 1475 to become a chorister in a ducal court in Milan. Thereafter we pick up the thread of his life at the Papal Chapel in Rome where he was a singer in the period 1486–1494. In the next years he was active in Florence and other cities of Italy, entered the service of Louis III of France, and then returned to Burgundy, becoming a Church provost and enjoying fame as a composer and much admired teacher of composition.

Josquin lived in the first part of the Renaissance, an important time in history. This was an "age of reason" and scientific inquiry which saw the end of knighthood, the discovery of the "new world," the rise of the great ruling families of Italian city-states, the inevitable struggles with the Church for freedom of thought and expression, and a blossoming of the arts, particularly in Italy with Botticelli, Leonardo da Vinci, and Michelangelo. Music reflected this spirit of rebirth as it became a vital part of society outside the Church, producing a vast quantity of secular music written for performance by amateurs and of choral music rich with contrapuntal imitation.

The Flemish composers were the musical giants of their day, and the greatest of them all was Josquin, prolific composer of masses, motets, and secular songs, and avowed master of contrapuntal technique.

Giovanni Pierluigi da Palestrina
(ca. 1525–1594).

■ Giovanni Pierluigi, named "da Palestrina" after his birthplace, was born in a village near Rome. He began as a chorister in the cathedral in Palestrina in about 1532. When his voice changed he furthered his study of music in Rome and then returned to Palestrina as organist and choirmaster. He married, had two sons, and when his Bishop was elected Pope Julius III, he joined him in Rome in 1557 as choirmaster of the Cappella Giulia, a choir of native singers in training for the choir of the Sistine Chapel. Three years later he published his first book of Masses, dedicated to the Pope who, in appreciation, appointed him to the Papal Choir. With a change of Pope, Palestrina and two others were dismissed, perhaps because they were married and thus ineligible for the position. Thereafter he served as musical director at St. John Lateran, where he composed his important *Lamentations* (musical settings of the Lamentations of Jeremiah), and later at St. Maria Maggiore, publishing his *First Book of Motets* in 1563.

In 1562 the Council of Trent decreed that Church music be purified of "anything lascivious or impure," agreeing that the text should predominate. More fervid reformers wanted to purge the literature of contrapuntal music, thought to be overly complex and not readily comprehensible. Emperor Ferdinand I intervened, however, and counterpoint remained. Palestrina created his most famous work—the *Mass for Pope Marcellus II*—about this time.

Palestrina—the greatest composer of the Catholic Church—created a richly melodious, contrapuntal music in which clarity of text and smooth, singable lines predominate.

EXAMPLE 8-8 JOSQUIN DES PREZ: "AVE MARIA," MOTET, MEASURES 1–17.

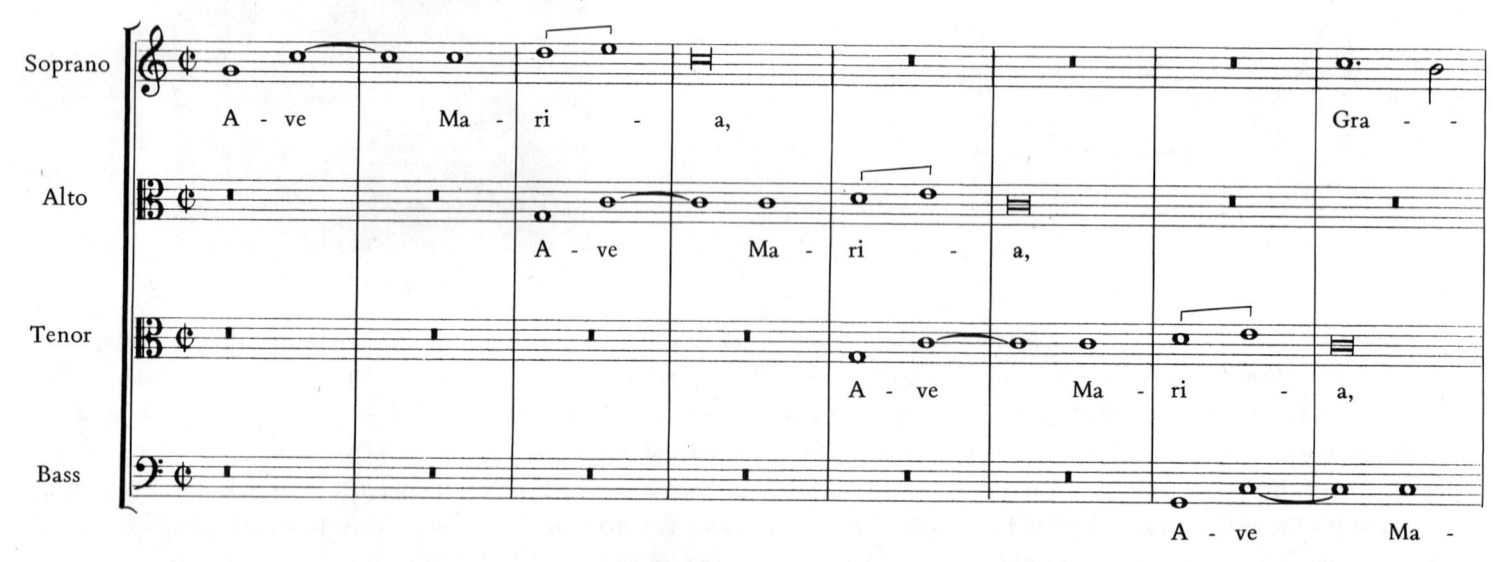

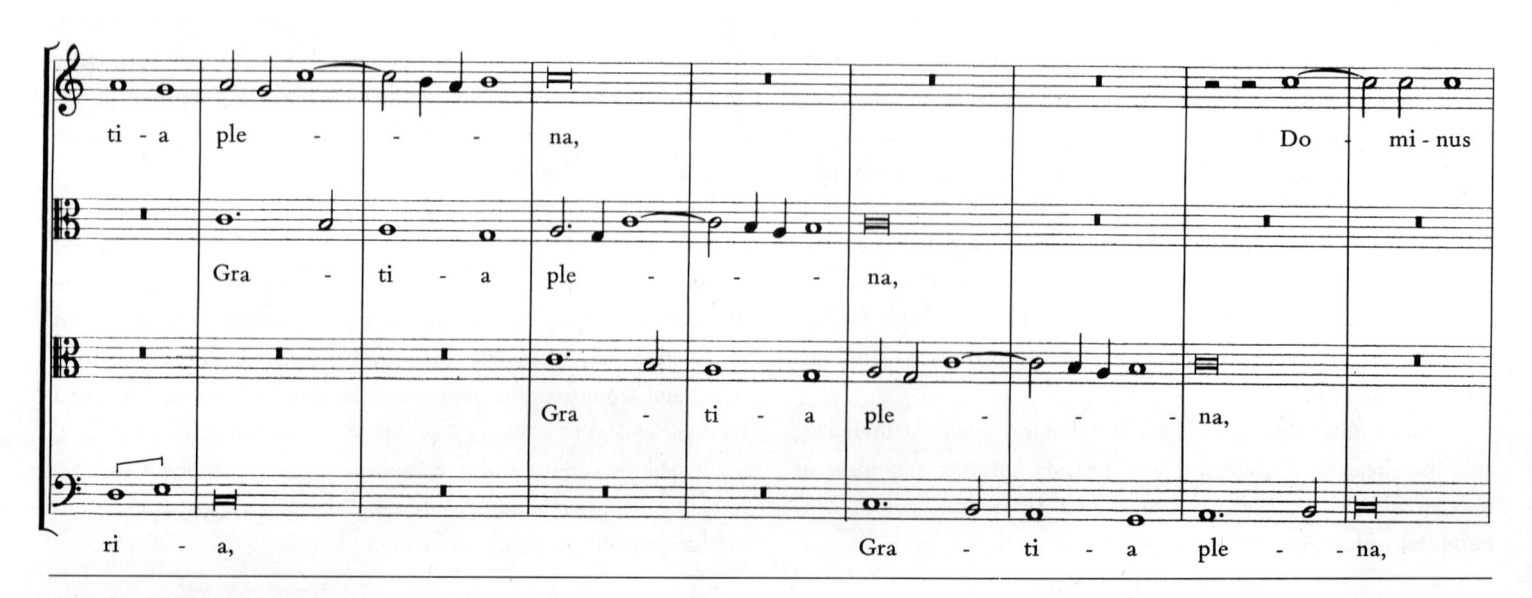

cappella [without accompaniment] music," it is now the conviction of most musicologists that this music was intended to be performed with the voices doubled by instruments.

Typical traits of Josquin's style, which appear here, are the imitation of pairs of voices. Sections in which this occurs alternate with other sections in which all four voices join together. This moving work, by a composer recognized by his contemporaries and by musicologists through the centuries as one of the most magnificent composers, will amply repay repeated hearings. Its polyphonic complexities do not yield up their treasures immediately upon first hearing, but can be heard with directed attention. The marvelous effect of the counterpoint of a master like Josquin comes from the fact that he is concerned both with vertical considerations (harmony) and horizontal considerations (melody). To assist you in following the lines, a portion of the music appears in Example 8-8.

Josquin des Prez was writing about the time that Columbus was discovering the "new world," and it could be said that Josquin conquered a "new world" of sound. Reformation and counter-Reformation were to mark the coming century. A little of this conflict may be heard even in the serene, expressive music of Josquin.

THE MADRIGAL

If our purpose were to describe musical landmarks and to honor musical greatness, we would certainly spend some time on the masters of sixteenth-century counterpoint, such as Orlando di Lasso (Roland de Lassus), Tomás Luis de Victoria, and Giovanni Pierluigi da Palestrina (ca. 1525–1594). Our purpose, however, is to show significant changes in stylistic development, and these masters were, for the most part, perfectors of inherited traditions rather than innovators. We must not, however, leave the sixteenth century without mentioning another important form that was to have a significant effect on the future developments of music in its own right—namely, the madrigal. This was a choral work in a free imitative form, written in the language of the country. Italy and England were the principal homes for this form. The madrigal ranged in style from the graceful simplicity of some of the early Italian madrigals to the rollicking good humor of the English madrigals, or "balletts" as they are more properly called, to the dramatic poignancy of some of the late madrigals of Carlo Gesualdo or William Byrd.

We shall end this section on Renaissance music with Thomas Morley's ballett "My Bonny Lass." We have quoted the work in full (Example 8-9) so that you may analyze various

EXAMPLE 8-9   MORLEY: "MY BONNY LASS," BALLET (MADRIGAL), COMPLETE.

Fa la la la la la la Fa la... Fa la la. la. Smile...
1. 2.
Fa la la la la la la la la. Fa la... Fa la... la. la. Smile...
la la la. Fa la... Fa la... la. la. Smile
la la. Fa la... Fa la... la. la. Smile...
la la la. Fa la la la. Fa la... Fa la...
And Fa la...
And... Fa la...
less dear love there - fore. And you shall love me more. Fa la la. Fa
And... Fa la la...
And... Fa la la. Fa
Fa la... Fa la...
1. 2.
Fa la... Smile la.
la la la. Fa la la. Fa la la la... Smile la.
Fa la... Smile la.
la... Fa la... la.

Thomas Morely (1557-ca. 1603) and William Byrd (1543-1623) were the chief representatives of the early English madrigal school, the former being the author of the first regular treatise on music published in England—A Plain and Easy Introduction to Practical Music.

aspects of it. More importantly, we have written it out in the hope that you will attempt a performance of at least the top melody line, if not all five parts.

SUMMARY

In closing, we will summarize some of the characteristic features in classic sixteenth-century style. Any such list of stylistic characteristics must be taken only as a group of general tendencies rather than absolute descriptions, but it is hoped that these characteristics may help you to identify typical music of the period.

Style Characteristics of Renaissance Music

Rhythm: Duple meter at moderate tempo is characteristic. Metric sense is frequently obscured by irregular groupings and by contrapuntal interplay of voices.

Melody: Modal scales are used, but the increasingly frequent usage of "musica ficta" (altered notes) points toward the eventual reduction to two modes, major and minor. Still at this point, in theory if not always in practice, the modal system is maintained. Melodies are generally of an average range with strong preference for movement by step. Occasionally leaps appear but are almost always balanced by steps in the opposite direction.

Harmony: Harmony is, at least theoretically, the by-product of contrapuntal lines, but there is clear evidence for the important shaping role of major and minor triads. Harmonic progression uses a balance of seconds, thirds, and fourths, but there is some emphasis on movement by fourths (fifths). Authentic and plagal cadences supplant the earlier modal cadences (except for the Phrygian). Dissonance is carefully controlled.

Texture: Four- or five-part imitative texture is the norm except for occasional passages in familiar homophonic style.

Timbre: Though written for voices alone, most authorities agree that instruments were used to double or replace voices in actual performance. There is a gradual emergence of an independent instrumental literature. Viol, lute, organ, harpsichord, and recorder are used, plus some use of early versions of trumpet, trombone, and oboe (i.e., zink, sackbut, shawm, etc.). Dynamics are rarely indicated.

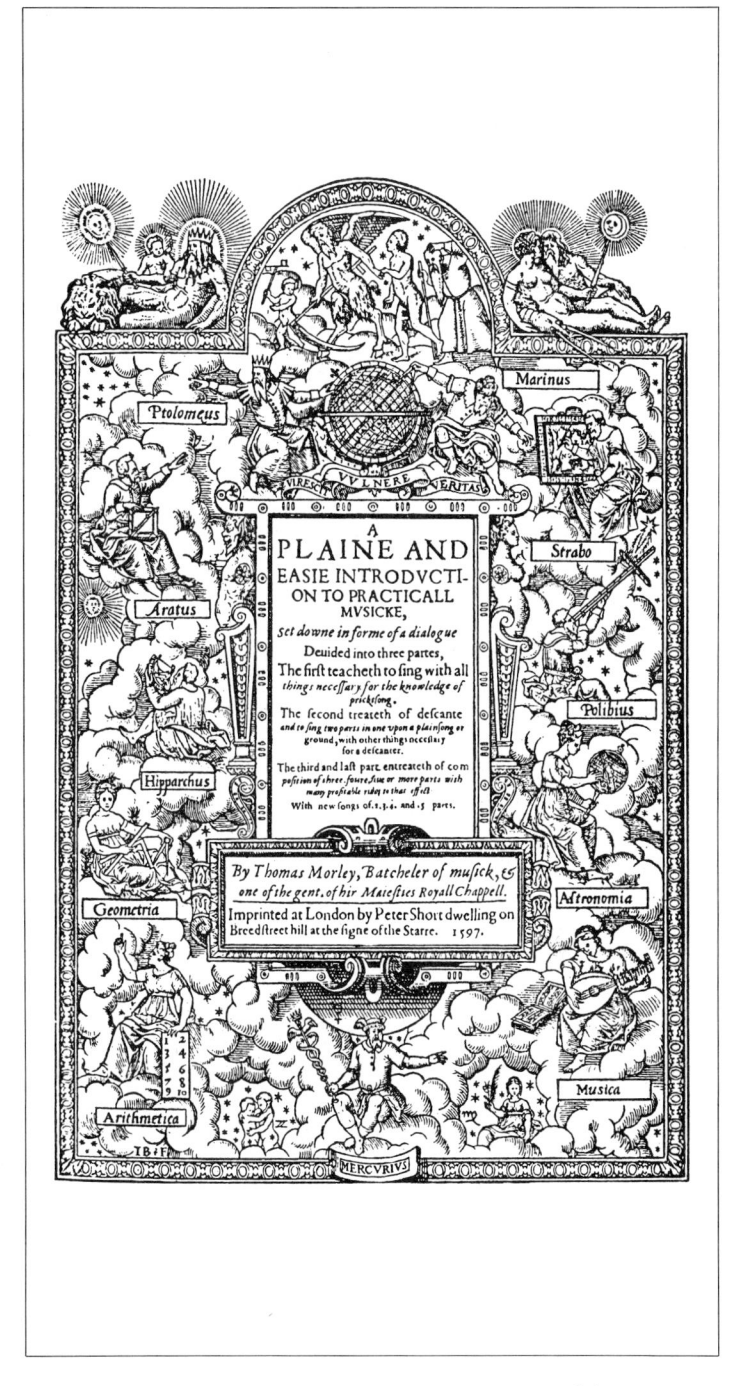

Forms: Mass, motet, madrigal, chanson, and chorale are among the important vocal forms. Fantasia, ricercare, prelude, toccata, and canzona are among the important instrumental forms.

9 Baroque Style (1600–1750)

We have traced some high points of the evolution of musical style up to the beginning of the seventeenth century—the crystalization of sacred monophony, the first tentative experiments in polyphony, the flowering of secular music, and the remarkable zenith of sixteenth-century music. In this chapter, devoted to music of the Baroque* period, our emphasis must shift from the evolution of style to the contrast of style. Indeed it may truly be said that the Baroque period was the birthplace of the concept of music style. In the Renaissance, despite subtle but interesting differences from composer to composer, there was one basic style, one set of fundamental compositional principles, which could be applied to various types of music. In the Baroque period, there were at least three distinct styles—one for the church music, one for theater music, and one for chamber music; and there were two distinct compositional practices—one based on the strict polyphonic principles of the Renaissance, and the other based on new principles which will be discussed later in this chapter.

OPERA

The Baroque period began with a phenomenon that was actually Renaissance in character. A group of noblemen in Florence sought to re-create a form of musical drama with some of the same effectiveness that ancient Greek dramas were reported to have. To say that they were trying to imitate or revise Greek dramas as some textbooks do is actually overstating the case. They wanted to accomplish with the music and drama of their own time what they imagined the Greeks had accomplished with the music and drama of their time.

The times were ripe for change and reform as church and state were dramatically altered. Christendom was divided into Protestant and Catholic, and the power of the Pope was waning. Scholasticism flourished in arts and letters, and there were significant new developments in the sciences. Although great art and music continued to remain within the domain of the church, there was also a popular strain concerned with more earthly matters, particularly in Italy.

*The French *baroque* derives from the Portuguese word *barroco*, which meant a pearl of irregular shape; it was used originally as a derogatory term denoting excessive decoration in art and music.

Whether considered a pearl of exquisite beauty or of vulgar extravagance, baroque works of art such as this of Jan Vermeer—17th century Dutch painter and master of the poetry of light—reflect the exuberant spirit of a flamboyant age.

This took the form of dramatic folk art called *commedia dell'arte*—the improvised comedy that was to influence comic opera to follow. These were improvised, staged works of numerous acts, involving a skeletal plot and stock characters in standardized costumes and masks—young lovers frustrated by their selfish, obstinate elders; zany (madcap) servants sympathetic to the young lovers and more clever than their masters; wealthy, miserly old merchants filled with thoughts of young love which are always shattered; bungling professional men (often lawyers or doctors), etc. These "situation comedies" impudently mirrored the blustering pretensions and humbling realities of life in a popular vehicle that permitted the "letting off of steam" in a time of considerable political and religious turmoil. Thus the stage was set in about 1600 for the appear-

Baroque Style (1600-1750) 141

ance of the oldest surviving musical art form, *opera*—a shortened version of *opera in musica* (a musical work)—which has prevailed for more than 350 years.

Recitative Style

A small group of noble intellectuals in Florence [which included the composers Jacopo Peri (1561-1633) and Giulio Caccini (ca. 1550-1618)] concerned themselves with reviving Greek tragedies, proceeding on the assumption that they had been sung or chanted originally in their entirety. They developed a new type of solo musical recitation that permitted the text to dominate, the music serving to heighten the meaning of the word. This was called *recitative,* a type of speech declamation set to sparse music, so created as to permit the text to be clearly intelligible. This became the trademark of the new musical practice, monody, which was characterized as *stile rappresentativo* (theatrical style). Pause for a moment to read the comments of Ottavio Rinucinni (1562-1621), librettist of the first opera *Dafne,* excerpted from the dedication of his second opera *Euridice* (1600), set to music by Jacopo Peri and first performed in the palace of the Florentine nobleman, Jacopo Corsi:

To the most Christian Maria Medici, Queen of France and Navarre.

It has been the opinion of many, most Christian Queen, that the ancient Greeks and Romans, in representing their tragedies upon the stage, sang them throughout. But until now this noble manner of recitation has been neither revived nor (to my knowledge) even attempted by anyone, and I used to believe that this was due to the imperfection of the modern music, by far inferior to the ancient. But the opinion thus formed was wholly driven from my mind by Messer Jacopo Peri, who, hearing of the intention of Signor Jacopo Corsi and myself, set to music with so much grace the fable of **Dafne** *(which I had written solely to make a simple trial of what the music of our age could do) that it gave pleasure beyond belief to the few who heard it.*

The musical genre that "gave pleasure beyond belief to the few who heard it" in 1597 continued, and continues, to give pleasure to those who are attuned to its message and not annoyed by its peculiar mannerisms. These early efforts, such as *Euridice,* were called *"rappresentazioni"* (representations) or *"favole pastorale"* (pastoral fables). Today we look back on those works and say that they were the beginning of *opera.* Mostly they consisted of solo sections in recitative style and some choral sections in simple homorhythmic or block-chord style.

Three aspects of those early works were to become significant for the whole period from roughly 1600-1750, a period that would eventually become known as the Baroque period. These were (1) a radical shift from polyphony to homophony with simple chords played on a keyboard instrument against a recitativelike melody, (2) a clear reliance on the triad as the generating force of the melodic line, and (3) a great attention to word painting. The last two aspects are, of course, not new; we have already encountered them at least to a degree in the sixteenth century.

The first aspect, the abandonment of polyphony for strict homophony, was a relatively short-lived novelty. Some aspects of polyphony, or at least a balance between polyphony and homophony, were restored by Claudio Monteverdi in his operas and madrigals, and, with this balance, genuine and powerful musical interest returned to infuse the new forms with artistic life. Monteverdi's masterpiece *Orfeo,* written only a few years after the works of Peri and Caccini, represents an enormous advance in terms of musical significance. In place of the excessive reliance on recitative and block-chord choruses, Monteverdi used a variety of vocal forms ranging from lilting dancelike arias to passionate ariosos, framed with instrumental pieces which effectively establish the mood of various scenes. Recitative was still used, but more sparingly and more effectively. Compare the excerpts of Caccini and Monteverdi (Example 9-1), noting the heightened effectiveness in word setting, and increased interest in harmonic and melodic aspects in the Monteverdi excerpt.

In later works, notably *The Coronation of Poppea,* Monteverdi shows even greater control of musical-dramatic expressiveness. Written for a public theater rather than a royal court, *Poppea* necessarily uses more modest forces, but uses them with telling effectiveness. The scenes are shorter, more contrasting,

EXAMPLE 9-1 (a) CACCINI: *Euridice*, RECITATIVE; (b) MONTEVERDI: *Orfeo*, RECITATIVE.

Baroque Style (1600–1750)

and the characters are more finely etched—Poppea is the first of a long line of utterly fascinating and delightfully wicked female characters who seem so effective for the medium of opera; indeed, the operatic stage is one place where it has seldom been necessary to argue for equal rights for women.

Monteverdi's concepts, if not his genius, were carried on by his pupils like Cavalli and by composers such as Carissimi, Luigi Rossi, and others. Carissimi carried operatic techniques over to sacred music in the form of the oratorio, which may be simply described as an opera without staging. *Jephthe* is one of the most effective and enduring of Carissimi's oratorios.

One of the significant stylistic developments of Monteverdi and his followers was in the aspect of texture. They frequently wrote for a combination of two high instruments (or voices) and one bass instrument or voice. The texture of two close high voices (often in thirds) and a separate low voice conforms to the distribution of tones suggested by the overtone series and perhaps for this reason tends to sound natural and effective. At the same time, it was an economical way to realize the three notes necessary for a triad. For whatever reason, this "trio texture" became a dominant textural type throughout most of the Baroque period, forming the basis for the trio sonatas of the Bologna school and other composers.

INSTRUMENTAL MUSIC

At the Church of St. Petronio in Bologna, it was the custom to augment the basic trio instrumentation with extra players on special occasions such as high holidays. The extra players or *ripieno* would join the trio players for loud sections and usually for easier sections, for it would be difficult to get good ensemble from this larger group on more difficult, fast passages. These passages were performed by the trio alone (with accompanying keyboard instrument). Eventually this alternation of solo (or *concertino*) and *tutti* (or *ripieno*) became not just a practical solution to a performance problem but an artistic convention.

The alternation of soloists and tutti, of loud and soft—i.e., of contrast in general—is often cited as a dominant characteristic of Baroque music. In this connection it is interesting to note that the two most popular instruments of the Baroque period, the organ and the harpsichord, were both equipped with two keyboards, and both had the possibility of striking changes in dynamics and timbre. By contrast, the most popular instrument of the sixteenth century was the lute, an instrument noted for its delicate, lovely sound but capable of only a limited range of dynamic and timbre contrast. Lute music did continue in the Baroque period, especially in France, but it was already in decline, and by the late eighteenth century its literature was virtually finished.

Music for organ or harpsichord was important in the sixteenth century with composers such as Cavazzoni and Cabezón, but it was at the beginning of the seventeenth century, with writers such as Sweelinck and Frescobaldi, that the great tradition of organ keyboard literature began its main continuous development. Though very important in Italy and in the Catholic service in the beginning of the century, the emphasis in organ music soon moved north in the middle of the seventeenth century to Germany and to Protestant composers such as Dietrich Buxtehude, Johann Pachelbel, and others. Most of the composers of organ music, like Buxtehude, were also active in writing sacred choral music.

CROSSCURRENTS IN THE MIDDLE SEVENTEENTH CENTURY

At this point in the middle of the seventeenth century, it is probably good to pause and take stock of the enormous variety of musical developments that were taking place. This is somewhat difficult to do, not only because the strands of development were so complicated and numerous, but also because, despite its intrinsic interest and historical importance, surprisingly little music of this period is known through present-day performances. The middle of the seventeenth century saw

Claudio Monteverdi (1567–1643)

■ The son of an Italian doctor, Monteverdi was born in Cremona where, at an early age, he became a chorister in the cathedral and began the study of music, including organ, the viol, singing, and composition. His first composition was published at the age of 16, and thereafter his star was to ascend as he became renowned as a composer and singer of madrigals, the imitative vocal works so popular at the time. He entered the orchestra of the Duke of Mantua about 1590, in whose service he remained until the Duke's death in 1612, becoming director of music. During this period he was to travel widely with his patron's court, compose many madrigals, and become acquainted with one of the first operas produced, probably Peri's *Euridice* in 1600. Seven years later his first opera, *La Favola d'Orfeo* (*The Fable of Orpheus*) was premiered and became an immediate success. This landmark work saw the wedding of the simple, archaic, declamatory style of the earliest operas with a more expressively dramatic mixture of melodies and choruses, utilizing contrapuntal techniques, brisk modulations, chromatic harmonies, and coloristic orchestral effects. This long-lived work has been revived a number of times with marked success.

Then followed many fruitful years highlighted by his appointment as master of music of the Republic of Venice in 1613 at age 46, a position he was to hold until his death. In Venice, successful and secure, he composed a vast array of masses and motets, madrigals, chansons, and various operas, only two of which are preserved, *L'Incoronazione di Poppea* (*The Coronation of Poppea*) and *Il Ritorno d'Ulisse* (*The Return of Ulysses*).

Although the music of the early founders of opera, the Florentine Camerata, is important for its historical significance, that of Claudio Monteverdi lives today because of its dramatic intensity and expressiveness, unorthodox dissonance, striking progression, abrupt contrasts, and vivid instrumental coloration. Monteverdi imbued his music with a dramatic intensity that reflected the spirit of the Baroque while adhering to the contrapuntal practices of the past. In so doing he created masterpieces that some four hundred years later are a part of the standard repertoire, earning for him the title "founder of modern opera."

Following its inception as an intimate spectacle for a select few in 1600, opera became a grand display requiring spacious theaters characterized by ornateness and elegance, where the drama on stage was matched in brilliance of array by the wealthy patrons, as illustrated in this presentation of Cesti's opera, Il Pomo d'Oro (The Golden Apple), for the imperial court in Vienna in 1667.

parallel developments in all the significant media and forms of the time. Let us list some of the more important of these:

Media	Forms
Secular vocal music	Operas, secular cantatas
Sacred vocal music	Cantatas, oratorios, masses, motets
Instrumental music	Solo sonatas, trio sonatas, concertos, concerti grossi, suites
Keyboard music	Dance pieces, variations, preludes, fugues, toccatas, fantasias

Not only was there great variety of media and forms, but also, for the first time in music history, there was really significant development of different national schools. In the sixteenth century one could still speak of an "international music"; it was difficult to tell the musical language of an Italian from a Netherlander except for very subtle nuances and tendencies. In the seventeenth century a consciousness of national stylistic differences began to become important, and is worth examining.

France

In France the court of Louis XIV provided magnificent opportunities for the development of music, and a young ambitious man named Jean Baptiste Lully (1632–1687) was quick to seize upon them. It mattered little that he was actually born Giovanni Battista Lulli in Italy; he soon learned to write music that was "more French than the French." The predilection for the dance and the proverbial "douceur Français" (French sweet-

Like his French compatriot, Lully, the painter Jean Antoine Watteau (1664-1721) reflected a dominant spirit of the Baroque in a langourous, sentimental style—here exemplified in Mezzetin, *a characteristic emotional expression executed in a marvelously direct and convincing manner.*

England

England enjoyed one of its periodic outbursts of musical glory in the latter half of the seventeenth century with the works of Henry Purcell (1659-1695), whose operas, sacred music, instrumental music, and keyboard works somehow manage to combine Italianate melody with a typically English sense of refinement and, at the same time, of adventure.

Germany

As we have indicated, the focus of musical development in Germany seemed to be in the church, and the music of the seventeenth-century German composers could be characterized in general as somewhat thicker and more complex in texture and somewhat heavier and more somber in character than the Italian music, although any such comparison obviously is subject to many individual exceptions. It is probably not too far-fetched to compare this characteristic difference in the music of Germany and Italy to characteristic differences in the weather of the two countries. One only has to spend a week or so in each country to be aware of the striking climatic differences, and yet it is still possible to have an occasional gloomy day in Italy and a gloriously sunny day in middle Germany.

The Suite

Example 9-2 provides us an opportunity to study one of the most important forms of the Baroque period, the *suite* form. In the Renaissance it had been the custom to write dance pairs such as the *passamezzo* and *saltarello*, or the *pavane* and *galliard*. Now in the Baroque period it became customary to have a group of four dances, played together as an integrated unit, and called a *suite* or *sonata da camera*.

The suite was, in effect, a compendium of national dance styles. The *allemande* was a German dance, usually in quadruple meter, and usually with a fairly slow or moderate tempo. The *sarabande* derived from a Spanish dance type. Though the original dance was fast and lascivious, by the time it had been assimilated into art music it had become a slow dance in triple meter, usually with an accent on the second beat. The *courante* was a French dance, or sometimes an Italian dance, and in

ness) found its quintessential expression in Lully's ballets and operas.

Italy

Opera continued to be a dominant mode of expression in Italy, and it is here that the Italian love for cantabile melody found unique expression, especially in the arias of Italian operas which always serve to show the composer's melodic gifts and the singers' vocal gifts more than they do to advance the story line of the plot. In Neapolitan opera the arias became stereotyped and one could almost predict that there would be one or two examples in each opera of such types as love arias (or duets), slumber arias, rage arias, etc., many of these in the standard da capo (A-B-A) form. Italian love of melody is also reflected in the instrumental music of the seventeenth century, especially in such writers as Corelli, Torelli, Vivaldi, and others at the end of the seventeenth century and beginning of the eighteenth.

EXAMPLE 9-2 BACH: *French Suite No. 5 in G Major.* (a) ALLEMANDE, MEASURES 1–13; (b) COURANTE, MEASURES 1–4; (c) SARABANDE, MEASURES 1–4; (d) GAVOTTE, MEASURES 1–4; (e) BOURRÉE I, MEASURES 1–3; (f) BOURRÉE II, MEASURES 1–3; (g) GIGUE, MEASURES 1–4.

(a) Allemande

(b) Courante

(c) Sarabande

(d) Gavotte

(e) Bourée I

148 Styles of Music

(f) Bourée II

(g) Gigue

keeping with the word (meaning "running"), it was usually a fast tempo in triple meter. The closing *gigue* was nothing more than an Irish "jig" marked by a lively tempo and written in a meter such as 6/8 or 12/8.

Between the sarabande and the gigue, composers sometimes inserted various types of optional dances. In Example 9-2 these optional dances consist of a gavotte and two bourrées; other optional dance types were the minuet, passepied, loure, and others. Occasionally the entire suite was prefaced with a prelude or an overture. For an example of the use of a minuet in a dance suite, see Example 9-3 excerpted from Bach's *French Suite in D Minor*. This minuet is a forerunner of the Haydn minuet (which we will discuss at the beginning of Chapter 10). The Bach minuet, like the later Haydn minuet, was written for a keyboard instrument, the harpsichord. This minuet occurs as the second of two appearing in a suite in D minor, the first of six suites from a collection composed about 1725, called *Six French Suites*. It is in triple meter and ABA form, as is characteristic of minuets, with the middle section usually being called a *trio*. Note the rhythmic pattern of the opening two measures and, as you listen to the work, be aware of subsequent uses of the same rhythm in unifying the piece.

THEORETICAL DEVELOPMENTS
Beneath the differences in character of the various media, forms, and national schools of the seventeenth century was a common ground of development in the basic musical grammar. This development has several related aspects. The most significant is the clear establishment of *functional major-minor tonality*. We might explain this most simply by saying that now music was governed not only by the triad, but also by certain conventional, goal-directed progressions of triads—in particular, progressions such as tonic to dominant and dominant back to tonic. The goal of progression and the clear center of a work was the tonic and its triad.

To recapitulate the developments in tonality and harmony to this point, we might say that early polyphony was marked by an emphasis on the relation of one line to another with chords as a more or less incidental by-product. Gradually, especially in the fifteenth and sixteenth centuries, triads became not just by-products but generative forces in their own right. There was little standardization of harmonic progressions except in some instances, such as cadential formulas. It was the unique accomplishment of seventeenth-century composers that they achieved a highly effective organization of those chord progressions. This organization may be seen not only in the movement of one chord to the next, but also, and perhaps even more significantly, in the movement from one large section of music to the next. Coincident with the organization of tonally directed chord progressions was the reduction of the modes to major and minor.

Clear and obvious tonal organization provided a stable framework of expectations. Even though composers may at some times have deliberately delayed or circumvented these for special effect, nevertheless the sense of directed motion was almost never completely lost in this music.

The Baroque harpsichord was not only a musical instrument but usually a highly attractive, ornate piece of furniture.

EXAMPLE 9-3 BACH: *French Suite in D Minor*, MINUET II, (a) MEASURES 1–8 AND (b) 17–24.

150 Styles of Music

Arcangelo Corelli (1653–1713)

■ Arcangelo Corelli, important violinist and composer of the mid-Baroque, was to lead an exemplary life as compared to such later unfortunates as Mozart, Beethoven, and Schubert, for example. Little is known about his early life up to age 21, except that he was trained as a violinist in Bologna, traveled to Germany and probably Paris, and settled in Rome, becoming a violinist at the French Church in 1675. Thereafter he played in a theater orchestra and in 1685, having won the respect of powerful Church officials, took up residence in the palace of the Cardinal Ottoboni, where he became greatly admired as composer, violinist, and teacher.

His position secure and his fame farflung, he led a contented life, conducting weekly concerts—attended by the cream of Roman society, including Queen Christiana of Sweden at the time she resided in Rome—composing the comparatively small body of works on which his fame rests, enjoying the friendship of his important contemporaries in music and art, and teaching some of the upcoming leaders of a new school of violin playing. Being the virtuoso that he was, he attracted outstanding students who were eager to copy his lyrical style and superb technique, he being the first to systematize bowing and one of the earliest to use double stops and violin chords.

Although his compositional output was limited, he developed compositional practices in his *sonatas da camera* and his *concerti grossi*, which foreshadowed the later sonatas and concertos of Bach and Handel, the latter having become acquainted with Corelli in Rome in his youth.

His music, all instrumental and contrapuntal in nature, exploited the violin's capacity for lyric expression, being generally characterized by compactness of form, imitative textures, melodic sweep and flow, and rhythmic inventiveness. This innovative composer who happily enjoyed success and security throughout most of his life left a sizable estate including a valuable collection of paintings. More importantly, he left a mark on music and musicians of far greater value.

Baroque Style (1600–1750) 151

Henry Purcell (1659–1695)

■ In the brief span of 36 years, Henry Purcell was to become one of the foremost English composers, the last of a grand tradition which had seen England rise to the fore among the musical nations of the world. Not until some two centuries later was there to be another native school of English composers that would regain a similar position of international prominence in a world largely dominated by the Continental Europeans.

The facts of Purcell's life are remarkably few and spotty, despite his importance. He was a natural genius, the son of a gentleman of the Chapel Royal and Choirmaster at Westminster Abbey. It is believed that he became a choir boy in the Chapel Royal at age six, where he received training and sang until his voice changed about 1673, at which time he was appointed assistant "Keeper of the King's Wind Instruments" without pay, subsisting on an allowance granted to choristers after change of voice.

He moved up rapidly, becoming first composer for the King's Band, then organist at Westminster Abbey, next at the Chapel Royal, and "Keeper of Instruments" and organ builder in 1683. (In the meantime he had written a number of choral works including *Ayres* (*Airs*), songs and music for the theater, and had acquired a wife.) That year was to see him emerge as composer-publisher of his *Sonatas of III Parts*, modeled after "the most fam'd Italian masters," so his preface reveals, and designed to acquaint his countrymen with their art, so dynamic, instrumentally conceived, and reflecting the new harmonic style and operatic innovations.

He mastered the art of song and choral writing, and of setting the English language, and poured forth tomes of music characterized by great vigor, freshness, and tunefulness, ranging from popular songs, catches, and rounds (often settings of ribald texts reflecting the spirit of the times) to colossal, religious, contrapuntal choruses of great breadth and grandeur.

In the last five years of his life he turned his attention to the theater, writing incidental music for plays and one opera only, *Dido and Aeneas*, a work presented in 1689 which still plays regularly, being a favorite of opera workshops in this country. One can only conjecture about what might have been had Purcell lived a long life, but from the success of his one operatic attempt it seems proper to assume that with a few additional years he might have established a tradition of opera in English, a tradition which was not to become established until this century.

Different writers on music may place the locus of development of functional tonality slightly earlier or later than we have, or they may place less emphasis on chordal aspects and more on melodic aspects, but all agree on the enormous importance this development had for the future course of music. Indeed, the other two developments we wish to examine in the seventeenth century, namely, the development of greater *textural strength and variety* and of greater *formal breadth and coherence,* may be regarded as vertical and horizontal outgrowths of the development of functional tonality. In texture, the stability of functional tonality provides a background against which composers can move contrapuntal lines without being excessively concerned with momentary clashes or dissonances between parts, especially inner parts. The outer parts, the two-voice framework, are of primary importance even in works such as fugues written for three, four, or five equal parts. In form, functional tonality makes it possible to organize relations between large sections and, therefore, to sustain a sense of interest and direction in a work of far larger dimensions than was previously possible.

Along with these three primary developments, there are other developments of interest. One of these is the development of the family of modern string instruments (violin, viola, cello), replacing the earlier viol family, and the development or improvement of wind, brass, and keyboard instruments. Another was the influence of dance music upon many forms of both instrumental and vocal music, which can be seen most clearly in the use of periodic, metrically regulated rhythms.

BACH AND HANDEL

As we leave the seventeenth century and enter the eighteenth, we encounter the monumental accomplishments of the two giants of the late Baroque, Johann Sebastian Bach (1685–1750) and George Frederick Handel (1685–1759). Until surprisingly recently, most of the music we have been discussing in this chapter would have been cavalierly dismissed as "pre-Bach," and therefore primitive and generally not worthy of serious study and performance. Fortunately modern scholarship and recording technology have combined to correct this attitude, and people are not only listening to this music, but there has been a great interest in its performance by amateurs and professionals alike.

None of this can diminish the greatness of Handel and Bach. To conclude this chapter, we shall seek to compare certain aspects of their musical style. Manfred Bukofzer has said that Handel represents the *synthesis* of national styles, Bach the *fusion* of national styles.* By this, he means that Handel, not unlike Orlando di Lasso in the sixteenth century, was able to write in several different styles, infusing each with his own genius and originality. Bach, on the other hand, though he certainly studied and admired his predecessors and contemporaries in other countries, did not so much write in their style as he did absorb their techniques into his own musical rhetoric.

There are other significant differences between these two men. Handel was a widely traveled and cosmopolitan figure. He achieved his first fame as a composer of opera, and opera remained important throughout his lifetime; even his other works are usually imbued with a dramatic sense. Bach never ventured beyond the borders of his native Germany and was little known even inside Germany during his lifetime, except perhaps for his knowledge of organs and his prodigious skill as an organist and improviser. He served most of his life as organist and director of music in several churches, culminating in St. Thomas in Leipzig. The focal point of his creative work was always religious music—cantatas, passions, organ music, etc.; even his secular works could be said to be imbued with a religious aspect. He once wrote that even an exercise in figured bass should be written for the glory of God.

Certain specific stylistic differences between these two composers grow out of these general considerations. Handel's dramatic nature is expressed frequently in bold melodic leaps, in powerful dotted rhythms, and occasionally in unusual harmonic progressions. Though a master of counterpoint, especially between outer voices, he does not show as strong an interest in writing extensive complex passages in pure polyphonic imitative writing. His choruses in his masterwork

---

*Manfred Bukofzer, *Music in the Baroque Era* (New York: Norton, 1947).

Johann Sebastian Bach (1685–1750)

■ The life of Johann Sebastian Bach was devoted to serving that early venerable patron of the arts, the Church. For more than a century and a half before J. S. Bach was born, the illustrious Bach family of Germany had supplied court and church musicians to Thuringia, and continued to do so well into the nineteenth century. No single family ever figured so prominently in the field of music, and none produced a more illustrious son.

J. S. Bach, true to the family tradition, began the study of music at an early age, studying the violin and viola with his father until he was orphaned at the age of ten. At that time he moved in with an older brother, continuing to prepare himself to assume the family vocation while furthering his general education in the local school. Because of economic necessity he enrolled as a chorister in St. Michael's Church in Lüneburg at age 15, studied organ and composition, and three years later began his professional career as church organist at St. Boniface in Arnstadt. The first of his many troubles with patrons began when the headstrong youth, according to the local authorities, refused to rehearse the choir, confused the congregation with his unusual hymn accompaniments and prolonged preludes, and, worst of all, "caused a strange maiden to be invited into the choir loft and let her make music there." Thus we are introduced to his cousin, Maria Barbara, whom he was to marry in 1707 after moving on to his first major post as organist of St. Blasius in Mülhausen. The next year, his fame growing faster than his income, he entered the service of the Duke of Weimar for the more lucrative position of court chamber musician and organist. There he remained for nine years, becoming recognized as an organ virtuoso and producing some of his greatest works—most of the great organ preludes, fugues, and toccatas.

Failing to be promoted to court conductor, he requested permission of the Duke to take another post. His request being denied, he protested, was arrested, and later "unfavorably discharged." In 1717, after this humiliating incident, he accepted the appointment of court conductor for Prince Leopold of Anhalt-Cöthen, a lover of instrumental music. In the five years there, Bach created such well-known orchestral works as the *Brandenburg Concertos,* and the compositions for keyboard including the *English* and *French Suites,* the *Well-Tempered Clavier, Part I,* and *Two-* and *Three-Part Inventions.* His musical style was established, a culmination of the contrapuntal practices of an earlier day which exemplified incredible technical mastery, spacious ornamental design, awesome grandeur, and powerful emotion.

Following the death of his wife in 1720, he married a young singer, Anna Magdalena, who was to bear him no less than thirteen children, his first wife having borne seven.

His fame at its height, he moved to Leipzig as cantor of St. Thomas, one of the most important music posts in Germany. There he stayed for the remainder of his life, composing, teaching, supervising the training of musicians for the city's two principal churches, and presiding at the organ. His responsibilities and squabbles with his superiors were many, and one wonders how, with such an exacting schedule and such a plethora of irksome duties and petty problems, he was able to produce such a flood of music: some 265 church cantatas, six motets, five masses, the *Mass in B Minor* being the most famous, four passions including the monumental *St. Matthew Passion,* three oratorios, one of which is the beautiful *Christmas Oratorio,* and keyboard masterpieces such as the *Goldberg Variations,* and *Clavier-Ubung (Keyboard Studies), Well-Tempered Clavier, Part II, The Musical Offering,* and *The Art of the Fugue.*

In his own time Bach was a relatively little-known church organist and composer. Now it is universally recognized that "the old wig" (as his sons affectionately called him), the devout churchman, dedicated family man, and industrious composer, devoted his life and his immense creative talents to constructing masterpieces excelled by none. No musician's name is better known, none more respected.

George Frederick Handel (1685-1759)

■ The twin giants of the late Baroque were both German and born the same year—George Frederick Handel and J. S. Bach. Although the career of Bach was generally confined to Church music and to his own country, that of Handel was to be identified with opera primarily and to become international in scope.

Handel was the son of a successful barber-surgeon of Halle who opposed a musical career. Carrying out his father's wishes, he began law study at the University of Halle in 1702, but withdrew the next year and departed for Hamburg to embark on a musical career.

Attracted to opera Handel obtained a position as violinist in the Hamburg Opera, where he became enamored of the Italian operatic style. He went to Italy and became thoroughly immersed in its music, befriended the leading composers and the best of society, and composed operas and oratorios that established him as a gifted young genius.

He returned to Germany in 1710, becoming Kapellmeister to the Elector of Hanover, a position from which he absented himself on two different occasions to go to England for the production of three new operas which were successfully received. Seeing a new world to conquer, and being ever alert to fertile financial opportunity, young Handel settled in England, was pensioned by the Queen, became a naturalized citizen, and lived out the remaining turbulent years. By a strange quirk of fate, he again became associated with the Elector of Hamburg, who became King George I upon the death of Queen Anne, and who, bearing no grudge, increased his pension.

From 1718-1720 he was musical director for the Duke of Chandos, for whom he wrote his first English oratorio, *Esther*, and the famed "Chandos Anthems," the beginnings of a series of large-scale works which were to further the grand choral tradition begun by Purcell.

He returned to his first love, the operatic stage, in 1720, when he was appointed one of three directors of the newly founded Royal Academy of Music, an institution dedicated to the production of Italian opera and backed by a group of wealthy nobles headed by the King himself. Handel at last had the opportunity to indulge Italian opera to his heart's content. These were amazing years highlighted by incredible bursts of creativity (he could compose a complete opera in a few weeks), monumental professional battles with prima donnas and rival composers (in which his fiery temper and overbearing nature were vividly paraded), and constant jockeying to stay in the public eye, despite the declining success of his works. It must be admitted that his personality often left much to be desired, but on the whole this commanding, independent spirit was good-humored, warm, and witty.

The Royal Academy lost its audience and Handel attempted to revive it, but to no avail. "Opera was dead!" or at least had been dealt a telling blow by a popular work called *The Beggar's Opera* (libretto by John Gay) attributed to Handel's rival, Pepusch. By parodying French opera and attacking high society, the pimps, pickpockets, and whores of *The Beggar's Opera* won the day with their naughty ballads in the language of the streets and with their insolence, cleverness, and charm.

Handel's life was in a shambles—he was hopelessly in debt and facing a debtor's prison when at age 52 he suffered a stroke and a mental collapse. These misfortunes might have felled a lesser man, but not Handel. He went abroad to recuperate and returned to reach a higher pinnacle of success in a different musical genre, the oratorio, the most popular of which is the immortal *Messiah*. Curiously enough, this oratorio, composed in twenty-four days by a German composer of Italian operas for a first performance in Ireland, was to become the most performed work in the repertoire of English choral music. Handel had found his forte and thereafter great choral masterpieces issued forth almost to the end, masterpieces of vocal style which along with his operas, cantatas, suites, sonatas, and concerti grossi earned him the supreme accolade of Beethoven—"He was the greatest of us all."

Although Handel's father intended for his son to make a career in law, this was not to be, as the precocious youth soon turned to music, finding ways to further this consuming interest.

Messiah, for example, are almost all a blend of polyphonic and homophonic writing.

Bach's melodies will usually be seen to consist of a striking "head" motive followed by a spinning-forth section. His rhythms are enormously varied but always vital and incisive. Whereas Handel usually painted his musical canvases with large gestures and sought to capture the essence of a particular emotion in the style of a whole movement, Bach frequently concentrated his expression into a single motive—representing death, for example, with a poignant diminished-seventh descent. A far greater proportion of Bach's output was devoted to works such as the fugues, especially *The Art of the Fugue* and *The Musical Offering,* which were designed to explore every possible aspect of the art of polyphonic writing. Both writers borrowed from themselves and from other composers, but where Handel was frequently content merely to appropriate a work without change, in a manner that today would probably earn him a lawsuit for plagiarism, Bach rarely took a passage from his earlier works or the works of others without reworking it to discover different facets and possibilities inherent in the musical material.

With Bach and Handel we have reached another stable point in the stylistic development of music. Indeed, at the risk of oversimplifying, we might note that the development of musical style frequently seems to consist of alternations of periods of stylistic instability and ferment with periods of stability and consolidation. On a smaller scale, this trend may also be seen in the life of an individual composer; although here it is usual to claim that the pattern is rather more a three-stage development consisting of an apprentice period, a journeyman period, and a master period. Helpful as these abstractions may be, they should never be allowed to substitute for an open exploration of an individual work of art.

Many characteristic features of Handel's musical style may be heard in the opening chorus of his *Brockes Passion* (Example 9-4), named after the eighteenth-century poet whose dramatic text on the suffering and death of Christ was set to music by no fewer than twenty Baroque composers.

The text of this chorus is given below in a translation that seeks to be literal rather than literary, in order to point out Handel's treatment of the text.

To free me from the chains of sins
My God was chained.
To heal me of the burden of my wounds
He let himself be wounded.

The orchestra, consisting for this movement of violins in unison and continuo, opens with a striking introduction marked by three of Handel's stylistic "fingerprints"—vigorous dotted rhythms, powerful melodic leaps, and (in the first five

EXAMPLE 9-4 HANDEL: *Brockes Passion*, "Von den Stricken meiner Sünden" ("Of the bonds of my sin"), measures 1–18.

1. Mich vom Strik-ke mei-ner Sün-den zu ent-bin-den, wird mein Gott ge-bun- -
2. Es muss, mei-ner Sün-den Flek-ken zu be-dek-ken, eig - nes Blut ihn far - -

Baroque Style (1600–1750) 157

measures) simple, strong harmonic movement back and forth between tonic and dominant (Example 9-4).

Naturally not all of these traits appear in every page of Handel, nor are they the exclusive property of Handel, but when they occur together, as they do here, the evidence is very strong that we are probably confronted with the works of this colorful and powerful musical personality. The wide leaps (sixths, octaves, even tenths) in the introduction may be explained in terms of their dramatic, emotional, "word-painting" function. In a strictly musical sense, however, we should point out that these leaps may also be explained as coming from the use of idiomatic instrumental writing (leaps that are very difficult to sing are relatively easy to play on a stringed instrument). They may also be explained by pointing out that the establishment of clear-cut harmonic progressions and functional tonality provides a solid background against which composers can be more adventurous in the melodic sense.

The thematic material of the introduction is now heard in two statements, first by the solo soprano and then by the solo alto. Following this, the basses take up the melody, but as they do, Handel adds the full chorus in a powerful block-chord harmonization of the theme. We might ask why Handel does this. Although we have no clear direct evidence from the master himself, study of other works by Handel and other contemporary composers suggests two possible answers. The first is Handel's marvelous ear for sonority and concern with projection of the text. It could be that a bass solo alone could not give the sense of ringing affirmation that Handel might have wanted at this point. A second possible explanation is the tendency to avoid three successive similar statements. This is one of countless examples that may be found not only in the works of Handel, but of other composers and other periods.

Returning to the chorus, Handel cadences on the dominant D minor and has a short four-measure orchestral interlude before beginning the second part of the work. In contrast to the essentially diatonic writing of the first part, there is some use of chromaticism in this section (Example 9-5). It would be tempting to link this chromaticism to word painting, since it occurs at the point of the text in which the word "wounds" (*Eiterbeulen*) appears. The only problem is that the same music is used for a second verse and this same chromaticism then occurs with the words, "Yes, it will give me eternal life." Actually this very fact reveals something of the creative personality of Handel. He was rarely overly concerned with minute details of text or music, but rather always more conscious of the overall effect.

We could contrast Handel's setting of this chorus with a setting of exactly the same text in the *St. John Passion* of J. S. Bach (Example 9-6), and we would find that Bach is much

EXAMPLE 9-5 HANDEL: *Brockes Passion*, "VON DEN STRICKEN MEINER SÜNDEN" ("OF THE BONDS OF MY SIN"), MEASURES 32–35.

158 Styles of Music

EXAMPLE 9-6 BACH: *St. John Passion*, "VON DEN STRICKEN MEINER SÜNDEN" ("OF THE BONDS OF MY SIN"), MEASURES 1–17.

Baroque Style (1600–1750)

more concerned with smaller details and that the work is more tightly knit in terms of concentration on imitative counterpoint, motivic development, and harmonic details. Much more complex in form and structure, the Bach work is unified by a melodic line in the bass that is repeated (with some variations and with some modulation to other key centers) several times throughout the work. Bach's setting is scored for two oboes, continuo, and alto solo.

Instead of discussing this work in any greater detail, we would urge you to listen to another masterpiece of Baroque music, Bach's *Brandenburg Concerto No. 4*, which shows us another facet of the musical style of the period. Bach wrote the six Brandenburg concertos while he was engaged as court musician in Anhalt-Cöthen. In all likelihood, he never heard the works performed during his lifetime. Each concerto is written for a different combination of instruments, and the

EXAMPLE 9-7 BACH: *Brandenburg Concerto No. 4*, FIRST MOVEMENT, MEASURES 1–21.

160 Styles of Music

Concerto No. 4 (Example 9-7), which we shall briefly consider, is written for a concertino group of two flutes (recorders) and solo violin, and a ripieno group of two violins (I and II), violas, cello, bass, and continuo (harpsichord). One of the most fascinating aspects of the work is the way in which these forces are deployed in a variety of textures. The very opening is characterized by a sustained note in one flute, arpeggio figures in the other flute, and short chordal punctuations in the ripieno and solo violin. This texture alternates with another in which the two flutes move in parallel thirds against chords in the continuo alone. After twelve measures the texture thickens somewhat both vertically (that is, there is more activity in the middle of the texture) and horizontally (that is, there is more continuous rhythmic activity; in effect a continuous motion of eighths is heard in some parts and sixteenths in others). At bar 23, the same sequence of alternations of textural types begins again. Repeated hearings of measures 1-23 of this piece can sensitize the ear to these changes of texture, which, in this piece and many others, are just as important as details of melody, rhythm, or harmony (9-7).

Later sections of the piece continue to emphasize these textural types. In addition, in some sections, such as measure

83, the solo violin is herd in arpeggio figurations against simple chordal punctuations in the continuo. The high point of rhythmic activity is reached in measure 186, approximately the middle of the movement, with the thiry-second-note scale passages in the solo violin. The slow movement (Example 9-8) presents many contrasts to the first movement. These are summarized in the table below.

The closing movement, marked *presto,* alternates fairly extended fugal sections for the entire ensemble (Example 9-9) with sections for the concertino or virtuoso sections for the solo violin. The light character of the two outer movements provides a symmetrical frame to the eloquent seriousness of the middle movement.

SUMMARY

We might summarize some of the principal stylistic characteristics of the Baroque period at this point. As was the case with the stylistic summary at the end of the chapter on Renaissance music, the reader is cautioned not to try to find each one of these characteristics in every work of the period, and yet the characteristics mentioned here should provide a frame of reference for the identification of most works of this period. In a sense, a list of stylistic characteristics such as this can be regarded somewhat as a list of clues in a detective story. A single clue by itself may not be significant, but several clues together may be. If you hear just one aspect of a composition—for example, the fact that it is in a steady triple meter—this will not be sufficient evidence for you to categorize it stylistically. However, if you hear several characteristics and can locate them on a particular list of stylistic features, you can be reasonably sure that the work belongs to that particular style period.

Comparison of Two Movements of the Brandenburg Concerto No. 4

	First Movement	Second Movement
Tempo	Allegro	Andante
Meter	3/8, but the virtually constant grouping of two bars creates the effect of compound duple meter	3/4—i.e., simple triple meter
Tonality	Major	Minor
	(In both movements there is naturally some modulation to related key areas and modes)	
Dynamics	No changes indicated	Some alternation of *piano* and *forte* indicated
Closing cadence	Perfect authentic creates definite conclusion	Phrygian (half cadence) creates impression of moving on, suspense, lack of clear ending
Thematic material	Several motives used throughout	Neighbor tone figure dominates the movement

EXAMPLE 9-8 BACH: *Brandenburg Concerto No. 4,* SECOND MOVEMENT, MEASURES 1–7.

EXAMPLE 9-9 BACH: *Brandenburg Concerto No. 4,* LAST MOVEMENT, MEASURES 1–6.

Baroque Style (1600–1750)

This delightful cartoon depicts Handel playing the flute, Bach in the garb of a Protestant priest, and Tartini with a violin, as well as Quanz, Gluck, and Jomelli.

Style Characteristics of Late Baroque Music

Rhythm: Both duple and triple meter are used in various tempi. However, once a tempo is established it will usually be maintained throughout the movement without change. (An exception is the *rubato* rhythm or freedom of recitative.) Though syncopations may occasionally be used, they rarely obscure the strong, ongoing sense of pulse which becomes a strong characteristic. Opening (head) motives are usually marked by strong, characteristic rhythmic patterns. Other sections may consist of flowing even-note patterns. Usually a strong sense of rhythmic drive and goal direction is present, even in slow movements.

Melody: Major and minor modes are clearly established with only rare allusions to church modes. Melodies are usually diatonic, but in some works chromaticism is used for affective or emotional purposes or for musical variety. The increasing importance of instrumental music is reflected in idiomatic melodies with larger range and more use of leaps. This is also true to a degree of vocal music. Interpenetration of vocal and instrumental idioms is evident. Written out or improvised ornamentation is used, especially in slow movements. Melodies are carefully organized, sometimes with sequential passages.

Harmony: Triads as well as seventh chords are used in theory as well as in practice. Harmony is regarded as the generator of musical events rather than as a by-product. Preeminence of root movement by fifths and frequent use of harmonic formulas or standardized progressions such as I-ii-V-I are hallmarks of a fully developed sense of functional tonality. Harmonic rhythm of one chord per beat in moderate tempo is characteristic.

Texture: A strong two-voice framework is the standard structural basis. Sometimes, as in a trio sonata, the top line will actually be shared by two lines. The middle of the texture may be filled in by continuo chords, other accompanimental lines, or other important voices, but the polarity of the outer voices is always apparent.

Timbre: There is an important development of instrumental music including members of modern string sections and most modern wind instruments except for clarinets. Contrast in terms of instrumental groups (concertino and ripieno) and in terms of dynamics (terraced dynamics) is important. The continuo (bass instrument such as cello, gamba, bass, bassoon, etc., and keyboard instrument such as organ or harpischord) is an essential ingredient in much vocal and instrumental music.

Forms: There is relative equality in importance of vocal and instrumental forms. Actually most vocal forms have some instrumental participation. Vocal forms include opera, cantata, oratorio, mass, and motet. Instrumental forms include concerto grosso, solo concerto, sonata, suite, overture, and prelude.

We began Chapter 8 with the year 800 and the Emperor Charlemagne, and we close this chapter in 1750 with the reign of Frederick the Great of Prussia. The former was the first great uniter of Europe, and the latter was one of the strongest princes of the small countries that emerged in the 1700's.

One of Bach's sons was a court musician for Frederick the Great, and in 1748 father Bach was invited to Frederick's palace in Potsdam. The King, an avid amateur musician himself, delighted in showing Bach his wonderful collection of instruments. Then he presented Bach with a theme upon which he asked him to improvise a six-part fugue. Bach improvised a three-part fugue and a four-part fugue, but was unable to supply the requested six-part fugue. Later, he returned to Leipzig and wrote out not only the six-part fugue, but also a whole collection of canons based upon the King's subject which became known as *The Musical Offering.*

We might take this as being typical of the Baroque attitude toward music in general, an attitude in which the structural element is highly important. Baroque music was not without feeling, but mere feeling was never allowed to replace a strong sense of craftsmanship and structure. On the other hand, Bach's sons were already committed to the new ideal of the coming Rococo period, in which feeling and emotions became foremost. They point us toward that next period in musical history, the Classical period, in which an almost miraculous synthesis of these two tendencies was to be reached.

10 Classical Style (1750–1825)

It has been said that the two opposing spirits in music are those exemplified by the terms "Classic" and "Romantic." In a very general sense, Classic music is exemplified by formalism, traditionalism, abstractness, impersonality, with emphasis on clarity, balance, and preciseness of form and technique, whereas Romantic music appeals more to the emotions by evoking subjective responses through emphasis on dramatic and descriptive effects, widely contrasting musical content and mood, fantasy, emotionalism, and invention. In fact, most music contains elements of both, and it is not crucial to the enjoyment of music for the perceiver to conceive of it in either of these terms. But since it will become apparent that composers do tend (and have tended) to favor one or the other, and in so doing become representative of a particular musical style and period, it does prove helpful for understanding to delve into the musical manifestations that differentiate these two points of view.

Consider first so-called "classic music," which has several meanings: art music as contrasted to folk or popular music; music of an earlier day whose masterpieces continue to be performed; contemporary works generally patterned after earlier great works; music of the Classical period. We shall concern ourselves with the last of these, a label used to designate that body of music, instrumental and vocal, composed about the second half of the eighteenth century. Some authors designate this time span as approximately 1750–1800 and others as 1750–1827. Such dating is imprecise, to say the least, since there is no abrupt, clearly discernible change from one to another period or style, nor is the rate or degree of change the same in all countries.

To gain a general impression of the tunefulness, elegance, and grace so typical of the music of this period we will pause briefly to consider two compositions by the twin giants of the periods, Joseph Haydn (1732–1809) and Wolfgang Amadeus Mozart (1756–1791).

The first work we will sample is the second movement of a piece for piano, Haydn's *Sonata No. 10 in G major,* which is cast in a minuet mold, a favorite of an earlier day. (Recall the discussion of the Bach minuet in the previous chapter.)

Elegantly poised at the two-manual harpsichord, popular keyboard instrument of the 16th through the 18th centuries, the French gentlewoman epitomizes the style, delicacy, refinement, and grace characteristic of much of the music of Haydn and Mozart.

The minuet (French, *menuet*) became popular in French courts in the seventeenth and eighteenth centuries. It is associated with the elegance and grace of court life and the festivity of the period. To a great extent the minuet of the French became obsolete after the revolution, even though some Viennese successors of Mozart and his contemporary, Haydn, composed minuets as late as the early nineteenth century.

The minuet is actually two minuets, as the Haydn piece suggests. It consists of an opening dance (minuet), usually divided into two similar sections, and a definitive close. A trio (actually a second, contrasting minuet) often follows, as happens here. After the trio the first minuet is usually restated. (These pieces were *not* as a rule composed to accompany dancing as such, but more to be performed and heard.)

Acquaint yourself with the excerpts (minuet and trio) in Example 10-1 and then listen to the entire movement, noting the triple meter, the rhythmic repetition, and that the contrast between minuet and trio is achieved, generally, by change of rhythm patterns and texture.

The second work is the first movement of a delightful piece by Mozart, his *Serenade in G Major, K. 525*, subtitled *Eine kleine Nachtmusik (A Little Night Music)*, for string orchestra. It is composed in a sonata-allegro form in which several contrasting themes are employed, the first of which is illustrated in Example 10-2. While listening to the movement, attempt to determine in what ways the themes relate and contrast. Further, note the variety of motivic activity, the changes of key, the diversity of rhythmic pace, and the dynamic changes. This beguiling work shows Mozart at his tuneful best as he crafts a piece filled with both varied and unifying elements created to be ever appealing, accessible, and popular.

POLITICAL AND SOCIAL SETTING

The mid-eighteenth century was ripe for a violent political change, the winds of change being formed by such great French intellectuals as Voltaire (1694–1778) and Rousseau (1712–1778). With his vitriolic pen, Voltaire punctured the hypocrisies of society about him and the egos of the mighty who peopled it. "The Baron was one of the most powerful lords in Westphalia, for his castle possessed a door and windows." "The Baroness weighed about three hundred and fifty pounds, was therefore greatly respected, and did the honors of the house with a dignity which rendered her still more respectable." Learned doctors of philosophy were fatally shafted. "Pangloss taught metaphysico-theologo-cosmolonigology. He proved admirably that there is no effect without a cause and that in the best of all worlds, my Lord the Baron's castle was the best of castles and his wife the best of all possible Baronesses." (From *Candide.*)

Rousseau proclaimed that "Man is born free, and everywhere he is in irons." (From *The Social Contract.*) Across the ocean a few years later, the immortal sequel was penned by Jefferson (1743–1826), "We hold these truths to be self-evident,—that all men are created equal." "Freedom" and "equality," then, were the fervent bywords of the times and no less fervent was an avowed appreciation for rational scientific inquiry of knowledge and truth. "Nature and nature's laws lay hid in night; God said, Let Newton be! and all was light." (Epitaph intended for Sir Isaac Newton, famed English physicist-mathematician of the seventeenth century, by Alexander Pope, 1688–1744.) "Knowledge is more than equivalent to

EXAMPLE 10-1 HAYDN: *Sonata No. 10 in G Major for Piano*, MINUET, MEASURES 1–8; TRIO, 1–10.

EXAMPLE 10-2 MOZART: *Serenade in G Major, K. 525 (Eine kleine Nachtmusik)*, FIRST MOVEMENT, MEASURES 1–10.

168 Styles of Music

force." (From *Rasselas*, by Samuel Johnson, 1709–1784.) "There is nothing so powerful as truth—and often nothing so strange." (From *Argument on the Murder of Captain White*, by Daniel Webster, 1782–1852.)

With this freedom came freedom to question existing institutions—artistic, religious, and political—culminating in the American Revolution and the overthrow of the monarchy in France, the weakening of the power of the aristocracy, and the emergence of governments functioning by the consent of the governed, in which the common man played a predominant role. A rational spirit pervaded the times despite the violence of bloody revolutions, a spirit grounded in belief that through reason all problems could be solved—social, governmental, artistic, or whatever. Reason, combined with enlightened knowledge accessible to all, held the answers to life's questions. Music reflected these changes and others, as will be seen, as it evolved in the hands of such composers as Haydn and Mozart, culminating in a classical artistic expression of rational balance, order, and restraint.

By the middle of the eighteenth century music had become cosmopolitan—that is, there was a commonality of practice in most of the industrial countries of Europe. Further, while men and women of enlightenment patronized the arts and made them available and popular to an ever-increasing middle class, the growth of the musical public furthered the decline of aristocratic patronage and an increase in public concerts and support. With this change came increased demands for more music, more performances, more understanding, leading to enormously increased publication and numbers of concerts. Thus greater quantities of music were readily accessible to an amateur public of listeners and performers, creating a need for critics and journalists dedicated to discussion, review, and criticism of music. Thus were established the basic components of the musical scene that persists to this day: public perfor-

"All mankind loves a lover" said the romantic American poet-essayist Ralph Waldo Emerson, and no more utopian love-setting was envisioned than that of the Frenchman Jean-Honore Fragonard, whose rococo style epitomizes such sumptuous hedonism in Lover Crowned.

CLASSIC COMPOSERS

It should be noted that to assign the general label of "Classic composer" to any individual, regardless of his place in the stream of time, can be misleading, if not incorrect, since almost all share in certain characteristics called "Romantic" in one work or another. For example, when one studies the overture to the oratorio *The Creation* by Franz Joseph Haydn (1732–1809), the epitome of "Classic composers," one finds that he indulges in a bit of Romantic "tone painting" through the use of unconventional sonorities and seemingly aimless chord progression (at least for that time) as he crafts a bit of tonal imagery suggesting the chaos that prevailed when "the earth was without form and void, and darkness was upon the face of the deep, and the spirit of God was moving over the face of the waters." Yet, in more general terms, one may properly say that Haydn is a Classic composer since a predominance of his works are devoted to less pictorial, more abstract, representations. More frequently his harmonies are basically diatonic and tonally oriented, yet spiced with occasional surprise dissonance and modulation. His melodies are typically based on simple chordal outlines or motives, chromatics being used relatively sparingly. His rhythms are generally regular, being sometimes varied by irregularities and unbalanced phrase lengths, and his textures evidence a mixture of homophonic and contrapuntal passages with a predilection for the former. Further, abrupt changes of dynamics, motion, and mood are likely to occur in his works more often than not at changes of theme or other important formal junctures. Take all such generalizations relative to musical style, then, with a "grain of salt" since they are just that, *generalizations,* which in no sense hold for all works of a composer—or period, for that matter.

Although the composers of the Classic period wrote many vocal works—songs, oratorios, cantatas, and operas—one may generalize that the more abstract realm of instrumental music occupied the major portion of their creative activities. One may conjecture that the composer in this "age of reason" was more interested than not in creating music with pure musical sounds divorced from the connotations of text. In any event, the major composers of the time created more symphonies, concertos,

mance of symphony, concerto, chamber music, and opera; mass music publishing and merchandising; and music journalism and criticism.

These changes posed real challenges to the artist who had both an elite and an untutored audience to reach. His art must be accessible, pleasurable in sound, and rational in structure, yet innovative to a degree sufficient to maintain the interest of the fickle listener. In reaction to the grandeur, ornateness, and contrapuntal complexities of the Baroque, now considered too obtuse for most, the composer was committed to create streams of sounds whose understanding must not be constrained by national boundaries or excessive technical complexities. The result was a music (instrumental being most popular) characterized by conciseness and symmetry of form, clarity of texture and harmonic progression, simple constancy of rhythms and tempi, lyrical melodies sectionally conceived, and tentative explorations of the timbral possibilities of choirs of instruments as well as other instrumental combinations. Some general stylistic features are presented in a more elaborate form in the outline appearing at the end of this chapter.

Franz Joseph Haydn (1732-1809)

■ The life of Franz Joseph Haydn illustrates a "Horatio Alger story" that seems almost too pat to be true. Of humble origin, born the son of a wheelwright in the village of Rohrau, Austria, Haydn left home at a tender age, educated himself under most trying circumstances, and through hard work and perseverance rose to the peak of his profession, famous and financially secure.

A robust, self-made man, he was at peace with himself and the world—a world whose pleasures he enjoyed and whose troubles he endured. Secure and content, Haydn immersed himself in his music while enjoying many of the "better things" of life—nature, hunting, fishing, good food and drink, and a bevy of beautiful women. "Papa Haydn," that amiable genius of the eighteenth century, created a music whose classic beauty, wit, humanity, freshness, polish, and craft continue to afford untold moments of "relief and relaxation" to all who are attuned.

After joining the family of a musical cousin to further his training, Haydn entered the choir of St. Stephen's Cathedral in Vienna at the age of eight, remaining there until his voice changed in 1749. While in the choir school he furthered his formal education, practiced violin and harpsichord, and studied composition on his own. Out of a job at age 17, virtually penniless and having few friends or acquaintances, he proceeded to make his own way by teaching children, and by writing for various itinerant street bands in which he played.

Haydn's big break came in 1761, the year following a marriage destined to fail, when he entered the service of Prince Esterházy, wealthy patron of the arts, becoming the conductor (Kapellmeister) of the court orchestra at the Prince's country estate in Eisenstadt. There he remained, out of the mainstream, for the next thirty years, perfecting his own style, little influenced by others, and thus, in his own words, "was made to become original." Perhaps no other composer has had such an easy time, with financial security and abundant time to compose, and an orchestra better than most to perform his compositions which could be tried out, revised, and perfected. He poured out a bounty of no less than 104 symphonies, 40 string quartets, 11 operas, 5 masses, 30 piano sonatas, numerous string quartets, and many other works as well. Included in the masterpieces of these three decades are such popular works as the *Symphony No. 45 in F-Sharp Minor* ("Farewell"), *Symphony No. 85 in B-Flat Major* ("La Reine"), and *Symphony No. 92 in G Major* ("Oxford"), three of the 104 symphonies he created in his lifetime which established him as the true "father of the symphony." In them one glimpses such broad stylistic features as appealing tunefulness, exuberant gaiety, and intense rhythmic drive coupled with angular motivic melodies, dynamic developments, and concise formal structures.

Upon the death of his patron, Haydn was pensioned, and he retired to Vienna, "freed" to captivate the world of music outside the confines of Eisenstadt. Then followed visits to London, his last twelve symphonies (the "London" symphonies, including the familiar "Surprise" *Symphony No. 94 in G Major*), and more than a dozen string quartets, among which are *Op. 74, No. 3* ("The Horseman") and *Op. 76, No. 4* ("Sunrise"). "Papa Haydn" remained admirably productive to the end, and during his last years he turned to choral writing, composing no less than six great masses and two ever-popular oratorios, *The Creation* and *The Seasons*. In the course of his seventy-seven fruitful years this son of a wheelwright had become the foremost musician of his day.

Early Viennese painter and member of the circle of bohemian friends of Franz Schubert, Moritz von Schwind accents the "romantic flavor" of Haydn's choral masterpiece with his fanciful illustration of The Creation.

sonatas, string quartets, and other chamber works than operas and other works for voice. In so doing they perfected a homophonic instrumental style which was to occupy the creative attentions of most composers in the century to follow.

Mozart and the Concerto

Let us turn now to an instrumental genre of music, the *concerto*, which in terms of today's standard repertoire may be said to have begun with the piano concertos of Wolfgang Amadeus Mozart (1756–1791). In them are manifest many of the Classic constraints of conciseness, formal balance, clarity, ready accessibility, tunefulness, sectionalization, relative constancy of rhythms, tempos, dynamics, and textures, as well as stereotypical chord progressions and key relations.

The term "concerto" is said to have derived from the Latin words *concentare* (to contend or fight) and/or *conserere* (to join together), and, indeed, one is immediately struck by the apparent "contest" between soloist and orchestra upon hearing one. Those concertos most frequently performed feature either piano or violin as the solo instrument against which the orchestra competes on equal terms, not simply as an accompanying body. Since Mozart's time the concerto is almost always a three-movement work, the first movement being a developmental form, concerto sonata-allegro (discussed in Chapter 7), featuring a double exposition and a dazzling cadenza near the end; a slow second movement often cast in a song form or theme-and-variations mold; a third movement, usually a repetitive form—a rondo. The concerto is a standard staple of many orchestral programs, not just for its intrinsic musical worth one suspects, but also because of our fascination with the eternal contest between a lone individual and a group.

Mozart, a brilliant pianist, created some of his most appealing musical utterances in his twenty-three sophisticated piano concertos. His *Concerto No. 23 in A Major for Piano, K. 488* was composed in 1786, a most productive year which was to see the creation of two other masterful piano concertos; *The Marriage of Figaro*, one of his more popular comic operas; the *Symphony No. 38 in D Major, K. 504* ("Prague"); the *Concerto in E-Flat Major for French Horn, K. 495*; a string quartet; a piano quartet; a piano trio; and various works for solo piano. He was at the height of his unequaled creative powers despite the fact that he was virtually overwhelmed with personal, domestic, and financial difficulties. It is a fitting testimony to his creative genius that Mozart surmounted such monumental difficulties to compose some of the greatest music ever penned. No one has characterized his genius better than the nineteenth-century Russian pianist-composer, Rubinstein, who wrote, "Eternal sunshine in music, thy name is Mozart."

In his *Concerto No. 23 in A Major for Piano, K. 488*, one hears the tunefulness, subtlety, and craft of the mature Mozart fully operating within the stylistic constraints of the period. The orchestra is small, being strings plus paired clarinets, horns,

172 Styles of Music

Wolfgang Amadeus Mozart (1756–1791)

■ Although Mozart once observed that people mistakenly assumed that his art came easily, it having been, so he avowed, the result of much study, thought, and familiarity with the great works of others, the fact remains that in the course of 36 hectic years this amazingly facile composer created a wealth of music—a bounty of musical works in virtually every genre—that has never been excelled.

Wolfgang Amadeus Mozart was born to a musical family, his father being an esteemed violinist in the private orchestra of the Archbishop of Salzburg. As was soon apparent, the young Mozart had an extraordinary talent for music—a talent not unnoticed by his ambitious father, who saw in it a commercial opportunity on which he was determined to capitalize. Mozart was tutored diligently by his father, and he accepted his rigid training with good grace and dedication. He began composing before age five and a year later performed on the clavier at the court of the Elector in Munich—and, most exciting of all, for the family of the Empress Maria Theresa in Vienna, then capital of the Holy Roman Empire itself. The next year saw him and his talented sister undertake a concert tour of the major cities of Europe, where they were well received.

Returning to Salzburg in 1767, exhausted and recovering from smallpox, Mozart honed his compositional skills. By now he had published a number of clavier works and had taught himself to play the violin and organ. Then began a period of rest and recuperation, study and composition, which saw him produce by age 13 two operas, a solemn mass which the "wunderkind" conducted, three symphonies, several concertos for piano and for violin, plus numerous sonatas and other works. In recognition of his talents he was "awarded" the post of Konzertmeister, without salary, in 1769, a position from which he was later to resign, after being dismissed and then reinstated following a running dispute with the tyrannical archbishop who replaced his original benefactor. In the next decade he was to go to Italy and overwhelm the musical intelligentsia with his mastery of composition and his extraordinary sight-reading and improvisational skills, receiving the Order of the Golden Spur conferred by the pope.

When the final rupture with the archbishop came in 1781, he left Salzburg, breaking both his court and family ties, electing to become a freelance musician in Vienna, where his earlier successes were not so easily duplicated now that the "child prodigy" had come of age.

The last ten years of his life were filled with many bitter disappointments, occasional successes, and a crushing struggle for financial security, as he was never able to regain the status achieved in his earlier years. They began with a great success, his first German opera, *The Abduction from the Seraglio,* commissioned by the Emperor Franz Joseph II, first performed in 1782. His touring days virtually over, he devoted his prodigious creative energies to composing while marginally subsisting on commissions and, belatedly, a niggardly salary paid him by the Austrian emperor for his service as chamber composer.

Although he composed for various performing media, it was his operas that were in demand. His greatest popular success came with *The Marriage of Figaro* in 1786 and thereafter such operatic masterpieces as *Don Giovanni, Così fan Tutte,* and *The Magic Flute,* some of the most-played works in the repertoire today.

When he went to his pauper's grave at age 35, he had created untold musical riches including the operas previously mentioned, nearly 50 symphonies, three of which were written in one year (1788) and never performed in his lifetime, over 20 piano concertos and string quartets, and a tremendous number of sonatas, arias and songs, masses, and other choral works.

No other composer has had greater compositional facility or gift for melody, or a finer sense of musical form, beauty, and elegance. When one knows his rich musical legacy, so diverse, copious, and appealing, one is persuaded of the rightness of the remark attributed to the composer Rossini, "There is only Mozart!"

Blessed with a musical gift bestowed on but few, a gift early realized by his ambitious father, Mozart (shown performing at the Court of the Princess Conti) was to surmount his innate precocity, leaving to the world a vast treasure of riches and receiving in exchange, a pauper's grave.

and bassoons. The timbre, consequently, is comparatively mellow and restricted in variety because of the lack of the more brilliant, penetrating sounds of trumpets and brasses and the rhythmic punctuation of the timpani.

Three basic sets of thematic materials constitute the melodic resources of the fast first movement (allegro) in quadruple meter, which is cast in a concerto sonata-allegro mold. The first exposition contains two of the themes which are restated by the piano in the second exposition. The first is a quiet, angular theme shaped in an inverted arch. Symmetrical in form, consisting of two four-measure phrases, it exhibits such typical features as prominent triadic and sequential figures and dotted rhythms (Example 10-3). In contrast to the first, the second subject is generally smoothly conjunct except for a few distinctive chordal figures, and it flows sequentially downward. It also moves relatively faster than the first because of shorter note values, and it contains some chromatic scalar elements (Example 10-4).

In comparing the two, one sees that Mozart has created two symmetrical themes, differing in contour, rhythmic motion, and scale. Thus he has set up two contrasting, though symmetrical, theme groups which will contribute needed elements of variety in what will prove to be a homophonic texture throughout. One notes that both themes contain repeated rhythm-pitch pat-

EXAMPLE 10-3 MOZART: *Concerto No. 23 in A Major for Piano, K. 488,* FIRST MOVEMENT, MEASURES 1–8.

EXAMPLE 10-4 MOZART: *Concerto No. 23 in A Major for Piano, K. 488,* FIRST MOVEMENT, MEASURES 31–38.

terns that will lend themselves to subsequent extension and developmental treatment, and that the themes are delineated by clearly defined cadences. Although the accompaniment is not illustrated here, in both instances it is clearly subordinate to the dominating melody and consists of characteristic diatonic harmonies inflected by occasional chromatic alterations as they progress between the tonal pillars of tonic and dominant. Both themes are first stated by the strings, hence the timbre is basically the same, yet contrast of tone color is provided when the winds repeat the first theme and join with the strings in bridging the gap between the two theme groups. One other element of variety is added as the orchestral exposition evolves: the bridge section between theme groups is loud in contrast to the soft statements of the themes themselves. Listen to the first exposition and verify the above stylistic generalizations.

Before proceeding further, familiarize yourself with these sets of thematic materials through repeated hearings, noting the variety achieved through use of contrasting melodic rhythms, motions and contours, and dynamic levels. Turn then to further stylistic considerations exemplified in the first exposition.

Theme 1, symmetrical in design, is set firmly in A major, the first section being stated initially by the strings in a compact homophonic texture tending toward the low part of their range. It is softly repeated in the same key by the winds, more widely spread in terms of texture. The contrasting period opens in A major and moves to the dominant in a loud, full-voiced statement by the orchestra. This movement from tonic to dominant is most typical of the style.

The first period of theme 2 is softly sounded in the home key by the strings and then repeated with the additional colors of flutes and bassoons. Thereafter the theme is completed with a loud, full-voiced orchestral statement of the second period in a more complex fabric of sudden dynamic contrasts, imitative exchanges, repeated chords, arpeggios, and running figures, the tonality being characterized by alternation between major and minor modes. In typical fashion Mozart thickens the texture, increases the motion, intensifies the dynamics, and clouds the home key to dramatize the appearance of the solo instrument.

In stark contrast, the piano softly and simply states the opening theme in the tonic key and, upon being joined by the strings, engages in decorative scalar embellishment as the texture thickens. Similarly, the piano alone sounds the opening of the contrasting theme, but in a new key, the dominant. The theme is completed in a brilliant texture of sixteenth notes of the soloist combined with thick chords of the accompanying body and imitative dialogue between piano and orchestra. It is apparent that variety of texture, timbre, dynamics, and rhythmic motion are integral to the style.

Typical of Mozart but not of Haydn, an unexpected new theme is abruptly introduced in the dominant key (Example 10-5). It contains the characteristic dotted-note figures and the chordal outlines cited earlier. More sustained than its predecessors, this theme and its contrapuntal companion constitute the sole thematic materials of the development, a practice anticipating the later works of Beethoven. Stated first simply and softly by the strings and then woven into a two-part fabric by the piano, the melodic fragments are melded into a

EXAMPLE 10-5 MOZART: *Concerto No. 23 in A Major for Piano, K. 488*, FIRST MOVEMENT, MEASURES 144–149.

rich contrapuntal tapestry of kaleidoscopic thematic fragments, textures, and timbres as a brilliant, modulatory dialogue between soloist and orchestra ensues. It was customary to work over themes and theme fragments in development sections, hence themes were designed with prominent rhythmic or melodic features that were readily recognizable and would lend themselves to various developmental processes—sequence, imitation, and the like. In typical fashion the orchestra comes to rest on the dominant seventh chord, and in a sweeping cadenza the piano leads the way to the important point of arrival, the reprise of the opening theme at the onset of a recapitulation.

Listen to the whole movement a number of times, concentrating first on thematic character and usage and then on such less-prominent stylistic features as change of key and mode, tempo and rhythmic motion, instrumental timbre, textures, and dynamics.

As one might expect in music of this period, the second movement differs markedly from the first: the tempo is much slower (adagio), the mode is minor, the meter is compound duple (6/8), and the form is sectional rather than developmental. The piano alone opens with a soft statement of the principal theme, whose wide-ranging line, rich with dotted-note rhythms, is supported by a simple chordal accompaniment (Example 10-6). Atypically, this is not a symmetric theme, as were those of the previous movement. It consists of a four-measure phrase plus one of eight measures.

The orchestra states the contrasting thematic material, smoother in melodic contour and rhythmic flow, in imitative dialogue as the dynamic level rises from piano to forte (Example 10-7). Again one is struck by the change of musical elements—the change of timbre, texture, rhythmic-melodic flow and dynamics.

A third set of thematic materials is heard, dramatized by a key shift to a major mode and a thinned texture limited initially to the upper winds in paired thirds above clarinet triadic arpeggios (Example 10-8).

While you are encouraged to listen carefully to this beautiful movement in its entirety and to savor its moments of pathos and tragic lyricism, little new will be revealed in terms

EXAMPLE 10-6 MOZART: *Concerto No. 23 in A Major for Piano, K. 488*, SECOND MOVEMENT, MEASURES 1–4.

EXAMPLE 10-7 MOZART: *Concerto No. 23 in A Major for Piano, K. 488*, SECOND MOVEMENT, MEASURES 12–16.

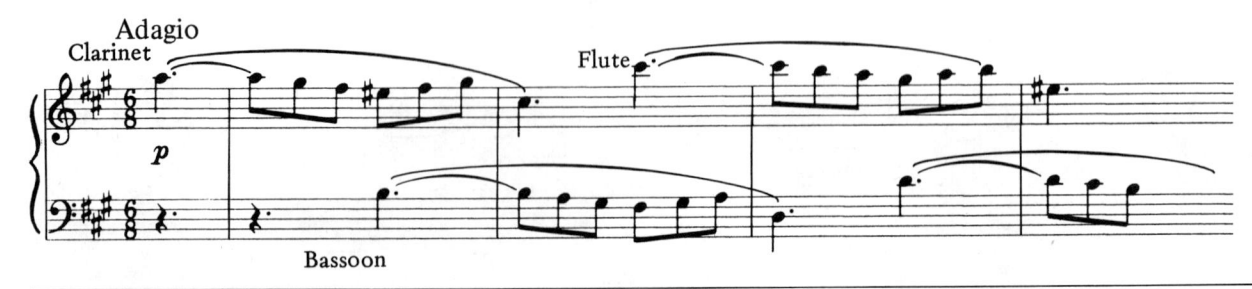

The piano forte replaced the harpsichord as the most popular keyboard instrument toward the end of the 18th century and this worthy successor inherited the delicacy of tone and touch and sameness of timbre of its progenitor, characteristics then suitable for the sparkling scale passages of the classic composers.

The more flamboyant musical statements of the Romantic composers, addressed to a sizably increased audience, created the demand for a piano capable of greater volume and wider, more varied dynamic range and timbre, resulting in a more massive instrument with thicker strings, more tautly strung, and pedals to control dynamics (soft-loud or piano-forte).

EXAMPLE 10-8 MOZART: *Concerto No. 23 in A Major for Piano, K. 488,* SECOND MOVEMENT, MEASURES 35–38.

of style features. Therefore, after hearing it a number of times, turn your attention to the closing movement.

Recall that we have moved from fast to slow, major to minor, and exuberance to somberness in the previous two movements. It is time for dramatic change, and change comes as Mozart launches one of his most exhilarating rondos, a racing perpetual motion of energetic musical utterances (allegro assai) brilliantly set in the key of A major (Example 10-9). Returning to the standard four-measure phrase pattern with clearly defined cadences, Mozart romps through this rapidly descending theme only to counter it suddenly with one less rhythmically energetic and soft (Example 10-10).

Another important thematic thread is introduced much later, being equally loud, in a minor mode, and moving faster than either of the other two (Example 10-11). Built into these basic thematic materials are the elements of contour mentioned, but, as more careful study will reveal, other contrasting elements are brought into play. Further, through the compulsive rush of scales up and down, the grace notes of the first two, and the impelling sequences of them all, the frolicsome spirit of the rondo is created in a manner so common to the style. One might analyze the "life" out of the movement in tracing the subtleties of change through the virtually unbroken rush of melodic-rhythmic motion. To do so would be a mistake as it is literally a kaleidoscope of readily accessible melodies flowing in a chain without a significant interruption from beginning to end. From this welter of melodies three themes emerge, cited below, which exemplify some of Mozart's most irresistible tunes and which appear ordered as follows in the movement as a whole: A-B-A-C-B-A. Most dramatically and characteristically the composer juxtaposes contrasting keys, modes, moods, and textures as piano and orchestra engage in a racing debate over the thematic materials presented. No movement better exemplifies the Classic composer's penchant for creating beguiling diatonic scalar tunes sparked by vigorous, accented rhythms and regularity of pulse which dominate the comparatively simple chordal accompaniments supporting them. Further, no work better represents the Classic, objective style of music mannered by carefully delineated design, balance of thematic content, and emotional restraint.

Beethoven and the Symphony

Let us next turn to a work of a musical titan who, looming large at the close of the Classic period, led the way to the more intensely subjective musical style that was to persist to the beginning of this century. In his early works he turned toward the "Classic" masters Haydn and Mozart, but soon abandoned their more restrained, elegant, and mannered style for one that

EXAMPLE 10-9 MOZART: *Concerto No. 23 in A Major for Piano, K. 488*, THIRD MOVEMENT, MEASURES 1–8.

EXAMPLE 10-10 MOZART: *Concerto No. 23 in A Major for Piano, K. 488*, THIRD MOVEMENT, MEASURES 62–69.

EXAMPLE 10-11 MOZART: *Concerto No. 23 in A Major for Piano, K. 488*, THIRD MOVEMENT, MEASURES 230–234.

Ludwig van Beethoven (1770–1827)

■ Few composers have made greater impact on the world of music than Ludwig van Beethoven, and none has more intrigued the mind and imagination than that heroic spirit who led the way into the Romantic period. Born to a family of musicians, his father being a singer at the court of the Elector of Bonn, Beethoven's precocious musical talents were soon recognized and vigorously cultivated. By the age of eight he made his first public appearance as a pianist. Three years later he composed his first published works (three piano sonatas) and in 1784 was appointed assistant court organist, a position he held until he was 22.

Lest one assume that this was the best of all possible worlds for Beethoven, it should be noted that the provincial German town of Bonn was hardly a musical mecca, Beethoven's father was scarcely an ideal parent because of his addiction to alcohol and the exploitation of his "wunderkind," and the young musician's genius, though recognized, was quite meagerly rewarded. Until 1792, however, he contented himself with assisting in the support of his mother and two younger brothers with a limited amount of composing, with his duties as court musician and harpsichordist and violist in the theater orchestra, and with broadening his taste for literature through his association with members of the local aristocracy.

Things changed drastically when at the age of 22 he went to Vienna, the musical center of Europe, to study with Haydn. He soon captivated the music-loving aristocracy with his great skill as pianist and his highly original style of improvisation, as well as with his compelling strength of personality and unique revolutionary views of their roles and those of the artist in society. "Prince! What you are, you are through the accident of birth. What I am, I am through my own efforts. There have been many princes and there will be thousands more. But there is only one Beethoven."

We may applaud his spirit or condemn his manners, but all surely agree that he was right. In Beethoven the creative artist finally found his rightful niche in society, at least in the nineteenth-century mind, where, supported by an admiring and enlightened "public," he was freed to explore the other world of heroic ideas and noble visions of what might be.

Firmly established in Vienna for the remaining 35 years of his life, he fashioned masterpiece after masterpiece—symphonies, concertos, string quartets and trios, piano sonatas, and vocal works—characterized by great breadth of dimension, dramatic intensity, variety, impact, and compositional craft. Lacking the ready facility of Mozart and the innate tunefulness of Schubert, Beethoven labored long with his basic musical materials, as his workbooks attest, until he had fashioned the precise personal statements to which he aspired. The result was a prodigious quantity of music distinguished by its expansive developmental treatment, expressive contrasts, vivid changes of pace and mood, and by its dynamic sweep and intense expressiveness as exemplified in the Third ("Eroica"), Fifth, and Ninth ("Choral") Symphonies, the *Missa Solemnis*, the Fourth and Fifth ("Emperor") piano concertos, the piano sonatas *C Minor, Op. 13* ("Pathétique"), *F Minor, Op. 57* ("Appassionata"), and *Op. 106* ("Hammerklavier"), the three string quartets *Op. 59* ("Rasumovsky"), and the last five *Op. 127, 130, 131, 132,* and *135,* and the piano trio, *Op. 97* ("Archduke").

It is ironic to realize that at the times Beethoven voiced some of his most heroic musical utterances, he was beset with some of the harshest realities of his life—total deafness, humiliating financial difficulties, and exhausting family problems. Not one to be defeated by life, this unimposing figure of a man—he was five feet four—was to assume gigantic stature in the world of music. True, "there is only one Beethoven."

Classical Style (1750–1825)

heralded the "new free spirit" of the future. No name is more familiar in terms of Western music that that of Ludwig van Beethoven (1770–1827), and few symphonies are more popular than his famous "Eroica" (Heroic) Symphony, *Symphony No. 3 in E-Flat Major, Op. 55*. In it one sees the emergence of a "new" spirit of musical expressiveness rooted in the practices of the past but anticipating those to follow with its more dramatic juxtapositions and contrasting extremes of tempo, rhythm, range, key, texture, dynamics, and timbre. Further, the Classic molds and harmonic language were enlarged by Beethoven to accommodate musical utterances of epic length and monumental proportion, all of which become apparent from study of this well-known masterpiece.

Despite his penchant for dramatic extremes, one finds his music "Classic" in terms of its adherence to the developmental and motivic interplay of the earlier forms set to a harmonic scheme with clearly defined, but long-delayed, points of tonal focus and arrival. Despite the increasing inroads of such unsettling "expressive" elements as those mentioned earlier, the music is dominated by the rational relationships, formal and tonal, practiced in the past and had not yet given way to a music more subjective and emotional in concept.

The "Eroica" Symphony is a monumental four-movement work of epic proportions consisting of a long, drawn-out, fast sonata-allegro first movement, a dirgelike slow second movement in A-B-A form, a bustling third movement (scherzo) cast in the same formal mold, and a final movement composed of a theme and a set of ten developmental variations. Although the forms of this work are those of the Classicists in general terms, one sees Beethoven stretch them to the point of bursting their bounds while still maintaining the earlier basic premise of balance of formal proportions. It is the very personal expressive nature of his music that presages the future—the dramatic intensity and drive, the extreme contrasts of range and dynamics, the striking sonorities and progressions, and the variety and richness of orchestral color. Beethoven lacked Mozart's gift of melody and Haydn's spontaneity, but he made up for these lacks with a stubbornness of spirit that enabled him to craft lasting musical monuments from less inspired melodies through prodigious effort. Born to be free, a man for all ages, Beethoven struggled mightily for self-expression and in so doing created some of the greatest, most personal of musical utterances, masterpieces that continue to this day to captivate all who learn to known them well.

The first movement of the "Eroica," *allegro con brio,* is quite extended, being a sonata-allegro form more than twice the length of its counterpart in Mozart's Piano Concerto in A Major, previously discussed. Except for the addition of a third horn, the instrumentation is that of a Classic symphony: pairs of woodwinds and trumpets (three horns), plus strings and timpani. In contrast to Haydn and Mozart, in this work Beethoven employs many, not two or three, theme groups, four of the most important being as shown in Examples 10-12 through 10-15.

Some stylistic features emerge from an inspection of these themes. Note that the first outlines a triad, the second and third consist of imitative fragments voiced by various instruments, and the fourth is rich with chromatic inflections. Further, as will become apparent as the movement is heard, the most significant of these theme groups are designed so as to provide developmental materials for what becomes the heart of the movement in Beethoven's sonata-allegro forms: the development section proper. Therein he demonstrates his unmatched genius at thematic extension, elaboration, and variation as he melds homophonic and contrapuntal webs with electric changes of mood, key, dynamics, timbre, tempo, and tessitura.

In the "Eroica" Beethoven goes even further in modifying the conventional sonata-allegro form when he suddenly extends the development section by introducing a new theme (see Example 10-15) and then goes further still when he invents an extended coda to close the movement, which in reality is a ssecond development. After familiarizing yourself with the important thematic elements, noting the prominent characteristics of each—the triadic chordal outline of the first, the sequential treatment of the second, the static reiteration of the third, and the flowing, conjunct movement of the fourth—concentrate

Mozart was so right! Beethoven overcame the musical world, with powerful strength of emotional expression and force of personality.

EXAMPLE 10-12 BEETHOVEN: *Symphony No. 3 in E-Flat Major, Op. 55 ("Eroica"), first movement, measures 3–8.*

EXAMPLE 10-13 BEETHOVEN: *Symphony No. 3 in E-Flat Major, Op. 55 ("Eroica"), first movement, measures 45–49.*

EXAMPLE 10-14 BEETHOVEN: *Symphony No. 3 in E-Flat Major, Op. 55 ("Eroica"), first movement, measures 83–91.*

Classical Style (1750–1825) 181

EXAMPLE 10-15   BEETHOVEN: *Symphony No. 3 in E-Flat Major, Op. 55 ("Eroica"),* FIRST MOVEMENT, MEASURES 284–288.

on certain broad, general organizational aspects, leaving more in-depth study for a later day when listening skills have been further refined.

Following two chromatic chords the cellos announce the principal theme (Example 10-12) in the tonic key. This theme is characteristically rich with rhythmic possibilities, being cast in triple meter which is most amenable to irregular accents, two-beat groupings, and rhythmic displacements. Further, the formal asymmetry is suggestive of the complexities to follow. As will become apparent, Beethoven utilizes these characteristics in the titanic struggle to ensue. Once the main theme is established, the composer digresses through a series of three sets of motivic transitional materials, the first of which appears in Example 10-13, because of its prominent use in the development section to follow. Following hard upon its heels comes the main contrasting theme (Example 10-14), which the winds (answered by the strings) lyrically set in the dominant key. Note that this tonality change from the tonic key of the first theme to the dominant key of the second is consistent with the stylistic practice of the time. Following a varied repetition the exposition terminates in typical fashion with a driving closing section highlighted by rhythmic agitation, dynamic crescendos and sforzandos, thickening of textural and timbral density, sharp dissonances, and brief references to fragments of the primary theme.

Beethoven, having fashioned his thematic materials well with their developmental potential in mind, sets out on a long exploration of the first transition theme (Example 10-13). The climax of the development is reached, but quite unexpectedly we are introduced to a new theme (Example 10-15) in a minor key. After this brief lyric interlude there suddenly occurs one of the great surprises of all music. In a master stroke of dramatic effect, Beethoven falsely recapitulates the opening fragment of the initial theme, softly voiced by the horn. Since this is not common practice, expectations are thwarted and concentration sharpened momentarily. Following this "false" entrance, the proper recapitulation occurs, being varied primarily in terms of orchestral timbres and changes of key. Master of the unexpected, Beethoven spices his lengthy works with piquant surprise elements that serve to recapture the attention of all save the most apathetic. What follows is the expected coda, which is longer than either the exposition or recapitulation. Herein Beethoven engages in further development of the principal theme, thus rounding out the ample form.

In retrospect one realizes that important structural points have been dramatically emphasized by dynamic weight or abrupt contrasts of textures, keys, timbres, or dynamics, or emphatic, obvious cadences. Further, Beethoven has greatly enlarged the Classic sonata mold by the addition of themes, development sections, and an extended coda, and has enriched it with tonal excursions far afield and with greater rhythmic, melodic, textural, and timbral variety.

As one might expect, the slow second movement, *marcia funebre (adagio assai),* is cast in a modified three-part mold with coda. The three primary sets of thematic materials appear in Examples 10-16, 10-17, and 10-18. One hears that the first is a somber funeral march in the minor mode; the second, a lyric melody in the parallel major mode; the third, a fugal theme. Again the composer has created a series of melodic materials characteristically different in terms of mood, mode, and rhythmic structure. In contrast to the explosive, motorific drive of the first movement, the second moves in somber cadence as the melodic materials unfold in a breadth of design in which the forward motion is slowed sometimes to a virtual halt. The climax is reached on a deceptive cadence; a coda ensues in a long decrescendo as the texture thins out. The movement closes with one last fragmentary reference to the dirgelike march softly voiced by the violin to pizzicato cellos and basses. Thus the movement is brought to a halting, tragic close. Again Beethoven has demonstrated his characteristic flair for creating dramatic intensity by the colorful juxtapositions of major and minor modes, the contrasting moods of the dirge and lyric themes, the mixtures of diverse textures, and the variety of orchestral timbres. This movement also shows his great skill

EXAMPLE 10-16 BEETHOVEN: *Symphony No. 3 in E-Flat Major, Op. 55 ("Eroica"),* SECOND MOVEMENT, MEASURES 1–4.

EXAMPLE 10-17 BEETHOVEN: *Symphony No. 3 in E-Flat Major, Op. 55 ("Eroica"),* SECOND MOVEMENT, MEASURES 69–73.

EXAMPLE 10-18 BEETHOVEN: *Symphony No. 3 in E-Flat Major, Op. 55 ("Eroica"),* SECOND MOVEMENT, MEASURES 114–118.

at expanding materials in that it opens as a three-part form in which themes 1 and 2 are presented in a simple A-B-A pattern, but he goes on to extend these brief germinal patterns into a movement of vast length.

The third movement in comparison to those previous is much simpler in design, although it, too, is quite extended. Beethoven replaces the Classic minuet with a derivative form called *scherzo,* a three-part form (scherzo-trio-scherzo) now greatly enlarged; the music is much faster in tempo (*allegro vivace*) and richer in vigor of rhythms, contradictions of meter, abruptness of contrasts of key, and harmonic instability. Further, one finds that this rollicking movement is clouded with moments of extreme gravity—for example, the return of the scherzo is disrupted by a loud fanfare mentioned below. The movement opens pianissimo with staccato strings establishing a lengthy, bustling theme, the headlong momentum and spirit of which dominate the movement (Example 10-19).

True to accepted practice, the second section is a contrasting one. It is loudly announced by a horn trio sounding a more sustained, triadic fanfare theme, each phrase of which is punctuated by comments of strings and winds (Example 10-20). In the second half of the trio the winds take up a more lyric, conjunct, descending theme in the home key, affording a further element of melodic contrast and greater harmonic stability. The repetition of the scherzo is literal until it is unexpectedly interrupted by an interpolated fortissimo fanfare figure. With this unexpected theatrical gesture the composer slows the rush toward closure and dramatizes its approach. In typical fashion Beethoven mixes impish humor with moments of compelling seriousness as he expresses his quixotic nature and views of life wherein gaiety and tragedy are a hairbreadth apart.

Recall if you will that to this point we have experienced a massive first movement, a dramatic, emotion-packed second movement, and a bustling third movement of sizable proportions. Beethoven chooses to use a theme-and-variations scheme to mold the close of this symphony. Following a dramatic flourish of rushing descending scale passages in the strings,

Classical Style (1750–1825) 183

the sparse skeletal theme is presented. What follows is a set of no less than seven developmental variations based on this "bare bones" bass and three based on a dancelike tune set counter to the bass theme in variation 3. For economy of space both the bass theme and lyric countermelody are cited together as they appear in variation 3 (Example 10-21).

As will become apparent from study of this movement and the works by others, few composers have had the compositional craft and inventive genius to make so much great music out of such simple basic materials. Since it is relatively easy to follow the themes as they are successively varied, after becoming familiar with them, listen to the movement and keep in mind such stylistic features as: extension of some variations by a number of measures in excess of the length of the theme proper; the variety achieved by contrasting textural density and type; instrumental colors, dynamics, key, and mode; and forthright thematic statement with developmental sections, including the fugal treatment in the fourth variation.

To sense the effect of the expressive extremes so characteristic of Beethoven, compare the first variation with the sixth. In the first the second violins softly state the theme in sustained notes to imitative passages by the cellos and first violins. This

EXAMPLE 10-19 BEETHOVEN: *Symphony No. 3 in E-Flat Major, Op. 55 ("Eroica")*, THIRD MOVEMENT, MEASURES 1–14.

EXAMPLE 10-20 BEETHOVEN: *Symphony No. 3 in E-Flat Major, Op. 55 ("Eroica")*, THIRD MOVEMENT, MEASURES 167–173.

EXAMPLE 10-21 BEETHOVEN: *Symphony No. 3 in E-Flat Major, Op. 55 ("Eroica")*, FOURTH MOVEMENT, MEASURES 76–83.

three-part texture is rather thin, the mode is major, and the mood quite calm and gentle. On the other hand, variation 6 is a vigorous, marchlike section set in a minor mode that climaxes the movement at this point. In a thick interwoven web the winds reiterate an ostinato dotted-note figure against the basses and cellos who boldly sound the skeletal theme in sustained notes. Obviously, the gentle thematic materials of the beginning have assumed a threatening martial character at the bidding of the master. One cannot minimize the importance of such dramatic divergences in considering Beethoven's style, as it is the prevalence of these, so apparent in his music, which differentiate his later works from those of the other Classical composers and which will so influence the Romantic composers to follow.

The merging of traditional (Classical) and sometimes explosively innovative stylistic materials and patterns in Beethoven's work produced numerous works of great depth of emotion as well as consummate musical craft. This merging of what are often described as Classical and Romantic attitudes and esthetic outlooks can be at once recognized in pieces such as his widely acclaimed *String Quartet in F Minor, Op. 95*. Like many compositions of Beethoven, Opus 95 reveals the master's great knack for creating dramatic, intense, and musically brilliant developments fashioned from a minimum of material. And in closing this discussion of Classical style, it appears appropriate to dwell briefly on a movement of a work which may be considered as a bridge to the future. While only the first nineteen measures of the opening movement of Opus 95 are cited in Example 10-22, you are encouraged to listen to the movement in its entirety, a sonata-allegro form, to hear how "the man who freed music" dynamically paves the way with his unsurpassed creative imagination and musical craft and developmental skills for the music of his Romantic successors.

EXAMPLE 10-22 BEETHOVEN: *String Quartet in F Minor, Op. 95*, FIRST MOVEMENT, MEASURES 1–19.

> Beethoven is depicted here rehearsing a chamber group of the Russian Count Rasumowsky, wealthy patron of the arts and chamber music lover, who commissioned Beethoven to write three of his greatest string quartets, Opus 59, the so-called "Russian" or "Rasumowsky Quartets."

186 Styles of Music

SUMMARY

In summation, please consider a brief listing of some of the prominent stylistic features of Classical music which became apparent from our study of the two works of Mozart and Beethoven. Keep in mind, of course, that such generalizations as follow are accurate only to a degree since they represent a synthesis of similar, different, and even contradictory practices within an objective style of music usually characterized by clearly delineated formal designs, balance of content, and emotional restraint.

Style Characteristics of Classical Music

Melody: Melody dominates the musical texture. It is generally tuneful, clearly sectional, usually symmetrical, and delineated by obvious cadences. It contains scale configurations melded with chord outlines and motivic patterns conducive to subsequent elongation and developmental treatment.

Rhythm: Rhythm flows in periodic streams interrupted by cadences, in contrast to the continuous motorific movement of the late Baroque. It is generally vigorous and regularly accented except for occasional metric displacement by interpolated syncopated figures. The rhythms abound with dance and march patterns and repeated dotted-note motivic figures, the regularity of movement being varied occasionally by accelerandos or ritards at climaxes and cadences.

Harmony: Harmony supports melody in a clearly key-oriented stream basically consisting of functional diatonic triads moving between the primary tonal pillars of tonic and dominant. It is impelled by movement to cadence, which movement is frequently intensified by sequences sharpened with occasional dissonance (seventh chords and nonharmonic tones) and heightened by chromatic inflections. Harmony functions most frequently within a major

Classical Style (1750–1825) **187**

key with modulations from and back to the tonic key to be anticipated, the most typical pattern being tonic-dominant-tonic.

Texture: Texture assumes a transparent homophonic character with melody dominating a basically chordal accompaniment varied by heterogenous groupings of melody and accompaniment, chord passages, running figures, imitative sections, and the like, thus superseding the basically homogenous contrapuntal textures of the Baroque. It is characterized by number and variety of densities (compacted or widespread, one line or many), alternation between the prevailing homophonic pattern and short episodic imitative sections, and animated and varied dialogue of thematic repetitions, variations, sequences, and interchanges in a music that is preponderantly repetitive and developmental.

Timbre: Timbre becomes valued for its expressive quality, the palette of instrumental colors being increased by the use of new instruments and instrumental combinations and effects. It is characterized by brilliance, clarity, and

Intending to counteract rococo fanciful excesses, painters such as the Englishman William Blake (1757-1827) turned back to classic Greek art (often sculpture) and, in so doing, fostered a romantic technique which, ironically, had no future.

variety of color as contrasted with the earlier more homogenous sounds. Timbre is made more colorful through alternation of orchestral choirs and different instrumental combinations and through the exploitation of extreme registers (high and low) and dynamics, muted sounds, various articulations (pizzicato, tremolo, staccato, legato), drum rolls and pedal points, brass fanfares and hunting calls, all wedded to create the timbral brilliance and variety of the Classical style.

Many of the stylistic generalizations pertaining to Classic music relate no less accurately to Romantic music. Thus the general observations about style closing the discussion of the Romantic period (Chapter 13) will *highlight differences* rather than similarities to the previous period. It should be noted that generalizations regarding the Romantic period are even more subject to dispute because of the tremendous variety of individual styles of music within the nineteenth century, which was to see both the climax and ultimate rejection of a musical tradition that had dominated for some two centuries. Therefore one will observe that the Classic composers were much more consistent in terms of stylistic practice than later Romantic composers who were both ending and beginning a new phase in the musical evolution of the Western world.

11 Romantic Style (1825–1900)

One might say that the nineteenth century, the Romantic period, was the "supreme ego trip"—a period in which people, engulfed in the cataclysmic wind of liberation that started whirling toward the end of the eighteenth century, sought to escape the harsh world of reality to find freedom of "self" in an idealized world of the spirit and nature. They envisioned ideal utopias in which all was reconciled—human and universe, past and future, sacred and profane, heaven and earth. People were suffused with a desire to be different, to find something else—"the best of all possible worlds." They sought what Victor Hugo called "a certain vague and indefinable fantasy." This "romantic" spirit had led to the founding of a "new world," the United States of America, a new government in France, the Union of Canada, and later another form of government in which "the proletarians have nothing to lose but their chains. They have a world to win. Workers of the world, unite." (From *Communist Manifesto,* 1847, by Marx and Engels.) Such social change occurred or was being advocated during a time that saw the advent of industrialism, Darwin's theories on evolution, Freudian psychology, the poetry of Goethe and Schiller, the literary works of Byron, Shelley, Wordsworth, and Thoreau, and the paintings of Cézanne, Millais, Friedrich, and Bingham.

ROMANTICISM AND MUSICAL EXPRESSION
We will leave it for history to determine the success of the struggle for emancipation, and turn to consideration of the forces brought into focus during the Romantic period that were manifest in the cultural activities of the time, particularly those in the field of music. As mentioned earlier, Romantic elements have always permeated arts and ideas, transcending all barriers geographic and historical, as people have always longed for a new and a better life whether on this planet or in the mind's eye. "Would you realize what Revolution is, call it Progress, and would you realize what Progress is, call it tomorrow." (From *Les Misérables,* 1862, by Victor Hugo.) Perhaps it is accurate to say that in no period of time did this eternal search for "tomorrow" become more strongly manifest than in the nineteenth century where the Romantic quest became so dominant.

Though of a classical school of French painting, Jean-Baptiste-Camille Corot (1796–1874) shared the sentiments of the romantic, creating landscapes such as The Lake, *which epitomized poetic revery and sensitivity.*

As one might assume when the search for freedom of expression prevails, there is no "typical" style or work—whether of music or other art forms. Intense individuality was the rule, and hence one finds a great disparity between the musical styles of composers such as Schubert and Brahms on the one hand, and Berlioz, Chopin, or Sousa on the other—to say nothing of the antithetical operatic styles of Verdi and Wagner. Perhaps the thread that prevails through the works of them all may best be described as one of *intensity of expression,* which differentiates them from those of the previous period so classically mannered, measured, and poised.

Regardless of the impetus, Romanticism pervaded the Western world and, interestingly enough, took different forms in different countries. In contrast to music of the Classic period, which was "universal" in style, at least in the Western world, in the period to follow a stream of the music became "regionalized" or "nationalized." That is, it became infused with themes, legends, and folk music indigenous to a particular country—Russia or Czechoslovakia, for example. This trend arose, no doubt, from the increasing consciousness of the identity of emerging countries that previously had been culturally overshadowed by Germany, France, and England.

Jean-Auguste-Dominique Ingres, French painter, drew telling portraits of the bourgeoisie, posing them in revealing ways so as to express their likenesses, personalities, and social stations.

ROMANTIC COMPOSERS AND STYLES

For sake of simplicity and brevity, consider the accompanying chart, which lists some dominant figures and suggests at least three identifiable streams, all springing from the progenitor Beethoven. Do not assume that these are discrete streams, because they often flow together, and do not assume that all composers listed did not on occasion move from one stream to another. In other words, such a listing has the same weakness (and strength) as generalizations about musical style.

To many the music of the nineteenth century represents the golden age of the art, a fact substantiated by the prevalence of such works in today's repertoire, whether orchestral, operatic, or solo. As was mentioned earlier, the century was one of revolution both socially and musically. With the decline of the power of the aristocracy and the advent of industrial revolution arose the bourgeoisie, the less sophisticated working class. This led to artistic independence of sorts and freedom of expression previously unknown by the musician. Beethoven, having thumbed his nose at his noble sponsors, became the folk hero of those to follow, thus launching a musical revolution which continues to this day. No longer a subservient artisan faced with the necessity of pleasing the patron, the musician became an emancipated artist with all the advantages and disadvantages this freedom entailed.

Having turned from a relatively sophisticated, knowledgeable elite, artists found a much greater public less attuned to their art. Thus they faced a serious problem of expressing their new-found freedom in a musical language that would relate to those less tutored. Two important things happened: one group sought to make their music more accessible by wedding it to a literary thread or pictorial association, or by filling it with nationalistic elements—idiomatic folk tunes and dances (waltz, mazurka, polka, etc.) of their native countries; the other group engrossed themselves in composing abstract music devoid of literal worldly association, being content to express their intense personal feeling and noblest emotions in music more international in scope, which might or might not be readily understood by the general public.

This "youthful" search for new modes and vehicles of musical expression saw the development of intimate miniatures, character pieces, which took the forms of solo songs and short works for piano. Further, artists became infatuated with the idea of fusing the arts, and indeed its painters made music, its composers created dramas, and its poets painted. Whistler considered his paintings to be "symphonies and nocturnes, harmonies in tone." From this concept arose "program music," for example, the *Symphonie Fantastique* of Berlioz, *Les Préludes* by Liszt, and *Prelude to the Afternoon of a Faun* by Debussy. One composer, at least, saw this new instrumental genre as being the epitome of art:

From time immemorial the sung word has occasioned or developed a connection between music and literary or quasi-literary works. The present attempt, however, is intended as a fusion of the two, which promises to become more intimate than any heretofore achieved. More and more the masterpieces of music will absorb the masterpieces of literature. (Liszt, 1882.)

And so, in a world where "without music life would be a mistake" (Nietzsche), and the composer's creed was "We believe as steadfastly in art as we do in God and man, both of whom find therein a means and type of elevated expression" (Liszt), music was to "progress."

(Beethoven)

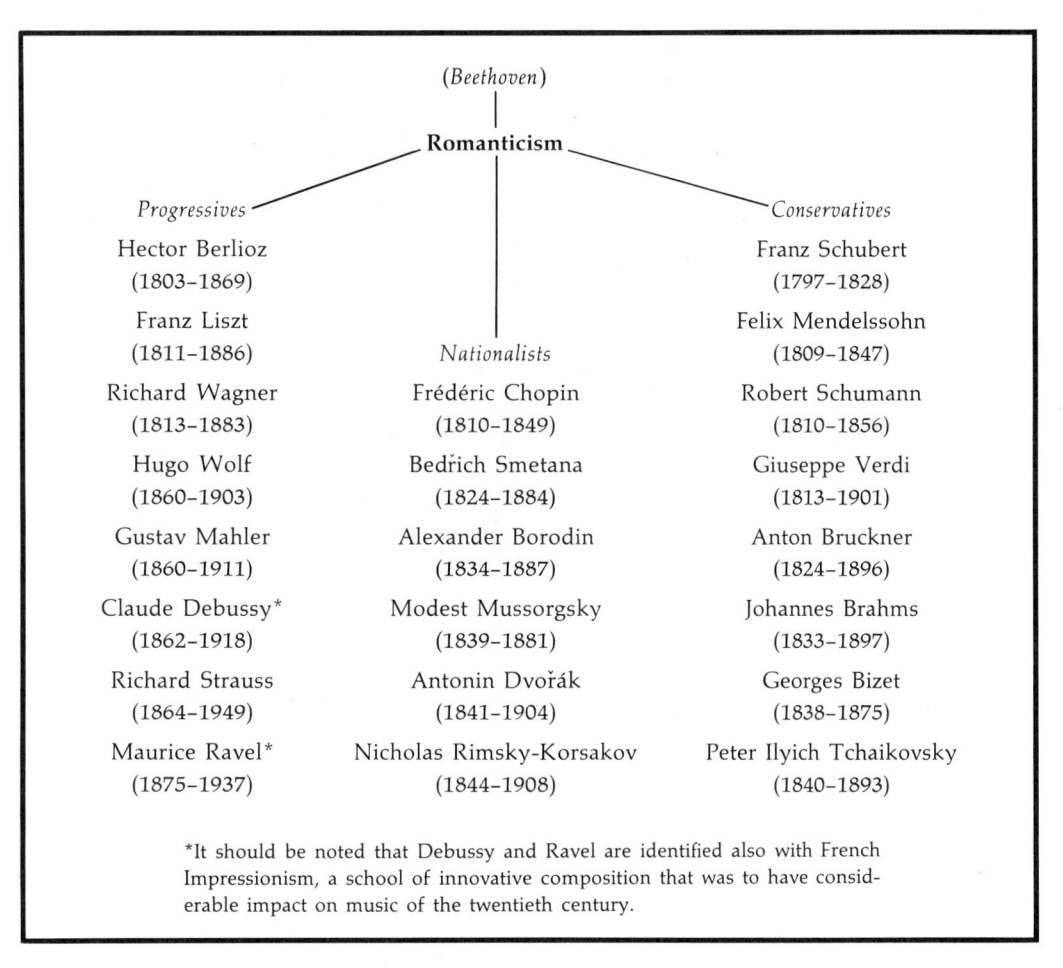

Romanticism

Progressives	*Nationalists*	*Conservatives*
Hector Berlioz (1803–1869)		Franz Schubert (1797–1828)
Franz Liszt (1811–1886)		Felix Mendelssohn (1809–1847)
Richard Wagner (1813–1883)	Frédéric Chopin (1810–1849)	Robert Schumann (1810–1856)
Hugo Wolf (1860–1903)	Bedřich Smetana (1824–1884)	Giuseppe Verdi (1813–1901)
Gustav Mahler (1860–1911)	Alexander Borodin (1834–1887)	Anton Bruckner (1824–1896)
Claude Debussy* (1862–1918)	Modest Mussorgsky (1839–1881)	Johannes Brahms (1833–1897)
Richard Strauss (1864–1949)	Antonin Dvořák (1841–1904)	Georges Bizet (1838–1875)
Maurice Ravel* (1875–1937)	Nicholas Rimsky-Korsakov (1844–1908)	Peter Ilyich Tchaikovsky (1840–1893)

*It should be noted that Debussy and Ravel are identified also with French Impressionism, a school of innovative composition that was to have considerable impact on music of the twentieth century.

When one surveys the vast array of music of the nineteenth century, one is struck by the incredible diversity of musical utterance—a virtual cornucopia of disparate types and styles. Instrumental music reigns supreme, but its sovereignty is almost equaled by opera. Art song and solo instrumental works flourish, and chamber music, once performed by and for a relatively small group of noble amateurs, becomes the expressive vehicle for the professional artist playing to a broader audience, though no less elitist in terms of understanding. Extended dramatic works prevail: spectacular operas and ballets, monumental symphonies, brilliant concertos, symphonic tone poems, massive concert oratorios, and the like. But, at the same time, intimacy of expression prevailed: short mood pieces for piano, art songs, and solo and chamber works for various media. Again one notes a cleavage between the grandiose, dramatic utterances of the former and the more personal, private statements of the latter.

Further, some music is cerebrally abstract—that is, non-referential—with the listener free to respond in a personal way to whatever meaning the music evokes. On the other hand, other works are programmatic, having a story line or other associative element that imposes certain constraints on the flights of fancy of the hearer. Thus one hears "Romantic music" which is both grandiose and miniature, abstract and story-oriented, national and universal, but through it all flows a strain of subjectivity evoking intense moods and emotions, the storms and stresses of life.

The composer, now "free" from the dominance of the patronage of church and nobility, often coming from a well-to-do cultural background himself, became a figure to be reckoned with in the musical world. Several of them were men of many talents, not all musical, and one sees such amazing figures as Richard Wagner—revolutionary, composer, dramatist, designer, and producer; Hector Berlioz—composer, author, and critic; Robert Schumann—pianist, composer, and critic; Felix Mendelssohn—composer and conductor, and the like. With the "new" music and audience arose the critic dedicated to explain it, publishers to produce it, entrepreneurs to sell it, and virtuosos to perform it. No previous century had seen such a vast wealth of creativity, such brilliance of virtuosity, and such mass consumption of the riches of music. To describe them all would take volumes, and to know them or their music

Franz Schubert (1797–1828)

■ While Bach was graced with the awesome capacity to create inspired masterpieces in great quantity and with amazing regularity, and Mozart, with incredible ease and great refinement, and Beethoven, with heroic effort and copious revision, Franz Schubert was endowed with a natural gift shared by few men, the gift of inspired melody. When asked how he composed, Schubert—that facile, melodic genius—replied simply, "I finish one piece and begin the next."

Schubert fits the popular conception of the Romantic composers: penniless, bohemian, divinely inspired but unappreciated, unfortunate in life and love, and sickly and short-lived.

He was born in a suburb of the then hub of the musical world, Vienna, a musical world dominated to that time by the so-called "Viennese masters"—Haydn, Mozart, and Beethoven. He came from a musical family, the son of a schoolmaster who furthered his training in music and prepared him for admittance to the imperial chapel and school for the training of court singers. Life there was spartan and uninviting, to say the least, and the shy Schubert found time there, except that devoted to music making, to be trying indeed. One colleague who supplied him with music paper he could ill afford observed, "He wrote music extraordinarily fast and the study hours he devoted unremittingly to composition." Composing soon totally absorbed him to the point that his other studies suffered, to the great consternation of his father. Nevertheless, he unswervingly pursued his first love, primarily instrumental composition at that time, and upon completing his formal music training at the age of 17, entered a normal school and thereafter secured a position in his father's school as an assistant elementary teacher. As one might assume, he was not fitted for the trying life of a schoolteacher, though it did seem an attractive alternative, at the time at least, to serving a fourteen-year stint in the Austrian army. In 1816 he quit his teaching position, never having given up composing. Some of his greatest songs, *Gretchen am Spinnrade* (*Gretchen at the Spinning Wheel*), *Der Erlkönig* (*The Elf King*), and *Heidenröslein* (*Heather Rose*) were created during that period in fleeting moments of spontaneous creativity and transcendent inspiration which saw the composition of no less than 144 songs in one year (1815) and as many as eight per day.

In the decade left him, he was cast loose in the colorful company of those painters, musicians, poets, and other literary figures who espoused the cause of Romanticism in Vienna. His mature life was that of a bohemian, wherein he teetered on the brink of poverty, often dashing off a masterful song, *Ave Maria,* for example, for the price of a drink or a meal. He created more than 600 solo songs and various song cycles and song groups, including *Die Schöne Müllerin* (*The Beautiful Miller's Daughter*), *Die Winterreise* (*The Winter Journey*), and *Schwanengesang* (*Swan Song*), made up of a group of his last songs.

Without doubt he was the supreme master of expressive Romantic *lieder,* songs in the German vernacular, and in this genre one sees manifest his genius for tuneful melody, some folklike and others quite sophisticated, and for his vivid accompaniments, generally based on uncomplicated harmonies, and above all his genius for dramatic and expressive musical utterance. He turned sporadically from his first love to compose eight symphonies, the "Great" *Symphony No. 9 in C Major* being one of the most beautiful; a number of operas, none of which was successful; numerous chamber works, such as the *String Quartet No. 14 in D Minor* ("Death and the Maiden") and the *Quintet in A Major, Op. 114* (the "Trout" Quintet); choral works, such as the *Mass in G Major;* and numerous works for solo piano—sonatas, waltzes, impromptus, *Moments Musicaux* (*Musical Moments*) and other such character pieces.

His unstable existence and incessant creative drive were to take their early toll; Schubert was only 31 when he died, and he departed an inhospitable world with few possessions, persuaded of his failure. Not until much later was the world to realize what the dying Beethoven perceived: "Truly, a divine spark lives in Schubert."

will take a lifetime. But the awards will be many for those who learn to know the music of the illustrious Romantic composers.

SONG

To sample the flavor of romanticism at its pictorial best, consider an ever-popular song by Franz Schubert (1797–1828), composed when he was only eighteen years old. *Der Erlkönig* (Example 11-1) could be translated as *The Elf King*, but since that hardly does justice to the malevolence of the title character, we shall leave the title untranslated. Though written for solo voice with piano accompaniment, the song is really a drama based on a ballad by Goethe, with a narrator, a child, a father, and the Erlkönig, a mythical figure representing death. In the following analysis the music is presented in slightly abbreviated form; the piano accompaniment is indicated only at the beginning of sections, even though it continues to play throughout. The translation is a literal one intended to assist in understanding how Schubert's music fits the original words, rather than to serve as a performing version. We suggest you study the song and the commentary first and then listen several times to the song to get the full meaning and impact.

Many of Schubert's songs are written in a simple strophic form in which each stanza of the poem is set to the same music. Others are set to modified strophic form, in which each stanza is set to basically the same music but with occasional variations in the voice part or piano accompaniment to meet the changes in mood or dictation of the later stanzas. As a typical Romantic composer, however, Schubert wrote many songs that do not follow rigidly prescribed patterns; instead the form of the music arises out of the form of the text. Frequently the term

EXAMPLE 11-1 SCHUBERT: *Der Erlkönig (The Elf King)*.

Measures 1–14: The rapidly repeated notes heard in the introduction (motive 1) and at key points throughout the song suggest the agitated sound of horses' hooves on the ground. Against this we frequently hear a low motive (motive 2) consisting of a rapid scale passage followed by three short notes outlining a descending minor triad. The motive is not sung, but heard in the piano. Even without words, however, we can sense its ominous, foreboding nature.

Measures 15–30: The voice enters in the somewhat neutral tones of the narrator, setting forth the essentials of the opening of the drama. The repeated notes and the ominous motive 2 are now heard as an accompaniment to the voice.

(Narrator)

Wer reitet so spät durch Nacht und Wind? Es ist der
Who rides there so late through night and wind? It is a

The accompaniment here continues in a similar manner.

Va - ter mit sei - nem Kind; er hat den Kna - ben wohl in dem Arm, er fasst ihn
fa - ther with his young child; He has the boy safe in his arm, He holds him

Measures 32–39: After a brief interlude for the piano with the motives 1 and 2, we hear the next phrase sung in the comforting tones of the father. Notice the generally lower range and the prominence of the interval of the perfect fourth.

si - cher, er hält ihn warm.
safe - ly, he keeps him warm.

196 Styles of Music

Measures 40–50: As the father's phrase concludes, we hear motive 2 twice in abbreviated form, only the ascending scale. This continues as the voice enters in the higher range of the young child. Notice how the ascending leaps fit so appropriately to the questioning nature of these phrases of the child.

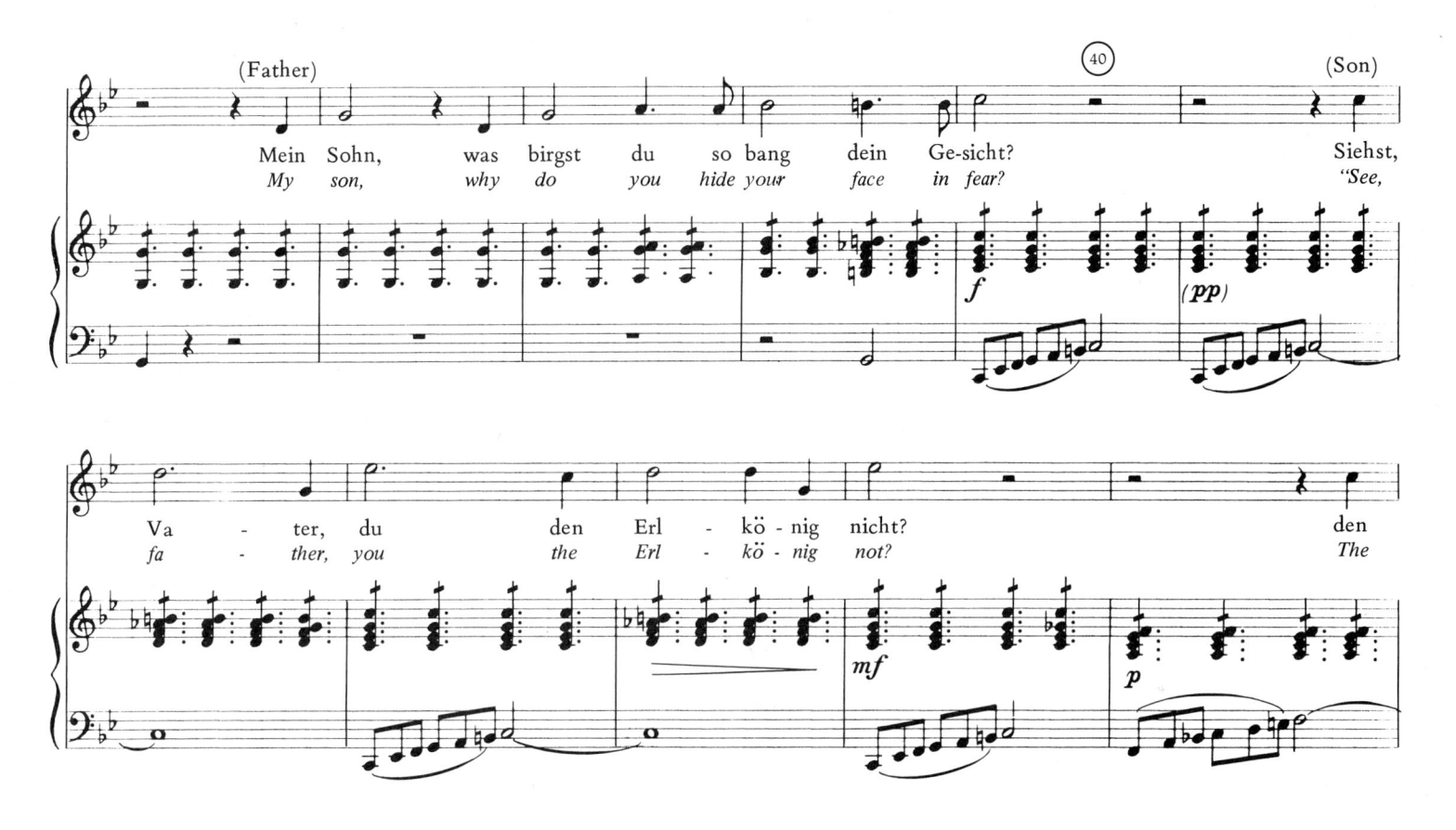

Measures 51–56: Now motive 1 drops out of the accompaniment for the first time, and against repeated notes we once again hear the lower tones of the father as he seeks to comfort the child.

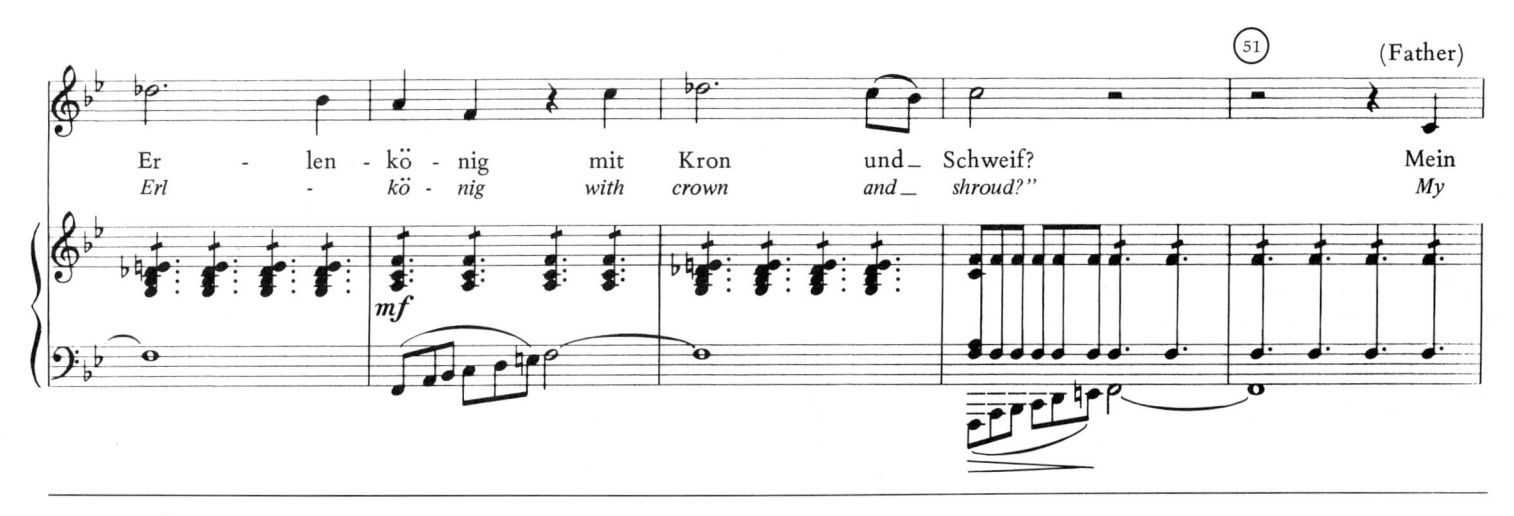

Romantic Style (1825–1900) 197

Measures 57–71: Suddenly the accompaniment changes to something almost like an extremely fast waltz accompaniment (bass note and two afterbeats). Over this we hear the sweet but somehow sinister song of the Erlkönig. To this point the song has been almost entirely in a minor tonality, but now it changes to major as the Erlkönig seeks to lure the child to him by rapturously describing the delights he will find. Notice the use of chromatic notes in the voice part in measures 66 and 67.

Measures 72–79: The Erlkönig's song is interrupted by the return of the repeated notes from the introduction. The child sings of his fear of the Erlkönig. Notice the poignant effect of the minor seconds in the motive of "Mein Vater" ("My Father"). The child's section ends with an ascending chromatic scale (all half steps).

Measures 80–85: The interval of the perfect fourth and the lower range signal the return of the voice of the father seeking to comfort his child.

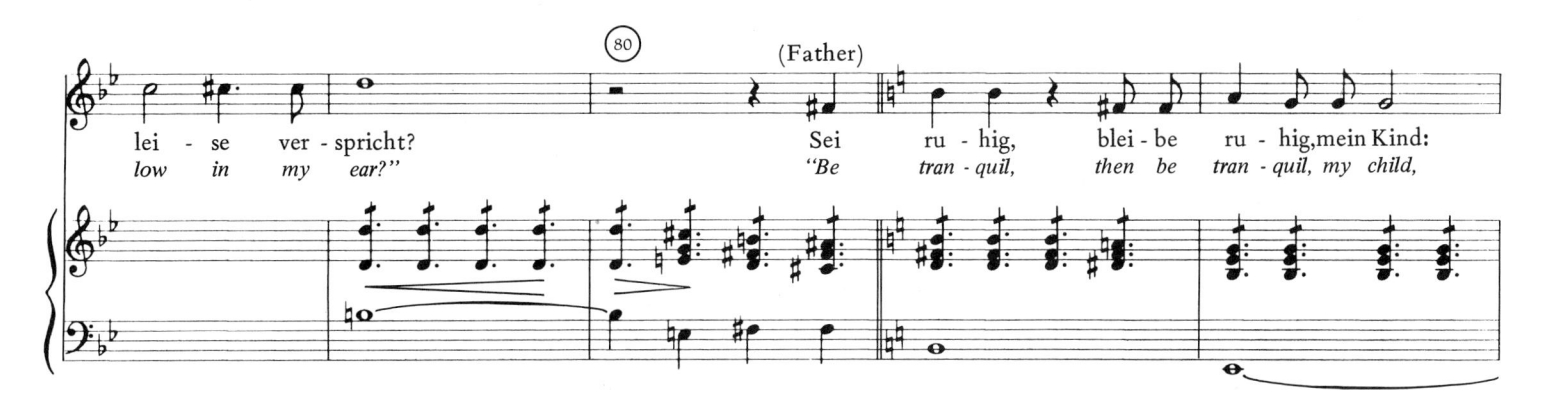

Measures 86–96: The Erlkönig returns, now to the accompaniment of major arpeggios that give the effect of a harp accompaniment. The melody of the Erlkönig now moves in more rapid notes, suggesting his impatience and his eagerness to take the boy with him to his kingdom.

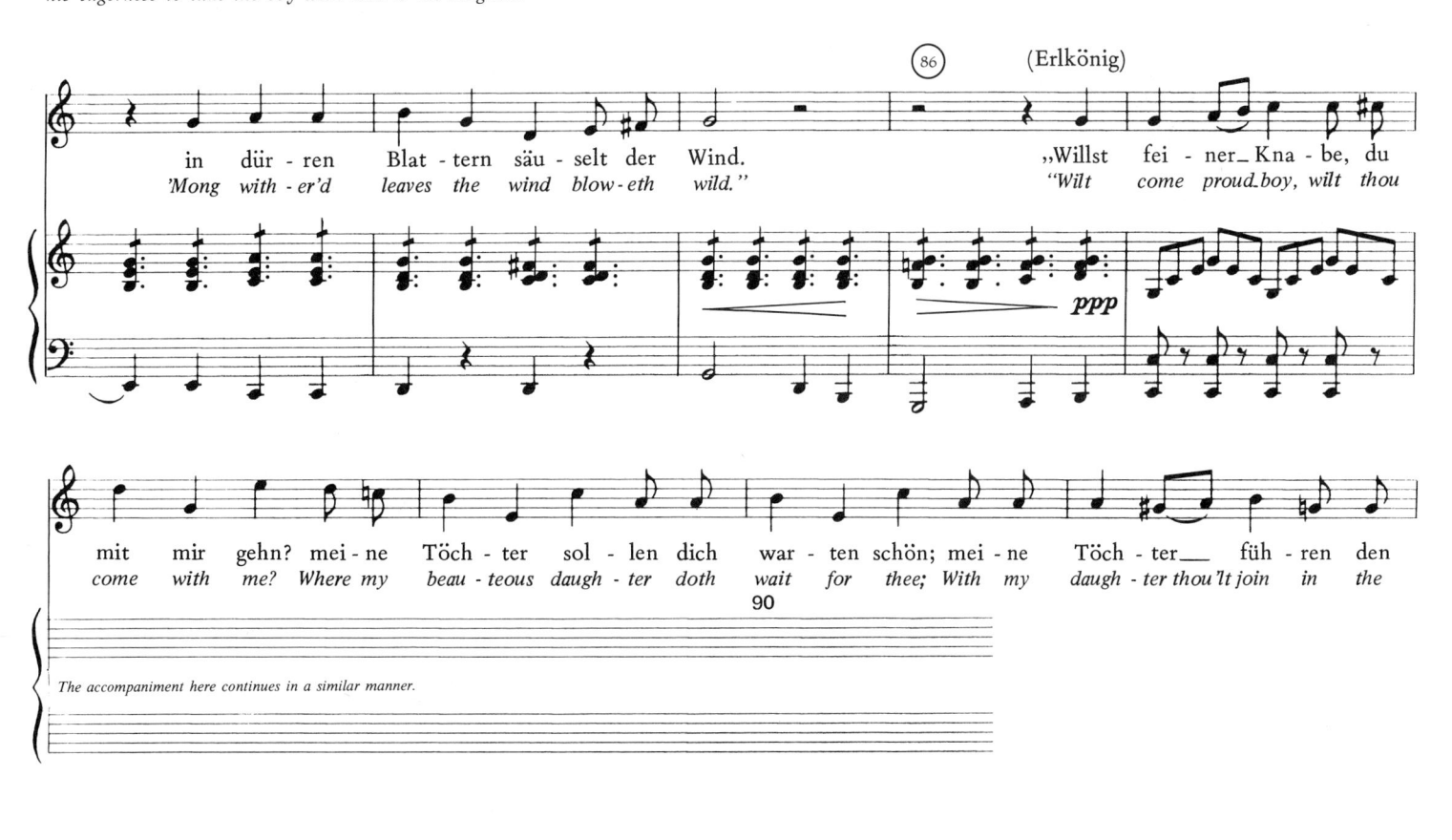

The accompaniment here continues in a similar manner.

Romantic Style (1825–1900) 199

The mysterious mood of Der Erlkönig (The Elf King) is vividly portrayed in this mid-19th century German engraving. Note the dimly perceived figures in the background of the picture.

Measures 97–104: *Again to the accompaniment of rapidly repeated notes, the son cries out for his father. He sings the same motive on "Mein Vater" as before, but now it is transposed to a higher pitch suggesting his intensified agitation.*

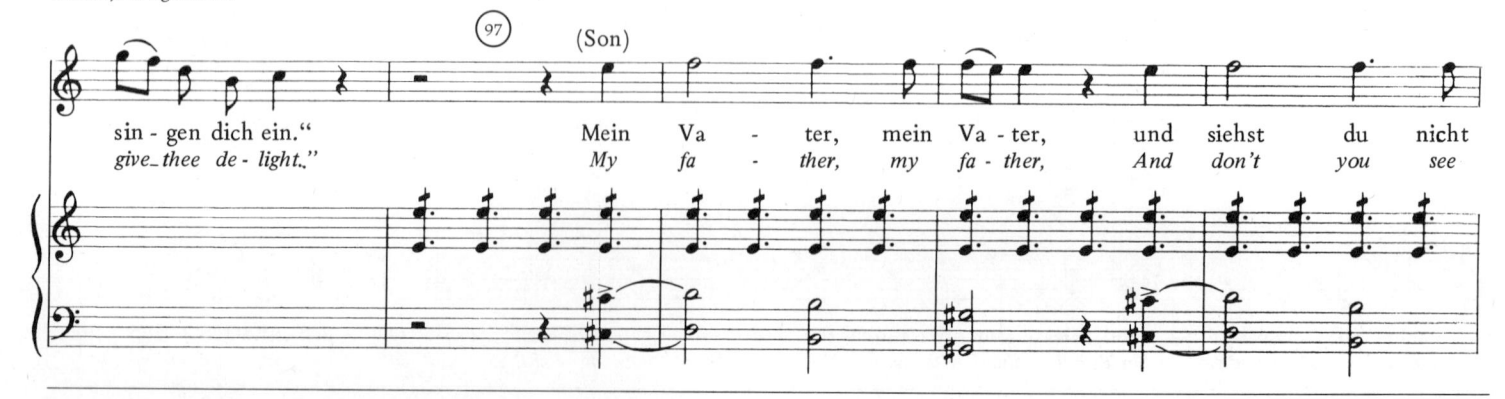

sin - gen dich ein."   Mein Va - ter, mein Va - ter, und siehst du nicht
give thee de - light."   *My fa - ther, my fa - ther, And don't you see*

200   Styles of Music

Measures 105–115: Again we hear the perfect fourth of the father's motive. It too has been transposed to a higher pitch level showing that he also is more agitated.

Measures 116–122: The Erlkönig returns for this last time and does not try to conceal his intentions. Brutally he seizes the child to take to his domain—which is, we now realize, the domain of death. Notice that the accompaniment here is not the false pleasantness suggested by the waltz accompaniment or the arpeggio accompaniment in the previous Erlkönig sections. Now it is the insistent repeated chords that have been used throughout the song to portray anguish and tension.

Romantic Style (1825–1900) 201

Measures 123–130: The voice of the child returns in one last desperate outcry. The half-step motive is now set at the very top of the singer's range.

willig, so brauch ich Gewalt." "Mein Vater, mein Vater, jetzt
will-ing, I seize thee by force!" "My father, my father! how

fasst er mich an! Erlkönig hat mir ein Leid getan!"
he is seizing me Erlkönig has hurt me.

Measures 132–148: Motives 1 and 2 now return and the voice of the narrator concludes the drama. The repeated notes stop shortly before the end. In the course of the song they have become identified with the life pulse of the child; their cessation signifies his death. The narrator, as though overcome by the tragedy, speaks rather than sings his last words, and two stark chords end the drama.

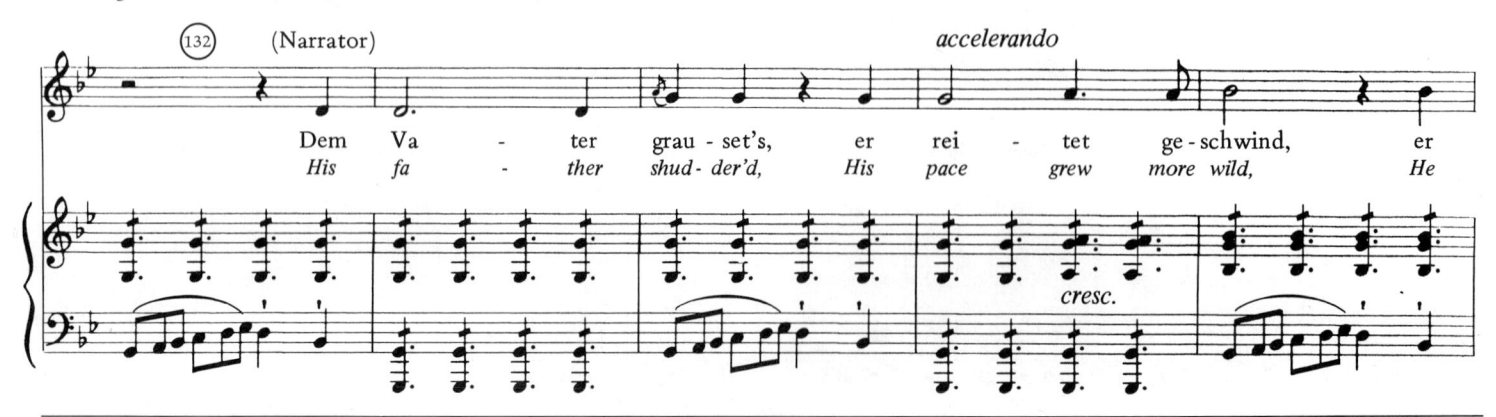

(Narrator) *accelerando*

Dem Vater grauset's, er reitet geschwind, er
His father shudder'd, His pace grew more wild, He

through-composed is applied to songs like *Der Erlkönig* that are written in a freer form. This should not be taken to mean, however, that there is no repetition or variation or restatement of material in such songs. We see in *Der Erlkönig* how Schubert uses these techniques not only for the sake of the drama but also for the sake of musical unity in the composition.

SONG LITERATURE AFTER SCHUBERT

Throughout the nineteenth century song literature was enriched by magnificent contributions from composers like Schumann, Brahms, and Wolf. The listener who has learned to appreciate the songs of Schubert should have no difficulty in approaching other art songs of this period, except perhaps for the language barrier. These songs are usually performed in the original German. It is difficult, if not impossible, to make an effective translation of German *Lieder* because the musical expression is so closely bound to the nuances and rhythm of the original language. This problem, however, can be turned into an opportunity. Many students have found that the study of songs in their original language can be an effective and enjoyable way to approach the study of foreign language.

At the end of the nineteenth century and the beginning of the twentieth century, composers like Gustav Mahler began to write songs with the accompaniment of full orchestra rather than just piano. Among Mahler's most famous works is *Das Lied von der Erde* (*The Song of the Earth*), a collection of six songs based on ancient Chinese poems and written alternately for tenor solo and alto solo with orchestra accompaniment. The first song, "Das Trinklied vom Jammer der Erde" ("The Drinking Song of the Misery of the Earth"), begins with the words "Schon winkt der Wein" ("Already the wine beckons"). These are preceded by a brief introduction for the orchestra which sets the mood for the beginning of the text just as the piano introductions of Schubert do. Mahler's introduction with its impetuous horn call and shimmering high woodwinds so effectively captures the essence of wine that one not only hears the music but can almost see and taste it. This brief outburst is followed by a lyric melody in the strings. Both the horn melody and the violin melody appear in Example 11-2.

In examining this fascinating melodic line we find that it is composed of only five pitches, or based on the pentatonic scale. This scale, which is characterized by the absence of half steps, forms the basis of much of the music of China and Japan as well as folk music from other cultures. Frequently in *Das Lied von der Erde* Mahler uses pentatonic elements, which add an exotic flavor to the work and contrast effectively with the diatonic or chromatic character of the rest of the work.

The first song is written in modified strophic form. Each of the three stanzas closes with the same text and music (see Example 11-3), but each time the music is transposed a half step higher so that the song closes in A minor, the tonality of the beginning introduction.

In the first stanza the poet announces that he will sing a song of sorrow. In the second he praises his host's wine cellar, then seizes a lute and sings that wine is "worth more than all the riches of the earth." The introduction to the third stanza features a brilliant high trumpet solo. In the text the poet contrasts the permanence of earth with the transitoriness of man's

EXAMPLE 11-2   MAHLER: *Das Lied von der Erde* (*The Song of the Earth*), No. 1, "DAS TRINKLIED VOM JAMMER DER ERDE" (THE DRINKING SONG OF THE MISERY OF THE EARTH"), MEASURES 1–10.

EXAMPLE 11-3   MAHLER: *Das Lied von der Erde* (*The Song of the Earth*), No. 1, "DAS TRINKLIED VOM JAMMER DER ERDE" ("THE DRINKING SONG OF THE MISERY OF THE EARTH"), MEASURES 81–89.

Gustav Mahler (1860–1911)

■ Gustav Mahler, son of a Bohemian Jewish shopkeeper, was destined to become the last of the incredible line of Viennese symphonic composers begun by Franz Joseph Haydn. Reared in very humble circumstances in a remote village, the precocious lad's talents first surfaced at age four when he could reproduce on the accordion the soldiers' marches heard at the local garrison, an early indication of his later propensity for the inclusion of folk elements and popular idioms of his native Bohemia in his deeply expressive, intensely personal musical utterances. He became an avid student of music, an accomplished pianist, and a precocious but rather erratic student of other subjects, being enamored of Germanic Romantic poetry and literature.

By age 15 his future was determined and he entered the Vienna conservatory where he turned his impressive talents to composition and conducting while continuing the study of philosophy and history at the university. It appeared that he was destined to conquer the world of musical drama, perhaps along the line of Wagner whose music he so greatly admired. After some unsuccessful early attempts in this genre, however, one of which was rejected by a jury chaired by Brahms, he abandoned this pursuit, turning to symphonic works which were to be epic dramatic compositions replete with richly colorful orchestral effects, the contrapuntal interweaving of melodious themes, surging unrest, and intense pathos typical of the last of the Romantic composers.

After his early failure as a composer, Mahler turned to opera conducting. In the next eight years, beginning in 1880, his great talents were to be recognized and his fame established as he gravitated from Halle, to Ljubljana, Vienna, Prague, Leipzig, and Budapest, to name but a few, before arriving at Frankfurt in 1891, having achieved recognition by the musical world and the admiration of such luminaries as Brahms and Strauss. One suspects that while he achieved these conductorial successes he sublimated his desires to compose, a thought that may help explain his reputation as a truculent tyrant who berated prima donnas and fought constantly with managers as he strove for performance perfection and faithfulness to the composer's intentions.

Having recovered from the dismal failure of his First Symphony in 1889 in Budapest while he was director of the Royal Opera House there, and having found a new champion in Strauss, famed composer-conductor, Mahler reentered the symphonic field, creating his next two monumental works, the Second Symphony ("Resurrection") premiered by Strauss in Berlin, and the Third Symphony, first performed in Krefeld with Mahler conducting. One wishes that the tides of public opinion might have turned and that these works, now enjoying the popularity they so richly deserve, might have assured Mahler the fame and security he sought. But, not so; Mahler was typecast as a conductor.

He became conductor, director, and then artistic director of the world-famous Vienna Opera (1897–1907), which through the force of his genius he was to see become among the greatest in the world. His operatic fame had not eluded the influential music lovers of this country, and in 1907 he became principal conductor at the Metropolitan Opera, making his debut with a monumental performance of Wagner's *Tristan und Isolde*.

Though world famous, Mahler was still a poor man who by age 47 felt rejected by his own country and bitter because of the lukewarm response to his music. Despite long-standing cardiac problems, he threw himself into his work with characteristic compulsion, taking on the additional arduous task of reviving the New York Philharmonic. By so doing he had hoped to acquire financial security and greater acceptance of his works—hopes that were never realized. Collapsing during a concert of the Philharmonic, he was rushed to Vienna for treatment but was declared hopelessly ill. He died a few months later, embittered and defeated, having left to the world nine monumental symphonies, plus a number of songs and song cycles, all fervidly tuneful works imbued with the richness of orchestral color, extravagance of pathos, and emotional expression so typical of the moody Romantic composer.

The fantasy and almost childlike nature of much folk music and art music are conjured up in Chagall's painting The Green Violinist.

life. The brief coda ends abruptly with the thud of a low chord.

The "sound world" of each song in this collection is unique and colorful (see the excerpts in Example 11-4). Mahler treats both voice and orchestra with the assured skill of a man who spent his life as a highly successful opera and orchestra conductor in Europe and the United States. Like a painter who can create a vivid illusion with just a few brushstrokes, Mahler can create a vivid orchestra timbre with just a few instruments, reserving the power and variety of the full ensemble for the high points of the work. He uses the voice with full awareness of its special strengths and color resources.

Mahler's melodic lines sometimes employ poignant motives created by an ascending leap followed by a descending step. This type of motive (called an *appoggiatura* or "leaning tone") is used effectively in song No. 5 after the voice has sung "If life is only a dream, why then all this effort and torture?" You will notice that the opening motive is almost identical in pitch with the opening motive of "Yesterday." In both cases the G is dissonant to the underlying F-major chord. This also contributes to the poignancy of the passages (Example 11-5).

We have excluded folk music and other popular forms of song in our discussion of Romantic music. To have done so may have created the impression that the venerable tradition begun by the ancient troubadours had died. But not so! Romantic humanity continues to voice personal views of life through the ever-popular mode of song—both in folk and art form—as it always has, does, and will.

EXAMPLE 11-4 MAHLER: *Das Lied von der Erde* (*The Song of the Earth*). (a) No. 2, "Der Einsame in Herbst" ("The Lonely One in Autumn"), measures 3–4; (b) No. 3, "Von der Jugend" ("Of Youth"), measures 3–4; (c) No. 4, "Von der Schönheit" ("Of Beauty"), measures 8–13; (d) No. 5, "Der Trunkene im Frühling" ("The Drinker in Spring"), measures 3–4; (e) No. 6, "Der Abschied" ("The Farewell"), closing chord.

EXAMPLE 11-5 (a) MAHLER: *ibid.*, No. 5, "Das Trunkene im Frühling" ("The Drinker in Spring"), measures 8–9; (b) LENNON AND MCCARTNEY: "Yesterday," measure 1.

12 Romantic Style (1825–1900) (continued)

PROGRAM MUSIC

This chapter discusses specific examples of instrumental music that are more or less directly related to other arts or at least to other life experiences. This type of music is generally called *program music,* but a better term might be *referential music,* since the identifying characteristic is that the music *refers* to some extramusical idea, to something outside the music, whether it be a specific story, poem, drama, historical event, painting, or simply a general mood, effect, or environment. We should first distinguish between true referential music—that is, music intended by its composer to refer to something extramusical—and "pseudo-" or "second-hand" referential music—that is, music that was not intended by its composer to be referential but that somehow was invested with a program, a nickname, or some other referential label by someone other than the composer. The "Moonlight" Sonata and the "Emperor" Concerto of Beethoven, for example, were not written as descriptions of moonlight or emperors.

We shall begin with a work that is generally recognized as the seminal work of nineteenth-century program music—the *Symphonie Fantastique* by Hector Berlioz (1803–1869). This work is based on a program written by the composer and incorporating, in a somewhat idealized and imaginative form, elements from Berlioz's own life. We shall first quote from the programmatic description and then suggest aspects of the use of instrumental color and other theoretical elements.

Berlioz: Symphonie Fantastique

I. Reveries, passions: *At first he thinks of the uneasy and nervous condition of his soul, of somber longings, of depression and joyous elation without any recognizable cause, which he experienced before the beloved one had appeared to him.*

The opening gesture is played by woodwind instruments entering rapidly one after the other on a pulsating triplet figure and ending on a minor chord (Example 12-1). Notice that the horns are treated as members, in effect, of the woodwind section.

The waltz, whose characteristic "embrace" was enthusiastically praised by the "swingers" and damned by the more staid of the 1800's, continues to capture the imagination of artists, composers, and dancers—as it did of two 19th century Frenchmen: the painter Pierre Auguste Renoir, whose Le Bal à Bougival appears here; and the composer Hector Berlioz, whose Symphonie Fantastique is discussed.

effect previously described. This chord is followed by a fortissimo dominant-seventh chord and then we hear, for one measure, a very effective alternation of staccato woodwinds and pizzicato strings (Example 12-2).

Then he remembers the ardent love with which she had suddenly inspired him, his almost insane anxiety of mind, his raging jealousy, his reawakening love, his religious consolation.

A few transitional measures take us into the main part of the movement, which begins with a statement of the idée fixe—that is, the recurring theme that represents the beloved. (Actually it probably represented Harriet Smithson, a beautiful actress with whom Berlioz had first a torrid love affair and then later a horrid marriage—fortunately only the former figures in this work.) The idée fixe is played legato by the first-violin section and the first flute. This is a typical orchestral device of doubling a string sound with a woodwind sound; the resulting mixture is more interesting than either sound alone would be. When we hear this melody we realize that the fragments we had been hearing in the introduction were really variants of motives from it. The melody is played without any accompaniment at first, except for repeated-note chords on the cadences in measures 7 and 8; later these repeated chords (played by spiccato strings) are placed under the continuation of the melody. In later sections of this first movement the idée fixe will be heard in fragments or in toto in such varied orchestral settings as doubled octaves in the low strings (measure 168), in triple octaves in solo flute, clarinet, and bassoon (measure 241), in varied version by the full orchestra (measure 412), in solo oboe changed to minor (measure 456), and in its final appearance in the first violins alone (measure 505). Most of this movement, in keeping with its reverie character, is played by the strings or by the woodwinds (with horns); the trumpets and timpani are used very sparingly and unobtrusively; the trombones, the tuba, and the other percussion are not used at all. The movement is cast in an adapted version of the sonata-allegro form. That is, the principles of an absolute form are combined with the expressiveness of program music.

Next come fragmentary gestures in the strings, con sordino, suggesting his longing. The mood of the music becomes more agitated as strings, now without mutes, and woodwinds share rapid sixteenth-note figures. At the very end of this introductory section we hear a sustained C-major chord with decrescendo and then crescendo played by the woodwinds and by the strings with the latter employing the tremolo

EXAMPLE 12-1 BERLIOZ: *Symphonie Fantastique,* FIRST MOVEMENT, MEASURES 1–6.

210 Styles of Music

EXAMPLE 12-2 BERLIOZ: *Symphonie Fantastique*, END OF INTRODUCTION, MEASURES 61–63.

II. A ball: *At a ball, amidst the confusion of a brilliant festival, he finds the loved one again.*

One of the most famous symphonic waltzes occurs in this movement of Berlioz's *Symphonie Fantastique;* the movement is appropriately titled "A Ball." The principal theme of the movement is quoted in Example 12-3.

The music of this excerpt is composed in such a way as to create an impression in the listener's mind of a gala ballroom scene filled with waltzing couples, handsomely dressed in the style of the early nineteenth century. Berlioz was a romantic and this work depicts musically the opium-induced fantasies of a young dreamer and the beloved one around whom his fantasies center.

EXAMPLE 12-3 BERLIOZ: *Symphonie Fantastique,* SECOND MOVEMENT, MEASURES 35–55.

212 Styles of Music

"At a ball, amidst the confusion of a brilliant festival, he finds the loved one again"—a scene from Berlioz' Symphonie Fantastique subtly revealed in this lithograph by Fantin-Latout.

the setting, the soft whispering of the trees stirred by the wind, some prospects of hope recently made known to him—all these sensations unite to impart an unaccustomed repose to his heart and to lend a smiling color to his imagination. And then she appears once more. His heart stops beating, painful forebodings fill his soul. "If she should prove false to him!" One of the shepherds resumes the melody, but the other no longer answers. Sunset . . . distant rolling of thunder . . . loneliness . . . silence.

The opening of this work is a unique study in timbre. Notice how similar are the sounds of the oboe and English horn and yet how subtly different their timbres. Berlioz called for these two parts to be played behind the scene or off-stage. At first heard alone, the two instruments are later accompanied by tremolo violas. The main melody of the movement is played by the same "mixture" of first violin and first flute that we found in the first movement, with pizzicato string chords appearing at the end of the first phrase. Once again the idée fixe appears in the middle section of the movement (measure 90), played by flute, oboe, and clarinet in octaves. Echoes of this appear in the flute in counterpoint to the main melody when it returns (measure 150). The form of the movement is A-B-A. (Recall the discussion of Sectional Forms in Chapter 5).

The mood evoked by this movement and its theme is elicited in part by the dance character of the music, a character clearly associated with the simple triple meter and tempo of the piece.

Clarity is achieved by a legato melody in the first violins and staccato accompanying chords in the other strings when the main waltz theme is stated (measure 39) and by the delicate use of staccato winds frequently throughout the movement in the middle of which the idée fixe is heard in the flute and oboe.

IV. March to the scaffold: *He dreams that he has murdered his beloved, that he has been condemned to death and is being led to the scaffold. The procession advances, accompanied by a march that is alternately somber and wild, brilliant and solemn, in which the sound of heavy steps follows without transition upon the most tumultuous outbursts. At last the fixed idea returns for a moment as the last thought of love is cut short by the fatal stroke.*

III. *On a summer evening in the country, he hears two shepherd lads who play the* ranz des vaches* *in alternation. This pastoral duet,*

Now for the first time the full resources of the orchestra are unleashed to match the powerful demands of the program. The opening is one of the most "modern" effects devised by this master of orchestration (Berlioz wrote the first extensive treatise on the art of orchestration). Two timpani are simultaneously played by two players; also heard are low strings pizzicato and fragments in low horns and bassoons. The main melody (the somber march) is finally stated by cellos and

---

*The *ranz des vache* is a type of Swiss folk tune often played on a primitive wind instrument, known as the alphenhorn or alphine horn. Mountain herders frequently use this horn for signaling over great distances.

Romantic Style (1825–1900) (continued) 213

EXAMPLE 12-4 Berlioz: *Symphonie Fantastique*, fourth movement, measures 21–28.

basses in octaves. Its power comes perhaps from its stark simplicity; it is nothing more than a descending minor scale. Later it will be heard in inversion—that is, ascending—and will lead to the "wild" march played in syncopated figures and dotted figures in the high brass and woodwinds, and changing in tonality from the G minor of the introduction and somber march to a bright B-flat major. These two ideas alternate throughout the piece, ending with a single statement of the idée fixe in the first clarinet that is terminated by a crashing fortissimo chord in the full orchestra, vividly suggesting the fall of the executioner's ax. The closing G-major chord is played by three timpanists.

V. Dream of a witches' sabbath: *He dreams that he is present at a witches' dance, surrounded by horrible spirits, amidst sorcerers and monsters in many fearful forms, who have come to assist at his funeral. Strange sounds, groans, shrill laughter, distant yells, which other cries seem to answer.*

The movement opens with tremolos in the high strings and scale fragments in the low strings. This is followed by eerie scales, first legato and then spiccato in the high strings, and then a trill figure in the low strings with pizzicato chords in the upper strings. Now fragments are wafted from one group of winds and brass to another, punctuated by a return of the first ideas in the strings.

The beloved melody is heard again but it has lost its noble and shy character; it has become a vulgar, trivial, and grotesque dance tune. She it is who comes to attend the witches' meeting. Howls of joy greet her arrival. She joins the infernal orgy.

This transformation of the idée fixe is effected first by having it played by the clarinet very softly with added grace notes and trills (rapid alternation between a main note and one a second above) and in a fast compound duple meter (like a jig) (Example 12-4). After a brief orchestral interjection (howls of joy), the transformation is made even more dramatic by having the melody played in the "raucous" timbre of the E-flat clarinet.

Bells toll for the dead, a burlesque parody of the dies irae. *The witches round-dance. The dance and the* dies irae *are heard at the same time.*

Orchestral bells toll the tonic and dominant of C minor. Against this the tubas and bassoons intone the Gregorian melody for the words *dies irae* (day of wrath) from the Requiem Mass or Mass for the dead. After each phrase a mocking version of the tune in diminution (in faster note values) is heard in the pizzicato upper strings and high woodwinds.

The witches' round dance changes to C major and is cast in the form of a fugue (recall the discussion of fugue in Chapter 3). The fugue begins in the low strings, moves through the upper strings, and gradually adds the full ensemble. Later the basically diatonic motion of the witches' theme is changed to a chromatic version (measure 363), and this is followed by the combination of the witches' theme in its original major version in the strings set in counterpoint against the dies irae in the woodwinds and brass (Example 12-5), a masterful stroke both dramatically and musically. It is followed by a brilliant, colorful coda calling on the resources of the full orchestra and providing a rousing conclusion to this exciting work.

EXAMPLE 12-5 Berlioz: *Symphonie Fantastique*, fifth movement, measures 414–422.

Hector Berlioz (1803-1869)

■ It is doubtful that the music of any composer has been more controversial than that of Hector Berlioz, highly praised on the one hand by its ardent admirers and ripped to shreds on the other by its virulent critics. "Powerful," "original," "brilliant," "innovative," "imaginative," "eloquent," say his supporters; "vulgar," "crude," "exhibitionistic," "banal," "grotesque," "grandiloquent," say his detractors. Nevertheless, all agree that this highly original innovator represents the epitome of the ebullient Romantic, certainly of France, and all admit his great genius as a daring orchestrator and astute music critic.

His music is now enjoying a new wave of popularity, highlighted by a recent performance of his colossal two-part opera *Les Troyens* (*The Trojans*) at the Metropolitan Opera in New York. Time seems to have vindicated his efforts to infuse music with more heady elements, dramatic and theatrical, and he has long since been forgiven his penchant for musical "strutting and fretting" on the concert stage.

Berlioz, son of a prosperous physician, was destined to follow in his father's footsteps. In fact, despite his obvious aptitude and love for music, he was forced to embark on a study of medicine, a course he pursued for some four years. Sent to Paris for medical training, he rebelled, began to compose, and then left the medical school and attempted to persuade his distressed parents of the wisdom of his erring ways. If this account sounds vaguely familiar, it is only because *it is*, since the pursuit of the arts as a means of fulfillment—and livelihood—has hardly been the course prescribed for a young lady or gentleman "with a future to consider." Berlioz obtained his father's permission to enter the Paris Conservatoire in 1826 but, in the process, lost his financial support. Thus began a tragic musical career that was generally fraught with frustration and disappointment, being only very infrequently relieved by a brilliant triumph.

He composed and studied while eking out a meager existence singing in a theater chorus and giving private lessons. During the next four years he became acquainted with Beethoven's music, competed unsuccessfully on two separate occasions for a Prix de Rome but won one on the third try, became immersed in the works of Shakespeare and Goethe, fell in love with an Irish actress, and composed his best-known work, *Symphonie Fantastique*. It seems appropriate to observe at this point that the love life of this flamboyant figure was no less troubled than his professional life in that he married twice, after tempestuous courtships, and became involved in a number of unfortunate liaisons, all of which were terminated by death or other unfortunate circumstances.

To compound the miseries of his life, his music, although occasionally a public success as was his dramatic symphony *Romeo and Juliet*, was not generally accepted and certainly was not profitable at the box office. He had to supplement his scanty income by turning to music criticism, at which he was a master but which, unfortunately, led to his political involvement and subsequently made his career in Paris even more precarious. In 1838 he was appointed assistant librarian at the Conservatoire de Musique, having been refused a post as professor of harmony because of his inability to play the piano. In 1852 he became chief librarian, a post which assured him a modest livelihood until his death.

During the last three decades of his life Berlioz divided his time between conducting his music in the major cities of Europe (having little acceptance in Paris), writing critical reviews, and composing. Ironically enough, few of the works for which he is best known were created after the age of forty. He died an embittered man, the greatest French composer of his time, though unappreciated by his countrymen. Berlioz left a rare musical legacy which, in his own words, is summarized as follows: "The prevailing characteristics of my music are passionate expression, intense ardor, rhythmic animation and unexpected turns." This "prophet without honor . . ." has now assumed his place among the musical greats of all times.

Other Program Music

The history of program music can be extended further back in history than Berlioz. Beethoven's Sixth Symphony, called the "Pastoral," was written in 1808, more than twenty years before the Berlioz *Symphonie Fantastique.* Beethoven subtitled the movements of this symphony as follows:

I. Cheerful impressions received on arriving in the country
II. By the brook
III. Peasants merry-making
IV. Tempest and storm
V. The shepherd's hymn—thanksgiving after the storm

The work has some highly interesting programmatic references associated with instruments, such as the depiction of the calls of the nightingale by the flute, the quail by the oboe, and the cuckoo by the clarinet, near the end of the second movement (measure 129); the delightful satirization of country musicians in the oboe and bassoon in the third movement (measure 91); the colorful representation in the fourth movement of thunder in the tremolo low strings (measure 1), drops of rain in the staccato eighth notes of the second violins (measure 3), and bolts of lightning in the full orchestra staccato chords (measure 33); and the peaceful serenity of the motives expressed by the clarinet and the French horn at the beginning of the fifth movement (measures 1, 5). Despite these and other explicit programmatic references, Beethoven stated that the work was "more an expression of feeling than painting." Probably what he meant by this was to emphasize the fact that this work was not like a host of inferior programmatic pieces written at this time, whose only interest lay in their programmatic references; Beethoven's "Pastoral," in contrast, stands on its own as a musical masterwork without any consideration of its programmatic content.

We could trace the history of program music back through such interesting examples as the Biblical sonatas of Kuhnau (1660–1722), in which, for example, the battle of David and Goliath is effectively represented, or other, earlier examples, but it will be more appropriate to carry forward our discussion through the nineteenth and twentieth centuries. The most frequently used type of program music of the nineteenth century was not the multimovement program symphony, though some significant examples did follow Beethoven and Berlioz, but rather the single-movement tone poem or symphonic poem. Franz Liszt is usually assigned the role of originator of this form. He wrote tone poems inspired by poems of Victor Hugo, Byron, and Schiller, but probably his best-known symphonic poem is *Les Préludes* (1854), based on Lamartine's *Méditations Poétiques.* The work is interesting not only for its brilliant, almost theatrical handling of instruments, but perhaps even more for the technique of transformation of themes which figures so prominently in it. A single thematic idea or germ, stated by the strings in the third measure, is not only varied in terms of the kind of motive variation techniques discussed in Chapter 2, but it is also transformed so that it has a different character or effect. Example 12-6 may make this clear.

So effective were works like this and other nineteenth-century programmatic pieces that they remained for years a fertile source of "background music" for radio, films, and eventually television. One of the best-known of these pieces is the *Romeo and Juliet Overture* by Peter Ilyich Tchaikovsky (1840–1893). (The familiar "love theme" is shown in Example 14-2a.) Tchaikovsky avoids a literal depiction of Shakespeare's tragedy of young love, instead he creates musical imagery that permits listeners to supply their own "story."

Composers developed such an ability in tone painting (i.e., using music for representational purposes) that Richard Strauss was able to boast that he could set anything to music, even a glass of beer. Strauss was in many ways the most successful and prolific writer in this genre, and his well-known tone poems *Don Juan, Till Eulenspiegel, Don Quixote, Death and Transfiguration, Thus Spake Zarathustra,* and others are among the staples of orchestral literature. Strauss sometimes attempted to conceal the specifics of the programs underlying these works, but most commentators now agree on analyses of their programmatic content. In *Don Quixote* Strauss provided very specific descriptions of the separate parts. The work is cast in variation form (recall Chapter 6), and in it the character

EXAMPLE 12-6 LISZT: *Les Préludes,* EXCERPTS.

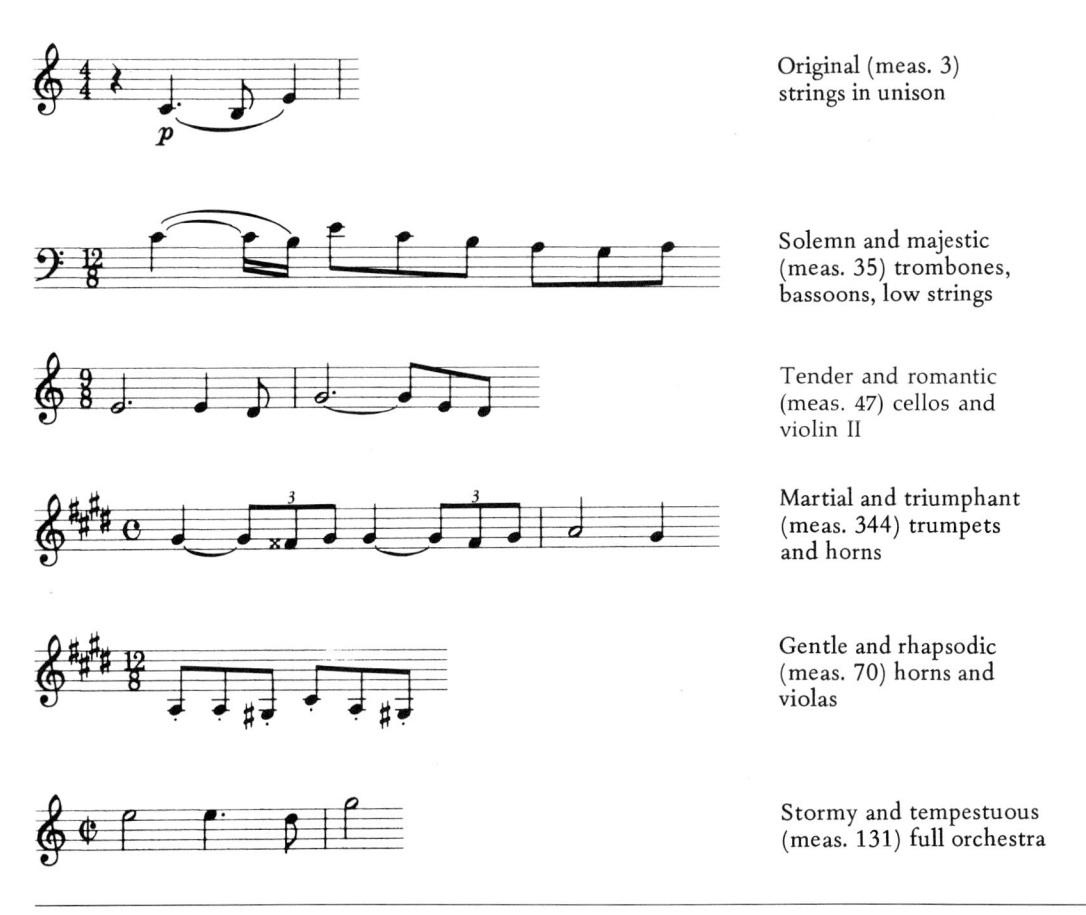

Original (meas. 3)
strings in unison

Solemn and majestic
(meas. 35) trombones,
bassoons, low strings

Tender and romantic
(meas. 47) cellos and
violin II

Martial and triumphant
(meas. 344) trumpets
and horns

Gentle and rhapsodic
(meas. 70) horns and
violas

Stormy and tempestuous
(meas. 131) full orchestra

of Don Quixote is always represented by the solo cello while his companion Sancho Panza is represented by the tenor tuba. The following guide to the opening indicates the approach taken by Strauss to this intriguing subject:

Prologue: Don Quixote's yearning for deeds of knighthood is suggested by the opening woodwind and string figures; his idealization of woman is suggested by the tender oboe theme; his yearning for adventure by the muted trumpet fanfares; and his confused state of mind by the following section of dense and complicated counterpoint. After this we meet first Don Quixote (solo cello) and Sancho Panza (tenor tuba) and we are ready for the following adventures, each of which is represented by a variation.

Variation I: The adventure with the windmills. At first we hear the themes of Don Quixote and Sancho Panza together in counterpoint. The windmills (which Quixote mistakes for his enemies) are introduced with *col legno* (notes played on the wood rather than the hair of the bow) low strings; Quixote's impalement on one of the windmill

Romantic Style (1825–1900) (continued) 217

Peter Ilyich Tchaikovsky (1840–1893)

■ Peter Ilyich Tchaikovsky, son of a Russian government mine inspector, trained for a career in law, but gave it up at the age of 23 to devote his life to music. Although his early years were spent in a remote province of Russia, he had a genteel upbringing, having a French governess and music teacher. After his parents moved to the city of St. Petersburg and he had completed his law training and four years of work in the Ministry of Justice, he made the decision to change careers, entering the newly founded St. Petersburg Conservatory in 1863. Having completed his studies in three years, and with the recommendation of the director of the Conservatory, Anton Rubenstein, famed Russian pianist and composer, he obtained his first music position in 1865, that of professor of harmony at the Moscow Conservatory. In the next twelve years there, he was to compose a great quantity of works including the *Swan Lake* ballet, the first three symphonies, the fantasy overture *Romeo and Juliet* (later revised), and the masterpiece of the period, the *Concerto No. 1 in B-Flat Minor for Piano, Op. 23* (world premiere in Boston in 1875), three quartets, 36 songs, and various works for piano.

As a closer study of his life will reveal, Tchaikovsky was a moody, often irrational person who suffered fits of depression and morbid self-disgust, which may have been occasioned by his homosexuality, as revealed in his letters to his brother. His life took an abrupt turn in 1877, when he became involved with two women: one, the widow of a wealthy industrialist, a lover of his music whom he never met, but who corresponded with him and provided him with financial support for thirteen years of his life; the other, a conservatory student who fell hopelessly in love with him and whom he married in an unfortunate act of charity and bravado perhaps, the unhappy outcome of which was an attempted suicide on his part, a separation, and her tragic death in an insane asylum some forty years later.

Leaving Russia at his doctor's orders, he moved to Switzerland, where he was to regain his equilibrium and decide to devote full time to composing, necessitating resignation from his professorship in the Moscow Conservatory. Thereafter he was to spend much of his life outside Russia, at times seeking peace and quiet to compose and otherwise enjoying the performance of his works at the major music capitals of Europe, since by now his fame was well established.

In the next decade he was to complete such important masterpieces as the celebrated *Concerto in D Major for Violin, Op. 35,* his most popular opera, *Eugene Onegin*, premiered in Moscow in 1879, the Fourth and Fifth symphonies, and *The Sleeping Beauty* ballet, as well as make a very successful concert tour as a conductor. The next big traumatic event of his life occurred in 1890 when his benefactress suddenly terminated her support and their curious relationship. Although he no longer depended on her monetary support, since by this time his fame had made him financially independent, he did suffer from the loss of an old friend and staunch supporter. This time he took the blow to his pride in stride, and busied himself with furthering his career as composer and conductor, venturing to the United States, where he conducted his own works for the opening of the now-famed Carnegie Hall in 1891. Received with great honor, this first Russian composer to achieve success in the West wrote about American "honesty, sincerity, generosity, cordiality and readiness to help," of the height of the houses, and of his conviction, "I am ten times more famous in America than in Europe."

Following his return to Russia, he settled in a country house near Moscow, venturing forth to receive an honorary degree from Cambridge and for one last conducting tour through Russia, Poland, and Germany. Nine days after he had conducted the first performance of his most popular symphony, *Symphony No. 6 in B Minor*, in St. Petersburg, he succumbed to cholera, an epidemic of which was ravaging the city at that time.

Said by Stravinsky to be "the most Russian of us all," Tchaikovsky left a legacy of music generally characterized by a tragic tone, exaggerated sentiments, ripe melodiousness, rhythmic vitality, and brilliant orchestration. And though his unabashed sentimentality may pall on some, the fact remains that this melancholy Russian continues to capture the minds of all who appreciate the poignant message of the avowed Romantic.

Perhaps best known for his almost 4,000 lithographs, Honore Daumier also found time to produce almost 200 paintings, of which this one of Don Quixote and Sancho Panza is one of the most interesting and well known.

arms and his subsequent fall are graphically depicted with ascending passages in the winds followed by a descending harp glissando. The sad state of the defeated knight is depicted by somber transformations of his theme.

Variation II: The adventures with the sheep. Undaunted, the pair seek new adventure and find it when they frighteningly mistake a herd of sheep for an army. The baaing of the sheep is portrayed with amazing realism by such devices as tremolo strings and flutter-tonguing in the winds and brass (a rapid, repeated articulation). Notice also the dissonant chords used in this section, sometimes referred to as *tone clusters* since the notes group or cluster together in half and/or whole steps.

Other variations: (III) a dispute between Quixote and Panza; (IV) the adventure with the religious procession; (V) Quixote's vigil in the night; (VI) the fair Dulcinea; (VII) Don Quixote's ride through the air (notice that the sustained low D indicates that he actually never leaves the earth though his theme soars four octaves higher); (VIII) the boat journey; (IX) the attack on the begging monks; (X) the duel with the knight of the pale moon; (XI) the epilogue and death of the hero.

Debussy's *Prelude to the Afternoon of a Faun* must be considered in any discussion of program music even though he (somewhat like Beethoven) rejected the idea that the work actually "depicted" something extramusical; instead he emphasized that, like his contemporaries in the visual arts (Manet, Monet) and literature (Mallarmé, Baudelaire), he sought to capture the evanescent essence of the impression that was made upon him.

A scene from Afternoon of a Faun is depicted in this pastel by Valentine Gross.

Romantic Style (1825–1900) (continued) 219

Franz Liszt (1811–1886)

■ Franz Liszt, dazzling piano virtuoso, far-sighted conductor of "the music of the future," brilliant composer of programmatic music, and indefatigable lover, captured the popular imagination of his day, becoming one of the legendary figures of the Romantic period. Liszt's imposing figure with his aquiline features, his magnetic personality, his flair for showmanship, and his incredible talents thoroughly captivated his audience. In scenes reminiscent of the adulation of popular superstars of our day, Liszt's female audience swooned and fought for souvenir bits of his clothing, inflamed by his music making and by the legend of the man himself.

Liszt was born in Hungary, son of a steward of the Esterházy estate (recall Haydn's earlier association with this wealthy family of music patrons). As a child prodigy he soon received the recognition and support of the music-loving nobility there.

First he went to Vienna where he met Beethoven and Schubert and then to Paris on a scholarship in 1823, where, like Chopin, he later joined with the intelligentsia who, caught up in the spirit of revolution, espoused the cause of Romanticism—Victor Hugo, George Sand, Berlioz, Rossini, Delacroix, and others. Soon lionized, he embarked on his tempestuous odyssey, performing in London, Vienna, Rome, and other major cities throughout Europe.

At the height of his concert career, Liszt withdrew to accept a position as court conductor for the Grand Duke Alexander at Weimar (1848). During the next eleven years there, he created his most important orchestral works—twelve symphonic poems including *Les Préludes*, the program symphonies, *Symphony after Goethe's Faust* and *Symphony to Dante's Divine Comedy*, and such virtuoso piano works as the *Transcendental Etudes*, *Hungarian Rhapsodies*, and others.

The intriguing life of this vaunted figure never waned during his 75 years, which saw him father three children, almost marry at age 50, and finally seek solace in the church, becoming Abbé Liszt in 1865. But more important is his legacy of richly rhetorical music, characterized by powerful lyricism, expressive transformation of a "fixed idea" (underlying theme), dazzling virtuoso passages, colorful orchestration, and striking harmonies and progressions. Like the life of the man himself, his music unfolds on a grand scale.

Richard Strauss (1864-1949)

■ Like so many of the world's great composers, Richard Strauss was German, a child prodigy and a member of a musical family. By the age of ten he had completed a number of promising compositions, and six years later, his first symphony, in a style that encouraged the staunch conservatives to deem him a worthy successor to Brahms. They were mistaken.

Having turned from the study of music briefly to enter the University of Munich, the Bavarian capital being his birthplace, he returned to his first love; after assuming various conducting posts and becoming thoroughly immersed in the music of Berlioz, Liszt, and Wagner, he proceeded to shock the musical world with the audacity and daring of his program music for orchestra—the extraordinary tone poems composed in 1886-1898, including *Don Juan*, *Death and Transfiguration*, *Till Eulenspiegel's Merry Pranks*, *Don Quixote*, and *A Hero's Life*. In these works, some of the most original of his output, he pursued to the highest degree the Romantic penchant for programmatic music—that is, music based on a story line or other nonmusical idea—and herein he demonstrated his genius for colorful pictorial depictions by the creation of a vast wealth of virtuoso orchestral effects, both sublimely inspired and frequently unbelievably trite. At his best he is the supreme master of the many-splendored colors of the orchestra.

During these years Strauss furthered a blossoming career as conductor of both orchestra and opera in Munich, Weimar, and Berlin, married a talented singer who was to become a champion of his inspired songs, and became a world-renowned figure.

At the turn of the century, Strauss, still an *enfant terrible* of music, turned to works for the stage and horrified audiences with his lurid operas, *Salome* and *Elektra*, and the decadent *Der Rosenkavalier*. One is struck by the arching melodies, unorthodox harmonies, and dramatic impact of the works of these years.

Unfortunately, in 1933, now a conservative and no longer representative of the "music of the future," he accepted the position of president of the notorious State Chamber of Music of the Third Reich. Although he was later completely exonerated of any wrongdoing as chief official of that body designed to protect "the purity" of German music—or for failure to leave his homeland in protest as Hindemith and others had done—Strauss, one of the great rebels of music and giants of our age, went to his grave under a cloud of suspicion never totally dispelled.

One of the most characteristic features of Debussy's music is his handling of the orchestral palette. In *Prelude to the Afternoon of a Faun* the lighter "pastel" colors of soft woodwinds, muted strings, muted brasses, delicate percussion such as antique cymbals, and harp dominate. Compare this to the bold theatricality of Berlioz and Liszt. The work is short and easy to follow in its broadest formal outlines. The opening section begins with a chromatic melody in the solo flute which is joined by woodwinds, horn, and harp (glissando); fragments of this opening section and other motives are introduced and the work builds to the contrasting middle section, a broad lyric melody in the violins. The work ends with a return to the mood and materials of the opening section.

Many of the great masterworks of Western art music were written as music for music's sake with no reference to any particular function, but many other equally significant works were written with a specific function in mind. And even if somehow it could be proved that the only purpose any music can have is to provide a realization of the experience of time, as Stravinsky suggests in his *Poetics of Music,* who could deny the importance—indeed, the necessity—of this function?

PIANO MUSIC

While the piano pieces of Romantic composers often were cast in Classic molds, for example, sonata or theme and variations, it is in their miniature "character pieces" (short works created to evoke a fleeting mood or to express a programmatic idea) that one best sees the poetic Romantic composer at work. Beethoven began this repertoire with his *Bagatelles* and others followed his lead with *Impromptus* (Schubert), *Songs without Words* (Mendelssohn), *Etudes, Nocturnes,* and *Mazurkas* (Chopin), *Ballades* and *Rhapsodies* (Brahms), *Préludes* (Debussy), and so on. In short, these capsule summaries became a characteristic form of piano music for the period, serving as a mode of expression of almost any poetic whimsy. No Romantic composer devoted more of his productive talents to the creation of such character pieces than did Robert Schumann (1810–1856), "the most romantic of them all," and no one created more appealing minute works of art.

Schumann's Carnaval

Schumann was truly a "split personality," a fact he chose not to minimize or hide, rather making it a part of his musical expression. This dual personality is exemplified in one of his more famous works for piano, *Carnaval, Op. 9* ("Little Scenes on Four Notes"), which shows both the whimsy and imagination of the composer. To fully understand the impact of these statements, one must realize that Schumann founded a music journal in which he espoused the cause of good music and attempted to discourage the bad being performed at that time. He not only edited the journal but also wrote articles, to some of which he signed the pen names Florestan and Eusebius, the former representing the capricious, tempestuous, passionate side of his nature and the latter the comtemplative, dreamy side. Florestan and Eusebius first appeared in his music in 1837 in the *Davidsbündlertänze, Op. 6* (*Dances of the David Leaguers*). The dances are a group of eighteen character pieces for piano, relating to an imaginary "League of David" which is dedicated to stamping out the mediocre music of the day. Herein one finds that the leader has not just one personality, but two, as the pensive pieces are signed "E" and the more impulsive ones "F." This scheme is carried out in the later *Carnaval* (1834–1835) where Schumann not only portrays his twin personalities but his friends, his beloved Clara, and assorted carnival characters—Pierrot, Arlequin, Colombine, Pantalon, and others. For the sake of brevity, excerpts of only a few are cited, but by comparing them in terms of contrasts of mode, mood, tempo, melodic and accompanimental features, expressive markings, characteristic melodic-rhythmic patterns, and textures, one will gain some insight into this highly subjective, poetic musical style.

The work opens loudly with a stately preamble (Préambule) of thick chords (characteristic of much of Schumann's music), but the scene changes abruptly to a brilliant one of racing imitative figures impelled by contradictory meters—two-beat in the left hand and three-beat in the right. Although the mode has not changed, the theme and mood have, as have the tempo, texture, and compositional technique (Example 12-7). Thereafter follows a series of epigrams suggesting im-

Robert Schumann (1810-1856)

■ Like so many Romantic composers, Robert Schumann was immensely gifted and tragically short-lived. He was truly the melancholy poet of Germanic Romanticism, with all its storms and stresses and unabashed emotionalism and expressive excesses, best portrayed in his smaller works for piano and solo songs.

Born the son of a bookseller and editor in Saxony, Schumann early developed a love for literature—especially such Romantic poets as Heine, Goethe, and Byron—which had a profound influence on the poetic musical statements he was destined to make. His childhood was marked by musical study, compositions by age seven, and the premature death of his father. At the insistence of his widowed mother, he entered Leipzig University and then went to Heidelberg to study law. After a desultory two years he persuaded his mother to permit full-time study of music, devoting himself to perfecting his piano technique (crippling a hand in the process) and to the study of composition, primarily for the keyboard. This early period (1829-1840) saw him become a renowned music critic and create some of his most representative works for the piano, the famed *Abegg Variations*, *Papillons*, *Intermezzi*, *Davidbündlertänze*, *Carnaval*, *Kinderscenen*, and other character pieces evoking fleeting moods or programmatic ideas.

In 1840 he married Clara Wieck, famed piano virtuoso and later inamorata of Brahms, and entered his "song year," during which he wrote a profusion of songs of bewildering variety and compelling beauty, creating more than 100 that year. Some of the more famous of these appear in the masterful song cycles *Frauenliebe und Leben* (*Woman's Love and Life*) and *Dichterliebe* (*Poet's Love*). With the beauty of his poetic utterance, soulful melody, and evocative settings, he gained a position of prominence beside Schubert as a master of German lieder.

Having devoted most of his compositional talents to relatively short character pieces, songs, and song cycles, Schumann now turned to chamber music, choral music, and ultimately the symphony. In these works, excepting those involving the piano—the popular *Quintet, Op. 44*, the *Quartet, Op. 47*, and the *Concerto in A Minor, Op. 54*—his genius is less apparent than in his earlier creations. It is conjectured, and hotly debated, that Schumann never mastered the larger developmental forms and the art of orchestration, but even if he had not, his smaller works would have assured him of immortality.

Schumann suffered from melancholia and emotional instability. He had several nervous collapses beginning in 1833, attempting suicide at one point, and finally ended his life in an insane asylum. Devoted to the cause of great music and champion of his contemporaries Chopin and Brahms, this tender poet of German Romanticism truly exemplified the age.

aginary characters whirling by at a masked ball, a theme which fascinated the composer.

We are first introduced to the character Pierrot, and one sees that the texture has become compacted, the tempo has slowed drastically, and the dynamic level is greatly reduced. As was true of the first, this piece is built of short sequential statements (Example 12-8). Arlequin, the clown, has a different mien. He skips about agitatedly to the misplaced accents (sforzandos) and wide leaps of a tune tied to an ostinato figure (Example 12-9).

The passionate side of the composer is revealed as Florestan appears to a soaring, restless theme set against thick, vibrant harmony. Note the dramatic change of tempo as the theme closes and a repeat is begun (Example 12-10).

Schumann contributes to the "masked ball" concept by fashioning a noble waltz, characterized by a soaring sequential line, dotted rhythms, and a "boom-chuck-chuck" accompaniment (Example 12-11).

Eusebius, the introspective one, is portrayed by a septuplet (seven-note group) sequentially repeated, which is clearly limited in scope. As opposed to Florestan, the more boisterous self, Eusebius is portrayed in soft pastel tones (Example 12-12).

Chiarina is someone special, his beloved Clara Wieck who was to become his wife some five years later. The tempo marking is *passionato*, the theme angular and sequential, the rhythms dotted, and the mood loud and impassioned (Example 12-13).

For a brief moment he turns to the pianistic style of his Polish contemporary, Chopin, to create an expressive minature suggesting Chopin's penchant for smooth, flowing melodies set to widely ranging arpeggiated chords in the left hand (Example 12-14).

Even more dramatic is the change of texture and tempo for the portrayal of two stock carnival characters—Pantalon, the wealthy, amorous old gentleman now arthritically impaired, and Colombine, the sassy servant lass who "knows all the answers"—and most of the questions (Example 12-15). Here

EXAMPLE 12-7 SCHUMANN: *Carnaval, Op. 9*, PRÉAMBULE, MEASURES 1–7 AND 26–33.

EXAMPLE 12-8 SCHUMANN: *Carnaval, Op. 9*, PIERROT, MEASURES 1–8.

EXAMPLE 12-9 SCHUMANN: *Carnaval, Op. 9*, ARLEQUIN, MEASURES 1–8.

EXAMPLE 12-10 SCHUMANN: *Carnaval, Op. 9*, FLORESTAN, MEASURES 1–11.

EXAMPLE 12-11 SCHUMANN: *Carnaval, Op. 9*, VALSE NOBLE, MEASURES 1–8.

Romantic Style (1825–1900) (continued)

EXAMPLE 12-12 SCHUMANN: *Carnaval, Op. 9*, EUSEBIUS, MEASURES 1–8.

EXAMPLE 12-13 SCHUMANN: *Carnaval, Op. 9*, CHIARINA, MEASURES 1–8.

EXAMPLE 12-14 SCHUMANN: *Carnaval, Op. 9*, CHOPIN, MEASURES 1–4.

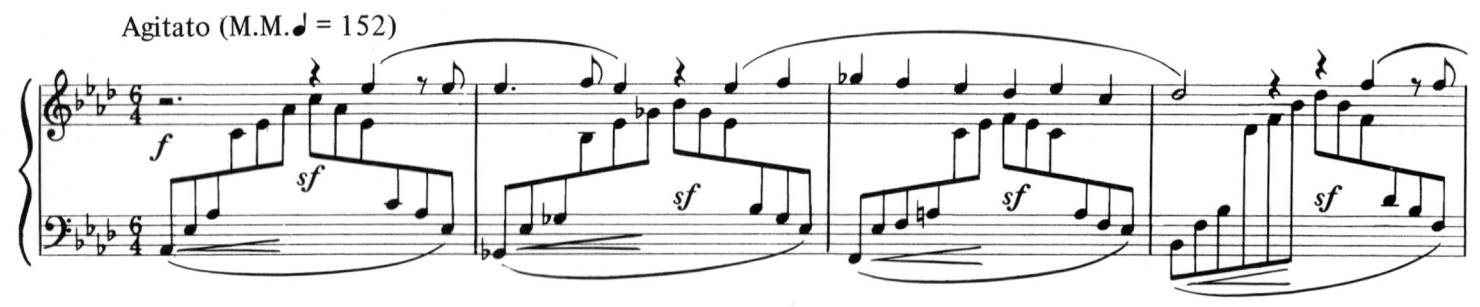

EXAMPLE 12-15 SCHUMANN: *Carnaval, Op. 9*, PANTALON ET COLOMBINE, (a) MEASURES 1–4 AND (b) 13–15.

(b) Meno presto

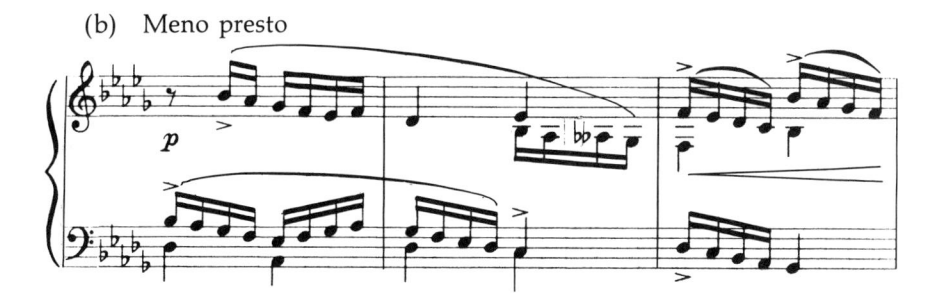

one sees a dazzling display of bustling staccato scales in contrary motion, suggesting the frivolous miss, countered with a more subdued section depicting the amorous but elderly merchant. The marvel of *Carnaval* is the incredible variety that Schumann achieves with such limited thematic materials. In brief epigrammatic statements he evokes a bewildering variety of characterizations and moods in a work considered by many to be the epitome of Romanticism.

Chopin's Mazurka, Op. 68, No. 3
Schumann and Frédéric Chopin (1810–1849) are said to represent the culmination of the Romantic movement in piano literature. Chopin, unlike his Viennese contemporary, composed almost exclusively for solo piano, turning often to the dance forms of his native land, thus infusing new nationalistic elements into music.

A large number of Chopin's pieces are short dances such as

Though classified as the leader of the Classical School of French painting, Ingres shared the visions of the romantics whose conceptions were epic, heroic, and highly subjective.

Romantic Style (1825–1900) (continued)

waltzes, mazurkas, and polonaises, the latter two being Polish national dances of folk or court origin. All three have in common the typical employment of simple triple meter. Like most dances all three reveal in their organization the use of recurring patterns such as the one shown in Example 12-16. Like most mazurkas this one employs a dotted rhythm (♪♩♩) that demands for performance accuracy the player's ability to relate a specific figure to the pulse levels it implies. Renotating the figure shown above shows the relation of the dotted figure to the implicit division of the quarter-note beat into sixteenths:

Establish recurring sixteenths at about ♩ = 90 and intone the rhythm of the first eight or so measures of Example 12-16; then listen to a performance of the piece from which the passage has been excerpted.

EXAMPLE 12-16 CHOPIN: *Mazurka, Op. 68, No. 3,* MEASURES 45–60.

Frédéric Chopin (1810–1849)

■ No composer was more "romantic" in terms of his life, life style, and musical creations than the short-lived Pole, Frédéric Chopin. This colorful figure, son of a Polish mother and French father, was to become the national composer of Poland despite the fact that he spent the adult half of his life in an adopted homeland, France. True to the stereotype of the Romantic musician, Chopin was a child prodigy of the piano, a frail, intense youth who became the pet of the aristocracy, and who, in a tragically short lifespan, was to move with the "in group" of the world of arts and letters, and vigorously continue to compose and perform despite unfortunate love affairs, financial uncertainties, and tuberculosis.

Chopin was born in a small village near the capital city, Warsaw, from whose newly founded conservatory he received his formal education. His precociousness was well recognized and little was done to discipline his high-flying originality—a mixed blessing, perhaps, since his works are criticized by some for the lack of intellectual development and praised by others for their daring innovations and extremely personal musical message. His lyrical, moody style, elegant, impassioned, and poetic, was fairly well established by the age of 20 when he departed Warsaw, never to return, to make his mark in the international music world.

Following a sensational introductory appearance at the salon of the Baron de Rothschild, he was embraced by the intelligentsia of Paris—nobles, high government officials, brilliant artists, musicians, and literary figures. George Sand, her real name being Mme. Aurore Dudevant, was to form a much talked-about liaison with Chopin which, in the course of its some eight years of tumultuous existence, covered the gamut of extremes from intense love to equally intense hostility.

His music, unlike that of most composers, is virtually confined to the piano for which he created some 200 compact works, characterized by beguiling romantic melodies, sumptuous harmonies—often daringly innovative—and subtle pianistic effects and fastidious embellishments (melodic and harmonic), of persuasive sentimentality and poetic reverie. It is accurate to say that Chopin freed the piano from conventional orchestral-choral influences and in so doing produced a music exploiting the tonal spectrum and effects peculiar to it, which make the piano such a superb solo instrument. He explored the popular dance rhythms of the day in his appealing waltzes and of his native land in his lively mazurkas and stately polonaises, examples being the ever-popular *Waltz in C-Sharp Minor, Op. 64, No. 2*, **the** *Polonaise in A-Flat Major, Op. 53*, **and the** *Mazurka in C Major, Op. 56, No. 2*. Further, he pursued his poetic flights of fancy in the melancholy *Nocturnes*, **the** *Nocturne in B-Flat Minor, Op. 9, No. 1*, **to name but one, the fragmentary** *Preludes, Op. 28*, **two dozen in number, the** *Etude in E Major, Op. 10, No. 3*, one of a number of such pieces designed for technical study but filled with musical inspiration, and in the epic *Four Ballades* and numerous other works.

Like his two contemporaries, Schumann and Mendelssohn, Chopin's peak of compositional achievement was reached in his youth when his romantic lyric nature found its noblest mode of expression and while his musical output was comparatively small. The meticulous miniatures of this unique composer were to greatly influence the changing course of music in the years ahead. Schumann was so prophetically right in 1831, when upon hearing Chopin's *Variations on "La ci darem la mano,"* he remarked, "Hats off, gentlemen: a genius!"

13 Romantic Style (1825-1900) (concluded)

OPERA

There is little doubt that the musical vehicle best suited to the realization of the emotional expressivity of many Romantic composers is that of opera. This is not surprising since no other genre of music is so directly wedded to a text which by its very nature is so dramatically conceived and no other single genre of art embraces such a diversity of modes of artistic expression—music, literature, dance, drama, and visual arts. The opera's extended length and dramatic text freed composers to explore a vast range of emotions—love, tragedy, irony, bitterness, hope, and despair—while fashioning music dramas peopled by characters bigger than life, but no less human, acting out the many vagaries of existence intensified by the combination of visual, textual, and musical elements.

The names first coming to mind as epitomizing the Romantic style are two: the German, Richard Wagner (1818-1883), and the Italian, Guiseppe Verdi (1813-1901). We have arbitrarily chosen to focus on the final act of an opera composed by Verdi about midcentury to exemplify many of the stylistic generalizations previously cited and to give you a brief taste of the unreal world of opera, peopled by noblemen and women, commoners, pimps, whores, heroes, and losers, which in its unreal way (who of us sings our way through life in stylized settings accompanied by a full symphony orchestra?) reveals some of humanity's greatest moments and most profound emotions.

However, in deference to the German genius, Wagner, we will first pause a few moments to observe that in this man the arts were indeed fused. Contemplate the incredible talents of a man capable of writing the libretto, composing the music, designing the sets, and conceiving the stage on which he could play out his epic tales, the most mammoth being the opera tetralogy *The Ring of the Niebelungs.* Since it is not possible within the scope of this introductory book to do more than sample a few works we will begin our discussion with an opera overture by Wagner.

Overtures are of three general types: those that are generally unrelated to the plot and serve simply to capture the attention of the audience or to evoke the proper mood for the

230 Styles of Music

Heroic figures, Gods, Goddesses, and Warriors brave, they were the stuff of German Romantic mythology, and no composer presented them more winningly than did Wagner, the epitome of the German Romantic musical mystic. And though far removed from the storms and stresses of Germanic Romanticism, Americans too heard the siren call of surreal subjectivism, as exemplified in Albert Pinkham Ryder's fantasy depicted here, Siegfried and the Rhine Maidens.

drama to follow, whether gay or sad; those that preview some of the important melodies to come; and those that give a capsule summary of the action to follow.

Wagner's Overture to Die Meistersinger

Extensive use of "preview" technique is made by Wagner in the Overture to *Die Meistersinger* (*The Mastersinger*), 1868, wherein he introduces the principal thematic materials (called *leitmotivs*—lead motives) used to identify various characters and emotions involved in the drama to unfold, and which appear throughout the work. The overture is composed of six principal thematic threads (Example 13-1).

The overture climaxes with an interweaving of all the themes, preparing the way for the opening curtain. Listen to

EXAMPLE 13-1　Wagner: *Die Meistersinger*, overture, six principal themes.

Majestic theme of the Mastersingers

Love motive related to the hero and heroine

Mastersinger's stately march

Sophisticated musical art of the Mastersingers

Hero's love song (called the "Prize Song")

Motive suggestive of "spring"

232　Styles of Music

Richard Wagner (1813–1883)

■ In the music dramas of Richard Wagner, the colossal conceptions of that "most German of Germans," one sees the spirit of Romanticism reach its culmination. To Wagner opera was the "universal art work," an expressive vehicle wherein music, drama, poetry, and painting should be organically melded to reflect the essential nature of humanity and society, and therefore its entertainment value was secondary to the idealized message it conveyed.

In pursuing his artistic creed, Wagner devoted his creative energies almost exclusively to music drama, often based on Nordic mythology, minimizing the traditional predominance of the singer for a musical fabric in which the orchestra assumed a more important role in the dramatic unfolding. He perfected a technique of composition wherein musical lead motives (*leitmotivs*) were identified with characters, moods, situations, and objects, and then used throughout the orchestral fabric in various forms, original and transformed, to intensify and unite the dramatic unfolding.

Wagner, that most complex and intriguing late Romantic, was born in Leipzig, son of a minor police official. His artistic talents were soon recognized and his musical training encouraged, but he proved to be a more apt student of the theater, of Greek and Roman tragedies. After a desultory period of study of piano, theory, and composition, becoming enamored with Beethoven's music, he abandoned the academic world of Leipzig University at age 20 to take his first professional post as chorus master of the opera at Wurzburg. Then followed a number of years in which he conducted opera at various provincial houses, married an actress, began a lifelong struggle with creditors, moved to Paris, and completed two early operas, *Der Fliegende Holländer* (*The Flying Dutchman*) and *Rienzi*.

Just as things were at their lowest ebb, his first break came: *Rienzi* was accepted for performance in Dresden, where it was an instantaneous success. His equally successful *Der Fliegende Holländer* was performed the following year and he was then appointed conductor of the court opera. However, his next production, *Tannhäuser*, was too advanced for the times and Wagner became alienated from his court listeners, joined a revolutionary group advocating the overthrow of the monarchy, and soon found himself without an audience or position. A revolution broke out which the troops of the King of Prussia crushed, and Wagner, marked for arrest, was forced to take refuge in Switzerland in 1849.

He began life anew, made new professional contacts and friends, became involved with another woman (one of many such affairs to follow), and entered upon the most productive period of his life. He wrote no music for the first four years, setting forth his theories in *Art and Revolution*, *The Art Work of the Future*, and *Opera and Drama*. Then followed *Tristan und Isolde*, *Die Meistersinger von Nürnberg* (*The Mastersinger of Nuremberg*), and the colossal four-opera cycle *Der Ring des Nibelungen* (*The Ring of the Nibelungs*).

His personal life became a shambles because of his involvements with other women—often wives or daughters of his benefactors and friends—his works gathered dust, being virtually unperformed, and his financial problems were overwhelming.

Again, in the very depths of despair, he was to find a champion in Ludwig II, the "mad king" of Bavaria, an opera "buff" and avid admirer of Wagner's music. He befriended the composer, commissioned the completion of *The Ring*, and established him in Munich. In typical fashion, Wagner became involved with the wife of the conductor appointed to conduct his works, the daughter of Liszt, and imprudently attacked the officers of the royal cabinet, leading to another exile to Switzerland.

In the end, however, Wagner had his day with the support of his ever-loyal friend King Ludwig II and of the new-found cult of Wagner music lovers; he was to return victoriously to his homeland and to see a musical shrine erected to his specifications, the opera house at Bayreuth, the site of the famous summer Wagner Festivals. In the truest sense, his genius triumphed.

In Die Meistersinger one sees the inevitable triumph of new over old as youth has its day in a world of change.

it, familiarizing yourself with the main motives, and noting the masterful mingling of the thematic strands as they fuse to triumphantly herald the opening of the first act. Further, listen to the first scene and note the unifying effect achieved by orchestral statements of the "love motive," the "spring motive," and the "Prize Song" interspersed with the vocal utterance of those on stage. One realizes that in this compositional style the orchestra assumes a major role in creating mood and color, and participates in the dramatic unfolding as well—that is, it becomes more than a mere accompanying body supporting the vocal declamation in that it actively engages in advancing the story line. In Wagner's hands the arts were melded into an organic whole to produce some of the most compelling works for the romantic operatic stage.

Verdi's A Masked Ball

When one studies Verdi's operas in greater detail, one realizes that his mannerisms, generally speaking, are typical of much Romantic music: bright tuneful arias sharply contrast with intense passionate ones; tuneful melodies, cadentially well defined, move to rather stable harmonies in comparatively thin, transparent homophonic textures enriched at points of theatrical importance with the intensification of harmonic and instrumental colors; the orchestra serves an accompanimental function but tellingly underscores dramatic events with masterful choices of instrumental timbres and effects; compelling vocal lines predominate with appealing melodies well suited to the voice and arranged in contrasting set numbers (arias, duos, trios, etc.) for different voice types and combinations; complex plots, usually ending tragically, unfold in patterns of melodramatically dissimilar scenes, moods, and emotions, set off by abrupt changes of pace and intensity of movement, harmony, tonality, and timbre.

The specific opera we will discuss is *A Masked Ball* (*Un Ballo in Maschera*), first performed in Rome in 1859. It is interesting to digress momentarily to comment on the unusual circumstances related to the composition and subsequent performance of this work, one of the melodramatic highlights of Verdi's middle period. Commissioned by the San Carlo Opera of Naples, Verdi based his libretto on a tragic historical event of the eighteenth century. However, his timing was bad. There was an attempted assassination of Napoleon III, and officialdom was hardly receptive to an artistic work based on murder, particularly of royalty, and political conspiracy. The official censors proposed a "modification" that virtually emasculated the original version and was unacceptable to the composer, leading to a lawsuit and threats of imprisonment. Compromise had to be reached, and reached it was by a bit of legerdemain in which the setting of the original story of European court intrigue was rather unceremoniously reset in, of all places, puritanical Boston. But such is the stuff of opera, and what does it really matter if the king becomes governor, titled the Count of Warwick, who dies tragically amidst French elegancy surrounded by Italians (Riccardo, Renato, etc.) in an austere provincial "new world" as foretold by a "Creole" fortune-teller. Accept opera for its idiosyncracies, for its stylized mannerisms and gestures, since that is what it is, and in doing so you will be led to many intriguing hours of musical exploration and involvement. Familiarize yourself first with the story line, the major arias, and the ensemble numbers, and then venture forth through the wondrous worlds of music drama the composer-librettist creates, being conscious of such differences of period and type as exist. Learn one opera well, and then another, and soon you will add your voice to the resounding "bravo" that occurs when the heroic tenor has a "good night."

The culminating assassination occurs in the third act, during a "court" masked ball held in the "palace" of the "governor" of Boston, Riccardo, "Count of Warwick." To this point the plot has revealed that the governor is in love with the wife, Adelia, of his devoted friend and secretary, Renato. The governor is being conspired against, his ultimate fate being revealed by the fortune-teller, Ulrica. Meanwhile, Adelia, the governor's

Giuseppe Verdi (1813-1901)

■ Born the same year as Wagner, Giuseppe Verdi, like his German contemporary, was to live a long, productive life devoted solely to opera, and to become a national hero of his country, Italy. Verdi shunned the symphonic character of Wagner's music dramas, choosing to exploit the Italian penchant for expressive vocal melody, dramatic action, and conflict, creating works of utmost directness, expressiveness, and immediate appeal which made him the most popular composer for the operatic stage.

Verdi was born in a small country hamlet, son of an innkeeper, where the poverty of village life left much to be desired in terms of his artistic developments. His precociousness was recognized, however, by a wealthy grocer in the neighboring city, the market town of Busseto, where Verdi had found employment, and through his assistance the young man was able to further his musical study. He applied for admission to the famed Milan Conservatory but was denied admission. Undaunted, he began private study of composition with a maestro at La Scala and two years later returned to Busseto where he was to hold various music posts and marry.

After several desultory years in which he became embroiled in some local political disputes, he left for Milan in 1838 and a year later his first opera, *Oberto*, was performed at La Scala. It attained sufficient success to merit the commission of three others, and he set about the task only to have his peace of mind destroyed by the unfortunate death of his beloved wife, his two children having only recently died. His next opera, a comedy, was a failure, and he was out of money. With superhuman effort he broke his vow never to compose again and created his first overwhelming success, *Nabucco*, which was premiered at La Scala in 1842. The timing was right. Italy was in the throes of becoming a nation by throwing off the yoke of the Hapsburgs, and the plot of *Nabucco*, concerned with the plight of exiled Jews at the time of the biblical king Nebuchadnezzar, fanned the flames of revolution. Verdi immersed himself in the movement for freedom and the next works, *I Lombardi*, *Ernani*, and *Attila*, embodied the political aspirations of his people, which were to culminate in the revolution of 1848.

His career now assured, his financial status improved, and his genius world-recognized, between 1851 and 1853 he was to compose three of his most popular works, *Rigoletto*, *Il Trovatore* (*The Troubador*), and *La Traviata* (*The Lost One*). He purchased a farm near Busseto to which he retired when his busy schedule would permit, and where he could enjoy the role of gentleman farmer and breeder of fine horses. Other great operas followed, including *Un Ballo in Maschera* (*A Masked Ball*), first played in Rome in 1859, the year in which he remarried, and *La Forze del Destino* (*The Force of Destiny*), commissioned for performance in St. Petersburg in 1862 during a five-year period.

His grandest of grand operas, *Aïda*, was commissioned by the Khedive of Egypt to commemorate the opening of the Suez Canal and the Cairo opera house in 1871. *Aïda* was then, and continues to be, a smashing success, as the master created a work typically replete with pageantry, orchestral color, and melodiousness.

Verdi was nominated a senator in 1875 and for the next decade virtually gave up music, but at age 74 he reappeared on the musical scene with his remarkable *Otello*, so dramatic and virile, and at age 80 with *Falstaff*, considered by many to be his most brilliant work.

Verdi's musical life may be considered to have ended with this comic masterpiece, but he created a second memorial by richly endowing a home for aged musicians in Milan. No composer ever did more to further the cause of his country and none ever created more popular works for the operatic stage than did Verdi.

mistress, obtains a "magic potion" from Ulrica to cure her infatuation, this deed being observed by the governor in hiding. Heavily veiled, Adelia proceeds as directed to gallows hill where she is to ingest the potion, only to be interrupted by the governor. Her husband arrives, not seeing through her disguise, to warn Riccardo that the conspirators are approaching to kill him. After much protest Riccardo departs asking that Renato accompany the "unknown" lady back to the city gates. In so doing they meet the conspirators, she is unveiled, and the second act closes as his courtier friends mock the shocked Renato, leading him to join the conspiracy and ultimately to kill Riccardo.

Act III curtain rises on Renato's library as a furious brass fanfare sets the stage for the stormy domestic quarrel to ensue. Renato enters, sword in hand, dragging his faithless wife. Adelia protests her innocence and Renato vows she must die in a tempestuous dialogue (soprano and baritone) highlighted by agitated strings and thundering brasses. Resigned to her fate, Adelia asks to see her son for the last time in a moving three-part aria (Example 13-2), "Morrò, ma prima ingrazia, deh"—"I die, but first implore you". In typical fashion Verdi underscores the dramatic intensity of the moment with a subdued "oom-pah" accompaniment as the solo cello sets the tender mood and then joins in obbligato with the soprano in voicing a plaintive melody rich with dotted-note rhythms, triplet figures, and sequences.

Suddenly realizing the true cause of his grief, Renato grabs his dagger and turns to a portrait of Riccardo, intimate friend become betrayer. In a thundering recitative, he declaims that "blood must flow—*your* blood!" With an abrupt change of tempo, key, and mood, the orchestra introduces agitated repeated chords shot through with ominous interjections of trumpet and trombone, and thus the way is prepared for the bitter aria "Eri tu" ("It was you"). Again the Italian master paints the background with the somber colors of the orchestra as he sets the agitated, angular theme homophonically (Example 13-3). His bitterness momentarily spent, and filled with self-pity, Renato poignantly recalls the joys of a love now lost, this moment being dramatized by abrupt change of timbre, texture, mood, and mode.

The conspirators (Samuel and Tommaso—both basses) enter to "cloak and dagger" music which exemplifies a Verdian mannerism often associated with stealthiness and intrigue: very soft staccato lower strings (*ppp*) moving agitatedly, in this instance as the strings weave a short fugato (Example 13-4). This theme serves as one of three important thematic threads woven through the opera for unifying effect, two of which appear in Act III.

Renato astounds them by revealing his knowledge of their plot to assassinate the governor (Riccardo) and pledges to assist in their nefarious plot. They join Renato in a resounding declaration of revenge, "Be the guilt and the shame divided"

EXAMPLE 13-2 VERDI: *A Masked Ball*, ACT III, SCENE 1, "MORRÒ" ("I DIE"), MEASURES 72–75.

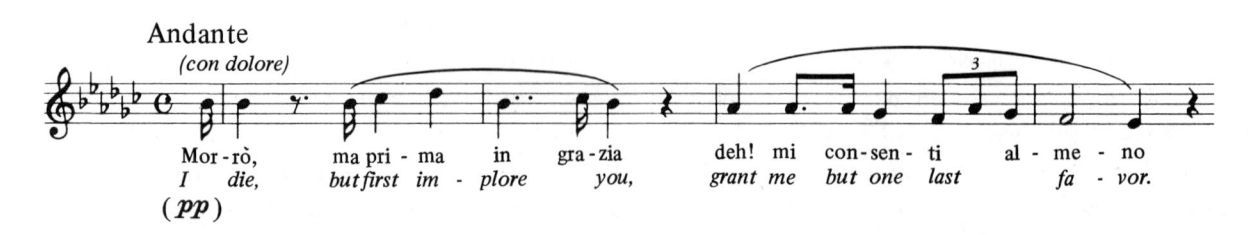

EXAMPLE 13-3 VERDI: *A Masked Ball,* ACT III, SCENE 1, "ERI TU" ("IT WAS YOU"), MEASURES 139–143.

EXAMPLE 13-4 VERDI: *A Masked Ball,* ACT III, SCENE 1, INTRODUCTION TO "DUNQUE L'ONTA" ("NOW THE SHAME"), MEASURES 178–182.

Romantic Style (1825–1900) (concluded)

(Example 13-5). This "vendetta music," too, is a Verdian cliché frequently employed and often characterized by thick staccato chords (now in the harp, later reinforced by the brasses) in marching cadence with pizzicato basses accompanying a stirring, virile theme.

In stark contrast to the mood of vengeance prevailing, the page (a boy's part, actually sung by a female) struts in gaily to an elegant orchestral march and begins a joyful, sparkling tune attended by the brilliant piccolo (Example 13-6). One is struck by the juxtaposition of contrasting moods and the masterful use of the orchestra for mood evocation. This leads to one of Verdi's most brilliant, overpowering ensemble numbers ("From what brilliance, what music"), in which all five characters join one by one in the simultaneous expression of four conflicting emotions: the lighthearted gaiety of the page envisioning the evening's festivities, the crushing misery of Adelia so hopelessly entrapped, the ecstatic jubilance of Renato anticipating swift vengeance, and the macabre rejoicing of the two conspirators at the prospect of "death in masquerade." Verdi is a master at depicting conflicting emotions in his ensemble num-

EXAMPLE 13-5   VERDI: *A Masked Ball*, ACT III, SCENE 1, "DUNQUE L'ONTA" ("NOW THE SHAME"), MEASURES 232–235.

bers (as will become apparent in the subsequent discussion of the quartet from *Rigoletto*).

Scene 2 is quite brief, serving to afford a few moments of relief from the tragedy to ensue. The governor is seated at his writing desk as cellos softly recall a "love theme," another of the three unifying themes previously mentioned. The "love theme" is first introduced in the opening short prelude (Example 13-7) to the first act, voiced by low flute, oboe, and clarinet, and closes off the scene under discussion. This use of recurring themes is typical of many Romantic composers of opera, who use this device to create both musical unity and dramatic intensity as one identifies a character or emotion from previous contact within a particular context. Having signed the order to send his beloved Adelia back to her homeland, Riccardo, overcome with emotion, sings of his anguish (Example 13-8). This brief aria shows Verdi at his melodic best as he spins an expressive melody to arpeggiated pianissimo strings, colored briefly midway along with the dark sonorities of clarinets and bassoons. With a stunning tonal shift downward a semitone, he launches the tenor voice in a soaring flight

EXAMPLE 13-6 VERDI: *A Masked Ball*, ACT III, SCENE 1, INTRODUCTION TO "DI CHE FULGOR, CHE MUSICHE" ("FFROM WHAT BRILLIANCE, WHAT MUSIC"), MEASURES 354–357.

EXAMPLE 13-7 VERDI: *A Masked Ball*, ACT I, PRELUDE, MEASURES 29–34.

EXAMPLE 13-8 VERDI: *A Masked Ball*, ACT III, SCENE 2, "MA SE M'È FORZA" ("BUT IT IS MY FATE TO LOSE YOU"), MEASURES 41–44.

Romantic Style (1825–1900) (concluded)

to climax and then brings the emotional aria to a quiet close.

As the end of the scene is approached, the mood is interrupted suddenly with the sound of gay dance music resounding from the ballroom. Again Verdi employs a colorful mannerism: the use of a stage band of winds, reminiscent of the village bands of his youth, perhaps, playing trivial dance tunes against which he interjects intermittent dialogue, usually of grim nature. This theatrical device, considered "corny" by some, permits the melodramatic combination of obviously conflicting forces and, in a sense, literally bridges the gap between the simple music of the people and that of the more sophisticated art world (Example 13-9).

A brilliant ballroom is revealed filled with a crowd of guests, most of whom are masked and wearing long, hooded cloaks. The country band, occasionally bolstered by the orchestra, grinds out an imperturbable tune, resting at important points so that the dialogue may be heard—another Verdi trademark. The conspirators enter in disguise.

With great theatrical flair, Riccardo's and Adelia's appearances are dramatized by the introduction of a minuetlike

EXAMPLE 13-9 VERDI: *A Masked Ball*, ACT III, SCENE 2, "AH! DESSA È LÀ" ("AH! SHE IS HERE"), MEASURES 78–85.

EXAMPLE 13-10 VERDI: *A Masked Ball*, ACT III, SCENE 3, INTRODUCTION TO "T'AMO, SI T'AMO" ("I LOVE YOU, YES, I LOVE YOU"), MEASURES 354–358.

The closing scene of Verdi's A Masked Ball represents opera at its most melodramatic height, as tragic love is cleaved by the assassin's knife.

dance played offstage by a small string ensemble and characized by ceaseless "boom-chuck-chuck" accompaniment (Example 13-10). To this stoic "death dance," mechanically repeated, will be acted out the ultimate tragedy. Disguising her voice, Adelia begs Riccardo to flee, but he refuses. Forgetting all pretense, she sings the beautiful "I love you, yes, I love you" in a typical Verdian line rich with expressive angular leaps and dotted-note rhythms (Example 13-11). Riccardo replies with a soaring song of love with the customary triplet figure and dotted-note rhythm (Example 13-12). Through it all the string ensemble grinds away dispassionately. Again it should be observed how dramatically effective is this much-used stylistic mannerism—the juxtaposition of disparate emotions, in this case intense boredom and intense love. To this grim accompaniment the lovers voice their final farewells. Death is met and the people recoil with horror as the curtain swiftly falls.

Before leaving Romantic opera, let us consider two other familiar operatic excerpts, a quartet and a duet. Thus, in the course of this book, we will have sampled most of the vital components that make up the kaleidoscopic world of opera.

EXAMPLE 13-11 VERDI: *A Masked Ball,* ACT III, SCENE 3, "T'AMO, SI T'AMO" ("I LOVE YOU, YES, I LOVE YOU"), MEASURES 390–394.

T'a - mo, si, t'amo, e in la - gri - me a' pie - di tuoi m'at - ter - ro,
Lov'd one, be-hold the flood of tears as here I kneel be - fore you,

Her amorous advances having been repulsed by John the Baptist, held captive by King Herod, the depraved princess Salome (heroine of the Strauss opera Salome) requests the severed head of the holy man. Bearing it on a tray, she smothers it with kisses after performing the seductive "Dance of the Seven Veils," dropping them one by one before the drooling king, who—lusting for his step-daughter, Salome—grants her perverse wish.

EXAMPLE 13-12 VERDI: *A Masked Ball*, ACT III, SCENE 3, "T'AMO, SÌ T'AMO" ("I LOVE YOU, YES, I LOVE YOU"), MEASURES 407–410.

Sin— che tu m'ami, A - de - lia, non cu - roil fato mi - o,
Since— thou with love hast blest me, all else my heart I ban - ish,

242 Styles of Music

No romantic opera is more popular than Verdi's Rigoletto, *a familiar tale of a dishonored daughter—the fair Gilda—and a vengeful father—the hunchbacked court jester Rigoletto—whose lives are melodramatically ruined by love and vengeance.*

Verdi's Rigoletto

One of the most familiar of opera *quartets* occurs in the tragedy *Rigoletto* (1851). In this, Verdi's fifteenth opera, the Italian master created one of his most appealing music dramas and some of his most popular music. The plot revolves around the following characters: the Duke of Mantua, a licentious nobelman; Rigoletto, his hunchback jester; Gilda, the jester's daughter; Sparafucile, an assassin for hire; and a number of supporting characters including Maddelena, the assassin's sister. The Duke seduces Rigoletto's daughter and leaves her for other conquests, and Rigoletto hires the services of the assassin to avenge this dishonor. The fateful climax comes in Act III, played out beside Sparafucile's wayside inn near Mantua. Rigoletto and Gilda approach, he intent on vengeance and she on saving her lover's life. She is horrified to see the Duke enter the inn and to hear him sing of the fickleness of women (the famous "La donna mobile"). The Duke attempts to make love to the compliant Maddelena, then all join together in their famous quartet to express their diverse emotions: Rigoletto, vengeance; Gilda, despair; the Duke, love; Maddelena, cynicism. This is a superb example of the portrayal of widely divergent emotions, all masterfully melded into a musico-dramatic whole (Example 13-13).

Puccini's La Bohème

The *duet* we will look at is by the sentimental successor of Verdi, Giacomo Puccini (1858–1924) who, inheriting the mantle of his fellow countryman, composed Romantic operas whose universal popularity has been unsurpassed. One of his most popular operas is *La Bohème*, produced in 1896.

The story of poor Mimi is too well known to warrant much elaboration here. She, a penniless flower girl, falls in with a group of gay but destitute Bohemian artist-intellectuals. One cold night she appears at their flat to have her candle relighted, since she has no matches of her own. She meets the poet Rodolfo for the first time. He comes to her aid, discovering that she is cold and ill. She lingers for a while as they become acquainted and soon they sense the first stirrings of love. Their voices movingly soar in the famous duet, a fragment of which appears in Example 13-14.

EXAMPLE 13-13 VERDI: *Rigoletto*, ACT III, QUARTET, MEASURES 25–28.

EXAMPLE 13-14   PUCCINI: *La Bohème*, ACT I, "O SOAVE FANCIUL" ("O GENTLE MAIDEN"), DUET, MEASURES 9–17.

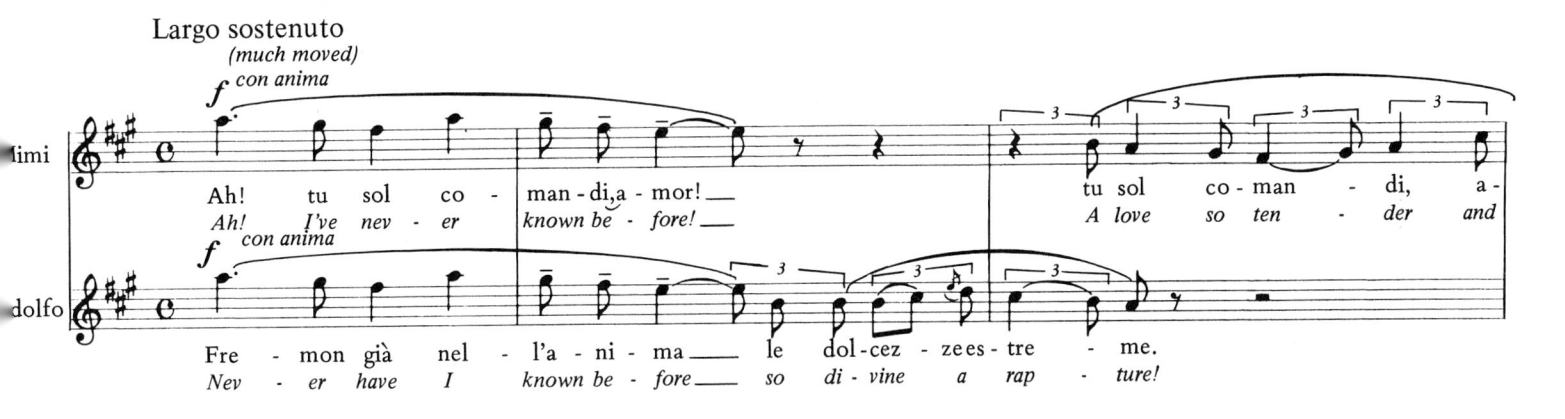

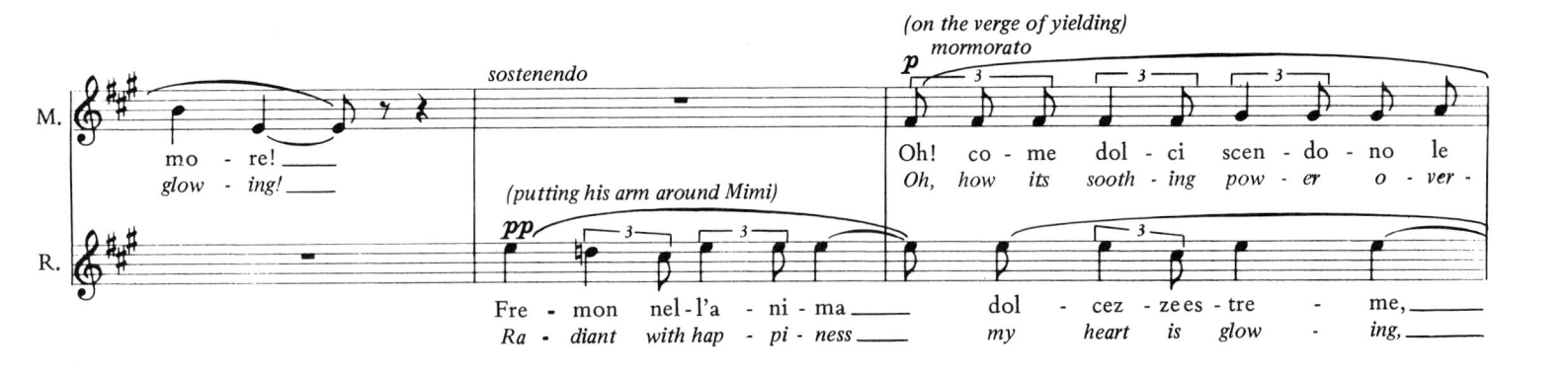

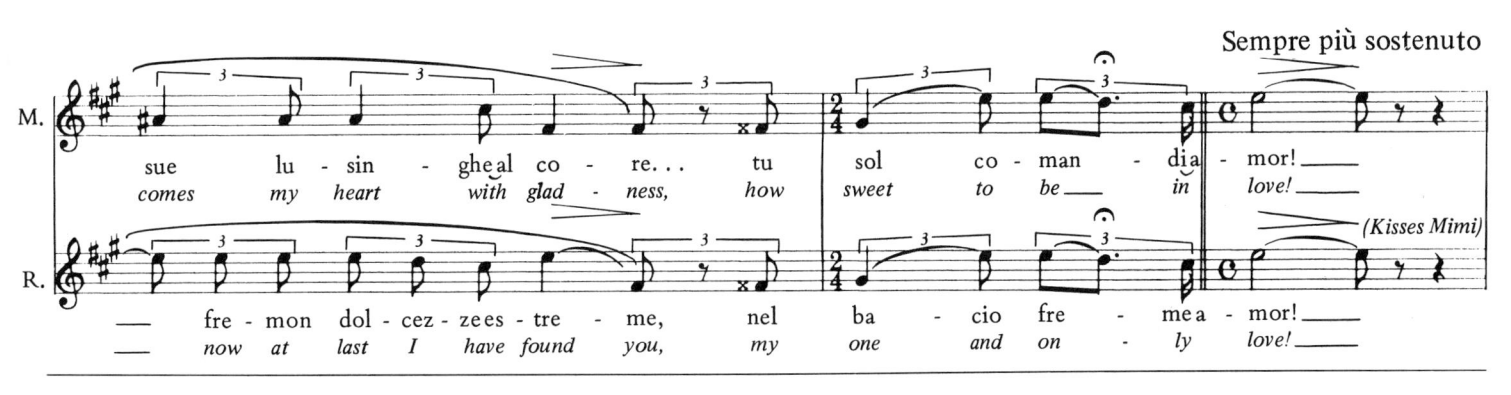

Romantic Style (1825–1900) (concluded)

Many disdain the unabashed sentimentality and "soap opera" melodrama of such Romantic works. Failure to explore them thoroughly, however, would be a serious mistake since, for many, they contain some of the most appealing of all musical utterances.

OTHER MUSIC

One might assume to this point that all music of the Romantic style is referential, that is, referring to some extramusical idea whether mood, effect, poem, story, or drama. But not all composers engulfed themselves in this "new music." Some still contented themselves with composing music devoid of extramusical implications. Such a composer was Johannes Brahms (1833–1897), a traditionalist considered to be "a man of the past" because he shunned this new wave that crested at the close of the nineteenth century. Brahms stood firm against the tide, preferring to couch his own inspirations in abstract musical terms. In so doing, he created a music uniquely his own, and whose popularity and universal appeal are unquestioned.

To sense the flavor of his highly individual style, we will briefly consider two of his most appealing works: *Piano Quintet in F Minor, Op. 34; first movement* and *Variations on a Theme By Haydn, Op. 56A.*

Brahms' Piano Quintet in E Minor, Op. 34

Brahms was one of the greatest masters of sonata form after Beethoven. His chamber works, among them three string quartets, three piano quartets (pieces for string trio and piano), two string sextets, two string quintets (with two violas), and a lovely piano quintet in F minor, create the peak of that genre after the monumental works of Beethoven's last string quartets. One of Brahms' most popular and appealing chamber pieces is his *Piano Quintet in F Minor, Op. 34.*

Listen to the opening movement with a particular ear for the presentation of materials in the exposition and their subsequent elaboration in the development section. The principal themes appear in Example 13-15. Having assimilated Brahms' presentation and development of the thematic ideas cited in Example 13-15, listen to the movement again, devoting special attention to their recall in the recapitulation and coda.

Following the development of the themes in a richly contrapuntal texture, Brahms recalls them all while moving far afield harmonically and then invests the subsequent rhythmically accelerated translation with a highly intricate and contrapuntal texture.

The introduction of a nine-measure *tonic* pedal in the piano signals the beginning of the coda of the movement. The melodic line stated in the first violin begins ten measures of imitative counterpoint in which all four strings contribute thematic statements. Material clearly recalling theme 1 is reintroduced to coincide with a return to the F-minor key of the movement, as well as a resumption of the opening tempo. The combination of these factors adds to the impression of return to the beginning or rounding that results, an impression that is given clearer definition by the fortissimo, tutti restatement of the characteristic broken triad sequence that acts as a kind of motto for the entire movement. Brahms maintains the minor mode to the final chord; doing so seems to heighten the effect of the continuity of mood, which at times approaches a hint of resignation, an effect that characterizes many of Brahms's works and which emerges as a kind of emotional "key" of many Romanticists.

Brahms' Variations on a Theme by Haydn

The final work we will consider exemplifies Brahms' retrospective nature as it is cast in a musical form dating back to the fourteenth century. Few composers have equaled Brahms' mastery of the variation form. His capacity for effectively elaborating and developing material in restatements can be observed throughout his compositions regardless of their formal mold. In his many variations for the piano, in his compositions for chamber groups such as his *String Quintet in G Major,* and perhaps above all in his symphonic *Variations on a Theme by Haydn,* Brahms matched if not surpassed prior attempts by other composers such as Haydn, Mozart and Beethoven to explore the variation principle in pieces for in-

EXAMPLE 13-15 BRAHMS: *Piano Quintet in F Minor, Op. 34*, FIRST MOVEMENT. (a) PRINCIPAL THEME 1, MEASURES 1–4; (b) PRINCIPAL THEME 2, MEASURES 47–51.

strumental ensembles. Brahms' unique capability to shape expressive and original material with the surehandedness and judgment of a classicist is generally apparent. In the latter regard he was unmatched in his time, that of the closing years of the nineteenth century, a century of unprecedented innovation, development, and intense emotionalism in music.

Brahms' approach to the problem of variations differed markedly from that of both Haydn and Mozart in that he utilized the theme as a point of departure for the invention of a whole succession of imaginatively contrasted and distinct variations which are almost like unique pieces in themselves, and their dependence on the initial theme as a source of melodic material is virtually obscured.

Fragments of the theme of Brahms' *Variations on a Theme by Haydn* are shown in a piano arrangement in Example 13-16a. Sing the melody and familiarize yourself with the accompanying chords and the phrase and cadence structure, and note the formal plan of the theme: A-A-B-A-coda. Listen to the entire movement before continuing.

The success of many variations often hinges on the essential simplicity and resulting playability of the theme itself. This piece is no exception. The extraordinary contrasts and changes of mood and character are tied together and given a logical order that is a product of the theme's basic formal-harmonic plan. It is through the elaboration of an adhered-to basic plan that a feeling of continuity—despite changes—is maintained. Two of the variations are dealt with here. You should also relate the following explanations and processes to the other variations.

The structure of the theme involves an initial section, composed of two five-measure phrases. The first, phrase a, closes with a progressive cadence on the dominant (V) and the answering (consequent) phrase (a variant of phrase a) reasserts the tonic B flat.

The second section begins with phrase b anchored to a dominant pedal and closing with a rhythmically weak arrival on tonic (V-I). Phrase b is repeated in varied form in the progression IV to V, elaborated by descending contrapuntal motion, which reemphasizes the dominant in preparation for a restatement of the opening phrase. Thereafter, a seven-measure coda brings the theme to a gradual close.

The basic layout of phrase structure and harmonic progression within the tonality of B flat constitutes the unifying, recurring basis for the eight variations that follow. To a great extent the details of harmonic progression—such as the measure-by-measure chord changes, pedal points, and to some

Johannes Brahms (1833–1897)

■ Johannes Brahms occupies a unique niche in music history because he remained a traditionalist at a time when the wave of the "new music," espoused by Liszt, Wagner, Strauss, and others, was cresting. He chose to preserve the long tradition epitomized by the works of Beethoven, contenting himself with the old forms and practices and leaving it to others more experimental to anticipate the future. Consequently his music, in a historical sense, has a retrospective flavor, imbued with a richness of lyricism and nostalgic Romanticism that gives it a character peculiar to Brahms. One is impressed by his rugged melodies, dynamic rhythms impelled by syncopation and cross-rhythms, the masterful interweaving of melodic lines, and the richness of sonority made mellow with a generous use of horns, low winds, and brasses. He may be faulted by some for being "after his day," but this impressive rhapsodist created a vast treasure of appealing works that assured his place among the greatest composers of all times.

Born in the waterfront district of Hamburg, the son of a string-bass player of the state opera, Brahms began the study of music at an early age and by age 14 gave his first public piano recital, including a set of variations he had composed. He made his own way, teaching, playing the piano in taverns, and playing backstage at the opera. He became acquainted with Schumann in 1853, a most fortunate event in the life of the precocious young man, as Schumann, recognizing Brahms's unusual talents and seeing him as the future standard bearer of the tradition he himself espoused, announced to the world in his prestigious journal, *Neue Zeitschift für Musik*, that a new musical force had arrived on the scene, the "young eagle" Brahms. Although Brahms failed to blaze a new trail as the title of Schumann's article, "New Paths," implied that he might, he did not fail to realize his great potential and the years ahead were to see him become a major figure in German music.

He became a close family friend of the Schumanns, but unfortunately became enamored with the wife of his benefactor, who at this time was at the very height of his fame. This circumstance wracked Brahms with suicidal guilt and remorse, but was resolved by the untimely death of Schumann. Brahms, for reasons best known to him, never married his beloved friend's wife, although they maintained a lifelong friendship; he remained a bachelor all of his life.

In 1863, having been unsuccessful in obtaining the post of director of the Hamburg Philharmonic, he left for Vienna, which was destined to be his final home. Then followed years of performing, conducting, and composing in Germany, Hungary, and Austria, years in which he struggled to gain attention in a world virtually dominated by the "new music." In time, however, he emerged as the logical successor of Beethoven, aided by some of Vienna's greatest musicians and, of course, by the performance of his own works.

His finest choral work, *A German Requiem*, was completed in final form and first performed in 1869 in the famed Gewandhaus in Leipzig. This choral masterpiece, which had been many years in progress and had been performed in incomplete form on two previous occasions, was the work above all others that was to establish his fame during his lifetime.

Until age 43 Brahms had shied away from composing for symphony orchestra, although this thought had been in the back of his mind for many years, during which he devoted his creative energies to choral pieces, piano and chamber works, and a vast quantity of songs. He startled and delighted the world with his *Symphony No. 1 in C Minor*, hailed as the "Tenth," a worthy successor to Beethoven's Ninth Symphony. Thereafter came three other such masterpieces in the next nine years, his beautiful concertos for violin and for piano, the popular *Academic Festival Overture* (written in acknowledgment of the doctor of philosophy degree awarded him by Breslau), and the *Tragic Overture*.

Brahms became a legend in his day, a mixture of crotchety bachelor with a caustic wit and warm-hearted man who loved the good life, his friends, and children. Ill with cancer, he caught a cold at the funeral of his beloved Clara Schumann, which started a series of complications leading to his death. Through his inspired creations he gained the supreme eminence of master among masters, so succinctly put in a phrase coined by a famous contemporary of his day, the "three B's of music—Bach, Beethoven, and Brahms."

Brahms was an accomplished pianist and some of his most inspiring works employ the piano, works in which his great richness of imagination, developmental craft, and intensity of expression are so abundantly revealed.

Refer to this diagram in relating the variations cited here to the harmonic and phrase structure of the movement.

Variation 1
This variation is composed of two contrapuntally woven lines over a supporting bass, measures 1-5. The two lines are contrasted by their respective rhythms, the one a duple-beat division, the other triple. This combined pattern is referred to as three against two (3 to 2). The structure of the theme is maintained despite the marked contrasts of tempo, texture, instrumentation, and mood. The sweeping legato articulation of the variation contrasts with the motivic character of the theme's melody (Example 13-16c).

Variation 2
This quicker-paced variation is based almost throughout on the reiteration of the opening rhythm of the theme, ♩. ♪♪ , but varied by legato articulation. The figure is assigned to the woodwinds for the most part, as in the theme, and the strings accompany in alternate pizzicato (plucked) and arco (bowed) passages. The harmonic structure of the theme is clearly maintained as is its phrase structure (Example 13-16d)

Most musically disposed persons find it hard to resist the persuasive melodies and siciliano rhythms of variation 7, which comes as a point of relaxation and sheer delight in lyrical melody that is rarely excelled in the symphonic repertoire. Although it is not cited here, you are encouraged to seek it out because Brahms' genius for variation and melodic invention is nowhere more apparent than in this section.

extent voice leading, which constitute the basic essentials of the work—are retained throughout. Each variation, however, unfolds a newly elaborated piece within the piece, clothed in changes of dynamics, texture, instrumentation, tempo, and mode. That Brahms' vision was such that he could reward the listener with such a remarkably free yet at the same time related and logically connected set of variations makes the piece all the more noteworthy. Shown in capsule form, the overall structure of the theme appears below:

	A		B		A (Coda)	
	Phrase a	Phrase a'	Phrase b	Phrase b'	Phrase a	
Harmony:	I V	I (V)I	V I	IV V	I	(V)I . . . I
Length:	5 meas.	5 meas.	4 meas.	4 meas.	4 meas.	7 meas.

Styles of Music

EXAMPLE 13-16 BRAHMS: *Variations on a Theme by Haydn.* (a) THEME MEASURES 1–5; (b) MEASURES 11–14; (c) VARIATION 1, MEASURES 1–5; (d) VARIATION 2, MEASURES 1–5.

Romantic Style (1825–1900) (concluded)

By the end of the nineteenth century, the ballerina had become the queen of dance with her bravura technique, full-skirted and tight-waisted tutu, and dazzling jewels. Degas, one of the greatest French painters of that century and very talented in depicting the human form in motion, captures a fleeting impression of ballerinas in rehearsal.

SUMMARY

Programmatic music dominated the Romantic period. For many, it is more readily understood and accessible than other more abstract forms. Although it should be carefully explored and valued for its intrinsic worth, careful study will develop listening skills that can lead to increased understanding and appreciation of the great abundance of less-representational music. If one concentrates on the treatments of the various parameters of sound and the compositional devices as exemplified in the works discussed in Chapters 11 through 13, one will begin to recognize some of the more obvious features of Romantic styles. One sees that melodies are greatly extended in range and dramatic scope, rhythms are more complex and varied than those of the Classical period, harmonies are thicker and more dissonant, textures are more varied, and, above all else, abrupt contrasts dramatize this subjective and emotional music.

Style Characteristics of Romantic Music

Melody: Melody dominates the musical texture; it is intense, broadly arching, frequently asymmetrical, angular, and sequentially derived, and enriched with chromaticism. Melody tends toward melodramatic changes of pace, mood, motion, and direction—thus being less homogenous than before—and contains more nationalistic elements—indigenous dance rhythms, melodic figures and folk tunes, and greater variety of scalar materials—modal, whole tone, and chromatic.

Rhythm: Rhythm flows generally in a periodic stream but with more deviation through the increased use of abrupt tempo and meter changes, syncopations, shifting accents, rhythmic complexities, retards, and accelerandos. It contains more imbalance in movement ranging from steady to impulsive to abrupt pause for dramatic effect dictated by the expressive nature of the theme.

Harmony: Harmony supports melody in a chordal stream still much oriented to the basic movement from tonic to dominant but now greatly enriched with nondiatonic harmonies, more dissonant tertian harmonies, nontriadic chords (quartal and whole tone), and mode changes. It is impelled by movement to cadence now less decisive, often obscure, frequently being weakened by metric placement on weak beats or elided with the opening of the ensuing phrase. Harmony contains greater variety and contrast of motion density, dissonance, abrupt changes of key and mode, and frequent modulations and restless tonal shifting.

Texture: Still predominantly homophonic, texture assumes thicker, more contrapuntal characteristics through use of sequential figures interspersed with a wide variety of chordal textures—thick, thin, and extremes of register. Texture is characterized by great variety of interweaving contrasting sonorities, being often virtually continuous, dramatically abrupt, pictorially descriptive and evocative of mood.

Timbre: Timbre becomes a predominant feature in much music, particularly programmatically conceived music in which expressiveness and wide variety of color are desired. Timbre is greatly enriched as wind and brass choirs are enlarged, the percussion battery increased, and extreme ranges and instrumental virtuosity exploited as in such coloristic effects as muting, tremolos, glissandos, plucking, and various types of unusual bowings (bouncing bow, back of the bow, etc.).

In closing it should be noted that, with the exception of the symphonic poem (tone poem), no new forms were devised by the Romantic composers; instead they expanded the old forms or, in the case of "character pieces," condensed them. New dance types were added to the repertoire, being derived from various indigenous folk or popular dances—waltzes, mazurkas, can-can, Slovak dances, and the like. Theme and variations, though still a staple of multimovement compositions, also became an independent work. The scherzo replaced the minuet in the symphony, the symphonic poem was developed, and the concepts of *idée fixe* and thematic transformation were perfected as form became more subservient to musical expressiveness, wherein inventive and "romantic" melody, harmony, dynamic, tempo, and textural changes replaced thematic development.

This was truly a time of experimentation and change that was to see the "new" threaten the "old," forcing one writer of the time to satirically observe, "It is a joy how the industrious Romantics apply the match to everything and tear it down, and push great wheelbarrowsfull of rules and Classical rubbish away from the scene of the conflagration." (Borne, 1830.)

14 Twentieth-Century Style (1900-)

STYLE CHANGES

It is important to approach the music of our time with an "open ear," so to speak, remembering that music making has always been a changing and developing art. Composers have seldom left music as they found it, but have constantly redefined and reshaped its materials and forms, stretching esthetic boundaries since the beginnings of Western music. It is a peculiarity of Western music that style change has been a musical-historical fact.

In this century the rate of style change and development has been drastically accelerated to the point that the listener or player may feel at times that the very basis for an involvement with music has been uprooted, redefined, or altered to an overwhelming degree. It may help to remind ourselves that music of our time is still as much an art of deploying sounds, rhythms, textures, timbres, chords, and other materials as it ever was. It is true, however, that the choice of materials as well as the means of deploying them artfully has widened considerably, to the point that many of us feel compelled to expand our own (narrow) definitions of music (what it is) and musical activity (what it may entail).

The goal of this chapter is to open the door to the wealth of little-explored art music of our time, written for and about *us* in our fast-changing era on this planet. A further and realistic aim is that you will develop a curiosity for, and willingness to become part of, the music of this century on its own terms—not because you should, but because you can hardly participate in the sweep of twentieth-century civilization without actively experiencing some of the music which in its own diverse ways helps to define and shape our time in history.

If nineteenth-century composers were concerned on the whole with individualism, extreme ranges of emotion, musical pictorialism, and a general commitment to musical effect—Romanticism—it seems no less accurate to generalize that twentieth-century composers returned to a more detached and objective approach to their art. This rededication, easily noted also in painting with the works of such renowned French painters as Monet, Gaugin, Seurat, and the Spaniard Picasso, is first observed in the music of Claude Debussy (1862–1918).

This Neo-impressionist painting by Georges Seurat (1859–1891), La Parade, conveys a veiled impression exemplifying a characteristic often associated with the music of his fellow countryman, Claude Debussy.

In his works for the piano and orchestra, Debussy fascinated the musical world at the turn of this century by creating a number of pieces whose attraction to audiences and impressionable fellow-composers lay primarily in their inventive sonorities, timbres, and textures that were both musically satisfying and unencumbered by Romantic emotionalism. Although Debussy's music by no means swept the world in the early twentieth century, it and other composers' works as well signaled an end, for practical purposes, of nineteenth-century Wagnerian Romanticism. This in turn set the stage for a period of unprecedented innovation, experimentation, and a general flood of musical ideas, most of which centered on essentially *musical* developments rather than ways of making music's expressive potential subservient to emotionalism and extramusical association. The difference in modern time is easily seen, for example, by contrasting the music provided as background to a film, often depictive music, with music such as a string quartet by Bartók or a blues improvisation by a jazz "combo," both of which are concerned in their own ways with a fundamentally free musical gesture not conceived to underscore or dramatize explicit emotions, ideas, or objects. It was the objective musicalness of Debussy's art and that of a number of his immediate successors or contemporaries that gave impetus to the innovational treatments of rhythm, line (melody), harmony, and timbre by three generations of twentieth-century composers such as Stravinsky (1882–1971), Bartók (1881–1945), Schoenberg (1874–1951), Webern (1883–1945), Hindemith (1895–1963), and many others. Some of the latter include a number of great jazz or "pop" artists of this century such as Duke Ellington, George Gershwin, Bix Beiderbecke, Fletcher Henderson, Eddie Sauter, Charlie Parker, and Dave Brubeck, to mention only a few.

Let us stop to consider one of the most appealing works created by such a composer, *Rhapsody in Blue* by George Gershwin (1898–1937).

JAZZ: A NEW IDIOM

Gershwin's Rhapsody in Blue

George Gershwin's famous *Rhapsody in Blue*, a twentieth-century example of sectional form, is interesting to study from several points of view. We might begin by mentioning the circumstances under which it was written. In 1924, Paul Whiteman, the great jazz orchestra leader, decided upon the then unprecedented step of presenting a concert of jazz works in the Aeolian Hall of New York. Before this, jazz was regarded as something to be heard in a dance hall or in a Broadway musical, but not in the concert hall. Whiteman realized that he needed a "major" work of jazz as the centerpiece of the program and asked his friend George Gershwin to write it. Gershwin had previously written only popular songs and Broadway shows, but he had a good understanding of classical techniques and forms, so he turned eagerly to the composition of a large-scale work. Here is the way he described the compositional process:

Suddenly an idea occurred to me. There had been so much talk about the limitations of jazz, not to speak of the manifest misunderstanding of its function. Jazz, they said, had to be in strict time. It had to cling to dance rhythms. I resolved, if possible, to kill that misconception with one sturdy blow. Inspired by this aim, I set to work composing.

I had no set plan, no structure to which my music could conform. The Rhapsody, you see, began as a purpose, not a plan. I worked out a few themes, but just at this time I had to appear in Boston for the premiere of **Sweet Little Devil.** *It was on the train, with its steely rhythms, its rattly-bang that is so often stimulating to a composer (I frequently hear music in the very heart of noise), that I suddenly heard—even saw on paper—the complete construction of the Rhapsody from beginning to end. No new themes came to me, but I worked on the thematic material already in my mind, and tried to conceive the composition as a whole. I hear it as a sort of musical kaleidoscope of America—of our vast melting-pot, of our incomparable national pep, our blues, our metropolitan madness. By the time I reached Boston, I had the definite plot of the piece, as distinguished from its actual substance.*

The middle theme came upon me suddenly, as my music often does. It was at the home of a friend, just after I got back to Gotham. I must do a great deal of what you might call subconscious composing, and this is an example. Playing at parties is one of my notorious weaknesses. As I was playing, without a thought of the Rhapsody, all at once I heard myself playing a theme that must have been haunting me inside, seeking outlet. No sooner had it oozed out of my fingers than I realized I had found it. Within a week of my return from Boston I had completed the structure, in the rough, of the Rhapsody in Blue.*

Though Gershwin said he had no set plan, the resulting piece is, in broad terms, a large three-part form. It consists of a first section in which the tempo ranges from moderate to fast and the character is generally lively; a second section which is slow in tempo and lyrical in character; and a third section, in which the fast tempo and lively character of the first section return.

To understand the thematic construction of the work, it is important to remember that Gershwin was primarily identified with the popular song, and when he wrote an extended composition it was as natural for him to turn to idioms and forms of the popular song as it was for Haydn to turn to the European folk song in his symphonic works. It can be shown that five melodies in the style of popular songs constitute the compositional core of the *Rhapsody in Blue*, shown in Example 14-1.

Part I consists of statements of themes A, B, C, and D with transition sections between. These transition sections are based on motives from the various themes.

Part II is devoted entirely to the lyric E theme, expressed first in the orchestra and then in the solo piano. A return to a faster tempo signals a return to the mood of the first part, but we must wait some before we hear a return to any of the thematic material of part I. At first we hear a new section which has been labeled *toccata* (literally a "touch piece") since it is devoted more to the percussive exploration of a rhythmic figure

---

*From David Ewen, *The Story of George Gershwin* (New York: Holt, Rinehart and Winston, 1943). Reprinted by permission of Holt, Rinehart and Winston.

EXAMPLE 14-1 GERSHWIN: *Rhapsody in Blue.* (a) MEASURES 38–41; (b) MEASURES 91–98; (c) MEASURES 115–118; (d) MEASURES 138–141; (e) MEASURES 303–310.

Twentieth-Century Style (1900–) 257

George Gershwin (1898–1937)

■ The Brooklyn-born George Gershwin was to first make his mark in "Tin Pan Alley" and then direct much of his creative energies toward bridging the gap between the music of Broadway and of the art world—a gap that was to be closed by later composers of so-called "third-stream" music. He was peculiarly fitted for this role, having been thoroughly trained in piano and music theory and possessing an inspired melodic flair and affinity for jazz rhythms and harmonies.

He began his career at 16 as a "song plugger" for a publishing house, but three years later his own lyric and rhythmic genius was to emerge, his first big popular success being "Swanee," a song which sold more than a million copies and more than two million recordings. Having been introduced to Broadway by Al Jolson, who interpolated "Swanee" in a hit show in which he was starring, Gershwin's career was cut out for him. In the next decade he conquered the world of musical comedy with such popular favorites as "Lady Be Good," "Strike Up the Band," "Girl Crazy," and "Of Thee I Sing."

Although he was thoroughly immersed in the jazz idiom as were so many composers of the time, and he had gained fame and great wealth in the field of popular music, Gershwin yearned to close the gap between the music native to this country, jazz, and that of the concert stage. His big opportunity came when the famed Paul Whiteman invited him to compose a symphonic work in the jazz idiom for a performance with his orchestra in Aeolian Hall. The result was the ever-popular *Rhapsody in Blue*, first performed in 1924 with the composer playing the piano part.

Relatively untrained in orchestration, he immersed himself in further study and four years later the New York Philharmonic performed his second such work, *An American in Paris*, a tone poem exemplifying his great wealth of accessible melodies and innate skill in treating jazz rhythms and progressions.

In the nine years remaining of his tragically short life, he attempted one opera, *Porgy and Bess*, a folk opera set in Charleston, South Carolina, and based on the unhappy lives of an unfortunate group of blacks. Its early success was mixed, but some of the tunes attained great popularity—"Summertime," "I Got Plenty o' Nuttin'," and "Bess, You Is My Woman Now." Today *Porgy and Bess* is internationally recognized as an American classic. Gershwin gravitated to Hollywood and tried his hand at film music, including *Shall We Dance* and *Damsel in Distress*, **but a brain tumor brought an untimely end to his brilliant career.**

than to a new thematic idea. This toccata figure continues then as accompaniment to an agitated version of the E theme in diminution and in minor. The music surges ahead with sequential repetitions of the head motive of the E theme, and finally reaches a climax. It gathers force once again and gradually broadens to a powerful statement of the C theme and then the concluding statement of the A theme.

Most listeners can easily hear the materials used and the formal structure created in the Rhapsody. It represents a "popular" stream of twentieth-century composition influenced by an American musical invention called *jazz*. And while it hardly is representative of the major thrust of art music of this century, having discovered the increased understanding, enjoyment, and appreciation that can come from this process of active, penetrating study of a relatively accessible work such as this, it is hoped that techniques and attitudes will be developed and carried over to other works, which at least on first acquaintance may not seem so accessible.

COMPARISON OF STYLES

The increasing number of stylistic streams that developed in the early stages of this century had in common, and for the most part still have, a commitment to musical sound free of the romantic and emotional references, allusions, and imageries of a hundred or so years before; but this change has been difficult for many music listeners and audiences to grasp. It does a disservice to much great music that today's listeners often seem to predicate their interest in and responses to music on an assumption of explicit extramusical meaning, even though such references and meaning are not commonly intended by many composers. That music has the power to move us while allowing for the interpretation of subjectively perceived meanings, musical or extramusical, is perhaps its greatest attraction. The twentieth-century listener must try to meet today's music on its own terms, not on those that might be assumed because of prior musical acquaintance.

A glimpse of the marked contrast of much of the music of this century with that of prior ones may be obtained by comparing the three melodies in Example 14-2. The first of these, by Tchaikovsky, typifies many nineteenth-century melodies in that it is quite expressive and outgoingly singable, while at the same time simply constructed and easily recalled. It is intended to underscore the feelings shared by Romeo and Juliet. The other two melodies, however, both products of the past fifty or so years, are not intended to have any specific extramusical association or references. The listener is invited to hear and react to them without any explicit or obvious associations.

The second melody in Example 14-2, by Webern, attracts our attention by virtue of its somewhat breathy and interrupted succession of durations. The pitch materials are those of the chromatic scale, each tone being of equal tonal importance and none emerging as a tonic. Melodies such as this are common in twentieth-century music; the absence of key feeling is generally called *atonality*. The expressiveness and melodic individuality of the melody is also attributable to the jagged contour that it traces, one constituted of a skillfully deployed balance of wide and small intervals begun and ended by static note repetition.

The final melody, one of a series of improvisations by a great jazz artist of the forties and early fifties, Charlie Parker, is indicative of the distinctly American expression of improvised jazz. The fluid quality of line, rhythmic propulsion, and idiomatic turns and figures of jazz are as uniquely a part of this century as Bach's music was to the eighteenth. From any point of view the last two melodies of Example 14-2 are worlds apart from the Romanticism of many nineteenth-century melodies. Taken as a whole they reflect a marked innovation in style, one that is indicative of the exploration and experimentation with musical materials that has typified the entire period. We shall see subsequently that the examples cited here represent only the beginnings of a pattern of marked diversity and change in the twentieth century that is still very much alive.

This pattern is a result of the responses of a whole generation of composers who became dissatisfied with the limitations of tonal music of nineteenth-century Romanticism and who felt that Romantic expression in music had reached a dead end.

EXAMPLE 14-2 (a) TCHAIKOVSKY: *Romeo and Juliet Overture,* MELODY ONLY, MEASURES 1–9; (b) WEBERN: *Symphony for Small Orchestra, Op. 21,* FIRST MOVEMENT, MELODY ONLY, MEASURES 1–11; (c) CHARLIE PARKER: "PERHAPS" (IMPROVISATION), MELODY ONLY, MEASURES 1–8.

The solution for twentieth-century composers lay in a renewed Classicism of a sort, at least insofar as this implied a revivified interest in musical sound for its own unique self as opposed to its association with Romantic imagery, fantasy, and theater.

THE MOVE AWAY FROM MAJOR-MINOR TONALITY

The first half of this century framed some of the most exciting activity in the history of Western music. Like the beginning of the Baroque period (ca. 1600), musical style and musical activity in general underwent numerous significant changes, the impacts of which are still being felt and assessed. The European unrest, strife, and dislocation of art and artists during the years surrounding the two wars provided a background for a number of developments and trends that have radically altered musical style. The music enthusiast, accustomed to expect some uniformity of practice in the music of different schools or composers of a given period, is likely to be confounded by the divergent styles and attitudes about music articulated by musicians of the period in question.

In attempting to get a grip on the striking contrasts of composers, styles, and attitudes current during the opening half of our century, it helps to try to identify some common thread or trait in most music of the time. Contrasts are often more apparent than those aspects of different styles that relate them and that act as a kind of common ground. At least one such common feature lies in the fact that most early twentieth-century composers of art music such as Debussy, Stravinsky, Schoenberg, Bartók, Hindemith, and subsequently the leading European-influenced American composers of the time such as Charles Ives, virtually abandoned *major-minor tonality*—that is, the organization of melodic and harmonic sounds into keys. Although this decisive step is far more apparent in some music than others, and the move away from the use of major-minor key organization is of much more far-reaching proportions in the works of Arnold Schoenberg, for example, than in the music of Igor Stravinsky, it can be perceived as an important feature of most of their works from as early as 1905 on.

The preceding statement needs some qualification because, as expressions such as *atonality, expanded tonality, neomodality,* and *polytonality* imply, the abandonment of tonality by early twentieth-century composers was by no means equally undertaken by all composers. Within the framework of such a general move toward the liberation of tones from the constraints of traditional harmonic and scalar patterns, one must note the radical attempts by Schoenberg and Webern in particular to avoid any semblance of key feeling or loyalty to a tonic. The majority of their works are, by general consensus, called *atonal,* meaning absence of tonality. By contrast, composers such as Hindemith, Stravinksy, Bartók, Ives, and others (especially non-Germanic composers) continued to organize their compositions with more or less systematic references to some kind of tonic focal point or tonal center. This was accomplished through any of a variety of techniques such as basing the pitch materials on those of a familiar major scale without the limita-

260 Styles of Music

tions of functional chord progressions (sometimes called *pandiatonicism*). Another tonal procedure involved the simple melodic or harmonic reiteration of one pitch (sometimes more), thus establishing a kind of focal pitch. In many passages two keys were combined (*polytonality*) so as to create a colorful superposition of tonalities. The possibilities for creating tonal feeling while exceeding the boundaries of major or minor diatonic scales and simple triadic chord progressions were (and still are) enormous. Bartók, Stravinsky, and Hindemith were extraordinarily gifted composers who worked for the greater part of their musical lives at attempting to reconcile in their compositions the use of all available *twelve* tones of the chromatic scale to some loyalty to a tonality, although not the tonality of the key system of the eighteenth and nineteenth centuries. The distinction may seem moot—it is not.

A better feeling for the generalized movement away from key organization that earmarks most music of the twentieth century can be gained by listening to the following three examples.

Example 14-3 presents the first section of the theme from the second movement of Stravinsky's *Octet for Wind Instruments.* Although the piece introduces all twelve available pitches within a rather short span, D emerges as a clearly felt tonic, defined by repetition in the bass. The chords sounded above the bass are by no means limited to triads functioning in the D scale.

The introductory measures from Hindemith's symphony *Mathis der Maler,* first movement (Example 14-4), show how the composer used clearly stated points of tonal emphasis to shape the piece and create tonal unity without relying on traditional keys to do so. Far removed from earlier practice in terms of variety of tonal materials, melody, and harmony, the piece nonetheless moves in the framework of expressly stated points of tonal stability and tension.

EXAMPLE 14-3 STRAVINSKY: *Octet for Wind Instruments,* OPENING OF SECOND MOVEMENT, MEASURES 1–8.

Copyright © 1924 by Edition Russe de Musique; renewed 1952. Copyright and renewal assigned 1951 to Boosey and Hawkes, Inc. Revised version copyright 1952 by Boosey and Hawkes, Inc. Reprinted by permission.

Twentieth-Century Style (1900–) **261**

EXAMPLE 14-4 HINDEMITH: *Mathis der Maler*, ENGELKONZERT, MEASURES 1–8.

Paul Hindemith (1895-1963)

■ No German composer of post-World War I days created more controversy than did Paul Hindemith, who early helped fan the flames of experimentation that boldly prevailed in the Weimar Republic. He later abandoned the role of musical *enfant terrible* to devote his boundless energy and talents to works less sensational, becoming one of the leading composers of this century.

Born near Frankfurt, Hindemith began the study and performance of music early in life, and by the age of 13 had mastered the violin. Having furthered his study at the Hoch Conservatory in Frankfurt, in the period from 1915-1929 he served as concertmaster of the Frankfurt Opera, switched to the viola, and founded and toured with an important string quartet. From 1927-1935 he taught composition at the famous Hochschule für Musik of Berlin, a post he abandoned when his music was banned by the Third Reich because of its radical "progressive" nature. As was true in many such cases, the United States was to benefit from this act of the Nazi leaders; Hindemith ultimately came to this country, joined the faculty of the Yale School of Music, lectured at Harvard, became an American citizen, and continued his most successful multifaceted career as composer, teacher, instrumentalist, and conductor. In 1953 he returned to Europe, settling in Switzerland where he spent his last years.

In summarizing his life one is struck by the immense diversity of his talents since one sees him revealed as a master teacher and skilled theoretician—*The Craft of Musical Composition*—**as a superb violist and conductor, and as one of the most prolific composers of the twentieth century, exemplified in such important works as the opera and symphony** *Mathis der Maler (Matthias the Painter),* **the ballet** *Nobilissima Visione,* **and the song cycle** *Das Marienleben (The Life of Mary).* Hindemith attempted to reconcile the old with the new by wedding the contrapuntal techniques of the past with the clashing dissonances of the twentieth century, thus crafting music in most genres and for most instruments and instrumental combinations.

Igor Stravinsky (1882–1971)

■ In 1913 the Ballet Russe in Paris performed a work without precedent in music to that time, a work that provoked not only a riot in the audience but also a revolution in music. The work was *Le Sacre du Printemps (The Rite of Spring)*, and the composer was Igor Stravinsky. Music was never to be the same.

Stravinsky was born not far from present Leningrad, where his father was a leading singer in the Imperial Opera. Like Handel and Schumann, he was destined for a law career, or so his parents believed. Also, since he was not a child prodigy, he received minimal musical training, although he was brought up in an artistic milieu. He did not have conservatory training, but received some private musical education. And despite his lack of precocity and spotty training, he emerged as a revolutionary leader in music.

Following training in law at the University of Leningrad (then St. Petersburg), he embarked on a career in the legal profession, a career that was aborted when at age 19 he met and subsequently studied with his famed countryman, the composer Rimsky-Korsakov, who, sensing his uncommon talents, encouraged him to enter the world of music. He conquered it ten years later when, at the age of 28, his first great ballet, *L'Oiseau du Feu (The Firebird)*, blazed onto the scene in Paris, premiered by the famed Ballet Russe and commissioned by the legendary Diaghilev. This Russian-based work, with its brilliant orchestration and folkloric elements, catapulted the composer into the musical arena. He followed it the next year with another highly successful ballet, *Petrushka,* whose violent rhythms, colorful orchestration, and innovative harmonies and key combinations foreshadowed the most revolutionary work yet to come—the aforementioned third ballet, *The Rite of Spring.* Although the first performance was riotous, soon after the furor subsided, the ballet became a favorite, a position it holds to this day.

With the outbreak of World War I, the scene changed dramatically. Sumptuous ballets declined and Stravinsky moved to Switzerland where in 1914–1920 he continued to compose, formulating a new concept of composition that tended toward works of modest dimension and those influenced by jazz idioms. One great work of that period was the chamber dance-drama, *L'Histoire du Soldat (The Soldier's Tale)* of 1918.

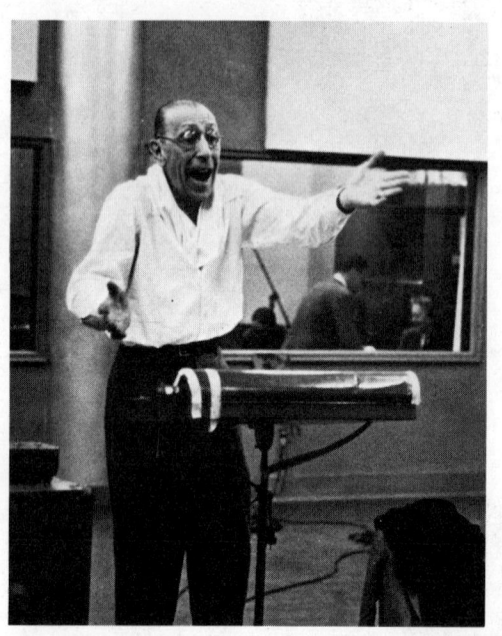

He returned to France in 1920, his ties with his homeland severed because of the Revolution, and remained there for nineteen productive years, successfully exploring the genres of jazz in *Ragtime for Eleven Instruments,* of chamber music in *Octet for Wind Instruments,* of choral music in *Oedipus Rex* and the *Symphony of Psalms,* of ballet in *Card Game* (a "ballet in three deals"), and numerous other works. During this period he toured widely as a conductor and performed his own works, first appearing in America in 1925 at which time he conducted the New York Philharmonic and performed with the Boston Symphony Orchestra.

Having enjoyed great success in America, and with the advent of World War II, Stravinsky elected to come to America, as did so many of his renowned contemporaries. First lecturing at Harvard, then marrying and becoming an American citizen, he engaged in a busy career as a conductor of his own works, ultimately settling in California where he proceeded to enjoy the world fame he so richly deserved and continued to the end to explore the musical world of the new and innovative. It is difficult to set Stravinsky in any particular stylistic mold because to the very end he continued to experiment. In the works written at about age 70 he dabbled with jazz in *Ebony Concerto* for jazz band and orchestra (first performed by Woody Herman), with opera in *The Rake's Progress,* with serial techniques in *Canticum Sacrum . . . (Sacred Song to Honor the Name of Saint Mark),* with ballet in *Agon* and *Threni . . . (Threnodies: Lamentations of the Prophet Jeremiah),* and then a television opera, *The Flood.*

Although his later works never enjoyed the popular success of the startling ballets of his youth, Stravinsky departed this world secure in the knowledge that he had turned the tide, had ridden the crest, and catapulted us all into the music of the future.

264 Styles of Music

Bela Bartók (1881–1945)

■ Béla Bartók, foremost Hungarian composer, might have contented himself to follow the nationalistic bent of others and concern himself solely with music for his own country. Although he became one of the stout champions of music of his native land, he had a broader mission, that of melding its elements into a musical language that would speak to an international audience. So in his music one hears Hungarian folk melodies, exotic scales, and barbaric rhythms, not common to most Western music, unfolding in rhapsodic musical strands sharply highlighted by pungent dissonances and striking syncopations. Though Hungarian by birth and steeped in the musical traditions of the Magyars and Slovaks, he transcended the national to create a music of universal appeal.

Born in Transylvania, then a part of Yugoslavia, the son of the director of a school of agriculture, the frail lad was soon to reveal a precocious talent for music. He played a piano recital of his own works at age 10 and was offered a scholarship at the Vienna Conservatory which he declined to enter the Royal Academy of Music in Budapest in 1894. There he established his reputation as a virtuoso pianist and abandoned the siren call of the "new music" of Wagner and Strauss, becoming involved in the nationalist movement then sweeping some countries of the world, especially those chafing under the yoke of the Austro-German empire. The height of his patriotic dedication was reached in 1903 when, having left the Royal Academy, he composed his first important work, Kossuth, a symphonic poem related to the life of the Hungarian patriot by that name and permeated with patriotic fervor.

About this time he and another important countryman, Kodály, becoming dissatisfied with the stereotyped view of ethnic Hungarian music having been so successfully established by Liszt and Brahms, embarked on a scholarly research project in which they explored the villages of Hungary and surrounding countries recording the folk tunes. This research culminated in a definitive work entitled *Hungarian Folk Music* and Bartók's becoming a leading authority in the field.

In 1907 he joined the faculty of the Royal Academy as professor of piano. Although he continued to create music, it was not well received at home because it departed so radically from the accepted repertoire of the day. He abandoned composing temporarily, contenting himself with teaching and further investigation of folklore. The climate changed rapidly near the close of World War I, Hungary having become independent of Austria. In an upsurge of national pride his mime-ballet, *The Wooden Prince*, was presented with resounding success at the Budapest Opera in 1917, followed the next year by the opera *Duke Bluebeard's Castle*, a work composed some seven years earlier. He had arrived.

Bartók's fame spread rapidly throughout the world, although at home he was at odds with the political regime that would in time espouse the Nazi cause. He held concerts widely, playing his own works, including a trip to the United States in 1927, during which he played from coast to coast. He continued teaching and composing in Budapest until 1940 when because of political developments he found it morally impossible to ignore the abhorrent blight of Hitler. Despite the perils of doing so, the loss of position and status, he became such an outspoken critic of Nazism that his friends, afraid of the consequences, persuaded him to return to the United States.

He had completed most of his masterworks by that time, which included, in addition to those mentioned already, *Music for Strings, Percussion, and Celesta*, six string quartets, the *Canta Profana*, *Mikrokosmos*, and concertos for piano, for violin, and for viola.

In America he wrote his most well-known work, the *Concerto for Orchestra*, commissioned and first performed by the Boston Symphony Orchestra in 1943. Bartók's last five years were miserable ones; he suffered from leukemia, had little money, and was exiled from his homeland. Through funds from ASCAP he was able to compose to the end, living in various nursing homes. Great fame finally arrived after his death, too late for the man now acknowledged as one of the greatest composers of our century.

Probably evolving from a Hungarian Soldier's dance, the czardas became a part of the folk tradition of Hungary, being danced with wild abandon.

Bartók's synthesis of the exotic melodies and rhythms of the folk music of his native Hungary with contemporary practices in art music earned him a place as one of the giants of the "new wave" in music.

While he is not an avowed atonal composer, his tonalities are tenuous and not always clearly defined. One is struck by the tensions of strident, percussive sonorities composed of fourths, seconds, tone clusters, and polyharmonies. All are poured into the musical molds of such classic structures as sonata-allegro and various sectional forms whose elements continuously evolve, enriched by colorful orchestral effects, resulting in a brilliant, lyrical, tightly knit contrapuntal tapestry which is Bartók's alone.

The *Concerto for Orchestra* (1943)—excerpted in Example 14-5—was commissioned and first performed by the Boston Symphony Orchestra. This five-movement work, although symphony-like in its proportions, is called a concerto because various instruments of the orchestra are treated soloistically, either singly or in groups in a virtuoso fashion.

The second movement, allegretto scherzando (in Example 14-5), shows Bartók at his urbane best. It is a game of instrumental pairs, highlighting the winds and brasses. The overall design is tripartite. Five brief sections featuring pairs of bassoons in sixths, oboes in thirds, clarinets in sevenths, flutes in fifths, and muted trumpets in seconds, are followed by a brief choralelike trio in the brasses and a return of the chain of five sections now given to enlarged instrumental combinations— the bassoons and oboes plus clarinets, clarinets plus flutes, flutes plus the remaining woodwinds, and muted trumpets plus harp. This is a tongue-in-cheek interlude kicked off by a sassy side-drum rhythm

which sets the mood of jocularity. The pairs march by, each displaying a dapper, jaunty savoir-faire, only to be brought up short by a solemn chorale. But the solemnity does not last long, and the dapper pairs, now chaperoned, file back to the whimsical beat. The result is a beguiling study of orchestral color and sonority done in a suave, debonair manner both subtle and obvious.

Bartók left us a heritage of marvelously imaginative and skillfully composed works, a number of which are keyboard pieces. Like his work in general, many of his keyboard pieces are based on folk dances or native Hungarian rhythms. The next example illustrates Bartók's commitment to dance in a simple yet effective piano composition, a portion of which is quoted in Example 14-6.

The excerpts quoted from Stravinsky, Hindemith, and Bartók reflect attempts by a number of early twentieth-century

EXAMPLE 14-5 BARTÓK: *Concerto for Orchestra*, SECOND MOVEMENT, MEASURES 123–126.

EXAMPLE 14-6 BARTÓK: *Bohemian Dance*, MEASURES 1–19.

composers to enrich and expand their tonal resources without completely abandoning all vestiges of tonality.

It is possible to summarize the preceding discussion by citing the following key issues that seem central to most of the music of the early twentieth century:

1. Composers changed their outlook from the intense emotionalism of the close of the nineteenth century to an interest in exploring and developing musical sounds in a more objective and detached way, disdaining, for the most part, romantic-affective expression.
2. The most immediate musical concomitant of this trend lay in the move, total or partial, away from traditional key usage.
3. The leading composers of the opening quarter of the century were Austrian (Schoenberg, Webern, and Berg) or Hungarian (Bartók) or French (Debussy, Ravel) or Russian (Stravinsky). With the exception of the American composer Charles Ives, few Americans of the time displayed either the vision or invention of their European peers.

TRENDS FROM 1900 TO 1945

By 1945 or so, twentieth-century composers had produced a stunning repertoire of works containing some of the most impressively original, imaginative, and skillfully fashioned music conceivable. The works produced up to this time by Bartók, Stravinsky, Hindemith, Ives, and Webern alone provide ample evidence of the musical riches of the first half of this century, many of which have become established standard repertoire for the great solo performers, opera companies, orchestras, and ballet companies of the world today. Inevitably the question is raised as to how and why music of our time seems so unlike more traditional music of the more widely familiar composers such as Beethoven, Haydn, Mozart, Brahms, Tchaikovsky, and to a lesser degree earlier composers such as Bach, Handel, and Vivaldi. Maybe the answer to this lies in one word—*communication.*

Composers and their music in past centuries had relatively little exposure; their works were known and heard by relatively small segments of the populace—sometimes just a gathering of friends or patrons comprised the audience for an important premiere. Many fine works, among them such masterpieces as Bach's *St. Matthew Passion,* lay hidden or undiscovered for years. A composer's opportunities for recognition were limited.

In this century of jet travel, radio, record players, and instant communication, the rapid spread of musical innovations and the ability to be in touch with artistic events through one or another means has narrowed the gap between the composer and public. Perhaps most important is the fact that composers themselves have had ready access through twentieth-century communication to the works of their contemporaries, thus making it relatively easy for composers to apply in their own works the developments and innovations of others. It is through such communication, along with more traditional means of sharing ideas through normal artistic discourse, that the contemporary insatiable appetite for novelty, invention, innovation, and originality has been appeased. The listener has in a sense been swallowed up by an overflow of highly varied styles and types of music. To a great extent it will remain for future generations to sort out and evaluate the production of twentieth-century composers. We can begin by familiarizing ourselves with some of the basic trends that have evolved to now.

Impressionism

The term *Impressionism,* the "unfortunate" invention of a French critic, has come to be associated with the early twentieth-century works of Claude Debussy and, to a lesser extent, Maurice Ravel. It originally referred to certain characteristics of the paintings of the French Impressionist painters of the same approximate period, among them Monet, Manet, and Cézanne. Monet's painting *Impression—Sunrise* prompted the use of the term. Some parallels do exist between the preoccupation with color blends, subtle lines, and the somewhat blurred and illusive images of Monet's work and Debussy's preoccupation with details of tone color, subtly orchestrated figures, motives, and counterpoints, and the lovely harmonic combinations of Debussy's orchestral pieces such as *La Mer, Prélude à l'aprés-midi d'un faune,* and *Images,* as well as two attractively innovative books of piano *Préludes,* to mention only a few of his many compositions.

Debussy appears at this stage to have been perhaps more important as a strong influence on numerous subsequent composers, among them Stravinsky, Bartók, and Hindemith, than for his own individual works per se. This is true despite the considerable popular appeal that many of his pieces such as *Prelude to the Afternoon of a Faun* have enjoyed. But Debussy does rank with such past harmonic innovators as Gesualdo, Schubert, and Chopin. His orchestral scoring and gift for instrumental figuration and line, gained partly from his study of Rimsky-Korsakov, Berlioz, and Wagner, have rarely been equaled, though frequently imitated. Although the message of his music is rarely of great emotional range, his compositions are hard to match for sheer pleasurableness of sonority and nuance. So much of Debussy's inventive scoring has been copied and cheapened by far less capable musicians that the skill and originality of his craft is unfortunately often overlooked if not unrecognized by modern audiences accustomed to suave television background scores and lush "pop" arrangements whose debt to Debussy is unacknowledged. Listening to either or all three of the pieces for orchestra mentioned above should help clarify some of the preceding assertions.

Several measures from the score of Debussy's orchestral poem *La Mer* are shown in Example 14-7. Some insight into his fondness for rich sonorities and idiomatic, motivic instrumental melodies can be gained from this short excerpt.

In listening to this section, follow the line begun by the English horn and note its growth and expansion into the other

Example 14-7 Debussy: *La Mer*, from measure 1 of number 16 to measure 3 after number 17.

Twentieth-Century Style (1900–) 269

Claude Debussy (1862–1918)

■ Claude Debussy was born in the outskirts of Paris, the son of a shopkeeper. He was to become the most renowned French composer after the turn of the century, the leader of a musical revolt that was to see the dissolution and eventual abandonment of a tonal system that had prevailed for some three hundred years. Following a few years of private piano study with a former pupil of Chopin, this sailor-to-be, as his father had planned, entered the Paris Conservatoire in 1873 and began a troubled voyage that was to see him scandalize his professors with his unorthodox harmonies and progressions, exotic scales, vague impressionistic miniatures, and general opposition to convention. Deemed surly, uncouth, and sarcastic, though obviously talented, this daring young innovator was to earn deserved recognition the hard way, one test being his efforts to win a Prix de Rome, at which he finally succeeded in 1884 after the third attempt with a cantata entitled *L'Enfant Prodigue* (*The Prodigal Son*). One might have wished that his one success would have smoothed the way for subsequent greater ones, as it has for so many great artists, but it did not.

He was to spend another decade of his life attempting to have his works performed, becoming identified with a French literary movement of symbolist poets (the Impressionists), learning first to appreciate and then reject the colossal Romantic music dramas of Wagner, finding a mistress, and perfecting a unique musical style replete with restless modulation and sensuous coloristic effects, but devoid of "developmental passages" in the conventional sense.

His next success, though a controversial one at best, occurred in Paris in 1893 with the premier performance of the familiar *Prélude à l'après-midi d'un faune* (*Prelude to the Afternoon of a Faun*). This voluptuous, symphonic poem, suggestive of fleeting thoughts of an afternoon spent in the warm, caressing sunshine, was to stamp him, rightly or wrongly, as the leader of the new musical cult devoted to evoking the illusory world of veiled impressions.

By the time his opera *Pelléas et Mélisande* was premiered in Paris in 1902 at the Opera Comique, he had become famous. He had labored over this work for some ten years, while composing such other masterpieces as his three *Nocturnes* for orchestra, a string quartet, the ever-popular *Clair de Lune* from the *Bergamasque Suite* for piano, and a number of his more than 60 songs, and while supplementing the income from his music by private teaching and writing critical reviews for various periodicals.

In 1899 he married for the first time, an unfortunate incident in his life which was to be terminated by his elopement with another woman and a subsequent divorce, after his wife had attempted suicide.

In the decade and a half of life remaining, he reached the height of his productive genius, conquering the world of music with a relatively small output of compositions, numbered among which are the orchestral works *La Mer* and *Ibéria,* the twenty-four *Preludes*, and twelve *Etudes*, and various other works for piano, as well as some of his most beguiling songs.

Prior to the outbreak of World War I, he traveled to London, Vienna, Budapest, the Hague, Amsterdam, Rome, and elsewhere, enjoying success as conductor of his own works. Not content to rest on his laurels, he composed his one ballet, *Jeux*, which was produced by the famed Diaghilev company in Paris in 1913 with Nijinsky as choreographer, and contemplated touring the United States. Unfortunately these plans had to be abandoned because of the ravages of cancer, discovered in London in 1909, and the ominous threat of the global cancer of war.

This "very exceptional, very curious, very solitary" innovator, the man who did as much as any other to close the book on the past and turn to the music of our century, died in his beloved Paris, being sung to his eternal rest by the voices of the approaching invaders.

With his illusory evocation of a veiled, misty dawn, Impression: Sunrise (1874), Claude Monet initiated the French Impression style of painting, which was to be reflected in the tone paintings of Debussy, Ravel, and other composers to follow.

winds, culminating in the high register of the oboe. This kind of fluid, rhapsodically evolving melody, skillfully highlighted and complemented by contrasting figures and dynamics in the accompanying instruments, reflects the composer's concern for lavish details of sonority and articulation. Listen to the entire work and try to note other techniques and processes that occur. The richly colorful passage cited here should suggest why Debussy's pieces have had such appeal to performers, composers, and perceptive listeners of his and our time.

Expressionism

French composers of the early twentieth century were reacting against the Romantic extremes of Wagnerian music-drama by concentrating their efforts on instrumental and keyboard works such as Debussy's *La Mer* or his *Rhapsody for Saxophone* or Ravel's string quartet and piano *Sonatine*; their Austrian counterparts were also composing works for *small* instrumental ensembles, for example, Webern's *Five Movements for String Quartet*, Alban Berg's *Chamber Concerto for Violin, Piano and 13*

In primordial expression of the agonies of modern man undoubtedly influenced by the works of Freud in psychoanalysis, painters and composers of the early 1900's rawly exposed the psychoneurotic world of hallucination, horror, and despair, a terrifying world earlier revealed by the Scandinavian artist, Edvard Munch, in The Cry (1893).

Winds, as well as Schoenberg's *Serenade, Op. 24*, for clarinet, bass clarinet, mandolin, guitar, and three strings. Although the Viennese composers of the opening of this century occasionally wrote pieces for large ensembles such as the orchestra or chorus, they seemed, particularly in the case of Webern, to be most at home with media of less imposing size, the more intimate vehicles for expression such as the piano, small chamber group, voice and piano, or small ensemble (as in Schoenberg's famous *Pierrot Lunaire*). It seems axiomatic that experimentation and innovation are more typically restricted to the less imposing genres; Beethoven, for example, seems to have experimented first with piano or chamber music before extending the fruits of such experimentation to the orchestra, certainly a very practical procedure.

The intensity and range of expression, frequently very highly charged, experienced in the works of Schoenberg, Berg, and to a lesser extent in the music of their more cerebral cohort Anton Webern, creates a marked contrast with the "cooler" music of Debussy. The contrast is further heightened by their development of a style of composition often called *free atonality*, which constituted a far greater digression from nineteenth-century practice than did the music of Debussy. How much reciprocity of influence took place between the two innovators, Debussy and Schoenberg, is a question of considerable speculation. Debussy's music received far more circulation and favorable acclaim that did Schoenberg's, Berg's, or Webern's. Practically speaking, the world has become acquainted with Webern's work only since his dramatic death in 1945. A good deal of the credit for the recent notoriety and acclaim given Webern is ironically due in part to an American musicologist from Spokane, Washington, named Hans Moldenhauer, who has made available a great many of Webern's sketches and has written a fascinating book, *The Death of Anton Webern*, on the events leading up to Webern's tragic and premature death at the hands of an American soldier.

Expressionism connotes the manifestation of the emotions and feelings of the inner self. Expressionism in early twentieth-century art was by no means limited to music. Many of the paintings of Matisse, Picasso, Kandinsky, Klee, Munch, and others create an aura of great personal emotional intensity—not so much reflecting explicit emotions, ideas, images, or actions, but occurring as a consequence of inner tensions, struggles, conflicts, and intense feeling. Contrary to the pleasurable and detached sonorities of the Impressionists, the sounds of the Expressionists—Schoenberg, Berg, and Webern—were commensurably more tense, frantic, whispered, and explosive. Expressionism in music called into play the widest range of dynamics possible—extremely difficult and demanding instrumental or keyboard timbres, unprecedented kinds of articulations such as flutter-tonguing by wind instruments (flute and trumpet especially), and the wedding to music of some of the most frightening, morbid, exotic, and mind-boggling poems and libretti ever conceived. Berg's opera *Wozzeck* and Schoenberg's monodrama *Erwartung* are good examples of Expressionist dramatic music.

272 Styles of Music

Arnold Schoenberg (1874–1951)

■ The same Vienna that provided the stimulus and background for the compositions of Haydn, Mozart, and Beethoven was also the home for one of the most significant developments of twentieth-century music—the twelve-tone system as exemplified in the works of Arnold Schoenberg, Alban Berg, and Anton Webern. Schoenberg, the founder of this school of composition, occupies a middle position in the musical trilogy. The majority of his compositions do not show such a strong link with the traditions of the past as do the works of Berg, nor do they show as clear a prefiguration of the innovations of the future as do the works of Webern. Though most of his significant works are within the twelve-tone technique, Schoenberg's earliest works such as *Verklärte Nacht* (*Transfigured Night*), *Op. 4*, written for string sextet or string orchestra, are in a rich post-Romantic or Expressionist style, and some of his later works, such as the *Theme and Variations for Band, Op. 43*, represent a return to diatonic, Neoclassic techniques.

Largely self-taught, Schoenberg himself was perhaps as important a teacher and theorist as he was a composer. He taught at music schools in Berlin and Vienna before he was forced by the Nazi regime to leave Europe in 1933. He came to California and continued private teaching and composing there.

Among his most important works are four string quartets; a piano concerto; a violin concerto; the *Variations for Orchestra; Pierrot Lunaire, Op. 21; Ode to Napoleon, Op. 41;* and numerous chamber works for miscellaneous combinations. His operas include the monodrama *Erwartung* (*Expectation*), *Die Glückliche Hand* (*The Lucky Hand*), *Von Heute auf Morgen* (*From Today to Tomorrow*), and *Moses and Aaron,* incomplete at the time of his death.

It is always difficult to make judgments about composers in their own time. The lack of overwhelming enthusiasm with which the Viennese public greeted the works of Haydn, Mozart, and Beethoven at the time they were written soon turned to acceptance and appreciation, and now these works are not only treasures of Viennese culture, but also actually staples of the Austrian economy. And these works have achieved recognition and favor throughout the world.

Whether or not a similar fate awaits the so-called "second Viennese school" of Schoenberg, Berg, and Webern depends on the judgment of history, but it seems certain that any future history of twentieth-century music will pay tribute to the artistic achievements as well as the path-breaking innovations of Arnold Schoenberg and his school.

One cannot help but relate in part the intense expression, tensions, and conflicts of the atonal music of the Austrian-Viennese Expressionists to the desperation, conflicts, and desolation that permeated Austrian life in the years surrounding World War I. As much as any prior movement in music, Expressionism reflected the power of music to communicate in *musical terms* the most keenly felt human emotions. Out of the tortured struggles of artists emerged new artistic achievements and modes of expression. In music these are perhaps most apparent in the high levels of dynamic, rhythmic, and harmonic tension. Further, a heightened textural tension results from the predominant use of counterpoint and sudden changes of texture. Listen to Schoenberg's *Pierrot Lunaire,* a striking setting for voice and small instrumental ensemble of twenty-one lyrics by a Belgian poet named Albert Giraud. Listen to the three sets of seven songs, one set at a sitting. The settings are absorbing and striking in their contrasts of texts and musical moods. There are few more original, indeed unprecedented, pieces in music literature. They demand repeated hearings.

Read the following lyric and then consult the music in Example 14-8. Note that the manner of vocalization for the piece is called *recitation*, denoting a combination of song and speech, *sprechstimme*, often used by the Expressionists, and allowing a singer far greater latitude of expression than a strictly observed rendition of pitches permits.

You somber, deathly-stricken moon,
There on the heaven's darkest couch,
Your gaze, so feverishly swollen,
Charms me like a strange enchanted air.

Of insatiable love-pangs
You die, die, by yearning overwhelmed,
You somber, deathly-stricken moon,
There on heaven's darkest couch.

The lover who, with rapturous heart,
Without a care to his mistress goes,
Is happy in your play of light,
In your pale and tormented blood,
You somber, deathly-stricken moon.

It would be hard to overestimate the impact and influence on Schoenberg's followers that *Pierrot Lunaire* and a number of other atonal pieces have had in the past fifty or so years since the completion of *Pierrot Lunaire* in 1921. The impact, however, was by no means universal. Many equally gifted musicians of the early twentieth century, such as Hindemith and Stravinsky, gave little evidence of their artistic acceptance of Schoenberg's theories* or practices in their compositions of the time. In later years (during the fifties and sixties), Stravinsky was to move far closer in his compositions to the acceptance of ideas that he rejected as a young composer still working under the influence of Tchaikovsky, Rimsky-Korsakov, and Debussy.

The various movements of Expressionistic pieces such as *Pierrot Lunaire* are characteristically short, emotionally high-keyed, and often, especially in the works of Anton Webern, quite compact and economically constructed. Webern's works avoid the characteristic and expected repetitions and restatements of material that audiences raised on nineteenth-century music had come to expect; for that reason, Webern's pieces often seem surprisingly brief. He attempted to avoid in his music the rehashing and redundancy of a generation before.

The short movement in Example 14-9 was composed during the first decade of this century; it is the second of five brief movements for string quartet. The piece telescopes into fourteen measures a most engaging series of events that are both highly unified and skillfully contrasted. Before listening to a performance of the piece, try to take in the linear motives—brief snatches of melody—that predominate in the upper two strings; be aware also of the consuming interest shown by the composer in details of timbre and dynamics as seen in the number of changes and shadings of dynamics in the first phrase, measures 1–5, and in the modifications of articulation such as *mit Dämpfer* (muted) in measure 1, the single pizzicato chord in measure 5 followed by a change to *arco* (bowed) after one eighth-note rest. Note also the tendency to heighten melodic tension by increasing the size of melodic intervals as a phrase unfolds, as

---

*Schoenberg was an active theoretical writer on music and was one of the few twentieth-century composers who attempted to spell out in books his own artistic, esthetic, and compositional principles.

EXAMPLE 14-8 Schoenberg: *Pierrot Lunaire*, No. 7, "The Sick Moon," complete movement.

EXAMPLE 14-9 WEBERN: *Five Movements for String Quartet, Op. 5, No. 2*, MEASURES 1–14.

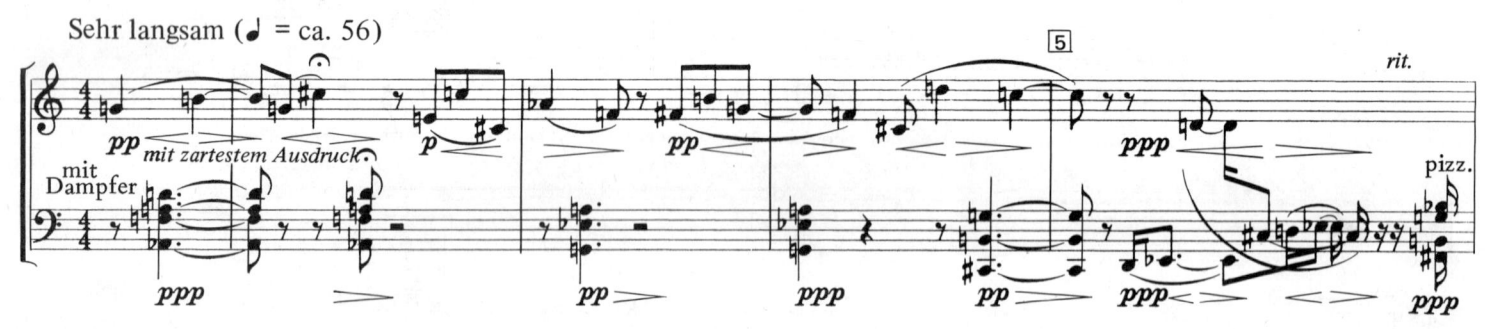

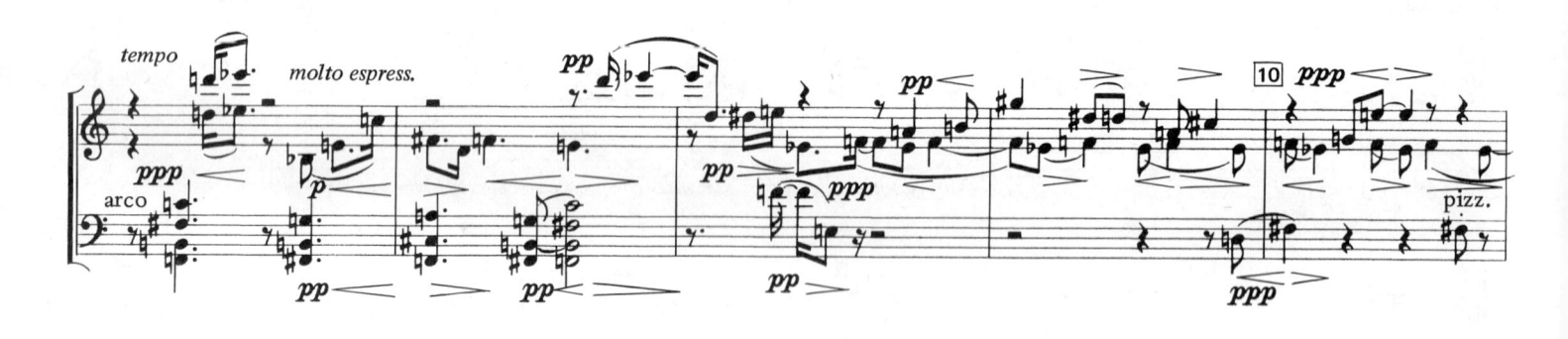

The leading painter of the American school of abstract expressionism, Jackson Pollock (1912–1956), liberated from the traditional constraints of the brush, dripped paints on canvas in intricate, forceful patterns—as in Autumn Rhythm—to express his unique inner visions.

in measures 1–5 of the top part. Every sound, line, and figure of this piece is intended to contribute meaningfully to the structure and emotional growth of the movement. There is no padding or extraneous material. Pieces such as this represent a very exacting and demanding musical experience for players and listeners alike. There is little music in the repertoire that aims at communicating more directly, demandingly, and subtly with the listener. You will probably find that this movement (Example 14-9), as well as the accompanying ones in Opus 5, will warrant repeated listening.

Many musicians agree that Webern has been the single most influential composer of this century. Had he not arrived on the scene when and as he did, contemporary music probably would have veered less sharply from paths of tradition; whether this is good or bad will have to be determined by later generations.

15 Twentieth-Century Style (1900-) (concluded)

NEOCLASSICISM

Classicism in almost any context refers to loyalty to traditional artistic values such as formal integrity, objectivity, clarity, and balance, intelligibility over expression, and a commitment by the artist to strive for economy of materials and cohesiveness of design above other artistic considerations. Classicism in music, applied in the broad sense, transcends the Classical period per se and alludes to the works of Bach and those of his predecessors which reveal such universal musical truths as those cited above.

Classicism is as much in the eye of the beholder as its antithesis, Romanticism. In common parlance, Neoclassicism in music denotes a period spanning about twenty or so years between approximately 1925 and the end of the war in 1945, during which time a number of composers, most important of whom were Hindemith and Stravinsky, created works predicated on a return to Classical models of textural clarity, formal coherence, and economy of means, as well as a return to pitch materials and organization implying tonality as contrasted with atonality. These composers' compositions of the period, such as Hindemith's symphony *Mathis der Maler* or *Ludus Tonalis* for piano and Stravinsky's *Octet for Wind Instruments*, *Symphony in C*, and the *Sonata for Two Pianos*, to name but a few, recalled in many ways formal models and masterpieces of the Baroque and Classical periods.

The Neoclassic movement in twentieth-century music gave decided evidence of the strong reactions of many composers to the unbridled emotionalism of Wagnerian Romanticism. Neoclassicism flourished in the United States during the forties especially, providing a mode of expression for a number of American composers such as Walter Piston, Roy Harris, Elliott Carter, and many others. These composers represented a more conservative stream of activity than that of Schoenberg and Webern, although they also created a great variety of styles and approaches to their craft. The term Neoclassicism has become somewhat questionable in value and meaning as the span from the time of Neoclassicism widens. However, Neoclassical music of this century alludes to a large number of compositions, among them many works written within the

The long-lived Picasso, artistic giant of the 20th century, created more than 20,000 imaginative works in a bewildering array of styles and techniques, among them Three Musicians. *Resulting from his association with the musicians and dancers of the Ballet Russe, for whom he designed sets, this work represents the culmination of his austere, straight-lined cubist ("little cubes") style.*

framework of such traditionally valued and accepted forms as the symphony, concerto, string quartet, opera, sonata, variations, fugue, or suite.

Twentieth-century composers have continued to explore and develop variation procedures, and the process of variation is perhaps more basic to much recent music than any other one process. Like the majority of twentieth-century composers, Igor Stravinsky has utilized variation procedures in a number of his instrumental or keyboard compositions. The piece cited in Example 15-1 is the second movement of Stravinsky's *Sonata*

Twentieth-Century Style (1900–) (concluded) 279

EXAMPLE 15-1 STRAVINSKY: *Sonata for Two Pianos*, SECOND MOVEMENT. (*a*) VARIATIONS (PITCHES OF THE THEME); (*b*) BEGINNING THEME (MEASURES 1–5) AND FIRST THREE VARIATIONS: VARIATION 1 (MEASURES 1–6), VARIATION 2 (MEASURES 1–4), AND VARIATION 3 (MEASURES 1–5).

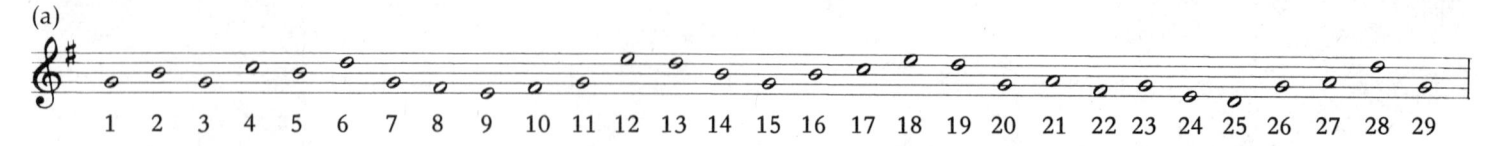

280 Styles of Music

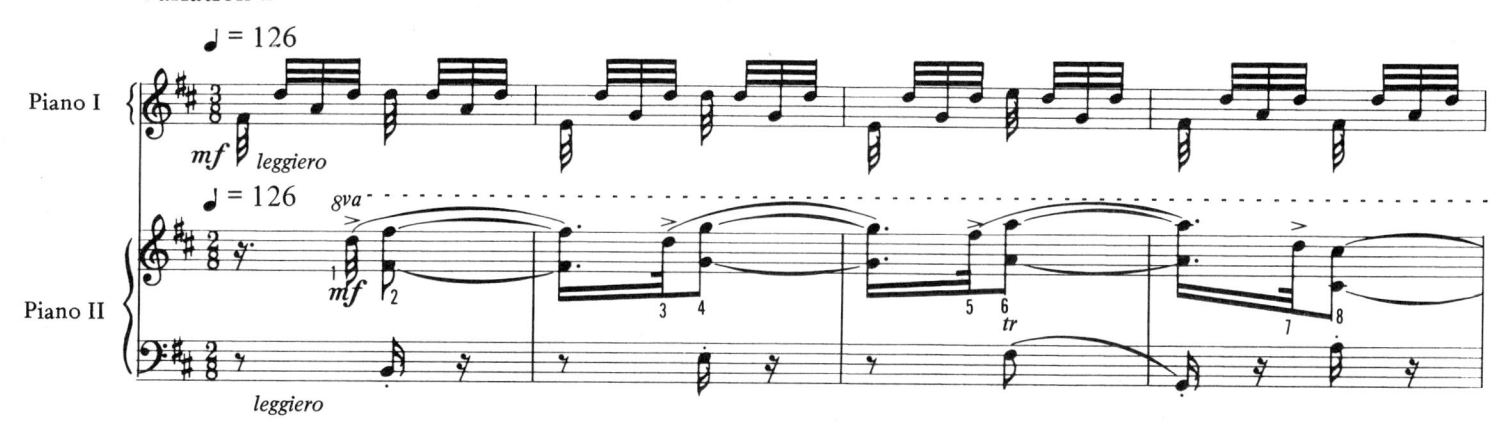

*10, 11, and 12 are omitted in variation 3.

---

for *Two Pianos,* completed in 1944. The piece is in variation form and is also called *Theme with Variations.*

Theme as used here by Stravinsky denotes a melodic line consisting of the notes in measures 1–5 in the top voice, shown here as a series of pitches which can easily be sung. The four variations on the 29-note series of pitches involve considerable variety of tempo, rhythm, texture, and exploitation of the resources of the keyboard. It is revealing and enlightening to be aware of the skillful ways in which the composer retains the original note series, virtually unaltered, in each variation, introducing thereby a marked limitation within which to invent the variations that follow. The procedure is quite similar to that of serialism found in many atonal pieces of the same period.

As a matter of fact, the movement amounts to a set of variations based to a great extent on a tonal note series that clearly defines a key, G major. Variations 1 and 2 are transpositions of the theme to the key of the dominant, which is D major in this case. Variation 3 is in the tonic key.

The first five measures of the largo theme section introducing the entire 29-note series of the melodic theme are shown in Example 15-1b, followed in turn by the beginnings of each of the first three variations which contain numbers for convenience in following the order of presentation of the basic pitch series insofar as it is quoted.

Listen to a performance of the sonata, concentrating on the second movement. Then consult the succession of section beginnings in Example 15-1 and familiarize yourself with the deployments of the theme in the variations. Try to identify aurally successive statements of the theme in the continuation of the different variations, the third of which you may recognize as a fugue. The subject of the fugue is skillfully fashioned out of the same note series, minus the notes numbered 10, 11, and 12.

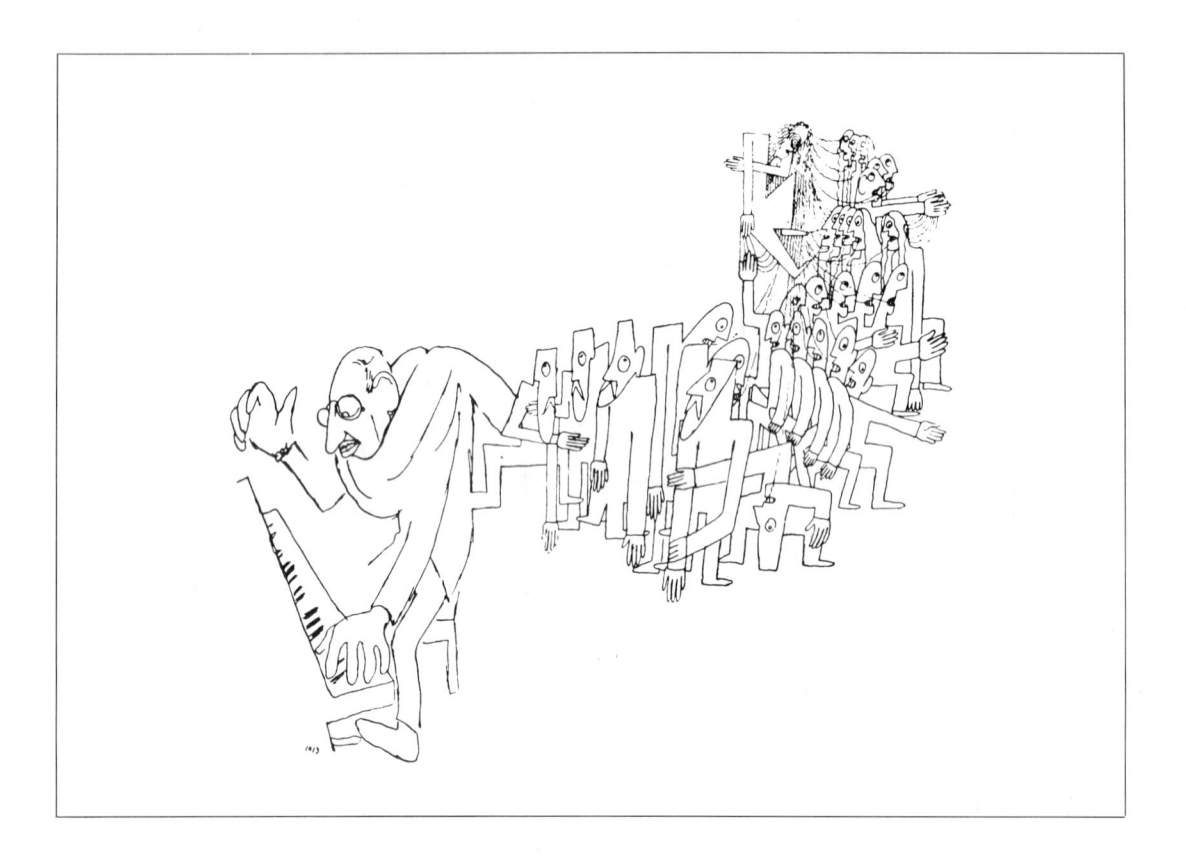

In hearing this work one is as much aware of the uniquely individual sounds and musical personality of Stravinsky as one is of the fact that such a piece offers striking evidence in the twentieth century of the flexibility and timelessness of the variation principle, which has served effectively the needs of composers whose styles differ as markedly as those of Bach and Stravinsky or Josquin and Webern.

One of the most positive outcomes of Neoclassicism lies in the fact that it represented a gradual, less radical change of style. Many of the compositions that resulted received great acclaim and were subsequently made part of the standard repertoire of many of the world's most outstanding performing organizations such as the Boston Symphony, New York Philharmonic, and Louisville Symphony, which commissioned a large number of such pieces by American composers. However, at the present time, Neoclassicism is a dead issue. But although the word itself has come to mean less and less, the movement helped audiences and musicians to adjust to many of the developments and innovations of the time via compositions that retained in part formal or tonal procedures and processes more readily associated with some of the traditions of the past than the more radical avant-garde pieces of the time.

For example, compare the passage by Paul Hindemith that appears in Example 15-2 with the selection by Webern in Example 15-4. The presence of tonality, the clear and direct melodic style, quite singable in character, the even-flowing rhythms and clearly fashioned phrases recall the formal clarity and essential simplicity of the Viennese Classicists. Listen to this example of Neoclassicism for other aspects that set it apart from the language and emotionalism of Schoenberg and Webern.

SERIALISM: TWELVE-TONE TECHNIQUE

Most listeners are aware of the fact that there are twelve half-steps (semitones) in the span of an octave:

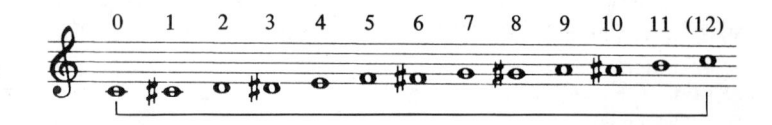

In a pen and ink sketch, Jean Cocteau graphically portrays Igor Stravinsky, that innovative genius of this century who shocked the musical world with his "pagan" ballet, Rite of Spring, in 1913.

EXAMPLE 15-2 HINDEMITH: *Sonata for Flute and Piano,* FIRST MOVEMENT, MEASURES 1–7.

I Heiter bewegt (♩ etwa 100)
Exposition

(*Note:* The notes shown with sharps may be notated as enharmonic equivalents—e.g., C sharp = D flat. In tonal music the determining basis for pitch selection is key; in atonal music the basis is context or composer's choice. Sometimes the selection is arbitrary.)

Composers had utilized all available twelve notes as early as the fourteenth century. Most traditional pieces of any length introduce all twelve pitches in one context or another, modulation being a primary means for creating tonal variety. In music written within a key such as C major or D minor—diatonic music—seven notes form the core of activity, and chromaticism involving any of the remaining members of the chromatic scale frequently functions in a melodic or harmonic decorative role. All the tones of a chromatic scale occur in the melody by Mozart in Example 15-3, for example, but the seven notes of the major scale clearly determine the *basic* melodic structure and tonality elaborated by chromatic alteration.

By the beginning of the century, composers such as Schoenberg and Webern had sought successfully to free pitch materials, melody, and harmony from the constraints of diatonic keys in their atonal pieces. It seems ironic that the same composers who were largely responsible for creating an im-

Twentieth-Century Style (1900–) (concluded) 283

EXAMPLE 15-3 MOZART: *Concerto No. 24 in C Minor for Piano, K. 491*, THIRD MOVEMENT.

pressive collection of pieces that successfully transcended the boundaries of tonality began searching immediately for a procedure that would again provide a rational basis for the systematic deployment of all twelve tones. It appears that Schoenberg and his contemporaries, having in effect wiped out diatonic tonality, felt a need for a systematic basis for organizing pitch in large atonal pieces such as symphonies, operas, sonatas, and so on. You may have noted already that most of the atonal works in the repertoire are brief, essentially undeveloped, pieces of small proportions.

In the 1920's Schoenberg and his contemporaries arrived at the formulation of a more disciplined and systematic means for coping with the entire twelve-tone scale. Essentially a compositional theory, the process, which has since gone largely out of vogue, was called the "twelve-tone system" or "composition with twelve notes"—in brief, "serialism." The effect on the composition of music was enormous during the forty or so years following its formulation. As usual, however, there were the typical holdouts, not the least of whom included such prominent composers as Prokofiev, Hindemith, Carter, and others who have resisted to this day Schoenberg's arguments and theories for serialism.

In his *Suite for Piano, Op. 25,* written in 1925, Schoenberg made use of a principle of organizing pitch materials, a twelve-tone or serial technique, that amounted to the systematic deployment of the various notes of the chromatic scale in such a way that no note recurred until all other remaining eleven had been sounded, thus guaranteeing a kind of maximal pitch variety. In its initial uses, twelve-tone technique carried with it a number of compositional constraints, many of which were essentially negative and some of which seem to have been applied more in theory than in musical practice, a common fault of many musical "rules" allegedly imposed to safeguard the musical consumer from technical lapses by composers straying from tradition.

Serial technique, predicated on the use of a specific pitch order or series—a *tone row*—provided the composer with a ready-made solution to the task of creating order out of the enormous number of possibilities of pitch succession and chord formulation. The notes of a given twelve-tone series were stated in both linear and vertical (harmonic) arrangements, and although some of the rules accompanying Schoenberg's introduction to serial technique seemed to dictate that suggestions of melodies and chords associated with tonal music were to be avoided, it was not long before composers found ways to adapt Schoenberg's principles to their own styles and idioms. Stravinsky, Dallapiccola, Berg, and others were among them. Despite statements to the contrary, twelve-tone technique was not a form of mathematical music, although mathematically determined music has become a reality during the past twenty or so years. On the contrary, twelve-tone music, like traditional music, was very much the result of the artistic invention and musical decisions of a composer attempting to solve familiar problems pertaining to the materials and designs of composition. It was the composer who determined the order of the pitches in the series and who planned the various rhythmic, timbral, and textural arrangements in which they occurred.

Although much more could be said about serial music, it may prove more interesting to turn our attention to a short atonal piece based on serial technique and composed by Schoenberg's student, Anton Webern. The relation between Schoenberg and Webern was one of great friendship, mutual

284 Styles of Music

respect, and reciprocity of influence, although both developed individual styles and their own unique "sounds."

That two composers, working as closely as did Schoenberg and Webern, were able to express themselves musically in quite different ways despite their common employment of serial technique testifies to the essential pliability and latitude of the technique. Turn to Example 15-4 and listen to a performance of Webern's *Kinderstücke* (*Child's Piece*), 1924. Note the delineation of phrases by brief silences, changes of dynamics, and registration. Vertical sounds, as opposed to linear, occur in measures 4, 8, 11, and in closing (as well as at other occasional points) to help define the ends of phrases. The piece is a child's piece and, as indicated at the end, may be repeated as many times as desired. It is a simple and letter-perfect model

EXAMPLE 15-4   WEBERN: *Kinderstücke* (*Child's Piece*) (FOR PIANO), MEASURES 1–17.

Twentieth-Century Style (1900–) (concluded)

Artists, like composers, reacted to the excesses of overblown romanticism and turned to non-objective, non-representational techniques of expression. In Nude Descending a Staircase, No. 2. *(1913), Marcel Duchamp revealed a multi-exposure cinematic technique which created a sensation in the art world.*

of serial technique. The row or set of the piece is shown below the music in the form of a series of pitches arranged without regard for their precise register or duration in the composition. All melodic and harmonic events in the piece result from different rhythmic and registral deployments of the tone row. In this piece the composer uses only the untransposed and unvaried form of the row, although it is possible to incorporate statements of the row based on any of the eleven possible transpositions of it. Statements of the basic set in inversion, retrograde (backwards), or in retrograde inversion (backwards in inverted form) are typically found in twelve-tone pieces, especially pieces of greater length than the *Kinderstücke*. Deploying the row in various forms or transpositions constitutes an essential means of creating tonal variety in twelve-tone music.

The piece cited here reveals two main sections, measures 1–12, and 13 to the end. The first section emphasizes linear statements of thematic material derived in the main from straightforward statements of the row punctuated by occasional vertical soundings of two or three notes simultaneously. Each of the phrases heard in the first section begins and ends so as to correspond with the beginning or ending of the row itself. The melodic activity of the section is elaborated through the use of a wide variety of intervals based on the row's pitches. Dynamic changes heighten the various figures and contours of the piece; rhythmic groupings by twos and threes contribute to the unity of the section.

The second section is differentiated by virtue of its quickened rhythmic pace, frequent use of note and chord repetition, and emphasis on harmonic as opposed to melodic material. Each phrase of both sections is separated in time by a brief caesura in the form of an eighth rest. As you become more familiar with this piece and others reflecting similar techniques, you may well admire Webern's capacity to create a highly varied yet convincingly unified musical shape based on a very minimal amount of musical materials.

The list of pieces recommended for supplemental listening given here represents a variety of individual approaches to serial technique as well as other aspects of musical style:

Berg: *Concerto for Violin and Orchestra*
Schoenberg: *Variations for Orchestra, Op. 31*
Webern: *Symphony for Small Orchestra, Op. 21*
Stravinsky: *Threni*
Schuller: *Fantasy for Violoncello Solo*
Dallapiccola: *Canti di liberazione*

You should keep in mind the fact that serial technique provided many composers working in the second quarter of this century with a working rationale for organizing pitch materials devoid of tonality. It provided a means of freeing pitch from the limitations of tonality, while at the same time accepting other lim-

The classicist of the Schoenberg School of abstract music, Anton Webern (1883–1945), sought the veritable essence of things, which he expressed in extremely short, succinct, epigrammatic statements, thus launching a new movement in musical composition.

itations. No composers of any significance have ever attempted to work without some self-imposed or inherited constraints.

During the past twenty years or so, serial technique has ceased to be of much service or concern to many practicing composers. Most young composers are shaping their pieces and styles without the use of serial technique, but the freedom of tonal materials that their works display, and that we accept, is in part a result of the attempts of the serial composers of the previous generation to achieve such freedom.

POST-ROMANTICISM

Russia has not contributed notably to the stylistic movements of the first half of this century with which we have dealt. Until recently, Russia's musicians had few opportunities to experience first-hand the music of such progressives as Webern, Bartók, Hindemith, and Stravinsky, let alone more recent avant-garde composers such as Boulez, Berio, Penderecki, Stockhausen, Xenakis, and others. The iron curtain has been tightly drawn and the political climate in Russia has been such as to discourage, if not entirely preclude, the airing of music reflecting Russian attempts to incorporate atonality, serialism, and other more recent innovations. It is unfortunate that this has been true in a country that has produced in the past such marvelously innovative composers and performers, not the least of whom include such geniuses as Tchaikovsky, Rimsky-Korsakov, Borodin, Mussorgsky, Stravinsky (who departed Russia at the age of 28), Rachmaninoff, Scriabin, Prokofiev, and Shostakovich.

This is not to say, however, that Russian musicians have played a minor role in this century. On the contrary, despite the essentially conservative and traditional elements in the works of her two leading twentieth-century composers, Prokofiev and Shostakovich, their compositions have been exceedingly popular in the United States and abroad. Several of Shostakovich's symphonies, and Prokofiev's concertos and symphonies, as well as a number of shorter pieces including ballets, chamber compositions, piano music, and operas, have been enthusiastically received by American and European audiences for half a century.

The works of Prokofiev and Shostakovich, although revealing many stylistic differences, continue to utilize to a great extent materials and forms inherited from and largely echoing the nineteenth century. Both have been tabbed Post-Romanticists. Both have been outspoken proponents of Russian nationalism, a trait at once recognizable in works such as Prokofiev's suite from the music for the film *Alexander Nevsky* (1939) and Shostakovich's *Symphony No. 7, Op. 60*, inspired by the siege of Leningrad by the Germans in 1941.

Both Shostakovich and Prokofiev are melodists. Prokofiev's pieces frequently reward the listener with attractive, moving melodies such as those found in his ballet *Romeo and Juliet* or in the second theme from the first movement of *Symphony No. 5 in B Flat*. Prokofiev stated in a letter, "I love melody, and regard it as the most important element in music."* Shostako-

*William W. Austin, *Music in the Twentieth Century* (New York: Norton, 1966), p. 459.

Aaron Copland (1900-)

Aaron Copland, one of America's most distinguished composers, was born in teeming Brooklyn, where he began the study of music in his early teens, later went to high school, and then composed his first published work, a piano piece entitled *The Cat and the Mouse*. At the age of twenty-one he went to Paris to study with the famed Nadia Boulanger, French composer and teacher, who was to sharpen the talents of so many celebrated composers of today.

In 1924 he returned to this country, where he has remained, and became a vigorous spokesman for the American composer and for the new American music, relatively unknown quantities at that time. Indefatigably, he organized contemporary composers' forums and societies, festivals and concerts, wrote articles and books, and conducted concerts, all espousing the cause of American music. It is accurate to say that no other single composer has done more to further recognition of the art music of our country than Aaron Copland. His fame as a composer continued to spread as he honed his skills and created a veritable cornucopia of compositions in the next half-century, works whose merits earned for him such awards as two Guggenheim Fellowships, a Pulitzer Prize, an RCA Victor Award of $5,000, a doctorate from Princeton, and an Academy Award—as well as universal recognition and acceptance.

Copland's music evidences a variety of styles and techniques that mirror the changing trends of the past fifty years, ranging from the jazz rhythms of some of his early works, *Concerto for Piano and Orchestra* (1927), through the recreation of American scenes, *Billy the Kid* (1938) and *A Lincoln Portrait* (1942), to experimentation with the serial techniques of twelve-tone composers in *Connotations for Orchestra* (1962).

Without doubt it was the music of the middle period, roughly the decade after *Billy the Kid*, which saw Copland rise to the peak of his popularity. Concentrating on American scenes, themes, and idioms, he created ballets such as *Rodeo* and *Appalachian Spring* (the orchestral suite that became his most popular work and won a Pulitzer Prize), and music for films such as *Of Mice and Men*, *Our Town*, and *The Red Pony*, plus other works too numerous to mention. Throughout them all one finds a mixture of folk-like tunes, lean harmonies spiced with acrid dissonances, and energetic rhythms melded into a personal idiom that is more restrained than emotional, more brittle than lush, but which is intensely vibrant and appealing.

As his style matured he became less dedicated to writing purely American music—i.e., using "conscious Americanisms"—and he turned toward a more universal idiom, creating one of his finest instrumental works, *Symphony No. 3*, first performed by the Boston Symphony in 1946 under the direction of Serge Koussevitzky and dedicated to the memory of the famous conductor's wife, Natalie.

He broadened his musical career to include concertizing as a pianist, conducting, and teaching at the New School for Social Research in New York City, lecturing at Harvard on several occasions, and serving as head of the Composition Department and then chairman of the faculty at the Berkshire Music Center at Tanglewood, in the period from 1940-1965.

Aaron Copland, this facile musician, pianist, conductor, and composer of works for the theater, movies, and concert stage, through his abundant creative talents and untiring efforts helped blaze the way for music representatives of this country—and of today. He has most certainly earned for himself the ultimate honorary title of "dean of American composers."

vich's *Symphony No. 5* reveals the composer's knack for soaring, driving melodies that have had great appeal. Like many of their musical predecessors, both Russians reveal in their works exceptional gifts for orchestration. Although many more forward-looking composers regard the Russians as outdated and insignificant insofar as the current scene is concerned, few question and most study intently their scores to gain greater insights into orchestrational craft. A good introduction to their music can be gained by listening to the Fifth Symphony of each. Their debt to the nineteenth-century Romantics should be easily perceived as manifested in a loyalty to tonality, clearly felt pulsatile rhythms, singable and memorable tunes, and engaging orchestral sounds as well as a dynamic range that is indicative of a high degree of emotion and intensity of expression. Traditional sonata forms abound as well as movements easily characterized as scherzi, marches, rondos, and so on.

Even though it is often regarded by some as naive to include these composers in discussions of music and musical changes in the currents of our time, it seems likely that the works of Prokofiev and Shostakovich may outlive those of some of their far more fashionable contemporaries from Germany, France, Italy, and the United States. Time will tell. The same statement may be made with equal implications for a great number of American composers of decidedly conservative and Post-Romantic leanings; among them are such popular contemporaries as Samuel Barber, Roy Harris, Howard Hanson, and Aaron Copland, to name only a few.

Copland's ballet *Appalachian Spring*, composed in 1943–44, stands as one of the best-known works of the first half of this century by an American composer. Copland's works, especially his *Symphony No. 3* and his music for the ballets *Appalachian Spring*, *Rodeo*, and *Billy the Kid*, have established him in the eyes of a large segment of the public as "the dean of American composers." He strove to make his music accessible to audiences—far more so than did a number of his more radical contemporaries—and his avowed dedication to jazz and American folk traditions comes through clearly in a variety of ways.

Copland first made his mark in the field of ballet, and his compositions in this genre have become standards of the literature. One of the most popular is *Appalachian Spring*, which was composed for Martha Graham and which the composer later adapted into a concert suite for orchestra. Consider for a moment an excerpt (Example 15-5) from this reflection of Americana by one of our best-known composers. The music and dancing of the section from which Example 15-5 is taken are meant to convey a sense of the elation and spiritual feeling associated with the celebration of spring in a community of early nineteenth-century Pennsylvania. The focal point of the community is a newlywed couple. One can easily hear elation and excitement in this brief, agitated melody (Example 15-5a). The spiritual devotion of the community is suggested by the melody in Example 15-5b, which contrasts markedly with the first.

Listen to the second section of this work and realize that a great number of interacting musical elements create the excitement and subsequent comparative calm of the passage; not the least of these are the ways in which the composer has utilized the resources of the orchestra to present in a colorful yet clear setting the series of musical events that constitute the work. The total affect is greatly enhanced, of course, by the presence and deployment of dancers in the ballet itself. Perhaps the most engaging feature of the music itself is its rhythm, and the passage's rhythm is itself composed of several competing and interacting elements.

Copland turned to the jazz of the twenties in pieces like *Music for the Theater*, but like many other composers caught up in the initial enthusiasm for bringing jazz into the symphony concert, his use of it was essentially short-lived. A better picture of his more fully developed and mature style can be obtained by listening to his *Symphony No. 3*, a work that reveals his fondness for a walloping full-brass sound, by no means unrelated to the more recent jazz and big-band developments in the forties, as well as very exhilarated tempi, intense contrapuntal developments, and exciting melodic play in the full-string orchestra. Like the Russians, Copland comes across well through the orchestra, a medium that he seems most able to command.

Aaron Copland is one of the last Americans to really assert himself through the large symphony orchestra. This is true in

EXAMPLE 15-5 (a) COPLAND: *Appalachian Spring*, MEASURES 1–4; (b) ibid., MEASURES 29–43.

Copyright © 1945 by Aaron Copland; renewed 1972. Reprinted by permission of Aaron Copland, copyright owner, and Boosey and Hawkes, Inc., sole publisher.

part because of the lack of attention given to contemporary American composers' orchestral works by most American conductors. It also results from the increasing lack of enthusiasm and encouragement for writing symphonies and large-scale orchestral pieces faced by the current generation of American composers. The picture is bleak at best.

OPERA

Since this chapter has been devoted primarily to instrumental music to this point, it is appropriate to pause briefly to pick up the thread of opera development. Opera has prevailed for more than 350 years and, rumors to the contrary, is still very much a part of the current musical scene. Up to the time of Wagner, it had been a singer's art, a genre dominated by voices in which the orchestra was assigned the secondary role of accompaniment. But twentieth-century composers have followed Wagner's lead, coming to depend more and more on the orchestra to intensify the dramatic action on stage and to afford cohesion, or even diversion, to the unfolding of the music drama. While space limitations preclude the possibility of more than brief mention of the operas of this century, let us consider two disparate examples that will at least suggest that "opera is not dead"—that it is still alive and playing to humanity's inherent love for the world of "make-believe," real though it is, and that it is continuing to entertain, inspire, and intrigue those who are attuned to its magic.

The first of our examples is the operatic masterpiece of the twentieth century, *Wozzeck* (1925) by Alban Berg (1885–1935). *Wozzeck* is the real-life story of an Austrian soldier whose life is ruined by an unfaithful mistress (Marie), his domineering captain, a sadistic doctor, and a lustful, brutish drum major. After his beloved has been seduced by the swaggering drum major and he has been ignominiously beaten by him, Wozzeck, now mad, kills his mistress and then himself. The opera may best be described as a music drama in that the composer has so skillfully wedded the stark drama to the dissonant music that neither overshadows the other. They become one.

Berg, who was both a follower of the serial composer Schoenberg and the German Romantics, has created condensed forms, taut contrapuntal structures, and jagged melodies and rhythms, of all which are elements of his unique lyric-dramatic style. The excerpt in Example 15-6 occurs in scene 3 of Act I. It exemplifies Berg's knack for expressive vocal writing, stark realism, and colorful use of palette of vivid orchestral timbres.

In the scene, a military band approaches, heralded by a bugle call, while Marie stands at a window watching and holding her son. She is attracted by the dashing drum major, but when derided by a neighbor, slams the window and sings a tender lullaby to her fatherless son. Her voice moves angularly through a wide range and is quietly wedded to muted strings, subdued horns, harp, and woodwinds to create a singular moment of intense expressiveness.

Our second example, of more recent vintage, is an opera written by an American composer. In *Postcard from Morocco** (1971) by Dominick Argento, the composer employs another type of instrumental interlude, a *divertimento*, midway through the work, which takes place in a Moroccan railway station in

*Available on Desto Records (DC 7137/38).

290 Styles of Music

Alban Berg (1885–1935), the lyric romantic of the Schoenberg School, revealed a vision of a tortured, common man in his opera Wozzeck, considered by many to be the greatest work of this century for the lyric theater.

the first quarter of this century. He labels the divertimento "Souvenirs de Bayreuth," and, in the usual sense of the word, the piece is meant to entertain, or divert the attentions (of the train-waiting passengers, in this case). Hence it is in a light vein as is typical of such divertissements. It is a potpourri of operatic tunes which in this case are those of Richard Wagner, creator of the famed opera house in Bayreuth, Germany. One tune in particular is used for a special reason, which the composer states as follows:

Somewhere towards the middle of Postcard from Morocco, *the onstage dance band entertains the waiting travellers with a medley of themes from Wagner's operas—the sort of musical farrago one might expect to find aboard a ship, or at a spa, or in a foreign railway station restaurant around 1914. Among the various bits and snatches, the "Spinning Song" from* The Flying Dutchman *occupies a central position. The selection is intended to conjure up more than local color: in* The Flying Dutchman, *Wagner's hero is doomed by supernatural forces to sail forever over the oceans until, through a stranger's act of*

EXAMPLE 15-6 BERG: *Wozzeck*, ACT I, SCENE 3, "MARIE'S LULLABY," MEASURES 372–387.

Twentieth-Century Style (1900–) (concluded) 291

compassion and love, the curse is lifted and the journey ended. Postcard from Morocco could, in a way, serve as a prologue to Wagner's opera, suggesting a different but equally possible origin of that journey: not launched by supernatural forces at all, but by very human ones, by people who fail to show charity or pity, love or understanding for a fellow creature. Perhaps this unkindness is self-protective or thoughtless and not malicious; perhaps it is the result of curiosity, suspicion, selfishness; or a form of grieving. Whatever the reason, when it does occur, another Dutchman is born and—if only in a swan-drawn boat or in a ship of one's own making—a new voyage begins.

The three following fragments appear in the divertimento: one evoking the dated jazz of the fox-trot era (Example 15-7); the "Spinning chorus" from *Die Fliegende Hollander* (*The Flying Dutchman*), 1843, sung by a chorus of maidens at the opening of act II (Example 15-8); and the famous "Valhalla theme" (Example 15-9), one of several used to unify the colossal four-opera *Ring* cycle, here cited from *Das Rheingold* (*The Rhine Gold*), 1853–1854. With tongue in cheek, Argento sets this majestic theme with a jazzy syncopated rhythm pattern recurring in the bass, which throws the picture "out of focus," thus maintaining the "unreality" of the drama unfolding.

The twentieth century has also seen the development of such public media as radio, film, and television, for which some important musical-dramatic works have been especially produced, thus making music and theater available to an audience of tremendous size. Operas, operettas, and musicals are playing to an ever-increasing audience, whether through the media or "live." And though the pessimist will say that "lyric theater is dead," or at least expiring, we can rest assured that this form of artistic expression will live on in old and new forms to satisfy our fundamental urge to glimpse the "real world" of "unreality," which is the magic spell of the theater.

EXAMPLE 15-7 ARGENTO: *Postcard from Morocco*, "SOUVENIRS DE BAYREUTH," MEASURES 1–8.

From *Postcard from Morocco* by Dominick Argento. Copyright © 1972 by Boosey and Hawkes, Inc. Reprinted by permission.

EXAMPLE 15-8   WAGNER: *The Flying Dutchman*, ACT II, "SPINNE, SPINNE" ("SPIN, SPIN"), MEASURES 20–23.

EXAMPLE 15-9   WAGNER: *Das Rheingold*, "VALHALLA THEME," MEASURES 1–2.

Twentieth-Century Style (1900–) (concluded)   293

SINCE 1945

We are living in one of the most exciting and unprecedented musical times since the end of the Renaissance. Music activity in the thirty years or so following the end of World War II has produced so much diversification, novelty, innovation, and change that to try to classify the various styles, genres, and trends is risky at best. While music of the mid-nineteenth century revealed certain common practices such as loyalty to metered rhythm, use of key, and dominance of triadic harmony, no comparable style universals exist three-quarters of the way through this century.

Possibly the greatest catalyst of change during the middle of the twentieth century was the war itself together with a number of related events or circumstances, not the least of which was the fact that a great many American musicians came into contact with European composers and developments immediately following the end of the war. Many Americans remained in France and Germany to study with such renowned teachers of composition as Nadia Boulanger in Paris. Because of the war, American musicians and those from other parts of the world as well had opportunities to become acquainted that would have been unlikely otherwise. Similarly many great European musicians were forced *out* of Europe because of their political or religious and ethnic backgrounds. This was particularly true in Germany and Austria, whose lists of artists who fled to the sanctuary of the United States are long and impressive, including such giants as Schoenberg, Bartók, and Hindemith. These men settled in the United States and shortly were engaged in the instruction of young American composers at such centers of musical activity as Yale, UCLA, Columbia, and others. Their impact on the development of music in this country was soon felt.

Developments in fields only secondarily related to music such as computer science, electronics, mathematics, communication, and others, influenced a number of musical developments, as we shall see. Another important influence on twentieth-century music lay in the great strides in musicological research that took place. A great deal of music from early times was discovered and made available for study by European and American scholars who had a reciprocal influence on each other and who brought to light music and musical processes that have had considerable influence on a number of composers such as Hindemith, Stravinsky, Orff, Messiaen, and many others.

Jazz reached new heights of virtuoso performance and compositional complexity in the forties and fifties. These developments had great impact on a number of younger composers such as Gunther Schuller. The dance and jazz arrangements of gifted musicians such as Eddie Sauter, Ralph Burns, and (later) Lalo Schiffrin featured innovations in instrumentation and scoring techniques as well as unprecedented demands on performers. These had considerable influence on the composing of scores by many of their peers in the field of concert music, some of whom had been exposed to such developments through the experience of playing in dance bands and jazz "combos." The number of competing and interacting trends that were, and some of which still are, stirring the imaginations of many young musicians during the years immediately following the end of hostilities in 1945 were staggering.

Most of the postwar centers of musical development, such as New York, Paris, Boston, Los Angeles, Cologne, Rome, and London, became accessible with a few hours travel. Record companies issued new works soon after their first performances. Composers were given grants for composition from foundations or they were commissioned to compose symphonies and concertos. Lecture series were established to provide a platform for the airing of new theories, philosophies, and analyses. Many young people returning from the service were afforded the opportunity for serious musical training in performance or composition by the G.I. bill.

The pace of change and the diversity of trends here and abroad during the second half of this century have decreased somewhat, but the maze of developments that resulted have left the listener with a staggering array of trends and countertrends to sort out and evaluate during a lifetime of involvement with music. The task is challenging but the opportunity is potentially rich and rewarding, however demanding.

Hostile to rationalism, Surrealists like Paul Klee, Swiss painter of Contact of Two Musicians *(1922), sought to evoke the strange world of the subconscious with non-representational abstractions and symbolic images.*

Taped Music and Experimental Trends

A number of the modules associated with this book are devoted to some of the divergent trends such as electroacoustic and aleatory music that became established in the period after the war, many of which are still actively pursued by some of the world's most gifted and resourceful musicians. Some composers have turned to the use of taped sounds, musical and extramusical, as new sound sources. Taped sounds have been used *alone* and in conjunction with *traditional* sounds. A piece called *Déserts* by Edgard Varèse illustrates the latter in a most exciting and imaginative juxtaposition of orchestral and taped (electronic) sounds. Other composers, Pierre Schaeffer in Paris and John Cage in New York among them, began experimenting with the use of recorded and distorted *non*musical noise as well as musical sounds. The name given to this trend, *musique concrète*, implies the need for an expanded definition of music. Schaeffer's efforts and imagination have as yet failed to produce any important works of art, but he has succeeded in convincing many younger composers of the potential for using both synthesized and natural sounds as building blocks for compositions. Among those who have incorporated studio techniques developed by Schaeffer in his experimentation with *musique concrète* is Karlheinz Stockhausen. His *Gesang der Jünglinge* is a well-known composition in which manipulation of taped sounds produced by a boy's singing and speaking voices supply the raw material for a most effective piece of work. It is a good introduction to this genre of twentieth-century music.

John Cage has played a role in the United States somewhat similar to that of Germany's Stockhausen. Cage has had considerable influence on a number of younger composers in this country, among them Earle Brown, Morton Feldman, as well as Pierre Boulez in France and Stockhausen in Germany. Cage has been perhaps the most provocative and controversial of the growing group of avant-garde composers clustered around New York City. He is often credited erroneously with having introduced the "prepared piano"—that is, a mechanically adapted piano utilizing pieces of metal or other gadgets fitted so as to modify the sounds of the hammers striking the strings.

Actually, Cage acquired and developed such procedures from his early teacher, Henry Cowell, a prolific composer of a generation earlier who was engaged in serious musical invention involving many kinds of treatments and alterations of the keyboard and other instrumentation as well, including electronic types. An early work of Cowell's, *The Aeolian Harp*, involves strumming on the strings of the piano with one hand while depressing the keys with the other. Cowell had considerable impact on a number of composers anxious to free music from the constraints of nineteenth-century traditions of instrumentation. A friend of Charles Ives, a brilliant musical innovator of the early part of this century, Cowell had a radical influence on Cage as well as a number of other contemporary musicians.

Cage's compositions have in common the use of many novel and imaginative sounds, procedures, and forms. Like a number of his younger contemporaries, Cage has professed a strong affinity for Eastern mysticism and philosophies such as Zen Buddhism. He has scorned the traditional relations between the composer, the public, and the functional roles of music in society to the point of extreme absurdity. Many of his compositions assume the form of theatrical stunts whose relation to music by any standards seems at best tenuous.

Cage is regarded as one of the leading composers and advocates of *aleatoric music*—that is, chance music. In such pieces a number of aspects for the realization of the piece are indeterminate—left to chance and not controlled directly by the compositional instructions and notations of the composer. In some works the player arbitrarily selects the ordering of sections or improvises his or her part on the basis of minimal instructions or a mere suggestion of what is to be played.

Cage's impact on the current musical scene has been more philosophical perhaps than explicitly musical. It is clear that although the ultimate significance of his output is far from determined, he has affected the musical thinking and esthetic ideas of a number of other gifted persons. Evidence of this can be found in the music of Earle Brown—for instance, in his set of pieces called *Available Forms*. In the first of these works, *Available Forms I*, composed for an ensemble of orchestral instruments, the ordering of a series of musical events involving considerable variety of tempo, texture, timbre, and linear detail is left to the whim of the conductor, who indicates with a signal to the performers the succession of events to be used. Since many of the details of each event are left to the invention of the players and the succession of events (sections) is decided upon during the performance by the conductor, it should be apparent that what results is partly a matter of chance. Listen to a recording of Brown's *Available Forms I* and evaluate for yourself the success of the piece. That the means for determining the performance involve chance elements in no way connotes that established values and principles of effective music such as unity, variety, change, and recurrence are irrelevant insofar as the listener is concerned.

Iannis Xenakis is the foremost of the many younger composers who have further relinquished compositional control over their pieces to such explicitly nonmusical procedures as probability theory, computer programming, and the application of various mathematical statistical formulas. Originally trained as an architect, Xenakis creates instrumental works such as *Pithoprakta* which involve the deployment of sound masses and blocks in a manner that clearly reflects architectural thinking. Disdaining most music around him, not to mention a great deal of the past, Xenakis may seem to echo in music the artistic models of another artist-architect, Fernand Léger, whose paintings such as his *Contrast in Forms* (1913) or *Nudes in the Forest* (1910) suggest a similar concern for the artistic arrangement of blocks and masses differentiated by color and texture.

There is no doubt that Xenakis serves as the spokesperson for a number of composers who, like Cage, view music composition as a far more objective and unemotional means of expression than did their predecessors of a hundred or so years ago. But the fact that Xenakis has applied his compositional theories to such traditional media as the brass ensemble or string orchestra helps the listener to find a footing where the use of more unconventional sound resources such as those of Cage might seem altogether disorienting. How far composers can go in applying and extending Xenakis's mathematical and stochastic (related to statistics) processes without almost totally excluding the role of the composer in decision making and artistic choice is an important concomitant question. Time will tell, in all *probability!*

Social Commentary and Commitment

Some of the most intense and moving contemporary music has come about as the result, direct or indirect, of composers' involvement in and reactions to war. The Polish innovator Krzysztof Penderecki, born in 1933 during the rise of Adolf Hitler, who subsequently ravished Poland, has assumed a position of deserved dominance by virtue of a number of works for traditional instruments and voices written in the sixties which symbolize a deep feeling for humanity and a sharp protest against the inhumanities of war and suffering. Penderecki's *Threnody for the Victims of Hiroshima* is a gripping and emotional outburst against the atrocities of the bomb. Although the instrumentation consists only of the traditional string sections of the orchestra, Penderecki's treatments and deployments of the string orchestra reveal the imagination and resourcefulness of a skilled inventor of new sounds. The strings are used in any number of innovative or unusual ways to produce an array of sustained or persuasive sounds varying from screaming, sirenlike outbursts to an onrushing shock wave of percussion-like plucked- and struck-string attacks. The impact of the piece is overpowering on first and subsequent hearings. The composer's *St. Luke Passion* echoes, with a distinctly new and expressive approach to choral writing, the great religious choral works of the past. Penderecki's appeal may be attributed in part to his dedication to fundamentally humanistic symbolism while at the same time representing a kind of middle ground between the avant garde of the twentieth century as represented by Cage, Stockhausen, Xenakis, and others, and the unabashed Romanticism of the nineteenth century.

Two contemporary Italians, Luigi Nono and Luigi Dallapiccola, have written a number of works reflecting a protest against war, atrocity, and inhumane acts. Nono's *Il Canto sospeso* is a highly moving piece for chorus, soloists, and orchestra, the text of which is based on letters written by members of the resistance prior to their execution. An opera of Nono's, *Intolleranza*, is a protest against conditions in a police state. The work combines the use of traditional resources such as chorus, soloists, and orchestra with electronic tape techniques and speaker amplification. Dallapiccola's works such as *Canti di Prigionia* are further evidence of the humanistic symbolism current in music of the years following 1945.

SUMMARY

Perhaps the most significant development in the last thirty years lies in the unforseen but influential adoption by Stravinsky of serialism in the latter stages of his artistic career. In view of the master's previous commitment to tonality and many other traditional processes and techniques, it can be regarded as indicative of the impact and sweeping influence of the Viennese composers—Schoenberg, Berg, and, above all, Webern—that a composer of such marked originality, inventiveness, and craft as Stravinsky was, like so many twentieth-century composers during the years following the war, caught up in the vogue of twelve-tone techniques. Any overview of this century must acknowledge the dominance of this trend over any other. It was the acceptance of twelve-tone atonality by the majority of twentieth-century composers, despite a number of highly important exceptions such as Bartók, Hindemith, and others, that sealed, at least for the time, the fate of tonality and a number of tonally related processes, forms, and techniques.

The music being written today has to a great extent been freed of the laws of serial techniques, just as atonal music represented a compositional liberation from tonality. Most of the current paths taken by composers such as Penderecki, Messiaen, Stockhausen, Carter, Boulez, Schuller, Henze, Xenakis, and Cage are clearly marked at their beginnings by a decisive turning away from tonality and many of its concomitant forms and procedures, the most clear-cut of which lay in the turn to serialism that flourished from about 1925 to 1960.

In closing this short study of the most provocative century in the development of Western music, it seems likely that a feeling for music now may be obtained by sampling a few contemporary works, insofar as they reflect some of the developments of the period. Listen to the works listed with an ear for the changing emphases that they reveal. Doing so should provide a frame of reference for comparison with, and assessment of, the entire gamut of activity in music of this century.

Developments in Twentieth-Century Music
Before 1945

Impressionism: Relaxation of musical emotionalism of Wagner based on more detached, objective handling (keyboard, orchestra, ensembles) of raw materials associated with nineteenth-century vocal (opera) extravaganzas; *sound as raw material* rather than emotional portrayal. (Example: Debussy, *La Mer*)

Expressionism: Emotional intensity, contrapuntal-textural complexity, often arbitrary sonority; motivic, brief, and highly intense. (Example: Schoenberg, *Pierrot Lunaire*)

Post-Romanticism: Continuation of non-Wagnerian nineteenth-century ideals; more diversified tonal arrangements, concentration on instrumental-timbral resources; very accessible melodic idiom, lyricism, traditional formal and rhythmic arrangements. (Example: Prokofiev, *Concerto No. 3 in C Major for Piano, Op. 26*)

Neoclassicism: Revivification of Baroque and late eighteenth-century Classical formal plans; modified tonality, melodic accessibility, and performance practicality. (Example: Hindemith, *Sonata for Flute and Piano*)

Nationalism: Essentially a nineteenth-century ideal involving the use of folk and traditional elements in an attempt to create an atmosphere or mood alluding to the composer's native land. (Example: Copland, *Appalachian Spring*)

Serialism: A systematic approach to atonality and pitch organization in general—later involving *all* parameters, featuring predetermined orders of note recurrence, usually involving all twelve tones. (Examples: Webern, *Cantata, Op. 29*; Stockhausen, *Zeitmasse for Five Woodwinds, Op. 5*; Stravinsky, *Threni*)

Individualism: Combines elements of Impressionism, Nationalism, Post-Romanticism, and others in most unique ways; unaffected by "isms" such as Serialism, Neoclassicism, etc.; rhythmic freedom, sometimes improvisatory harmonic inventiveness; bi- or polytonality. (Examples: Bartók, *String Quartet No. 4*; Ives, *Symphony No. 4*)

After 1945

Indeterminacy-aleatory: Events or facets of them not determined or controlled by composer—"play as fast as possible for 30 seconds," "conductor will select order of events by throwing dice," "tune radio for 20 seconds"; improvisatory elements, unrhythmicized pitches, etc. (Example: Brown, *Available Forms I*)

Third stream: Combines jazz elements with traditional idioms. (Example: Schuller, *Concertino for Jazz Quartet and Orchestra*)

Electronicism: Sounds produced by nontraditional media, pitched and nonpitched. (Example: Varèse, *Déserts*)

Humanism: Traditional and innovative sounds deployed in rational and imaginative ways: compositions revealing in spirit a renewed dedication to faith, humanism, and love of fellow humans. (Examples: Penderecki, *St. John Passion*; Argento, *A Letter from Morocco*)

Previous chapters in this section have ended with a summary of style characteristics for the particular period of music literature. The diversity and complexity of the twentieth-century styles listed above make such a summary impractical for these chapters. Moreover, any generalizations about music of today may prove invalid for music of tomorrow. We cannot foresee with any degree of certainty the future developments of music, but we can be sure that they will require not only the creative genius of inspired composers and the artistic commitment of dedicated performers, but also the understanding appreciation of informed and involved listeners.

Appendix

The Notation of Pitch

The following illustration shows the designation of pitches as related to the keyboard. Notice that black keys may be designated with either a sharp name or a flat name, for example c sharp or d flat.

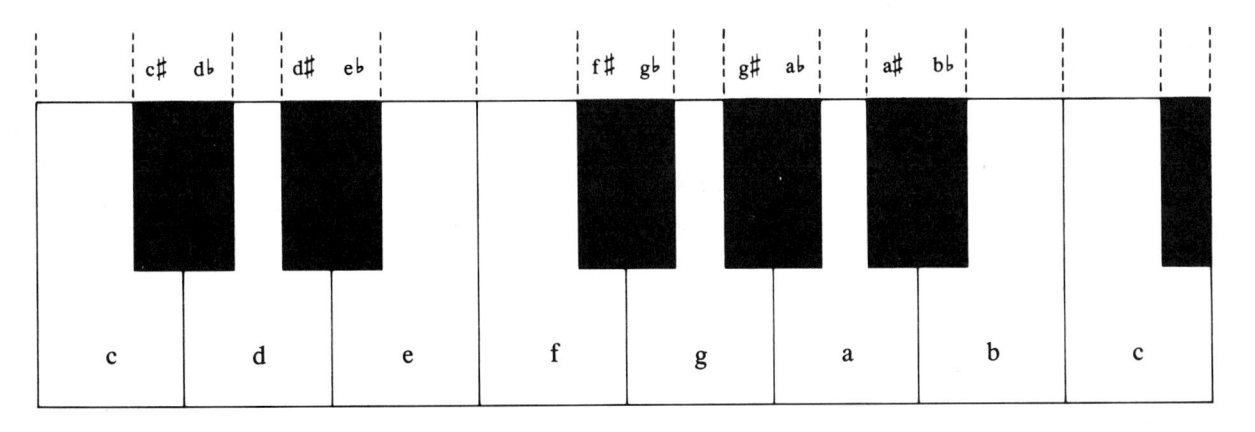

The designation of natural pitches over the entire range of the keyboard is shown below. Notice that the designation (lower case or capital, subscript or superscript) changes each time at the pitch C.

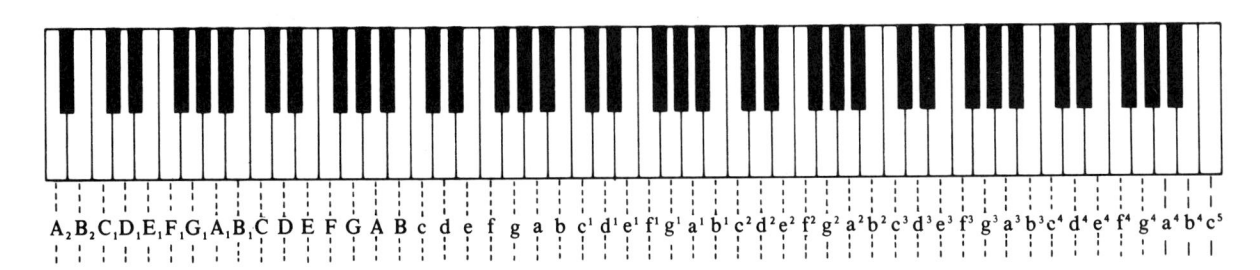

The following example shows the notation of pitches on the treble staff. Notice that the loop of the treble-clef sign indicates the location of the pitch g^1.

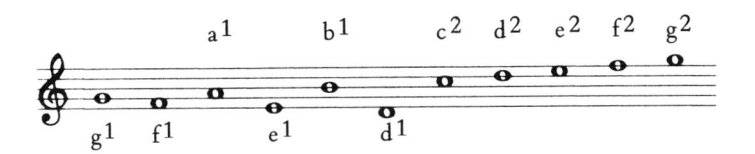

Appendix 299

The notation of pitches on the bass staff appears below. Notice that the two dots of the bass-clef sign indicate the location of the pitch f.

The following illustration shows the notation of pitches on ledger lines above and below the treble and bass staves. Notice that the ledger lines are the same distance apart as the staff lines.

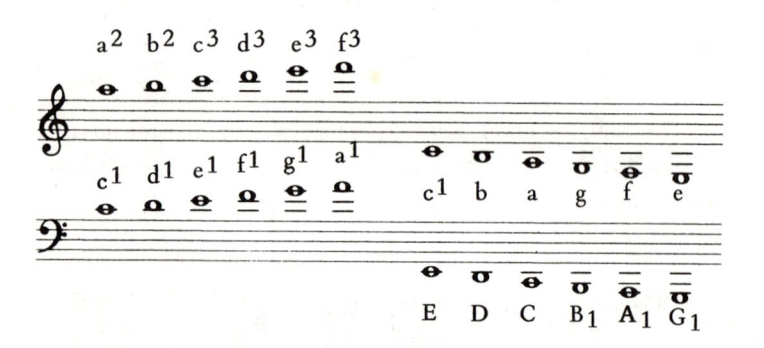

The key signatures of major keys in treble and bass clef are indicated below. The same signature would apply for the minor key with the tonic a minor third below that of the major key.

For information on rhythm notation, see Chapter 2. For fuller information on all aspects of pitch and rhythm notation, see the module *How to Read Music*.

300 Styles of Music

Voice-Leading Rules

1. Most pieces or sections reveal a great variety of motion—that is, directional patterns between parts. Part independence is most apparent as a rule when contrary motion occurs.
2. Wider intervals, such as fifths, sixths, octaves, tenths, etc., are more commonly observed between the lower (bass and tenor) as opposed to upper (soprano and alto) voices. As such, they reflect somewhat the natural spacing found in the overtone series.
3. Both open and close spacing occur. The former is present when the tenor and soprano voices are separated by more than an octave. Close spacing results when less than an octave separates tenor and soprano. Rules of spacing are far less likely to be applied without exception in keyboard and instrumental music, since the spacing and registral capabilities of those media are more diverse and flexible than those of vocal music.
4. Parallel motion involving successive octaves, unisons, or perfect fifths between any pair of voices reduces part individuality and is usually avoided in traditional tonal music. Instrumental octave doublings common to both keyboard and instrumental ensemble music are exceptions to the preceding.
5. When three-note chords are distributed between four or more voices, it is necessary to double some triadic member; chord *roots* most often serve as doubled tones. As a rule, both the tonic and dominant notes of a given key are effective doubled notes as well.
6. The most active members of a key are the seventh and fourth scale degrees, which together form a *tritone*. When these two scale members occur as part of the dominant or leading tone function, in progressions to the tonic especially, the leading tone usually ascends by step to tonic, and fourth scale degree, the subdominant, descends by step. The former is most observed when the leading tone is in the soprano.

Study the following Bach Chorale, noting with care the movement of the individual parts as well as the vertical sonorities that they create. Check out the applicability of the six rules of thumb just cited.

Appendix 2

Annotated Bibliography

Chapter 1: Varieties and Aspects

Christ, William B., and Richard DeLone, *Introduction to the Materials and Structure of Music* (Englewood Cliffs, N.J.: Prentice-Hall, 1975). Students can use this source to augment their study of the parameters of musical raw materials as well as to survey the main stylistic features of the various historical periods and musical genres.

Lang, Paul Henry, *Music in Western Civilization* (New York: Norton, 1941). Selected readings from Lang's treatise can effectively relate a student's awareness of music and musical style to trends and developments in the sister arts.

Chapter 2: Rhythm, Melody, and Accompaniment

Winold, Allen, and John Rehm, *Introduction to Music Theory* (Englewood Cliffs, N.J.: Prentice-Hall, 1969). This source provides a wide variety of materials for developing skill in the interpretation of rhythm via both reading and listening procedures.

Chapter 3: Music and Words

Christ, William B., et al., *Materials and Structure of Music,* Vols. 1 and 2, 2nd ed. (Englewood Cliffs, N.J.: Prentice-Hall, 1971). Both volumes present a useful basis for study of voice leading, contrapuntal devices and forms, and techniques of chord connection associated with both traditional and contemporary music.

Chapter 4: Instruments and Voices

Apel, Willi, *Harvard Dictionary of Music,* 2nd rev. ed. (Cambridge, Mass.: Harvard Univ. Press, 1969). See the articles dealing with "Song" and "Song Cycle" for added perspective.

Cannon, Beekman, Alvin Johnson, and William Waite, *The Art of Music* (New York: Crowell, 1960). See the informative discussion of Schubert's songs in Part II, Romanticism, pp. 349–353.

Liepmann, Klaus, *The Language of Music* (New York: Ronald Press, 1953). This basic text contains excellent discussions of timbral and expressive resources as well as practical illustrations.

Winold, Allen, and John Rehm, *Introduction to Music Theory* (Englewood Cliffs, N.J.: Prentice-Hall, 1969). This book provides ample materials for developing basic skill in the reading and aural recognition of tonal pitch materials in melody.

Chapter 5: Sectional Forms

Berry, Wallace, *Form in Music* (Englewood Cliffs, N.J.: Prentice-Hall, 1966). This book gives more detail and fuller illustration than the Fontaine book (see below). It is a first-rate source.

Christ, William B., et al., *Materials and Structure of Music,* Vols. 1 and 2, 2nd ed. (Englewood Cliffs, N.J.: Prentice-Hall, 1971). Both volumes contain detailed discussion with illustrations of complete pieces representing all of the traditional sectional and developmental forms.

Fontaine, Paul, *Basic Formal Structures in Music* (New York: Appleton-Century-Crofts, 1967; reissued by Prentice-Hall, 1974). This is a supplementary source of information relative to the traditional forms. The illustrations are accessible, playable, and well chosen.

Hardy, Gordon, and Arnold Fish, *Music Literature,* 2 vols. (New York: Dodd, Mead, 1963). These two volumes provide a wealth of examples for study and illustration of traditional form types.

Chapter 6: Variational Forms

Apel, Willi, *Harvard Dictionary of Music,* 2nd rev. ed. (Cambridge, Mass.: Harvard Univ. Press, 1969). See the article entitled "Variations."

Berry, Wallace, *Form in Music* (Englewood Cliffs, N.J.: Prentice-Hall, 1966). This book gives more detail and fuller illustration than the Fontaine book (see below). It is a first-rate source.

Christ, William B., et al., *Materials and Structure of Music,* Vols. 1 and 2, 2nd ed. (Englewood Cliffs, N.J.: Prentice-Hall, 1971). Both volumes contain detailed discussion and illustrations of variational forms.

DeLone, Richard, *Music Patterns and Style* (Reading, Mass.: Addison-Wesley, 1970). See the chapter dealing with variations for further illustration of the process of variation in a wide cross section of literature.

Fischer, Kurt von, *Anthology of Music* (ed. Gustave Fellerer) (Cologne: Arno Volk Verlag, 1962). The anthology contains a wide spectrum of examples as well as detailed discussion of the various processes involved.

Fontaine, Paul, *Basic Formal Structures in Music* (New York: Appleton-Century-Crofts, 1967; reissued by Prentice-Hall, 1974). This is a supplementary source of information relative to the traditional forms. The illustrations are accessible, playable, and well chosen.

Chapter 7: Developmental Forms

Apel, Willi, *Harvard Dictionary of Music,* 2nd rev. ed. (Cambridge, Mass.: Harvard Univ. Press, 1969). See the articles entitled "Development" and "Sonata Form."

Berry, Wallace, *Form in Music* (Englewood Cliffs, N.J.: Prentice-Hall, 1966). A first-rate source book.

Christ, William B., et al., *Materials and Structure of Music,* Vols. 1 and 2, 2nd ed. (Englewood Cliffs, N.J.: Prentice-Hall, 1971). Both volumes contain detailed discussion with illustrations of complete pieces representing all of the traditional part and developmental forms.

Cuyler, Louise, *The Symphony* (New York: Harcourt Brace Jovanovich, 1973). This book provides a well-organized survey of the symphonic repertoire spanning three centuries of development.

Fontaine, Paul, *Basic Formal Structures in Music* (New York: Appleton-Century-Crofts, 1967: reissued by Prentice-Hall, 1974). This is a supplementary source of information relative to the traditional forms. The illustrations are accessible, playable, and well chosen.

Grout, Donald, *A History of Western Music* (New York: Norton, 1960). This book can be effectively used to add to a student's knowledge of various developmental forms and significant composers, periods, and genres.

Longyear, Rey M., *Nineteenth-Century Romanticism in Music* (Englewood Cliffs, N.J.: Prentice-Hall, 1969).

Chapter 8: Medieval and Renaissance Style

Apel, Willi, *Historical Anthology of Music,* Vol. 1 (Cambridge, Mass.: Harvard Univ. Press, 1962). The music in this anthology can be used for additional study, listening, and class performance.

Bukofzer, Manfred F., *Studies in Medieval and Renaissance Music* (New York: Norton, 1950). This is a useful reference for both teacher and student, particularly as a source for detailed research into certain aspects of the periods.

Crocker, Richard, *A History of Musical Style* (New York: McGraw-Hill, 1966). This source provides added perspective and detail as well as excellent musical documentation.

Reese, Gustave, *Music in the Renaissance,* rev. ed. (New York: Norton, 1959). A far more detailed picture of the working relation between musicians and the Church as well as the music of the period of Church domination of music can be gained from this study.

Chapter 9: Baroque Style

Apel, Willi, *Historical Anthology of Music,* Vol. II (Cambridge, Mass.: Harvard Univ. Press, 1962). Volume II is as appropriate for further study and performance of Baroque music as the preceding volume by Reese is for the Renaissance.

Bukofzer, Manfred F., *Music in the Baroque Era* (New York: Norton, 1947). This is perhaps the best source for the study of the music and various stylistic streams of the period. There are also numerous musical examples.

Christ, William B., et al., *Materials and Structure of Music,* Vols. 1 and 2, 2nd ed. (Englewood Cliffs, N.J.: Prentice-Hall, 1971). Both volumes present a useful basis for study of voice leading, contrapuntal devices and forms, and techniques of chord connection associated with both traditional and contemporary music.

Crocker, Richard, *A History of Musical Style* (New York: McGraw-Hill, 1966). This source provides added perspective and detail as well as excellent musical documentation.

Grout, Donald, *A History of Western Music* (New York: Norton, 1960). This is perhaps the best source for further study for nonmusic majors.

Chapter 10: Classical Style

Apel, Willi, *Historical Anthology of Music,* Vol. II (Cambridge, Mass.: Harvard Univ. Press, 1962). An excellent source for the further study and performance of Classical music.

Cannon, Beekman, Alvin Johnson, and William Waite, *The Art of Music* (New York: Crowell, 1960).

DeLone, Richard, *Music Patterns and Style* (Reading, Mass: Addison-Wesley, 1970).

Rosen, Charles, *The Classical Style—Haydn, Mozart, Beethoven* (New York: Norton, 1972). This is a penetrating study of Classical music by a world-renowned musician-scholar.

Ward, William, *Examples for the Study of Musical Style* (Dubuque, Iowa: Brown, 1970). This is an excellent source for the teacher for supplementary illustrations and added commentary about the music.

Wold, Milo, and Edmund Cykler, *An Outline of History of Music* (Dubuque, Iowa: Brown, 1963). Reference to this basic text may help students fit chronology into place with a minimum of wasted effort. The references to discography are also valuable.

Chapters 11, 12, and 13:

Christ, William B., et al., *Materials and Structure of Music,* Vol. 2, 2nd ed. (Englewood Cliffs, N.J.: Prentice-Hall, 1971).

Cone, Edward, *Musical Form and Musical Performance* (New York: Norton, 1968). This is an excellent source of reading for the teacher.

DeLone, Richard, *Music Patterns and Style* (Reading, Mass.: Addison-Wesley, 1970).

Grout, Donald, *A History of Western Music* (New York: Norton, 1960). This is perhaps the best source for further study for nonmusic majors.

Longyear, Rey M., *Nineteenth-Century Romanticism in Music* (Englewood Cliffs, N.J.: Prentice-Hall, 1969). This book is a useful supplement to the study of the Romantic period in which timbre and dynamics assume very significant roles in music for the first time.

Ward, William, *Examples for the Study of Musical Style* (Dubuque, Iowa: Brown, 1970). This is an excellent source for the teacher for supplementary illustrations and added commentary about the music.

Chapters 14 and 15: Twentieth-Century Style

Austin, William, *Music in the Twentieth Century* (New York: Norton, 1966). This book is a good reference for teachers as well as an excellent source of bibliography for students.

Glossary/Index

In addition to providing page references to topics, names, and works discussed in the text, the Glossary/Index provides other information for use as a quick reference or review. Specifically, the Glossary/Index provides the following:

1. A guide to pronunciation is given for foreign words and names.
2. Nationality, year of birth, and year of death is given for all composers. Short biographies appear on page numbers set in *italic* type.
3. Under each composer entry there is a list of the musical works by this composer discussed in the text. An asterisk indicates the location of musical examples.
4. Following most musical terms is a brief definition. For full information please consult the body of the text or such standard musical reference works as the *Harvard Dictionary of Music*, 2nd rev. ed., edited by Willi Apel (Cambridge, Mass.: Harvard Univ. Press, 1969).

GUIDE TO PRONUNCIATION
Approximate pronunciations of foreign words and proper names are indicated in parentheses after the main entry. A key to the sounds is given below.

Vowels
a—as in *hat*
ah—as in *palm*
ai—as in *maid*
e—as in *get* (in final German syllables it should be pronounced almost like the *a* in *ago*)
ee—as in *see*
i—as in *hit*
o—as in *hot*
oh—as in *go* (in final Italian syllables it should be pronounced very short)
oo—as in *too*
u—as in *but*

Diphthongs
ie—as in *lie*
oi—as in *ointment*
ou—as in *house*

Foreign Vowels
The following vowels have no equivalent sounds in English, but they may be approximated as indicated.

ö—*ai* (as in *maid*) through closely rounded lips
ü—*ee* (as in *see*) through closely rounded lips

Consonants
The following consonants are to be pronounced according to normal English usage: b, d, f, h, j, k, m, n, p, t, v, w, y, z.

g—hard as in *go*
l—generally brighter and more "palatized" (with the tongue closer to the roof of the mouth)
r—generally to be "rolled," especially at the beginning of syllables.
s—always sibilant as in *so*

Foreign Consonants
The following consonants have no equivalent sounds in English, but may be approximated as indicated.

kh—like the guttural Scotch *ch* in *loch*
nh—the nasal French *n*
xh—place the tongue as for the vowel *ee* (as in *see*) and emit a strong current of breath
zh—like the *s* in *measure*

Accent is indicated by CAPITAL letters. As a general rule vowels are long for accented syllables, short for unaccented syllables. The glottal stop is indicated with a diagonal line (/).

Absolute music, 15
A cappella (ah-kah-PEL-lah) (without accompaniment), 134, 137
Accent (stress or prominence created by such aspects as loudness, length, or radical change in pitch, harmony, orchestration, or texture), 21
Accidental (sign such as sharp, flat, or natural—♯, ♭, ♮—used to alter the pitch of a particular note), 19
Accompaniment (subsidiary or less important elements of a musical texture), 31–35, 49–50

African music, 123
Aleatory music, *see* Chance music
Allegro (ahl-LAI-groh) (cheerful or fast), 18, 112
Allemande (AHL-le-mahnd) (German dance in quadruple meter, moderately slow), 147–148*
Alto (AHL-toh) (low female voice), 68
"America the Beautiful," 22*
Animé (Ah-nee-MAI) (animated), 18
Answer (fugal), real (literal transposition of a theme), 49
  tonal (intervallically altered theme), 49
Apel, Willi, 119

Apollonian (restrained and objective), 120, 121
Appoggiatura (ahp-po-jah-TOO-rah) (leaning tone, a nonharmonic tone approached by leap and left by step), 206
Arabian music, 122
Arch, inverted arch, 26–27*
Arco (AHR-koh) (bowed), 274
Argento, Dominick (American, 1927–)
  Postcard from Morocco, "Souvenirs de Bayreuth," 290–292*, 298
Aria (AH-ree-ah) (song for one or two singers, with accompaniment, in operas, cantatas, etc.), 62–72

Arioso (ah-ree-OH-soh) (work for solo voice and accompaniment in a style between a recitative and an aria), 142
Aristotle, 120
Armstrong, Louis, 2
Arpeggiation, 93, 99, 101
Arpeggio (ahr-PED-joh) (the notes of a chord sounded successively rather than simultaneously), 34, 59
Articulation, 100
Art music, 126
Atonality (absence of a tonality, *q.v.*), 259–260
Augmentation (rhythmic) (stating theme in longer note values while retaining original tempo), 48, 99
Aulos, 120
Avant-garde composers, 4, 287
Avant-garde music, 87, 295

Bach, Johann Sebastian (YOH-hahn se-BAHSS-tee-ahn bahk) (German, 1685–1750), 5–10, 38, 40, 44, 49, 88, 93, 95–96, 106, 115, 153, *154*, 156, 158–160, *163*, 278
 The Art of the Fugue, 156
 Brandenburg Concertos, 86
 Brandenburg Concerto No. 4, 160*–161*, 162*–163*
 Cantata No. 80, "Ein' Feste Burg ist unser Gott" ("A mighty Fortress Is Our God"), 6–8, 10*
 Es ist gewisslich an der Zeit (chorale), 49, 50*–51*, 52
 French Suite No. 1 in D Minor, 149–150*
 French Suite No. 5 in G Major, 147, 148*–149*
 Mass in B Minor, 154
 The Musical Offering, 38–40*, 156, 165
 St. John Passion, 158–159*
 Two-Part Invention No. 13 in A-Minor, 40–41*, 42–43
 Well-Tempered Clavier, Book II, Fugue in C Minor, 44, 45*–49*, 52, 55
Bach, Wilhelm Friedeman (VIL-helm FREE-demahn bahkh) (German, 1710–1784), 8
Bacharach, Burt, "Close to You," 90, 91*–92*
Background music, for radio, films, television, 216, 255
Bagatelle (short character piece for piano), 222
Balance, *see* Symmetry and balance

Ballade (bahl-lahd) (an early form of poetry and its musical setting), 128–129* (a somewhat extended character piece for piano), 222
Ballet (theater performance by a dance group accompanied by music), 134
Ballett (bah-LET) (an early English madrigal), 137
Bania (an African plucked-string instrument, a predecessor of the banjo), 58
Barber, Samuel (American, 1910–), 289
Baritone (middlu-ranged male voice), 70
Barnes, Alfred, 102 *fn.*
Baroque binary dance form, 106–109
Baroque music, 55, 81, 84, 86, 93, 95–96, 99, 106, 119, 147, 170
Baroque orchestra, 60
Baroque style, 140–165
Baroque trio sonata, 90
Bartók, Bela (BAI-lah BAHR-tohk)(Hungarian, 1881–1945), 4, 79, 260–261, *265*–267, 294
 Bohemian Dance, 266–267*
 Concerto for Orchestra, 1, 22*, 265–266*
 Kossuth, 265
 String Quartet No. 4, 298
 The Wooden Prince, 265
Bass (low male voice), 70–71
Bass clarinet, 59
Bass drum (percussion instrument with low, booming, indefinite pitch), 58–59
Bassoon (low woodwind instrument played with a double reed), 58–59
Beat (regularly recurring stimulus or point in time), 9–10, 90
Beatles, The, 3, 30 *see also* Lennon, John, and McCartney, Paul
Beethoven, Ludwig van (LOOD-vig fahn BAIT-hoh-fen) (German, 1770–1827), 5–6, 86, 106, 108, 155, 177, *179*, 180–187, 272
 Bagatelles, 222
 Concerto for Violin in D Major, Op. 61, III, 80, 84, 85*–87*
 Emperor Concerto, 208
 Moonlight Sonata, 208
 String Quartet in F Major, Op. 59, No. 1, I, 52, 53*–54*
 String Quartet in F Minor, Op. 95 ("Serioso"), 5–6, 10–11*, 185*–186*

Beethoven, Ludwig van (*continued*)
 Symphony No. 3, in E-Flat Major, Op. 55 ("Eroica"), 180–181*, 182*–184*
 Symphony No. 6 in F Major ("Pastoral"), 216
 Symphony No. 7 in A Major, 84
Beggar's Opera, The, 155
Beiderbecke, Bix, 255
Bellini, Vincenzo (veen-CHEN-dzoh be-LEE-nee) (Italian, 1801?–1835)
 Norma, Act I, "Casta diva" ("Chaste Goddess"), 63–65*
Berg, Alban (AHL-bahn bairk) (Austrian, 1885–1935), 272–273, 284
 Woozeck, 272, 290–291*
Berio, Luciano (loo-chee-AH-no BAIR-ee-oh) (Italian, 1925–), 287
Berlioz, Hector (HEK-tor BAIR-lee-ohz) (French, 1803–1869), 193–208, *215*
 Romeo and Juliet, 215
 Symphonie Fantastique, 192, 208–209, 210*–212*, 213–214*
Bernstein, Leonard (American conductor, composer, pianist, 1918–), 61
Binary form, 47, 81–82, 84, 106–114
Bizet, Georges (zhohrzh bee-ZAI) (French, 1838–1875), 193
 Carmen, 67
Blake, William, 189
Blues, 90, 103, 105, 255
Blues progression, 90, 96, 103, 105*
Bologna school, 144
Borodin, Alexander (ahl-leks-AHN-der BOR-oh-deen) (Russian, 1834–1887), 193
Botticelli, Sandro, 8–9
Boulanger, Nadia (NAH-dee-a boo-lahn-ZHAI) (French, 1887–), 294
Boulez, Pierre (pee-AIR boo-LEZ) (French, 1925–), 287, 297
Bourree (boo-RAI) (a fast French dance, usually in duple meter), 148*–149*
Brahms, Johannes (yoh-HAHN-ness brahmz) (German, 1833–1897), 4, 26, 193, 246, 248, *249*, 250
 A German Requiem, 249
 Academic Festival Overture, 249
 O liebliche Wangen (*O Lovely Cheeks*), Op. 47, No. 4, 27*
 Piano Quintet in F Minor, Op. 34, 246, 247*–248*

308 Glossary / Index

Brahms, Johannes (continued)
    Symphony No. 1 in C Minor, 249
    Symphony No. 4, 99 fn., 103-104*
    Variations on a Theme by Haydn, 99, 246, 248, 250-251*
Brasses (instruments sounded by setting a column of air into vibration with a "lip buzz"; include French horn, trumpet, trombone, tuba), 58-59
Breughel, Pieter, 133
Bridge (the middle melody of a popular song), 24
Brown, Earle (American, 1926-), 295-296
    Available forms, 296, 298
Brubeck, Dave, 255
Bruckner, Anton (AHN-tohn BROOK-ner) (Austrian, 1824-1896), 193
Buffo (BOOH-foh) (comic), 71
Bukofzer, Manfred, 153
Burns, Ralph, 294
Buxtehude, Dietrich (DEET-rixh books-te-HOO-de) (German, 1637-1707), 144
Byrd, William (English, 1543-1623), 7, 139
Byzantine music (music of the eastern branch of early Christianity), 121

Cabezón, Antonio de (ahn-TOHN-ee-oh ka-beh-THON) (Spanish, c. 1500-1566), 144
Caccini, Giulio (JOO-lee-oh kah-TCHEE-nee) (Italian, c. 1545-1618), 142
    Euridice, 142-143*
Cadence (a musical point of conclusion), 31, 76*, 93, 139, 162
Cadenza (kah-DEN-zah or kah-DEN-tsah) (a virtuoso passage in a concerto or other work; it may have the character of a development or an elaborated cadence), 115
Caesura (si-ZHOOR-a) (a pause or break in a line of music), 286
Cage, John (American, 1912-), 295-297
Canon (the consistent imitation of one part by another), 36-37, 39-40*, 49
Cantabile (kahn-TAH-bee-lai) (songlike, singing), 72
Cantata (a work in several movements for solo voice or voices and/or chorus with orchestral accompaniment), 7-8, 10*

Cantata (continued)
    secular, 146
Cantus, 50
Cantus firmus (KAHN-tooss FEER-mooss) (fixed melody: a preexisting theme used as the compositional core of a work or section), 93
Caravaggio, Michelangelo Merisi da, 119
Carissimi, Giacomo (JAH-koh-moh kah-REES-see-mee) (Italian, 1605-1674)
    Jephthe, 144
Carter, Elliott (American, 1908-), 178, 284, 297
Cavalli, Piero Francesco (pee-YAIR-oh frahn-CHESS-koh kah-VAHL-lee) (Italian, 1602-1676), 144
Cavazzoni, Marco Antonio (mahr-koh ah-TOHN-ee-oh kah-vah-TSOH-nee) (Italian, c. 1490-1560), 144
Cello (CHEL-loh), *see* violoncello
Cesti, Marcantonio (Italian, 1623-1669)
    Il Pomo d'Oro (The Golden Apple), 146
Chaconne and passacaglia (shah-KOHN and pah-sah-KAHL-yah) (terms used almost interchangeably to describe dance forms and variation types in the Baroque and other periods; modern writers suggest using *chaconne* for a variation form based on a repeated harmonic progression and *passacaglia* for a variation form based on a repeated melodic idea, or *ostinato*), 93, 96-97
Chagall, Marc, 206
Chalameau (SHAH-le-moh) (lower register of the clarinet), 58
Chamber music, 60, 109, 193
Chance music (music in which some aspects of the composition or performance are determined by chance operations), 295-296
Chanson de geste (shahnh-sonh de zhest) (song of heroic achievement), 128
Character piece, 252
Cherubini, Luigi (loo-EE-jee ke-roo-BEE-nee) (Italian, 1760-1842), 5
Chinese music, 122-123
Chopin, Frédéric (FRED-e-rick shoh-PANH) (Polish, 1810-1849), 5, 88, 193, 227, 229
    Mazurka, Op. 68, No. 3, 228*
    Prelude in C Minor, Op. 28, 52*

Chorale, 49, 50*-51*, 55
Chord (two or more pitches sounded simultaneously), 11-13, 31-32, 34, 95-96
Chorus, 15, 88-89
Christian music, 121-126
Chromatics, 29, 283
Church modes (a system of diatonic pitch sets classified according to their range or ambitus, tonic or final, and intervallic makeup, consisting of those basic patterns shown as unaltered or white-note scale patterns:
    Aeolian: abcdefg(a)
    Dorian: defgabc(d)
    Lydian: fgabcde(f)
    Mixolydian: gabcdef(g)
    Phrygian: efgabcd(e), 124
Circle of fifths (an arrangement of pitches or chords by successive fifths), 97
Clarinet (middle-to-high-range woodwind instrument played with a single reed), 58-59
Clarion (upper register of the clarinet), 58
Classical music, 15-17, 166-189
Classicism, 278
Clavichord (a very quiet keyboard instrument whose strings are struck by small metal tangents attached to the keys), 59
Close spacing (the separation of tenor and soprano voices by less than an octave), *see* Appendix
Coda (ending or conclusion of a work), 81, 112-113, 115
Codetta (a short coda or ending), 112
Col legno (kohl LAI-nyoh) (played with the wood rather than the hair of the bow), 217
Coloratura (koh-loh-rah-TOO-rah) (highest, most agile and brilliant type of soprano —occasionally tenor—voice), 62-64, 68
Coltrane, John, 88, 103
Commedia dell'arte (kom-ME-dee-ah del-LAHR-te), 5, 141
Common-practice period, 119-120
Common time, 19
Common tone (tone common to two successive chords), 52
Communications, effect on music, 268
Composite rhythm, 46-47

Composition, in painting, 22
Compound duple meter, 84, 100, 214
Computer and music, 294, 296
Concertino (kohn-chair-TEE-noh) (the solo group in a *concerto grosso*), 144
Concertmaster (leader of the first violins in an orchestra), 60
Concerto (kohn-CHAIR-toh) (a work for solo instrument and orchestra in several movements, frequently three), 84–85*, 115, 172, 177
Concerto grosso (kohn-CHAIR-toh GROSS-soh) (a Baroque instrumental form featuring alternation between solo group—concertino—and the full ensemble—ripieno or tutti), 146
Conducti (processional songs), 126
Conducting, 60–62
Consequent phrase, see Antecedent and consequent phrases
Conservatives (composers), 193
Consonant (euphonius, blending well), 11–12
Contemporary music, see Twentieth-century music
Continuity, 22, 75, 95
Continuo (kohn-TEE-noo-oh) (the accompaniment supplied by a keyboard instrument and a low string or wind instrument), 164
Contour (the overall shape of the pitches of a melody), 25–26, 49
Contrabass (double bass, string bass) (a large, low-stringed instrument of the violin family), 59
Contrabassoon (a larger, lower version of the bassoon), 59
Contradictory meter, 222
Contralto, see Alto
Contrapuntal, see Counterpoint
Contrary motion (the movement of two parts in opposite pitch directions), 23, 50–52
Contrast, 24, 75, 82
Copland, Aaron (American, 1900–), 4, 74, 288–290
  A Lincoln Portrait, 288
  Appalachian Spring, 18–19, 21*–23*, 288–290*, 298
  Billy the Kid, 288–289
  Concerto for Piano and Orchestra, 288
  Connotations for Orchestra, 288

Copland, Aaron (*continued*)
  Music for the Theater, 289
  Rodeo, 288–289
  Symphony No. 3, 288–289
Corelli, Arcangelo (ahr-KAHN-je-loh koh-REL-lee) (Italian, 1653–1713), 106, 151
  Sonata da camera, Op. 5., No. 8, Prelude, 81–82*
Corot, Jean-Baptiste-Camille, 191
Count Basie, 103
Countermelody, 78, 93
Counterpoint (two or more melodies sounded simultaneously), 12–13, 23, 36–55, 106, 137–138, 274
Counterrhythm, 42
Courante (koo-RAHNT) (a moderately fast Baroque dance in triple meter), 147–148*
Cowell, Henry (American, 1897–1965), 295
Crescendo (kre-SHEN-doh) (getting louder), 8
Crocker, Richard, 127
Cymbals (percussion instruments consisting of two concave metal plates that are clashed together with a sharp ringing sound), 58–59

Da capo aria (dah-KAH-poh AH-ree-ah) aria in the form A-B-A), 147
Dallapiccola, Luigi (loo-EE-jee dahl-lah-PEEK-koh-lah) (Italian, 1904–), 284, 297
  Conti di Prigonia, 297
Dance music, 15, 133–134, 147–149
Daumier, Honore, 219
Davis, Miles, 103
Debussy, Claude (klohd de-büs-SEE) (French 1862–1918), 193, 219, 222, 254–255, 260, 268, 270–272
  Images, 268
  Jeux, 270
  La Mer, 268–269*, 287
  Prélude à l'après-midi d'un faune, 192, 219, 268
  Preludes, 268*
Decibel, 8
Decrescendo (dai-kre-SHEN-doh) (getting softer), 8
Degas, Hilaire Germain Edgar, 19, 26, 252
De la Halle, Adam (French trouvère of the thirteenth century)
  Le Jeune Robin et Marion (*The Play of Robin and Marion*) "Robin m'aime" ("Robin My Love"), 128–129*

Development (the processes by which a composer expands, varies, and restates materials; used in the middle section of the sonata-allegro form and elsewhere), 102–115
Developmental forms, 15, 102–115
Diatonic (the seven basic pitches of a given major, minor, or modal scale or tonality), 29, 158, 177, 214, 283–284
Dies irae, 214
Digression, 42, 47, 112
Diminished interval (an interval a half step narrower than a perfect or minor interval), 25
Diminuendo (dee-mee-noo-EN-doh) (getting softer), 8
Diminution (rhythmic), 214
Dionysian (emotional and subjective), 120–121
Directional patterns (contrary motion, oblique motion, parallel motion, similar motion, *q.v.*), 50–51
Dissonant (noneuphonious, not blending well), 11–12
Dittersdorf, Karl Ditters von (karl DIT-erz fahn DIT-erz-dorf) (German, 1739–1799), 5
Dominant (the fifth scale degree of a tonality or key, usually the second most important pitch), 11, 29
Dominant seventh chord (a chord consisting of a major triad plus a minor seventh above the root), 209
Dorian, 120
Dot (used following a note to extend the duration of the note by one-half its normal value; used above a note to indicate staccato), 19, 20 (table)
Double bar, 82, 112
Double bass (or string bass or bass viol) (a low, stringed instrument of the viol family), 56–57, 59
Double exposition, 115
Double stop (playing two notes simultaneously on a stringed instrument), 84
Doubling, 209
Dramatic coloratura (a soprano—or tenor—voice of weighty quality but of extreme agility), 63–64
Dramatic soprano (a soprano voice with some of the darkness and intensity of the lower mezzo soprano and yet with high

Dramatic Soprano (*continued*)
range and brilliant sound), 62, 64, 66
Dramatic tenor (a tenor voice with the range of the lyric tenor but with a heavier tone quality), 68–69
Duchamp, Marcel, 103, 286
Duet (a composition for two performers), 243, 245
Durations, 20 (table)
Durer, Albrecht, 126
Dvořák, Antonin (AHN-toh-neen DVOR-zhahk) (Czech, 1841-1904), 193
Dynamics (levels of loudness or change in loudness), 8

Eakins, Thomas, 64
Eastern music, 3, 121–123
Egyptian music, 122
Eighteenth-century music, 153–189
Elaboration, 93, 95
Electronicism, 298
Electronic music, 3–4, 9, 56, 295, 297–298
Ellington, Duke, 255
Embellishment, 88, 93, *see also* Figuration
Embouchure (ahnh-BOO-shur) (the mouthpiece of a wind instrument; the shaping of a player's mouth to such a mouthpiece), 58
Emerson, Ralph Waldo, 170
English horn (a larger, lower version of the oboe), 58–59
Enharmonic pitches (pitches that sound the same but are spelled differently), 438
Ensembles, 15, 88–90
Episode (a theme that represents a departure or digression from the principal theme), 42–43, 47
Estampie (ess-stahm-PEE) (an instrumentally performed melody in the style of a dance), 133
Etude (AI-tüd) (study; short piece for solo instrument, usually devoted to a study of one musical idea or performance technique), 222
Expanded tonality, 260
Expansion techniques, 93
Experimentation, 255, 295–296
Exposition (the opening section of a sonata-allegro form, which presents the main theme of the movement and provides a

Exposition (*continued*)
modulation from the tonic to a related key), 47, 113
(the opening section of a fugue in which each voice successively states the subject), 44
Expression, intensity of, 191
Expressionism (musical style associated with Schoenberg and other—mostly Austrian —composers in the early twentieth century), 271–272, 274, 277, 297
Extramusical considerations (or associations), 255

False recapitulation, 182
Fantasia, 146
Fantin-Latour, Henri, 213
Favola pastorale (fah-VOH-la pah-stoh-RAH-le) (pastoral fable), 142
Feldman, Morton (American, 1926–), 295
Fermata (fair-MAH-tah) (a symbol, ⌒, indicating the duration beneath or above it is to be held or sustained for sufficient time to create a distinct musical pause), 19
Fibonacci series, 79
Fifth (interval between two pitches represented by letters five letters apart, counting first letter as one: C-G, etc.; in staff notation, counting from line to second next line, or from space to second next space), 24–25
Figuration (embellishment of basic pitches of theme's rhythm and contour), 99
Figure (a group of notes used briefly in a melody or more extensively in an accompaniment), 24
Figured bass (a musical shorthand code used to denote chords to be played over given base notes), 93, 95–96, 99
Film music, 216, 255
Fitzgerald, Ella, 103, 105
Five-part form, 84
Flat (a sign, ♭, that indicates a note is to be played one half-tone lower), 29
Flute (high woodwind instrument played with embouchure or mouth hole), 58–59
Flutter-tonguing (playing rapidly repeated notes in woodwinds or brass instruments), 58, 219
Focal pitch, 261

Folk music, 109, 206, 298
Form (that aspect of music concerned with specific schematic designs or general principles), 13, 71, 73–115, 146, 153, 165
developmental, 102–115
sectional, 74–87
variational, 88–101
Formal activity, levels of, 81
Formal diagrams, 80–81
Forte (FOR-tai) (loud), 8, 19
Fortissimo (for-TEESS-see-moh) (very loud), 8, 58
Forward motion, 76
Fourth (interval between two pitches represented by letters four letters apart, counting first letter as one: C-F, etc.; in staff notation, counting from line to adjacent line plus space, or from space to adjacent line plus space), 25
Fragmentation (dividing a theme into small units, motives, or fragments), 81
Fragonard, Jean-Honore, 170
Free counterpoint (nonimitative), 40
Free imitation, 13
Free sectional form (a form in which there are clear sections and some element of return but no adherence to a strict, established pattern), 87
French horn (a middle-range brass instrument), 58–59
Frescobaldi, Girolamo (jee-ROL-ah-moh fress-koh-BAHL-dee) (Italian, 1583-1643), 144
Frets (thin strips of metal or other material used on the finger board of guitars, viols, and other instruments to indicate the placement of the fingers), 57
Fugue (polyphonic composition with imitation of one or more themes by the several voices, combined with nonimitative material, usually in accordance with fairly specific principles), 42, 44, 46–49, 105
Functional tonality, 153
Function and structure, 80–81
Funeral march, 182
Fusion of the arts, 192

Galliard (gahl-YAHRD) (a lively sixteenth-century dance form in duple meter), 147

Glossary / Index 311

Gamelan (a Javanese instrumental group), 15
Gavotte (ge-VAHT) (a moderately fast old French dance in quadruple meter), 148–149
Gay, John (English, 1685–1732)
  Beggar's Opera, 155
Gershwin, George (American, 1898–1937), 255–256, 258
  An American in Paris, 258
  Porgy and Bess, 258
  Rhapsody in Blue, 87, 256–257*, 258–259
Gesualdo, Carlo (KAHR-loh gez-ZWAHL-doh) (Italian, c. 1560–1613), 137
Gigue (zheeg) (a fast Baroque dance in compound duple meter), 149*
Gillespie, Dizzy, 88
Glissando (performed with a slurring or gliding effect by running one or more fingers rapidly across the keys of a piano or strings of a harp, or by sliding one finger along the strings of a stringed instrument), 59, 219
Goliard (GOH-lee-ahrd) (wandering student-musican of the eleventh and twelfth centuries), 127–128
Goodman, Benny (American, 1909–), 4
Gothic, architecture, 6
  and music, 10
  musical style, 119
Grace note (embellishing note), 177, 214
Greek music, 120–121
Gregorian chant (early monophonic liturgical Catholic music based on Church modes), 122, 124, 125*–126
Gross, Valentine, 219
Guitar, 57

Half step (the smallest interval in Western music), 24–25
Hampton, Lionel, 4
Handel, George Frederick (in German the name is Georg Friedrich Handel) (GAI-ohrk FREED-rixh HEN-del) (German, 1685–1759), 93, 95–96, 106, 151, 155–158
  Brockes Passion, "Von den Stricken meiner Sünden," 156, 157*–158*
  Messiah, 155–156
  Passacaille (Chaconne), 96–97*
Hanslick, Eduard, 13

Hanson, Howard (American, 1896–), 289
Harmonic intervals, 93
Harmonic progression (chord connection), 51, 90, 96, 149, 153
Harmonic rhythm, 43, 164
Harmony (that aspect of music concerned with simultaneous pitch combinations or chords), 11–12, 23, 36, 38, 40, 42–43, 126, 164, 187–188, 252
Harp (a musical instrument with strings stretched in an open triangular frame, played by plucking with the fingers), 59
Harpsichord (a keyboard instrument played with keys connected by a jack mechanism to quills that pluck the strings), 59, 146, 150
Harris, Roy (American, 1898–), 278, 289
Harrison, George, 3
Haydn, Franz Joseph (frahnts YOH-zef HIE-dn) (Austrian, 1732–1809), 5, 36, 106, 108, 113–115, 170–*171*
  The Creation, 170
  Sonata No. 10 in G for Piano, Minuet, 166–167, 168*
  String Quartet in G Major, Op. 17, No. 5, I, 109*–112*, 113–114
  String Quartet, Op. 76, No. 2, "Quinten," III, 36–37, 38*–39*
Head motive (a characteristic opening motive), 112
Heldentenor (HEL-den-ten-OHR), *see* Heroic tenor
Henderson, Fletcher, 255
Henze, Hans Werner (hahns VAIR-ner HEN-ze) (German, 1926–), 297
Heroic tenor, 69–70
Heterophony (the simultaneous presentation of two versions of the same melody in two different parts), 121
Hindemith, Paul (poul HIN-de-mit) (German, 1895–1963), 4, 260–261, *263,* 278, 282, 284, 294
  Ludus Tonalis, 278
  Mathis der Maler, Engelkonzert, 261–262*, 278
  Sonata for Flute and Piano, I, 282–283*, 298
Hoffmann, E. T. A., 15
Homophony (one main melody with accompanying or subsidiary parts), 13, 23, 106, 142

Homorhythmic (block-chord style, all voices moving together in the same rhythm), 142
Huang chung (basic standard pitch in Chinese music, approximately D), 122–123
Hugo, Victor, 190, 216
Humanism, 298
Hurrian song, 127*
Hymn, 126

Idée fixe (ee-dai feeks) (a recurrent theme), 209, 213–214, 253
Imitation (a musical process involving the sounding of the same or a similar melody in different parts of a piece at different times), 13, 37, 40, 42, 137, 139
Impressionism (musical style associated with Debussy and other—mostly French—composers in the late nineteenth and early twentieth centuries), 193, 268–272, 297
Impromptu (short character piece for piano), 222
Improvisation (spontaneous musical invention), 88, 90, 92–93, 96, 259–260*
  in painting, 89
Incipient ternary form, *see* Binary form
Indeterminacy, 298
Indian (American) music, 123
Indian music, 3, 12, 122
Indiana School of Music, 16, 53
Ingres, Jean-Auguste-Dominique, 192, 227
Instruments, 56–60, 120–122, 139
  see also Brasses, Percussion, Strings, Woodwinds
Interval (the musical distance between two pitches), 11, 24–25 (table)
Introduction, types of, 81
Invention (a short contrapuntal piece usually based on one theme), 40–41*, 42, 44
Inversion (reversal of pitch direction in repeating a motive; ascending lines become descending and vice versa), 26–28, 286
Ives, Charles (American, 1874–1954), 260, 267, 295
  Symphony No. 4, 298

Japanese music, 204
Jazz (a branch of twentieth-century music featuring improvised expression with an ongoing beat and an underlying

312   Glossary / Index

Jazz (*continued*)
harmonic progression), 1, 4, 8, 88, 90, 92–93, 103, 255–256, 259, 289, 294
Jefferson, Thomas, 167
Jewish music, 121–122
Jig (an Irish dance in compound duple meter), 149, 214
Johnson, Samuel, 169
Jongleur (zhohnh-glor) (professional entertainer of the Middle Ages), 128
Josquin des Prez (zhoss-KANH dai prai) (Flemish, 1450–1521), *135*, 137
"Ave Maria," motet, 134, 136*

Kandinsky, Vasili, 89, 272
Keppelmeister (kah-PEL-mies-ster) (music director), 7
Kern, Jerome (American, 1885–1945)
"Yesterdays," 30*
Key (a term referring to the particular pitch used as tonic and to the mode, major or minor), 43, 81, 86, 260–261
Keyboard instruments (including piano, organ, harpsichord, and clavichord), 5, 95, 144, 146
Key signature (a collection of accidentals following the clef sign at the beginning of a line of music to indicate the key), 28*–29
Kithara, 57, 120
Klee, Paul, 272, 295
Koto (a Japanese plucked-string instrument), 58
Krupa, Gene, 4
Kuhnau, Johann (YOH-hahn KOO-nou) (German, 1660–1722)
Biblical sonatas, 216

Lai (an old French form of poetry and music), 130
Landini, Francesco (frahn-CHEES-koh lahn-DEE-nee) (Italian, 1325–1397), 130
Lasso, Orlando di (or-LAHN-doh dee-LAHSS-soh), also called Lassus (LAHS-sooss) (Flemish, 1532–1594), 137
Laudes (festive ceremonial songs), 126
Leading tone (the seventh scale degree, which leads to the tonic), 29
Leaning tone, 206
Leap (relatively wide interval), 11, 24, 49, 51, 158

Lebhaft (LAIP-hahft) (lively), 18
Legato (lai-GAH-toh) (smoothly connected notes), 56
Léger, Fernand, 296
Leit motiv (LIET moh-TEEF) (leading motive used to identify characters and emotions in an opera, especially Wagnerian), 231
Lennon, John, and McCartney, Paul, "Yesterday," 3, 23, 24*–25*, 26, 27*–29*, 30–31, 207
Lieder (LEE-der) (songs), 194, 203
Liszt, Franz (frahnts list) (Hungarian, 1811–1866), 9, 88, 192–193, 216, *220*
Les Preludes, excerpts, 192, 216–217*
Liturgy (the public rites and services of the Christian Church, such as the Mass and the Office in the Catholic Church), 124–125
Loudness, *see* Dynamics
Loure (loor) (a seventeenth-century dance form in triple meter), 149
Love duet, 147
Lully, Jean-Baptiste (zhahnh bah-TEEST LU-lee) (French, 1632–1687), 146
Lute (loot) (a plucked-string instrument of the Medieval and Renaissance period), 144
Luther, Martin, "A Mighty Fortress Is Our God," 6
Lyre, 127
Lyric soprano (high, light, clear soprano), 62, 64
Lyric tenor (a light, clear, supple tenor voice), 68–69
Lyric theater, 292

Mauchaut, Guillaume de (gee-OHM de mah-SHOH) (French, 1300–1377), 130–131
"Quant ma Dame," rondeau, 130, 132*
Madrigal (a secular choral work in the vernacular), 137–139
Maelzel's metronome (MM), 18 *fn.,* 20
Mahler, Gustav (GOOSS-tahf MAH-ler) (Austrian, 1860–1911), 108, 193, 203, *205*
Das Lied von der Erde (The Song of the Earth), 203–204*, 206–207*
Major (a qualitative name for intervals indicating that the top note is in the major scale of the bottom note), 24–26
Major and minor triads, 31*
Major-minor tonality, 29–30, 260–261

Major scale (a scale consisting of all whole steps except for half steps between the third and fourth and seventh and eighth degrees), 29
March, 10, 18
Marimba (a pitched percussion instrument with wooden bars struck by mallets, and with resonators underneath), 58
Marx and Engels, 190
Mass (the liturgy and musical setting for the Eucharistic service in the Catholic Church), 7, 124
Mathematical and statistical procedures in music, 294, 296
Matisse, Henri, 21, 27, 272
McLuhan, Marshall, 56, 87
Mediant (the third scale degree), 29
Medieval and Renaissance style (800–1600), 118–139
Mehta, Zubin, 3
Meistersinger (mie-ster-ZING-er) (master singer, middle-class poet-musician in fifteenth and sixteenth century Germany), 128
Melodic inversion (reversal of direction of each interval, retaining all integral sizes), 99
Melodic variation and development, 96–97, 99–100
Melody (a succession or horizontal arrangement of pitches), 10–11, 18, 23, 164, 187, 252, 259
"Melody types" (short melodic patterns or formulas), 122
Mendelssohn, Felix (FAI-liks MEN-del-zohn) (German, 1809–1847), 193
Italian Symphony, finale, 121
Menuhin, Yehudi, 3
Messiaen, Olivier (oh-lee-VYAI mes-YAHN) (French, 1908–), 3, 294, 297
Meter (the organization of beats into groupings on various levels), 10, 19–20, 99
Mezzo forte (MED-zoh FOR-tai) (moderately loud), 8
Mezzo piano (MED-zoh pee-AH-noh) (moderately soft), 8
Mezzo soprano (lower voice than soprano with a dark, thick, quality of sound), 62, 66–67
Middle Eastern music, 121–122

Minnesinger (MIN-ne-ZING-er) (courtly medieval German poet-composer), 128
Minor (a qualitative name for intervals a half step narrower than major intervals), 24–26
Minor scale or tonality (a scale characterized by a half step between the second and third degrees; the sixth and seventh degrees are variable in different forms of the minor scale), 29–30*
Minstrel (professional musican of the Middle Ages who sang to instrumental accompaniment, 128
Minuet (French: menuet) (a dance form in triple meter), 78–79*, 80
Mit Dämpfer (muted), 274
MM, see Maelzel's metronome
Modal scales, 139
Mode, change of, 99
Modulation, 47
Moldenhauer, Hans, 272
Monet, Claude, 254, 271
Monophonic songs, 130
Monophony (one melody sounded alone), 12–13, 22–23, 124
Monothematicism (use of only one significant melodic subject), 113
Monteux, Pierre (pee AIR mohn-TO) (American conductor born in France, 1876–1964), 62
Monteverdi, Claudio (KLOU-dee-oh mohn-te-VAIR-dee) (Italian, 1567–1643), 142, 144–145
  Il Ritorno d'Ulisse (The Return of Ulysses), 145
  L'Incoronazione di Poppea (The Coronation of Poppea), 142, 144–145
  Orfeo, "Possente Spirito" ("Mighty Spirit"), 142–143*, 145
Moog Synthesizer, 9, 56
Morley, Thomas (English, 1557–1603)
  "My Bonny Lass," ballett (madrigal), 137*–138*, 139
Motet (a polyphonic choral composition with a sacred text, usually unaccompanied), 42, 55, 134, 136–137
Motive (a relatively short, self-contained unit, rhythmic or melodic, used as a building block in a melody), 21–22
Movement (a piece within a larger work), 99

Mozart, Wolfgang Amadeus (VOLF-gahng ah-ma-DAI-oos MOH-tsart) (Austrian, 1756–1791), 6, 83, 86, 100, 106, 115, 167, 172, 173, 174
  The Abduction from the Seraglio, 173
  Concerto No. 23 in A Major for Piano, K. 488, 172, 174*–176*, 177, 178*, 180
  Concerto No. 24 in C Minor for Piano, K. 491, III, 283–284*
  Don Giovanni, Act II, "Il mio tesoro" ("My treasure"), 6, 9, 13, 15, 68–69*, 71, 173
    No. 7 duettino, "La ci darem la mano" ("Give me your hand"), 11*
  G-Minor String Quintet, K. 516, 6
  G-Minor Symphony, K. 550, 6
  The Magic Flute, Act II, Scene 3, "Queen of the night" aria, 63*, 65, 173
  The Marriage of Figaro, 67, 172–173
  Melodic variational techniques, 97–98*, 99
  Requiem Mass, 6
  Serenade in G Major, K. 525, "Eine Kleine Nachtmusik" ("A Little Night Music"), 167, 168*–169*
  Sonata in A Major for Piano, K. 331, I, 99–101*
  Sonata in D Major for Piano, K. 284, 82–83*
  Symphony No. 38 in D Major, K. 504 ("Prague"), 172
  Symphony No. 40 in G Minor, 22*
    Minuet, 78, 79*–80*
  Symphony No. 41 in C Major, IV, 76–77*
Munch, Edvard, 272
Musica ficta (MOO-zi-kah FEEK-tah) (music altered by the use of chromatic notes), 129
Musical genres, 15, 17
Musical terms, 7–8
Musical theater, 15
Music-drama, 140
Musique concrete (moo-ZEEK kohn-KRET) (music incorporating recorded and distorted noise), 295
Mussorgsky, Modest (MOH-dest moo-SORG-skee) (Russian, 1839–1881), 9, 193
  Pictures at an Exhibition, 9

Nationalism, in music, 192, 252, 298
Nationalists (composers), 193
National styles, 146–147

Neighbor tone (a tone moving away from and back to a given tone), 100, 162
Neoclassicism (musical style—roughly 1925–1945—based on a return to Classical models), 278–282, 298
Neomodality, 260
Neume, 125
"New music," 119, 249
Nietzsche, 192
Nocturne (night piece: short character piece for piano, usually in a quiet, nocturnal mood), 222
Nondiatonic harmony, 252
Nonimitative counterpoint, see Free counterpoint
Nonlinear structure, 87
Nonmusical procedures, in twentieth century compositions, 295
Nono, Luigi (loo-EE-je noh-noh) (Italian, 1924–), 297
  Il Canto sospeso, 297
  Intolleranza, 297
Nontriadic chords, 252
Notation, 7, 19–20, 28–29
Note-against-note, 52
Notre Dame school of music (c. 1200), 134
"Now form," 87

Oblique motion (the movement of one part sounding against a stationary or repetitive part), 23, 50–51
Oboe (Middle-to-high-range woodwind instrument played with a double reed), 58–59
Octave (interval between two pitches represented by the same letter name but eight letters apart, counting the first letter as one), 25
Open spacing (involves the separation of tenor and soprano voices by more than an octave), see Appendix
Opera (a drama sung with instrumental accompaniment and presented with appropriate scenery, costumes, and staging), 62–72, 142–147, 230–246, 290–293
Opera buffa (OH-pai-rah BOOF-fah) (comic opera), 6
Opera in musica (a musical work), 142

Opera seria (OH-pai-rah ZAIR-ee-ah) (serious opera), 6
Oratorio (an unstaged opera, either sacred or secular), 144
Orchestra, 15, 59-62
Orchestration (that aspect of music concerned with assigning musical material to instruments or instrumental groups), 289
Orff, Carl (German, 1895-),
Carmina Burana, 128
Organ (a keyboard instrument with sound produced either by forcing air through tuned pipes or by electronic means), 59, 144
Organum (OHR-gah-noom) (early polyphonic work using parallel motion in perfect fourths or fifths), 126
Ornamentation, 164
Ostinato (ohs-tee-NAH-toh) (a persistently recurring motive or melody; basso ostinato is a recurring short melody in the bass over which other parts are written), 93, 95-96, 184
Overtone series, 144
Overture (the opening piece or movement of an opera, ballet, or instrumental work; also used for independent instrumental movements, often of a programmatic nature), 149, 231-232*

Pachelbel, Johann (YOH-hahn pahkh-EL-bel) (German, 1653-1707), 144
Paganini, Niccolo (NEEK-koh-loh pah-gah-NEE-nee) (Italian, 1782-1840), 9
Caprice No. 24 in A Minor, 26-27*
Palestrina, Giovanni Pierluigi da (Joh-VAHN-nee pee-air-loo-EE-jee dah pah-les-TREE-nah) (Italian, 1525-1594), 6-7, 135, 137
Mass for Pope Marcellus II, Kyrie, 13-14*, 15, 135
Pandiatonicism (using the pitches of a major scale without the limits of functional chord progressions), 261
"Pants roles" (men's roles sung by women in opera), 67, 238
Parallel major-minor mode, 99
Parallel motion (the movement of two parts in the same direction and at the same

Parallel motion (*continued*)
distance from each other), 23, 50-52
Parker, Charlie, 88, 103, 255, 259
"Perhaps" (improvisation), 259-260*
Parody technique (the incorporation of a section of one work into another—e.g., a motet into a Mass in the fifteenth or sixteenth century), 134
Part writing, 50
Passacaglia (pahss-sah-KAHL-yah), see Chaconne and passacaglia
Passamezzo (pahs-sah-MED-zoh) (a slow Renaissance dance in duple meter), 147
Passepied (PAHS-pee-ai) (a lively dance in triple time), 149
Passing tones (notes that connect two basic pitches), 50-51, 100
Pavane (pah-VAHN) (a slow, stately Renaissance dance in quadruple meter), 147
Pedal point (a long, sustained tone, often in the lowest part, providing an unchanging pitch reference for the other, moving voices), 23, 246
Penderecki, Krzystof (KRZHEEZ-tof pen-der-ETS-skee) (Polish, 1933-), 287, 296-297
Pentatonic scale (a five-note scale characterized by the absence of half steps), 123, 204
Percussion instruments (instruments on which the tone is sounded by striking, including instruments with definite pitch such as timpani or xylophone and instruments with indefinite pitch such as snare drum or cymbals), 58-59
Perfect (a qualitative name for intervals; used for unison or prime fourth, fifth, or octave, and indicating that top note is in the major scale of the bottom note), 24-25
Performance media, 15
Peri, Jacopo (yah-KOH-poh PAIR-ee) (Italian, 1561-1633), 142
Euridice, 142-143*
Perotin (pair-oh-TANH) (French composer, twelfth century), 134
Phrase (a relatively complete musical utterance, often four measures long), 30-31
Pianissimo (pee-ah-NEESS-see-moh) (very soft), 8, 58

Piano (pee-AH-no) (soft), 8
(a keyboard instrument sounded by hammers striking metal strings), 59, 177
music, 222-229
Piano forte, 177
Piano trio (chamber music group consisting of piano, violin, cello), 15
Picasso, Pablo, 74-75, 254, 272, 279
Piccolo (a small, high flute), 58-59
Piston, Walter (American, 1894-), 278
Pitch, 9-11, 24-29, 122-123, 283-284
Pitch notation, see Appendix
Pizzicato (peet-see-KAH-toh) (plucked-string instruments), 56-57, 209, 213-214, 250
Plainsong (ancient monophonic chant used in liturgical music), 122
Plato, 120-121
Pollock, Jackson, 277
Polonaise (pohl-oh-NAIZ) (a stately national Polish dance in triple meter), 228
Polyphony (two or more melodies sounded simultaneously, 12-13, 23, 34, 126, 134, 137, 142, 156
Polytonality (simultaneous use of two or more keys), 260-261, 298
Ponticello (pohn-tee-CHEL-loh) (notes played near the bridge on stringed instruments), 56
Pope, Alexander, 167
Popular music, 15, 17, 109, 268
Post-Romanticism (twentieth-century musical style based on a return to, or continuation of, some musical concepts and techniques of the preceding century), 287, 289-290, 298
Prelude (PRAI-lood) (the opening piece of an opera or instrumental work; also, an independent instrumental movement, usually in a fairly free form), 146
Prepared piano, 295
Presentation, 80
Prima, Louis, 4
Prime or unison (two pitches that are the same or repeated), 25, 38
Prime symbol, 81
"Primitive" music, 123
Probability theory, in music, 296, 298
Program music (music based on a story, poem, or other extramusical idea), 15, 192, 208, 222

Glossary / Index 315

Progressives (composers), 193
Prokofiev, Serge (SAIR-gai proh-KOH-fyev) (Russian, 1891-1953), 284, 287, 289
Concerto No. 3 in C Major for Piano, Op. 26, 298
Romeo and Juliet, 287
Symphony No. 5 in B Flat, 287, 298
Proper of the Mass, 124
Puccini, Giacomo (JAH-koh-moh poo-CHEE-nee) (Italian, 1858-1924), 243
La Boheme, Act I, "O soave fanciul" (O gentle maiden"), duet, 243, 245*
Madame Butterfly, Act II, "Un bel di" ("One fine day"), 64-65*
Tosca, Act II, "Mi dicon venal" ("I'm called venal"), 70-71*
Pulse (regularly recurring stimulus or point of time), 9-10, 19-20, 47, 49
Purcell, Henry (English, 1659-1695), 93-94*, 95-96, 147, 152
Ayres (Airs), 152
Dido and Aeneas, "Thy hand, Belinda," 93-94*, 95-96, 152
Sonatas of III Parts, 152

Quartal chords (chords based on fourths), 252
Quartet, 243-244
Quintet, 246
Quintolet (division of a given metrical unit into five notes of equal duration), 92

Rachmaninoff, Sergei (SAIR-gai rakhk-MAHN-nee-nof) (Russian, 1873-1943)
Rhapsody on a Theme of Paganini, 26-27*
Raga (a melodic formula used in Indian music), 3, 11-12, 122
Range, 164, 252
Ranz des vaches (rahnz dai vahsh) (a Swiss mountain melody used to call the cows), 213
Raphael, 6
Rappresentazioni (rah-prez-zen-tahts-ee-OH-nee) (representations), 142
Ravel, Maurice (moh-REESS rah-VEL) (French, 1875-1937), 9, 193
Recapitulation (the concluding section in sonata-allegro form, consisting of a restatement of material from the exposition in tonic key), 108, 112-113

Recitation (a combination of song and speech), 274
Recitative style (re-see-tah-TEEV) (a speech declamation set to sparse music so created as to permit the text to be intelligible), 142-143*, 164
Recorder (a Renaissance and Baroque transverse flute), 46
Referential music, *see* Program music
Register, voice (a specific part of the voice range, such as the head register), 52, 58
Rehearsals, 61
Religious music, 15, 120-126
Renaissance instruments, 16
Renaissance music, 7, 55, 118-119
style characteristics of, 139
Repeat sign, 78
Repetition (the immediate reuse of musical material), 21, 75-76, 78, 81-82, 286
Requiem mass (Mass for the dead), 214
Rest, values of (table), 20
Restatement (delayed reuse of musical material with intervening contrasting or varied material), 21, 30, 42, 113
Retrograde (repeating the pitches of a motive or melody in reverse order), 28, 99, 286
Return, to original musical material, 108, 112-113
Rhapsodie (character piece usually in a free sectional form), 222
Rhythm (that aspect of music concerned with the duration, accentuation, and temporal grouping of musical sounds), 9-10, 18-22, 26, 28, 48, 90, 92-93, 164, 187, 252
Ricercare (ree-kair-CHAR-re) (a study), 139
Richard Coeur-de-Lion, *Ja nuns hons pris,* ballade, 128-129*
Rimsky-Korsakov, Nicolai (NIK-oh-lie rim-skee-KOR-sah-kof) (Russian, 1844-1908), 193
Rinucinni, Ottavio, 142
Ripieno (ree-pee-AI-noh) (the full orchestra), 144
Ritornello form (ree-tor-NEL-loh) (an instrumental form characterized by the return of opening thematic materials—often in different keys—with intervening contrasting material), 86, 115

Rock-and-roll, 134
Rock music, 8
Rococo period, 165
Romantic music, 118, 190-253, 255, 259-260
Rondeau (rohnh-doh) (a medieval vocal form with a specific arrangement of two musical ideas: AB, AA, AB, AB), 130
Rondo form (a sectional form characterized by recurrences of a principal theme or theme group with contrasting material between these recurrences and transitional sections between the thematic sections: A-B-C-A, etc.), 84, 86-87, 105
Root (the fundamental note of an interval or chord), 31
Root movement, 164
Rossi, Luigi (loo-EE-jee ROSS-see) (Italian, 1598-1653), 144
Rossi, Salomone (1587-1630), 121
Rossini, Gioacchino (joh-AH-kee-noh ross-SEE-nee) (Italian, 1792-1868)
The Barber of Seville, 71
Round (one melody restated by two or more parts), 37
"Frère Jacques," 12*, 37
"Three Blind Mice," 12*, 37
Rounded binary dance form, 106, 112-113
Rousseau, Jean Jacques, 167
Rubato (roo-BAH-toh) (freely), 164
Russian music, 287, 289
Ryder, Albert Pinkham, 231

Saltarello (sahl-tah-REL-loh) (a fast Renaissance dance in triple meter), 147
Sarabande (SAH-rah-bahnd) (a slow Baroque dance in triple meter), 147-148*
Sauter, Eddie, 255, 294
Saxophones (woodwind instruments in a variety of ranges, played with a single reed), 58-59
Scale (an arrangement of a group of pitches in successive ascending or descending order), 29
Scarlatti, Domenico (doh-MEN-ee-koh skahr-LAH-tee) (Italian, 1685-1757), 108
Andante for Klavier, 106*-107*
Schaeffer, Pierre, 295

316 Glossary / Index

Scherzo (SKAIR-tsoh) (joke; a lively triple-meter movement, often in a humorous style), 84, 183, 253
Schiffrin, Lalo, 294
Schoenberg, Arnold (AHR-nolt SHON-bairk) (Austrian, 1874–1951), 260, 272, *273*, 274, 282–286, 294
  Erwartung, 272
  Pierrot Lunaire (Moonstruck Pierre), 274–275*, 297
  Suite for Piano, Op. 25, 284
  Theme and Variations for Band, Op. 43, 273
  Verklärte Nacht (Transfigured Night), 273
Schubert, Franz Peter (frahnts PAI-ter SHOO-bairt) (Austrian, 1797–1828), 31, 193, *194*, 195
  Ave Maria, 27*, 32–33*, 194
  Aufenthalt (Resting Place), 32*
  Das Wandern (Wandering), 34*
  Der Erlkönig (The Elf King), 194, 195*–203*
  Der Tod und Das Mädchen (Death and the Maiden), 32*
  Heidenroslein (Heather Rose), Op. 3, No. 3, 29–30*, 32–33*, 194
  Lob der Thränen (Praise of Tears), 34*
  Morgengruss (Morning Greeting), 32*
  Rastlose Liebe (Restless Love), 34*
  Standchen (Serenade), 27*
  Wohin (Whither), 34–35*
Schuller, Gunther (American, 1925–), 294, 297
  Concertino for Jazz Quartet and Orchestra, 298
Schumann, Clara Wieck, 222–224
Schumann, Robert (ROH-bairt SHOO-mahn) (German, 1810–1845), 5, 10, 193, 222, 223, 224, 227, 229, 249
  Carnaval, 222–223, 224*–227*
  "Chopin," 10
Schwind, Mortiz von, 172
Scriabin, Alexander (ah-leks-AHN-der skree-AH-bin) (Russian, 1872–1915), 287
Second (interval between pitches represented by successive letters of the alphabet: A-B, etc.; in staff notation, line to adjacent space or space to adjacent line), 24–25
Section, 24, 43, 74–87, 93, 112–113
Sectional forms, 15, 74–87, 105, 256
Sectionalization (the division of a composition into sections and subsections), 13, 15, 76–78, 112

Semitone, or half step, 95
Septuplet (the division of a given time unit into seven equal-lengthed durations), 224
Sequence (repetition of the same motive or phrase at a different pitch level), 26–28, 40, 224
Serialism (a process or pitch organization based on consideration of serial order of notes), 282–287, 298
Set, 286
Seurat, Georges, 254–255
Seventh (interval between two pitches represented by letters seven letters apart, counting the first letter as one: C-B, etc.; in staff notation count from line to third next line or from space to third next space), 25
Seventh chord, 25, 164
Shankar, Ravi, 3
Sharp (a sign—♯—that indicates a note is to be played one half-tone higher), 29
Shofar (a ram's horn used as a trumpet in battle and religious ceremonies in ancient times and still used in synagogues on specific occasions), 122
Shostakovich, Dimitri (dee-MEE-tree shoss-tah-KOH-vich) (Russian, 1906–), 287, 289
Siciliano rhythm (a compound dotted rhythm: $^6_8$ ♩. ♫), 250
Sight reading, 49–50
Similar motion (the movement of two parts in the same direction but not with the same intervals between them), 50–51
Sitar (an Indian string instrument played by plucking), 3, 58
Sixth (interval between two pitches represented by letters six letters apart: C-A, etc.; in staff notation, line to second next line plus space or space to second next space plus line), 25
Smetana, Bedrich (BAID-rixh SMET-ah-nah) (Czech, 1824–1884), 193
Snare drum (percussion instrument with indefinite pitch and crisp metallic sound), 58–59
Solo song, 192
Sonata (a multimovement instrumental form), 146–147

Sonata-allegro form (a single-movement instrumental form), 75, 106–115
  table, 113
Sonata da camera (soh-NAH-tah dah KAH-mai-rah) (chamber sonata; a composite instrumental work based on dance forms), 147
Song cycle (a more-or-less unified collection of songs), 194
Song literature, 203
Song without words (short character piece for piano), 222
Soprano (high female voice, high range in general), 62–68
Spiccato (spee-KAH-toh) (short bouncing notes on stringed instruments), 56, 214
Spinning (flowing figures usually following a head motive, *q.v.*), 156
Sprechstimme (SHPREXH-shtim-me) (speaking voice), 274
Stability, 43
Staccato (stah-KAH-toh) (short), 62, 209, 216
Standard pitch (the pitch A of the tuning fork kept in the American Bureau of Standards—today, 440 double vibrations per second), 122
"Star-Spangled Banner, The," 12*, 28*
Statement, 42–44, 48–49, 158
Step (relatively close interval), 11–12, 24–25, 100
Stile rappresentativo (STEE-le rah-pre-sen-tah-TEE-ooh) (theatrical style), 142
Stockhausen, Karlheinz (kahrl-hients shtok-HOU-zen) (German, 1928–), 3–4, 11, 287, 295
  Gesang der Junglinge (Song of the Youth), 3, 11–12, 194
  Mikrophonie I and II, 87
  Zeitmasse for Five Woodwinds, Op. 5, 298
Strauss, Johann, Jr. (YOH-hahn shtrouss) (Austrian, 1824–1899), 4–5
  Die Fledermaus, Act II, "Mein Herr Marquis" ("My dear Marquis"), 64, 66*
  Kaiser-Walzer (Emperor Waltz), Op. 437, 9, 11*
Strauss, Richard (RIXH-ahrt shtrouss) (German, 1864–1949), 193, *221*
  Death and Transfiguration, 221
  Der Rosenkavalier (The Knight of the Rose), 69, 221
  Act I, opening, 67–68*, 71

Glossary / Index 317

Strauss, Richard (*continued*)
  Don Juan, 221
  Don Quixote, 216–217, 219, 221
  Salome, 221
    "Dance of the Seven Veils," 242
  Till Eulenspiegel, 221
Stravinsky, Igor (EE-gohr strah-VIN-skee) (Russian-American, 1882-1971), 60, 221, 260–261, 264, 278–279, 281–284, 287, 297
  Ebony Concert, 264
  Firebird, 264
  Octet for Wind Instruments, II, 261*, 278
  Petrushka, 264
  Rite of Spring, 264, 283
  Sonata for Two Pianos, II, 278–279, 280*–281*, 282
Stretto (imitation of one part by another before the first has concluded), 48–49
String bass, *see* Double bass
Stringed instruments, 56–60, 153
String quartet (chamber-music group consisting of violin I, violin II, viola, cello), 15, 109
Strong and weak beats, 76*
Strong pitches (tonic and dominant), 11
Strophic form (a song form in which each stanza of a poem is set to basically the same music), 204
Structural interrelations, 75–87
Structural pitch (a basic pitch of a melody), 92–93
Structure, 74–75, 80
Structure hunger, 74–75
Style, musical, 118–120
  table, 119
Subdominant (fourth scale degree), *see* Appendix
Suite (sweet) (in Baroque music a collection of dances; in later music a collection of pieces, sometimes drawn from an opera or ballet), 147–150
Sweelinck, Jan Pieterszoon (yahn PEE-terszohn SVAI-link) (Dutch, 1562-1621), 144
Symmetry and balance, 13, 75, 78–79
Symphonic poem, 216
  see also Tone poem
Symphony (an instrumental work in several movements, frequently four), 84, 90, 180–184
Syncopation (a rhythmic displacement that occurs when the accents of a rhythmic

Syncopation (*continued*)
  grouping are arranged so as to fall on weak beats, or weak parts of the beat), 21–22, 46
Synthesized sounds, 9, 295

Tabla (a percussion instrument from India), 3
Taped music (use of tape-recorded sounds in original or distorted form in musical composition), 295, 297
Tarantella (a lively Neapolitan dance in 6/8 time), 121
Tchaikovsky, Peter Ilyich (PAI-ter IL-yitch chie-KOF-skee) (Russian, 1840-1893), 218
  Concerto No. 2 for Piano, 17
  Nutcracker Suite, "Dance of the Reedpipes [or Mirlitons]," 76–77*, 78, 80*, 193, 218
  Romeo and Juliet Overture, 216, 259–260*
Tempo (the rate of speed at which basic beats are heard: the pace), 10–11, 18–20, 100–101
Tenor (high male voice), 62, 68–70
Ternary form (three-part form: A-B-A, A-A-B, etc.), 75, 81–82, 84, 105
Terraced dynamics (sudden changes from one dynamic level to another without crescendo or decrescendo), 164
Tertian chords (chords based on thirds), 252
Texture (that aspect of music concerned with the way individual elements of sound are woven together to form a musical fabric), 12–13, 22–23, 36, 52, 55, 76, 78, 153, 164, 188, 252
Textural density, 52
Theater music, Baroque, 140
Thematic organization, in the fugue, 47–48
Thematic presentation, 81
Thematic sections, 80–81
Thematic transformation, 253
Theme (a well-formed melody or musical idea that plays a significant role in a composition), 76, 86, 99–100
Theme and variations, 75, 99
Theoretical developments, in the seventeenth century, 149
Third (interval between two pitches represented by letters three letters apart, counting the first letter as one: C-E, etc.; in staff notation, line to adjacent line or space to adjacent space), 25

Third-stream music (music combining elements of traditional Western art music and jazz), 298
Thorough bass, *see* Figured bass
Three-against-two rhythm, 250
Through-composed song (a song form that is freer and more varied than strophic form), 126, 203
Tie (a curved line that connects two notes of identical pitch and denotes a continuation of the sound), 19
Timbre (tone color or tone quality), 8–9, 56, 62, 76, 78, 164, 188–189, 252
Timpani (kettle drums; low-pitched drums), 58–59
Toccato (toh-KAH-toh) (a free-style improvisational composition), 256
Tonal basis of composition, 96
Tonal center, 260
Tonal instability, 106
Tonality (that quality in music according to which one tone, the tonic, is heard as a focal pitch on which the other pitches of a particular piece or section all focus), 11, 28–30, 43, 76, 78, 86
  change of, 76, 86
  twentieth century, 260–261
Tonal organization, 149, 153
Tonal shift, 252
Tonal stability, 47
Tonal unity, 261
Tone cluster (a combination of three or more consecutive seconds), 219
Tone color, *see* Timbre
Tone painting, 170
Tone poem (a single-movement instrumental work, based on some extramusical idea or event), 216, 252
  see also Symphonic poem
Tone row (a series of twelve pitches in which no pitch of the chromatic scale is repeated; basic set of pitches for twelve-tone technique), 284
Tonic (the keynote or central pitch of a composition; the first note of the scale), 11, 25–29
Tonic-dominant relationship, 29
Tonic key, 84, 115
Tonic triad, elaboration of, 43
Torelli, Giuseppe (joo-ZEP-pe to-RELL-lee)

Torelli, Giuseppe (*continued*)
  (Italian, c. 1650–1708), 147
Toscanini, Arturo (ahr-TOO-roh tahs-kah-NEE-nee) (American conductor, born in Italy, 1867–1957), 61–62
Tovey, Sir Donald, 17
Transcription (process of changing a work from one medium to another), 8–9
Transformation of theme (the use of variation technique to create a different characteristic emotion), 253
Transition (a passage of music connecting two thematic units), 84, 209
Transposition (moving a melody from its original pitch location to another, preserving the relative interval structure and the rhythm), 26, 28
Tremolo (TRAIM-oh-loh) (rapidly repeated notes), 56
Triad (a chord made up of three different pitches), 31*, 149
Triadic harmony, 38–39
Triad progressions, 149
Triangle (a percussion instrument of indefinite pitch, made in the shape of a triangle and struck with a metal rod), 58–59
Trill (rapid alternation between two notes, usually a major or minor second apart), 214
Trio (a work for three performers), 15
  (the middle section of minuets, marches, and other works), 78, 149
Trio sonata (a work of the Baroque period for two melody instruments and *continuo*—a keyboard and a bass instrument, hence for four performers), 144
Trio texture, 144
Triple meter, 19
  in mazurka, polonaise, and waltz, 228
Triplet (a group of three notes of equal duration performed in the span of a unit normally divided into two), 100
Tritone (augmented fourth—three whole steps—or diminished fifth), 25
Trombone (a middle-to-low-range brass instrument), 58–59
Troubadour (TROO-bah-dohr) (poet-composer in medieval southern France), 128, 130
Trouvère (troo-VAIR) (nobleman poet-composer in medieval northern France), 128, 130

Trumpet (a high-range brass instrument), 58–59
Tuba (a low-range brass instrument), 58–59
Tutti (TOO-tee) (the entire ensemble), 144
Tutti-solo alternation, 144
Twelve-tone music (compositions based on the manipulation of the twelve tones of the chromatic scale), 282–287
Twentieth-century music, 119, 254–298
Two-keyboard instruments, 144
Two-part counterpoint, 93, 95
Two-part form, 81–82
  see also Binary form
Two-voice framework, 36–37, 50–52

Unison, or prime or same note, 39
Unity and variety, 13, 28, 30, 75, 78, 82

Van Gogh, Vincent, 13
Varèse, Edgard (ed GAHR vah-REZ) (American, 1885–1965), 295
  Déserts, 295, 298
Variation (modified or altered repetition), 24, 26, 88, 90–93, 96–97, 99–101
Variational forms, 15, 88–101
Verdi, Giuseppe (joo-ZEP-pe VAIR-dee) (Italian, 1813–1901), 234–235
  Aïda, Act I, "Celeste Aïda" ("Heavenly Aida"), 68–70*, 235
  Attila, 235
  Don Carlo, Act III, "Dormiro sol" ("I'll sleep alone"), 71–72*
  Ernani, 235
  Falstaff, 235
  I Lombardi, 235
  Il Trovatore, Act II, "Stride la vampa" ("The flames cry out"), 67*
  La Forze del Destino, 235
  Nabucco, 235
  Oberto, 235
  Otello, 235
  Rigoletto, Act II, quartet, 239, 243–244*
  Un Ballo in Maschera (*A Masked Ball*), 68, 234–242
    Act I, Prelude, 239*
    Act I, Scene 2, "Re dell' abisso" ("King of the night"), 68–69*
    Act III, Scene 1, 236*–239*
    Act III, Scene 2, 239*–240*
    Act III, Scene 3, 240*–242*
Vermeer, Jan, 141

Vibraphone (a pitched percussion instrument with wooden bars, resonators, and electric amplifying and vibrating devices), 58
Vibrato (vee-BRAH-toh) (a rapid sharping and flatting of the pitch, produced by rolling the stopping finger of the left hand back and forth), 62
Victoria, Tomas Luis de (tohm-MAHS loo-EES de vee-TOH-ree-ah) (Spanish, c. 1548–1611), 137
Viennese Classicism (1750–1827), 119
Viennese composers (twentieth century), 297
Vigoroso (vee-goh-ROH-soh) (vigorously), 18
Viol (VIE-ohl) (early stringed instrument with sloping shoulders and frets), 57
Viola (vee-OH-lah) (a middle-ranged instrument of the violin family), 56–57, 59
Viol family, 56–57, 59
Violin (a high-ranged stringed instrument), 56–57, 59
Violoncello (vee-oh-lohn-CHEL-loh) or cello (a middle-to-low-range stringed instrument of the violin family), 56–57, 59
Virelai (VIR-e-lai, also veer-LAI) (an old French form of poetry and music), 130
Vivaldi, Antonio (ahn-TOHN-yoh vee-VAHL-dee) (Italian, 1669–1741), 147
Vocal ensembles, 15
  see also Chorus
Voice leading (the rules for writing the various voices in contrapuntal music), 37, 42, 49–55
Voices, 62–71
Voltaire, 167

Wagner, Richard (RIXH-hart VAHG-ner) (German, 1813–1883), 71, 193, 230–231, 233–234, 290–293
  Das Rheingold, "Valhalla theme," 292–293*
  Der Fliegende Holländer (*The Flying Dutchman*), Act II, "Spinne, spinne" ("Spinning Chorus"), 233, 291–292, 293*
  Der Ring des Nibelungen (*The Ring of the Nibelungs*), 66, 230, 233, 292
  Die Götterdammerung (*The Twilight of the Gods*), Act III, "Starke Scheite" ("Mighty Pyre"), 66*

Wagner, Richard (continued)
  Die Meistersinger, 231–232*, 234
  Rienzi, 233
  Siegfried, Act I, "Nothung," 70*
Waltz (a dance form in triple meter), 4, 209
Watteau, Jean Antoine, 147
Webern, Anton (AHN-tohn VAI-bern) (Austrian, 1883–1945), 259, 272–274, 277, 282–287
  Five Movements for String Quartet, Op. 5, No. 2, 274, 276*–277
  Kinderstücke (for piano), 284–285*, 286
  Symphony for Small Orchestra, Op. 21, I, 259–260*

Webster, Daniel, 167
Western music, 3, 24, 114, 126, 222, 254, 297
Whiteman, Paul, 256
Whole-tone scale, 252
Wilson, Teddy, 4
Wolf, Hugo (HOO-goh volf) (Austrian, 1860–1903), 193
  Mörike Lieder, "In der Frühe" ("In the Early Morning"), 29–30*
Woodwind quintet (chamber-music group consisting of flute, oboe, clarinet, bassoon, French horn), 15
Woodwinds (instruments sounded by the breath blown through a mouthpiece,

Woodwinds (continued)
  sometimes with single or double reed; include flutes, oboes, clarinets, bassoons, and others), 58–59
Word painting, 142, 158

Xenakis, Iannis (YAHN-nis zen-NAH-kis) (Greek, 1922–), 287, 296
  Pithoprakta, 296
Xylophone (pitched percussion instrument with wooden bars struck by mallets), 58